QUANTITATIVE

AND STATISTICAL

RESEARCH METHODS

From Hypothesis to Results

WILLIAM E. MARTIN

KRISTA D. BRIDGMON

JOSSEY-BASS
A Wiley Imprint
www.josseybass.com

Published by Jossey-Bass
A Wiley Imprint
One Montgomery Street, Suite 1200, San Francisco, CA 94104-4594—www.josseybass.com

Jossey-Bass books and products are available through most bookstores. To contact Jossey-Bass directly call our Customer Care Department within the U.S. at 800-956-7739, outside the U.S. at 317-572-3986, or fax 317-572-4002.

Wiley publishes in a variety of print and electronic formats and by print-on-demand. Some material included with standard print versions of this book may not be included in e-books or in print-on-demand. If this book refers to media such as a CD or DVD that is not included in the version you purchased, you may download this material at http://booksupport.wiley.com. For more information about Wiley products, visit www.wiley.com.

Library of Congress Cataloging-in-Publication Data

Martin, William E. (William Eugene), 1948-
    Quantitative and statistical research methods : from hypothesis to results / William E. Martin, Krista D. Bridgmon. — First edition
        pages cm.— (Research methods for the social sciences; 42)
    Includes bibliographical references and index.
    ISBN 978-0-470-63182-9 (pbk.); ISBN 978-1-118-22075-7 (ebk.); ISBN 978-1-118-23457-0 (ebk.);
    ISBN 978-1-118-25908-5 (ebk.)
        1. Psychology—Methodology.   2. Social sciences—Methodology.   3. SPSS (Computer file)
    I. Bridgmon, Krista D., 1979-   II. Title.
    BF38.5.M349   2012
    150.72'7—dc23
                                                                                                        2012010748

Printed in Singapore

FIRST EDITION
PB Printing   10 9 8 7 6 5 4 3 2 1

 M WEP170712 131222

CONTENTS

TABLES AND FIGURES

TABLES

FIGURES

PREFACE

Working through a solution to a research problem is a stimulating process. The focus of this book is learning statistics while progressing through the steps of the hypothesis-testing process from hypothesis to results. The hypothesis-testing process is the most commonly used tool in science and entails following a logical sequence of actions, judgments, decisions, and interpretations as statistics are applied to research problems. Statistics emerged as a discipline with the purpose of developing and applying mathematical theory and scientific operations to enhance human understanding of phenomena experienced in life. For example, William Gossett developed the t-statistic while working at the Guinness Brewery in the late 1800s. He worked to explain the factors that contribute to Guinness beer remaining suitable for drinking and what fertilizers produce the best yield of barley used in brewing. Analysis of variance is the most widely used family of statistics in the world, and Sir Ronald A. Fisher developed the procedure in 1921 while researching the factors contributing to better yields of wheat and potatoes.

The research problems used in the book reflect statistical applications related to interesting and important topics. For example, research problems for students to work through include findings on the efficacy of using cognitive-behavioral therapy to treat depression among adolescents and evaluating if support partners added to weight loss treatment can improve weight loss among persons who are overweight. It is hoped that students will find the problems that they work through to be interesting and relevant to their field of study. The research problems presented are consistent with findings in the field.

The format for each chapter on a major statistic is to cover the research problem by taking the student through identifying research questions and hypotheses; identifying, classifying, and operationally defining the study variables; choosing appropriate research designs; conducting power analysis; choosing an appropriate statistic for the problem; using a data set; conducting data screening and analyses (IBM SPSS); interpreting the statistics; and writing the results related to the problem.

It is the intent of the authors to provide a user-friendly guide to students to understand and apply procedural steps in completing quantitative studies. Students will know how to plan research and conduct statistical analyses using several common statistical and research designs after completion of the book. The quantitative methodological tools learned by students can actually be applied to their own research with less oversight by faculty.

Students will develop competencies in using IBM SPSS for statistical analyses. Computer-generated statistical analysis is the primary method used by quantitative researchers. Students will have the opportunity to also calculate statistics by hand for a fuller understanding of mathematics used in computations.

Moreover, the curriculum includes having students analyze research articles in psychology using a research analysis and interpretation guide. These learning experiences allow students to enhance their understanding of consuming research using the information they have learned about statistical and research methods.

ACKNOWLEDGMENTS

The authors would like to gratefully acknowledge the outstanding editorial leadership and support provided by Andrew Pasternack, Senior Editor; Seth Schwartz, Associate Editor; and Kelsey McGee, Senior Production Editor, all of Jossey-Bass. We also wish to thank the following reviewers for their thoughtful and valuable feedback in the early stages of the manuscript: Joel Nadler, Kathryn Oleson, Richard Osbaldiston, and Joseph Taylor.

THE AUTHORS

William E. Martin Jr. is a professor of educational psychology and senior scholar in the College of Education at Northern Arizona University. His areas of teaching include intermediate, computer, and multivariate statistics; research methods; and psychodiagnostics. His research relates to person-environment psychology and psychosocial adaptation.

Krista D. Bridgmon received a PhD in educational psychology from Northern Arizona University with emphasis in counseling. She is an assistant professor of psychology at Colorado State University—Pueblo. She has taught undergraduate courses in abnormal psychology, child psychology, clinical psychology, statistics, tests and measurements, and theories of personality, and has taught graduate courses in appraisal and assessment, clinical counseling, ethics, and school counseling. Her doctoral dissertation examined the stress factors that all-but-dissertation (ABD) students encounter in the disciplines of counselor education and supervision, counseling psychology, and clinical psychology. The study created an instrument using multivariate correlational methods to measure stress factors associated with being ABD, named the BASS (Bridgmon All-But-Dissertation Stress Survey).

To my wife Susan and my children and their spouses:
Neil and Jennifer, Kurt and Michelle, and Carol and Kyle
To my grandchildren: Grace, Adriana, Hudson, Lillee,
Uriah, Naaman, and Isaac

—W.E.M. Jr.

To Jerrad and Coltin: Thank you for always making me laugh!

—K.B

Chapter 1

INTRODUCTION

AND OVERVIEW

LEARNING OBJECTIVES

○ Understand the purpose of the book and the structure of the book.

○ Review independent, dependent, and extraneous variables and their scales of measurement.

○ Review measures of central tendency and variability.

○ Review visual representations of data, including the normal distribution.

○ Review descriptive and inferential statistical applications of the normal distribution.

The **purpose** of this book is to provide a hands-on approach for students to understand and apply procedural steps in completing quantitative studies. The book emphasizes a step-by-step guide using research examples for students to move through the hypothesis-testing process for commonly used statistical procedures and research methods. Statistical and research designs are integrated as they are applied to the examples. The structure of each chapter covers the following nine quantitative research procedural steps:

1. A description of a research problem, taking the student through identifying research questions and hypotheses.

2. A method of identifying, classifying, and operationally defining the study variables.

3. A discussion of appropriate research designs.

4. A procedure for conducting an a priori power analysis.

5. A discussion of choosing an appropriate statistic for the problem.

6. A statistical analysis of a data set.

7. A process for conducting data screening and analyses (IBM SPSS) to test null hypotheses.

8. A discussion of interpretation of the statistics.

9. A method of writing the results related to the problem.

The underlying philosophy of the book is to view the quantitative research process from a more holistic and sequential perspective. Concepts are discussed as they are applied during the procedural steps. It is hoped that after completion of the book readers will be better able to plan research and conduct statistical analyses using several commonly used statistical and research designs. The quantitative methodological tools learned by students can actually be applied to their own research, hopefully with less oversight by faculty.

The use of statistical software is an essential tool of researchers. Psychological, educational, social, and behavioral areas of research typically have multifactor or multivariate explanations. Statistical software provides a researcher with sophisticated techniques to analyze the effects and relationships among many independent variables (factors) and dependent variables (variates) in various combinations all at once and instantly. We will use IBM SPSS statistical software, which has been developed over many decades and is one of the most widely used statistics programs in the world.

Statistical techniques may have more meaning, understandability, and relevance when learned within the context of research. One needs to have an understanding of statistical analyses to consume and construct professional research competently. Knowledge of quantitative research methods is especially important today because of the emphasis on evidence-based practice in psychology (EBPP) to improve clinical work with clients. EBPP refers to using the best available research with clinical expertise in the context of patient characteristics, culture, and preferences (American Psychological Association, 2006).

Ideally, the goal is to help a student achieve self-efficacy in understanding, planning, and conducting actual independent research. Information and skills grow, leading to advanced understanding. We next present a review of foundational information related to research and statistics that will be useful to review prior to completing the chapters that follow.

REVIEW OF FOUNDATIONAL RESEARCH CONCEPTS

A review of foundational concepts related to research and statistics is presented next. Quantitative research involves the interplay among variables after they have been operationalized, allowing a researcher to measure study outcomes. Essential statistical methods used to assess scores of variables include central tendency, variability, and the characteristics of the normal distribution.

Independent, Dependent, and Extraneous Variables

At the core of quantitative research is studying and measuring how variables change. Kerlinger and Pedhazur (1973) stated, "It can be asserted that all the scientist has to work with is variance. If variables do not vary, if they do not have variance, the scientist cannot do his work" (p. 3). Even the father of modern statistics, Sir Ronald Fisher (1973), said, "Yet, from the modern point of view, the study of the causes of variation of any variable phenomenon, from the yield of wheat to the intellect of man, should be begun by the examination and measurement of the variation which presents itself" (p. 3).

An *independent variable (IV)* in a study is the presumed cause variable. In experimental research, the IV is designed and employed to influence some other variable. It is an antecedent condition to an observed resultant behavior. Changes in the independent variable produce changes in the dependent variable.

All variables need to be able to vary. Kerlinger and Lee (2000) identified two types of independent variables: active and attribute. An *active independent variable* is one that is manipulated by the researcher. For example, a researcher designs a study with an IV that has a researcher-specified treatment condition compared to a no-treatment control condition. Other terms used for an active IV are stimulus variable, treatment variable, experimental variable, intervention variable, and *X* variable.

A second type of IV is called an *attribute independent variable*, which is not manipulated but is ready-made or has preexisting values such as gender, age, or ethnocultural grouping. Other terms used are organismic or personological variables.

The terms *classification variable* and *categorical variable* are often used as an IV label. They can be used as either active or attribute types. For example, a manipulated IV that has a treatment condition and a control condition could be called a classification variable. Also, an attribute variable such as gender (male or female) may be referred to as a classification or categorical variable.

A *dependent variable (DV)* is the presumed resulting outcome in research. It is usually observed and measured in response to an IV. We look for changes in a DV caused by an IV. A DV is also referred to as a response variable or a *Y* variable.

An *extraneous variable (EV)* is an unwanted and contaminating variable. An EV acts on a dependent variable like an independent variable does but in a confounding way that confuses an understanding of how the IV is changing the DV. An extraneous variable is undesired noise in a research study. A researcher wants to control an extraneous variable to neutralize its effects.

Variables need to be assigned meaning by specifying activities or operations necessary to measure the variable, which is known as an *operational definition (OD)*. A comprehensive operational definition entails all of the activities and operations that define the variable. For example, an active IV psychotherapy approach might have two conditions (Gestalt therapy and control condition). We can say there are two operational definitions for the IV psychotherapy approach for the sake of brevity. However, each condition has a detailed, comprehensive operational definition that is clearly and fully specified. A brief operational definition of a dependent variable of depressive symptomatology may be scores on the Beck Depression Inventory (BDI). However, the comprehensive OD would detail key psychometric research used in validating the BDI.

In correlations research, an independent variable is often called a *predictor variable (PV)*, and a dependent variable is called a *criterion variable (CV)*.

Scales of Measurement of Variables

Variables can be assigned scales of measurement. A variable does not have an absolute scale of measurement. The scale of measurement of a variable can change depending on how the variable is being used in different studies and even within the same study. Therefore, there is a research contextual consideration that helps determine the scale of measurement of a variable. The process of thinking through the connection between scales of measurement and variables helps the researcher more clearly see how variables can be measured in a study. Also, the scales of measurement assigned to a variable can be useful in selecting appropriate statistics to use in research.

There are two general classifications of scales of measurement, each having two subcategories; they are *discrete scale* (nominal and ordinal) and *continuous scale* (interval and ratio).

A variable using a *discrete-nominal scale* of measurement has mutually exclusive categories. For example, gender has mutually exclusive categories of male or female, and political affiliation has categories of Republicans, Democrats, or independents. A *discrete-ordinal scale* of measurement variable has ordering along some continuum. It is rank scaled. For example, the order (first, second, third, etc.) in which runners complete a race reflects an ordinal scale.

A *continuous-interval scale* of measurement variable has numerical distances on a scale that are considered approximately equal numerical distances of the attribute being measured. There is no true zero point on the scale; it is considered arbitrary. For example, scores on the Wechsler IQ test are considered interval scaled, and there is an arbitrary zero, but the test does not measure a total absence (true zero) of intelligence. A *continuous-ratio scale* of measurement variable has a true zero point, and the numerical distances on the scale are equal to the attribute being measured. Weight is an example of a ratio-scaled variable. A zero number of pounds is meaningful, and 100 pounds is one-third as heavy as 300 pounds. Other examples of ratio-scaled variables include height, length, and time.

There are times when ordinal-scaled variables such as Likert-type scales are statistically analyzed as a continuous-interval variable (Tabachnick & Fidell,

2007). Howell (2010) states, "We do our best to ensure that our measures relate as closely as possible to what we want to measure, but our results are ultimately only the numbers we obtain and our faith in the relationship between those numbers and the underlying objects or events" (p. 8). A more important gauge of understanding the meaning of scores on dependent variables in a study has to do with their distributions. Measures of central tendency and variability of scores of distributions are discussed next.

REVIEW OF FOUNDATIONAL STATISTICAL INFORMATION

One of the most important tasks of quantitative researchers is to understand the data they are working with. Researchers need to assess their data for issues including dishonest data, cases with atypical scores, and noncompliance with appropriate use of statistical requirements. Also, it is important for researchers to understand the uniqueness of their data sets by examining typical scores, variability among scores, and characteristics and shapes of distributions of scores related to variables in a data set.

Measures of Central Tendency

Measures of central tendency are values that represent typical scores in a distribution or set of scores. We will be using the data in Table 1.1 to demonstrate how to calculate the three most common measures of central tendency: mode, median, and mean.

TABLE 1.1 Values Used to Illustrate Measures of Central Tendency and Variability

$X(N = 6)$	X^2	$(X - \overline{X})$	$(X - \overline{X})^2$
48	2,304	$48 - 49 = -1$	1
43	1,849	$43 - 49 = -6$	36
52	2,704	$52 - 49 = 3$	9
50	2,500	$50 - 49 = 1$	1
48	2,304	$48 - 49 = -1$	1
53	2,809	$53 - 49 = 4$	16
$\Sigma X = 294$	$\Sigma X^2 = 14,470$	$\Sigma(X - \overline{X}) = 0$	$\Sigma(X - \overline{X})^2 = 64$
$(\Sigma X)^2 = (294)^2 = 86,436$			

Mode (M_o)

The *mode* (M_o) is the score that occurs most often in a set of scores. The mode is the highest point on a graph such as a frequency distribution or a histogram and is referred to as *unimodal*. If there are two scores in a sample that are equally the most frequently occurring, then the distribution is called *bimodal*. The column headed by X (individual score) and $N = 6$ represents six individual scores in the distribution of scores example. The only score that is represented more than once is 48. Thus, the $M_o = 48$ and it is a unimodal distribution.

Median (M_{dn})

The *median* (M_{dn}) is a value in the set of which 50 percent of cases fall below and 50 percent above. If the number of a set of ordered scores from low to high is odd, then the score that has half of the other scores below it and half above it is the median. For example, in the set of numbers 4, 5, 7, 8, and 9, the number 7 is the median.

In the set in Table 1.1, the number of scores is even. The six scores ordered are 43, 48, 48, 50, 52, 53. To obtain the median requires calculating the average value between the score at $N/2$ and the score at $(N/2) + 1$. So, $N/2 = 6/2 = 3$ (i.e., the third score) and $(N/2) + 1 = 3 + 1 = 4$ (i.e., the fourth score). The third score in the set is 48 and the fourth score is 50. The average of 48 and 50 is $(48 + 50)/2 = 98/2 = 49$. So, the median of the data set in Table 1.1 is 49.

Mean ($\overline{X}$ or M)

The *mean* ($\overline{X}$ or M) is the sum of individual scores (ΣX) in a data set divided by the number of scores (N). The mean is typically a more precise measure of central tendency than the mode or the median, because the specific value of each score is used to calculate the mean. Also, the mean has the properties of being continuously scaled as an interval or a ratio. The mean is more stable than the mode or median when it is used as a sample measure of central tendency drawn from a population. On the downside, when a sample has extreme scores (skewed), the mean is drawn way from the clustered scores toward the extreme scores. In these situations, the mean may not be the most typical score in a data set. For example, an analysis of salaries of company employees that includes the high salaries of executives can produce a company employee mean salary that the vast majority of employees are well below. The median might be a better indication of the typical employee salary in the company. Presented next is the calculation of the mean of our sample data in Table 1.1.

$$\overline{X} = \frac{\Sigma X}{N}$$

$$= \frac{294}{6}$$

$$\overline{X} = 49.00$$

where

$\Sigma X =$ sum of the individual scores

$N =$ number of scores

Measures of Variability (Dispersion) of Scores

Foundational to quantitative research is the study of the *measures of variability (dispersion) of scores* in a sample data set. Here we review common measures of range, mean deviation scores, sum of squares, variance, and standard deviation using the data set from Table 1.1.

The *range* of scores in a data set is simply the difference between the highest and lowest scores ($score_{highest} - score_{lowest}$). In the example data in Table 1.1, the highest score is 53 and the lowest score is 43; $53 - 43 = 10$, which is the range.

A measure of variability that is used as a component in many statistical formulas that are used in fundamental statistics is called the *total sum of squares*, which is the sum of squared differences of all scores in the data set from their overall mean, $\Sigma(X - \overline{X})^2$.

Variance of the Sample (s^2)

The variance of the sample (s^2) is the *total sum of squares* divided by the number of scores, $\frac{\Sigma(X - \overline{X})^2}{N}$. The symbol of the variance of the population is sigma squared (σ^2). If all the cases are the same value, the variance will equal zero. The larger the variance value, the more the values are spread out in the distribution.

We will be using $N - 1$ as the denominator rather than N since the primary focus of this book is to use samples to estimate populations. The use of $N - 1$ is a more accurate estimate (*unbiased estimate*) of a population parameter. We do not know what the population mean is, so the sample values have less variability. We use the sample mean instead and with $N - 1$ as a compensation for not knowing the population mean. This use of $N - 1$ also is referred to as *degrees of freedom (df)*, a practice used in most statistical analyses. As Hays (1963) states, "Thus we say that there are $N - 1$ degrees of freedom for a sample variance, reflecting the fact that only $N - 1$ deviations are 'free' to be any number, but that given these free values, the last deviation is completely determined" (p. 311). If the goal of studying a sample is to describe the sample and not to estimate a population, then N may be used and not $N - 1$. The variance is calculated next using the data from Table 1.1.

$$s^2 = \frac{\Sigma(X - \overline{X})^2}{N - 1}$$

$$= \frac{64}{5}$$

$$s^2 = 12.80$$

Standard Deviation of the Sample (*s*)

The *standard deviation of the sample (s)* is the square root of the variance. The symbol for the standard deviation of the population is σ. The standard deviation is a more useful explanatory measure of variability when compared to the variance because it is in the same units as the original data. For example, when presenting the mean and the standard deviation together, they are both in the same metric.

$$s = \sqrt{\frac{\Sigma(X - \overline{X})^2}{N - 1}}$$

$$= \sqrt{\frac{64}{5}}$$

$$= \sqrt{12.80}$$

$$s = 3.58$$

Coefficient of Variation (C)

The *coefficient of variation (C)* is a ratio of the standard deviation divided by the mean. The coefficient of variation can be used to compare the variability of different variables as well as the means of the variables. Using the $s = 3.58$ and $\overline{X} = 49$ from the data in Table 1.1, the coefficient of variation is calculated here as a ratio and as a percentage:

$$C = \frac{s}{\overline{X}}$$
$$= \frac{3.58}{49}$$
$$C = .073$$
$$C \times 100 = 7.30\%$$

The coefficient of variation for the DV is 0.073, and converted to a percentage it is 7.30 percent. The standard deviation is approximately 7.30 percent of the mean.

Visual Representations of a Data Set

There are many charts available to assist researchers in more fully understanding their data. Illustrations of a bar chart, histogram, and normal Q-Q plot are presented.

A data set of scores on a dependent variable of depressive symptoms is presented in a *frequency distribution* in Table 1.2. There are scores from 145 participants and there are no missing data. Hence, the data set has complete scores and the values in the Percent and Valid Percent columns are the same. The values in the first column are the scores representing depressive symptoms. For example, the score of 17 has a frequency of nine scores ($9/145 = 6.2\%$) in the data set. The value 17 represents a cumulative percentage of 49.7 percent, which is the closest value to the 50th percentile rank of the distribution of scores.

This data can be shown as a *bar chart* (see Figure 1.1). The horizontal line of the bar chart is called the *abscissa* or *x-axis*, and in this example each number represents a value for depressive symptoms in the data set. The vertical line, also called the *ordinate* or *y-axis*, represents the frequency of scores by participants at each value for depressive symptoms in the data set. For example, you can see the most frequently scored value (16) and the least frequently scored values (5, 7, 9, 35) by participants in the sample.

TABLE 1.2   Frequency Distribution of Scores of Depressive Symptoms

Statistics		
DV		
N	Valid	145
	Missing	0

		DV			
		Frequency	**Percent**	**Valid Percent**	**Cumulative Percent**
Valid	5	1	0.7	0.7	0.7
	7	1	0.7	0.7	1.4
	8	4	2.8	2.8	4.1
	9	1	0.7	0.7	4.8
	10	7	4.8	4.8	9.7
	11	5	3.4	3.4	13.1
	12	11	7.6	7.6	20.7
	13	6	4.1	4.1	24.8
	14	7	4.8	4.8	29.7
	15	5	3.4	3.4	33.1
	16	15	10.3	10.3	43.4
	17	9	6.2	6.2	49.7
	18	13	9.0	9.0	58.6
	19	2	1.4	1.4	60.0
	20	7	4.8	4.8	64.8
	21	6	4.1	4.1	69.0
	22	4	2.8	2.8	71.7
	23	6	4.1	4.1	75.9
	24	3	2.1	2.1	77.9
	25	4	2.8	2.8	80.7
	26	4	2.8	2.8	83.4
	27	4	2.8	2.8	86.2
	28	3	2.1	2.1	88.3
	29	5	3.4	3.4	91.7
	30	2	1.4	1.4	93.1
	32	7	4.8	4.8	97.9
	33	2	1.4	1.4	99.3
	35	1	0.7	0.7	100.0
	Total	145	100.0	100.0	

FIGURE 1.1 Bar Chart of Scores of Depressive Symptoms

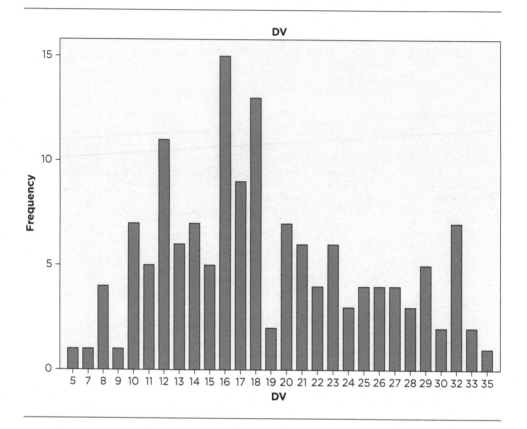

A *histogram* of the data set is presented in Figure 1.2. In a histogram the *x*-axis depicts intervals of scores and the *y*-axis still represents frequencies of scores. However, the scores on the *x*-axis are reported as falling within intervals. In this graph, the intervals are 10-point intervals, so all scores in the data set between 0 and 9 are represented by bars in this interval. Using Table 1.1 for assistance, the scores by frequencies in the data set interval 0—9 are score 5 (frequency = 1 score), score 7 (frequency = 1 score), score 8 (frequency = 4 scores), and score 9 (frequency = 1 score). Therefore, a total of seven scores in the data set are within the range of 0—9. The total numbers of scores within the intervals are interval 0—9 (seven scores), interval 10—19 (80 scores), interval 20—29 (46 scores), and interval 30—39 (12 scores).

A histogram of a data set provides the researcher with a quick visual inspection of the shape of the distribution of scores. For example, we can see

FIGURE 1.2 Histogram of Scores of Depressive Symptoms

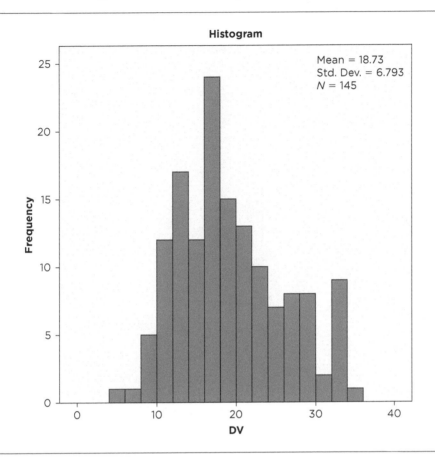

that scores cluster around the mean and there is reasonable *symmetry* (balance) of scores on either side of the mean. Also, there appear to be no extreme scores to the negative side (left) or the positive side (right) of the distribution.

The same histogram of the data set is presented in Figure 1.3 with a normal curve superimposed on the graph. This provides additional information about how well the sample distribution of scores fits a normal curve. If the data set scores were a perfect fit to the normal curve, then the bars would fit fully within the superimposed normal curve.

An example of a useful plot to assess normality of a data set is called a *Q-Q (quantile-quantile) plot* (see Figure 1.4). The Q-Q plot is derived by first subtracting each observed score from the group mean. Then, these *residuals*

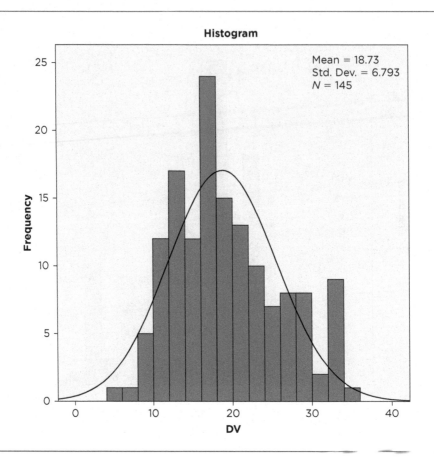

(differences) are plotted against the expected observed scores if the data are from a normal distribution (Norusis, 2003). Normality exists in the sample distribution of scores if the points on the Q-Q plot fall on or near the straight line. In this example, it appears that the data set shows reasonable normality among the scores.

THE NORMAL DISTRIBUTION

The *normal distribution* (bell curve) is the most studied and widely used curve in the field of probability (Tabak, 2005). Many measurements of human activities have been shown to be normally distributed. A great deal has been discovered about the normal curve over the past 300 years since Abraham de Moivre formulated a

FIGURE 1.4   Q-Q Plot of Scores of Depressive Symptoms

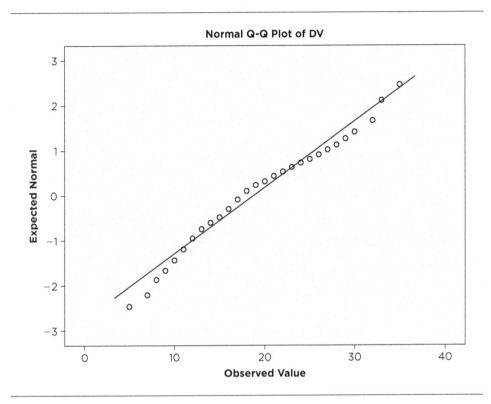

mathematical proof of the normal distribution. The normal distribution has useful properties. If two random variables have a normal distribution, their sum has a normal distribution. In general, all kinds of sums and differences of normal variables have normal distributions. So, many statistics derived from normal variates are themselves normally "distributed" (Salsburg, 2001). The normal distribution has two parameters (constants): the population mean (μ) and the population standard deviation (σ). There are many different normal curves that are based on these two parameters (Snedecor & Cochran, 1967).

Characteristics of the Normal Distribution

The normal distribution has a *peak* (highest point on the curve), *tails* (the extreme left and right points of the curve) and *shoulders* (the left and right sections of the curve between the peak and the tails) (see Figure 1.5). The right side of the

FIGURE 1.5   The Normal Distribution and Standardized Scores

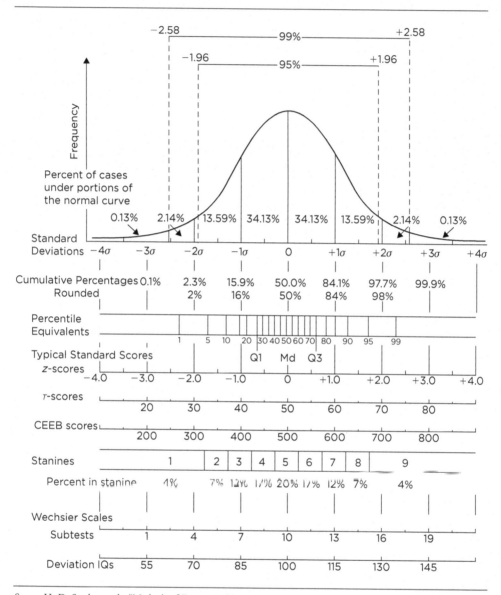

Source: H. D. Seashore, ed., "Methods of Expressing Test Scores," *Test Service Notebook* 148, January 1955. Reprinted from The Psychological Corporation, NCS Pearson, Inc.

curve is also called the *positive side* of the curve, and the left side is referred to as the *negative side*.

The base of the curve is called the abscissa (horizontal axis, *x*-axis) and sections off measurements in standard deviation units of constant percentages such as percentile ranks, *z*-scores, and *T*-scores. The height of the normal curve is called the ordinate (vertical axis, *y*-axis), which represents the percentage of cases under portions of the normal curve.

The area within the normal curve is referred to as a density of 100 percent or a unit of 1.0 for using probability. While the tails on both sides of the normal curve extend to infinity (∞) and never touch the abscissa, 99+ percent of the curve falls within ± 3 standard deviations of the curve. Most of the area is in the middle of the curve at the highest point where 68.26 percent is between ± 1 standard deviation of the normal curve. The percentage of the area under the curve decreases as the shape of the curve moves toward the tails.

The normal distribution is symmetrical, and each half of the curve is exactly 50 percent density. The mean, median, and mode of the normal curve are the same, as represented by 0 at the midpoint of the curve. Illustrations of using the normal curve in descriptive statistical analyses are discussed next.

Descriptive Statistical Applications of the Normal Distribution

We will assess an individual's measured IQ score compared to the IQ scores of others who are part of a normative sample of individuals whose scores reflect a normal curve. Bob has a measured IQ score on a standardized IQ test that is 80. The population mean of the normative sample is $\mu = 100$, and the standard deviation is $\sigma = 15$.

A *z-score* can be used with this information to compare Bob's score with the normative sample. A *z*-score is a standard score that shows the relative standing of a raw score in a normal distribution. The formula for a *z*-score is $z = X - \mu/\sigma$, where X is an individual score, μ is the population mean, and σ is the population standard deviation. The *z*-score of Bob's individual IQ score is $z = 80 - 100/15 = -1.33$. One can visualize where $z = -1.33$ is placed on the normal curve in Figure 1.5.

Next we will find the *percentile rank* of Bob's *z*-score $= -1.33$ (raw score of 80). A percentile rank is the score that indicates what percentage of persons being measured fall equal to or below the particular score. The exact percentages in the normal curve associated with *z*-scores are found using an online statistics calculator.

1. Go to www.danielsoper.com, where there are several free statistics calculators.

2. On the home website > click on *Statistics Calculator* > scroll down and click on the *Normal Distribution* button > click on the *Cumulative Area Under the Normal Curve Calculator.*

3. Type in Bob's *z*-score of −1.33 > click on the *Calculate* button > the *Cumulative area:* is .09175914.

If you take .09175914 times 100 or move the decimal two places to the right, you obtain 9.175914, which is approximately 9.18%. So a *z*-score = −1.33 indicates that equal to or less than 9.18 percent of the norm group obtain an IQ score of 80, when the mean is 100 and the standard deviation is 15. Bob's percentile rank is 9.18.

In another example, Jean scored 105 on the same IQ test. Jean's *z*-score = 105 − 100/15 = +.33. A *z*-score = +.33 is to the right of the center point mean.

1. Go to www.danielsoper.com, where there are several free statistics calculators.

2. On the home website > click on *Statistics Calculator* > scroll down and click on the *Normal Distribution* button > click on the *Cumulative Area Under the Normal Curve Calculator.*

3. Type in Jean's *z*-score of .33 > click on the *Calculate* button > the *Cumulative area:* is .62930002.

If you take .62930002 times 100 or move the decimal place two places to the right, you obtain 62.930002, which is approximately 62.93 percent. So a *z*-score = .33 indicates that equal to or less than 62.93 percent of the norm group obtain an IQ score of 105, when the mean is 100 and the standard deviation is 15. Jean's IQ score of 105 represents a percentile rank of 62.93.

Inferential Statistical Applications of the Normal Distribution

We just showed how the normal curve can be used in a descriptive statistical analysis. The normal curve also plays a key role in *inferential statistics*, which involves inferring information about samples to generalize to populations.

Inferential probability statements made about populations' characteristics (*parameters*) from analysis of sample characteristics (*statistics*) is statistical inference. Parameters are any measurable characteristic of a population, and statistics are any measurable characteristic of a sample. Inferential statistics are estimators in the sense that they estimate parameters. When a random sample is selected from a population with the purpose to understand the population, there is likely to be a difference between the population mean (μ) and the sample mean ($\overline{X}$). The difference between a population parameter and a sample statistic is *sampling error*. If you were able to select an infinite number of sample means from a population, the mean of the sample means would equal the population mean. The infinite number of sample means forms a *sampling distribution of the mean* that is distributed as a normal curve. This is the foundation of one of the most important theorems in statistics. The *central limit theorem* says that "whatever the shape of the frequency distribution of the original population of X's, the frequency distribution of $\overline{X}$ in repeated random samples of size n tends to become normal as n increases" (Snedecor & Cochran, 1967, p. 51). Thus, all that is known about the normal distribution can be applied to the sampling distribution of the mean, including the probability of obtaining a mean by chance and testing hypotheses. The z-test is used to test hypotheses when the parameters (μ and σ) are known. A sample mean can be compared to these parameters to see if it belongs to that population. One use of a z-test is in situations using test norms where σ and μ are identified in the standardization process.

For example, a researcher wants to determine if a sample of adults who have a learning disability in math would have an average full-scale (FS) IQ score that is different from the normative sample of the Wechsler Adult Intelligence Scale−IV (WAIS-IV). The WAIS-IV norms are: mean $= 100$ and standard deviation $= 15$. Since the researcher is not indicating a direction as to whether the average FS IQ score will be higher or lower than the normative sample, it is referred to as *nondirectional* and we can designate the *alternative hypothesis* as H_a: $\mu \neq 100$. The *null hypothesis* is tested, and it is written as H_0: $\mu = 100$. The population mean symbol (μ) is used because we are using the sample mean as an estimator of the population mean in the hypothesis.

A random sample of 50 adults who have a learning disability in math have a mean FS IQ score of 86 on the WAIS-IV. We want to test the null hypothesis that 50 adults with a learning disability in math are a random sample from a population of adults represented by the standardized norm sample of the WAIS-IV.

A criterion (*critical value*) is identified to compare to a calculated z-test statistic before calculating the z-statistic. We will use a commonly used *alpha level* of $\alpha = .05$. This is a *two-tailed test* since there is no specification that the outcome will show that the sample mean is higher or lower than the norm mean. We will therefore be using both the left (negative) and right (positive) sides of the normal curve to find significance. In this case, if the z-statistic produces a negative value, then we would look in the negative side of the distribution; and if a positive value is found, then we would look in the positive side. Since we are using $\alpha = .05$ and the alternative hypothesis is nondirectional, creating a two-tailed test, we need to distribute half of the alpha (.025) in each tail of the normal curve. We are going to find a z critical value that is located on the abscissa (horizontal axis) of the normal curve where .025 of the curve density falls beyond at either end of the normal curve. We are going to use an online calculator to find the z critical value at .025 in the left tail and right tail of the normal curve using the following directions.

Go to www.danielsoper.com > click on *Statistics Calculators* > scroll down and click on *Normal Distribution* > click on *Standard Normal Distribution z-score Calculator* > beside *Cumulative probability level:* type 0.025 > click the *Calculate!* button and the answer is z-score: -1.95996398.

Rounded, the z-value is -1.96, corresponding to the $\alpha = .025$ on the negative or left side of the curve. The other half of the $\alpha = .05$ is on the positive or right side of the normal curve since it is a two-tailed test. So, if you followed the same online calculator directions but typed in .975 ($1 - .025$), you would get a rounded $+1.96$ that is a positive value. Thus, the critical value that we will use to compare to the calculated z-statistic is $z_{cv} = \pm 1.96$ ($\alpha = .05$, two-tailed). The formula and calculations of the z-statistic are presented next. The numerator of the formula $\sigma / \sqrt{n}$ is the *standard error of the mean* that is the index reflecting the sampling distribution of the mean.

$$z\text{-statistic} = \frac{\overline{X} - \mu}{\sigma/\sqrt{n}}$$

$$= \frac{86 - 100}{15/\sqrt{50}}$$

$$= \frac{-14}{15/7.07}$$

$$= \frac{-14}{15/7.07}$$

$$= \frac{-14}{2.12}$$

$$z\text{-statistic} = -6.60$$

The z-statistic $= -6.60$ is greater than $z_{cv} = -1.96$, so there is a significant difference in FS IQ between the sample mean (86) of adults who have a learning disability and the mean (100) of the normative sample. The 50 adults with a learning disability in math are not a random sample from a population of adults represented by the standardized norm sample of the WAIS-IV.

One-Sample t-Test (Student's t-Test)

The z-statistic is not often used since we rarely know the population parameters. A more commonly used statistic that evolved from the z-statistic is used more often and is known as the *one-sample t-test (Student's t-test)*. The originator of the t-test was William Gossett, who worked for the Guinness Brewing Company. He used the pseudonym Student when he wrote the seminal scientific article titled "The Probable Error of the Mean," published in the 1908 issue of *Biometrika* (Student, 1908). Gossett had to use the pseudonym Student since, to protect proprietary interests, it was against company policy for employees to publish studies about Guinness.

Gossett developed a new probability distribution called the t-distribution that he assumed had an initial normal distribution. In large samples the t-distribution is nearly normal, but it is less so when the sample is less than 30. The t-distribution works well with all sample sizes as long as statistical assumptions are present. Not only is the t distribution useful for small samples, but the sample standard deviation and mean can also be used to estimated population parameters.

The one sample t-statistic is very similar to the z-test except that the sample standard deviation (s) is substituted for the known σ and the t-distribution is used to identify probability estimates to compare to obtained statistical values.

For example, a school district wants to assess whether third graders in a particular school perform in reading similarly to all third graders in the school district. The average score on a reading achievement test of third graders in the school district is 105. The sample of 25 third graders from the particular school had an average score of $\overline{X} = 124$ and standard deviation of $s = 13$. The one-sample t-test is used next to test the null hypothesis that H_0: $\mu = 105$ at $\alpha = .01$. The alternative hypothesis is nondirectional, H_a: $\mu \neq 105$. First, we will obtain a critical value using an online calculator to compare to the calculated one-sample t-test. The degrees of freedom $N - 1$ (24) and alpha ($\alpha = .01$) are needed to identify the critical value.

> Go to www.danielsoper.com > click on *Statistics Calculators* > scroll down and click on *t-Distribution* > click on *Student t-Value Calculator* > type in 24 beside *Degrees of freedom:* > click 0.01 next to *Probability level:* > click on *Calculate!* and the answer is *t-value (two-tailed):* ±2.79693951.

Rounding the t critical value for the two-tailed test is 2.797. Next, the one-sample t-test is calculated.

$$t = \frac{\overline{X} - \mu}{s/\sqrt{N}}$$

$$= \frac{124 - 105}{13/\sqrt{25}}$$

$$= \frac{19}{13/5}$$

$$= \frac{19}{2.6}$$

$$t = 7.31$$

The obtained t-value $= 7.31$ is larger than the critical value $= 2.797$, so we reject the null hypothesis ($p < .01$). We conclude that 25 third graders from a particular school had a significantly higher average score on reading achievement when compared to the average reading achievement score of all school district third-grade students.

The *t*-distribution also is used for two commonly used statistics to compare two means for differences, which are the *dependent t-test* and the *independent t-test*.

Dependent *t*-Test

A comparison is made between two sets of dependent scores when a dependent *t*-test (paired-sample *t*-test) is used. The pairs of scores between the two sets are linked together. A dependent *t*-test is used in the following four situations.

1. A comparison of the pretest and posttest scores of the same participants.

2. A comparison of the scores of one group of participants with another group of participants who are matched on one or more extraneous variables.

3. A comparison of the scores of the same group of participants under two different conditions.

4. A comparison of the scores of naturally occurring correlated pairs, like twins.

We will illustrate the use of the dependent *t*-test related to research that compares pretest scores with posttest scores on self-compassion from the same 16 participants who received a mindfulness treatment program. Self-compassion is measured by the Self-Compassion Scale (SCS; Neff, 2003), and high scores reflect higher self-compassion. The alternative hypothesis is H_a: $\mu_{preSCS} \neq \mu_{postSCS}$ and the null hypothesis to be tested is H_0: $\mu_{preSCS} = \mu_{postSCS}$.

We start by obtaining a *t* critical value to compare to an obtained *t*-value using the online calculator.

> Go to www.danielsoper.com > click on *Statistics Calculators* > scroll down and click on *t-Distribution* > click on *Student t-Value Calculator* > type in 15 beside *Degrees of freedom:* > click 0.05 next to *Probability level:* > click on *Calculate!* and the answer is *t-value (two-tailed):* ±2.13144955.

The rounded value is $t_{CV} = \pm 2.131$ using an $\alpha = .05$ with 15 *df* ($N_{pairs} - 1$, $16 - 1 = 15$). The scores and difference measures used for the analysis are in Table 1.3.

TABLE 1.3 Scores and Difference Measures for Dependent *t* Analysis

ID Number	Pretest	Posttest	Difference (*D*)	D^2
1	65	114	−49	2,401
2	106	120	−14	196
3	45	74	−29	841
4	116	129	−13	169
5	75	105	−30	900
6	46	97	−51	2,601
7	54	95	−41	1,681
8	79	103	−24	576
9	55	109	−54	2,916
10	99	101	−2	4
11	52	94	−42	1,764
12	73	76	−3	9
13	51	77	−26	676
14	88	98	−10	100
15	76	86	−10	100
16	68	88	−20	400
	$\overline{X}_{pre} = 71.75$	$\overline{X}_{post} = 97.88$	$\Sigma D = -418$	$\Sigma D^2 = 15,334$
		$\overline{D} = 71.75 - 97.88$		
		$\overline{D} = -26.13$		

$$\text{Dependent } t\text{-test} = \frac{\overline{D}}{\sqrt{\dfrac{\Sigma D^2 - \dfrac{(\Sigma D)^2}{N}}{N(N-1)}}}$$

$$= \frac{-26.13}{\sqrt{\dfrac{15,334 - \dfrac{(-418)^2}{16}}{16(16-1)}}}$$

$$= \frac{-26.13}{\sqrt{\dfrac{15,334 - 10,920}{240}}}$$

$$= \frac{-26.13}{\sqrt{18.39}}$$

$$= \frac{-26.13}{4.29}$$

$$t = -6.09$$

The calculated dependent $t = -6.09$ is greater than the $t_{CV} \pm 2.131$, so the null hypothesis is rejected and we conclude that there is a significant difference between the pretest and posttest self-compassion scores. The pretest $\overline{X}_{pre} = 71.75$ and the posttest $\overline{X}_{post} = 97.88$. Since a high score represents higher self-compassion, we conclude that there was a significant gain in self-compassion following the mindfulness treatment.

Independent *t*-Test

The independent *t*-test is used to test if two sample means are significantly different from each other from two independent samples. This is a between group analysis. We are testing whether the two means from independent samples are from different populations. The sample means as estimators of the population parameters based upon the sampling distribution of differences between means.

An independent *t*-test analysis will be demonstrated comparing a randomly assigned group of 16 participants who received a psychotherapy intervention on their changes in thought suppression to a control group ($n = 16$) who received the treatment later. Thought suppression is measured using the White Bear Suppression Inventory (WBSI) (Wegner & Zanakos, 1994), and high scores represent higher perceived thought suppression. The alternative hypothesis is H_a: $\mu_{pschotherapy} \neq \mu_{control}$ and the null hypothesis is H_0: $\mu_{psychotherapy} = \mu_{control}$. The mean and variance of WBSI scores and group sizes for the psychotherapy group of participants were $\overline{X} = 39.75$, $s^2 = 95.67$, $n = 16$, and for the control group $\overline{X} = 53.06$, $s^2 = 130.73$, $n = 16$.

First, we obtain a *t* critical value.

Go to www.danielsoper.com > click on *Statistics Calculators* > scroll down and click on *t-Distribution* > click on *Student t-Value Calculator* > type in 30 beside *Degrees of freedom:* > click 0.01 next to *Probability level:* > click on *Calculate!* and the answer is *t-value (two-tailed):* ±2.74999566.

The rounded value is $t_{CV} = \pm 2.750$ using an $\alpha = .01$ with 30 df ([$n_1 - 1$] + [$n_2 - 1$], [$16 - 1$] + [$16 - 1$] = 30).

$$\text{Independent } t\text{-test} = \frac{\overline{X}_1 - \overline{X}_2}{\sqrt{\dfrac{s_1^2}{n_1} + \dfrac{s_2^2}{n_2}}}$$

$$= \frac{39.75 - 53.06}{\sqrt{\dfrac{95.67}{16} + \dfrac{130.73}{16}}}$$

$$= \frac{-13.31}{\sqrt{5.98 + 8.17}}$$

$$= \frac{-13.31}{3.76}$$

$$t = -3.54$$

The calculated independent $t = -3.54$ is greater than the $t_{CV} = \pm 2.750$, so we reject the null hypothesis of no differences. The treatment group showed significantly lower thought suppression scores than control group participants who did not receive the treatment ($p < .01$).

We used equal-sized groups in this example of an independent t-test. A pooled variance, $S_p^2 = \dfrac{S_1^2(n_1 - 1) + S_2^2(n_2 - 1)}{n_1 + n_2 - 2}$, is used if the sizes of groups are unequal and the independent t formula becomes $t = \dfrac{\overline{X}_1 - \overline{X}_2}{\sqrt{S_p^2\left(\frac{1}{n_1} + \frac{1}{n_2}\right)}}$.

SUMMARY

This chapter has presented the purpose of the book and information related to the foundations of research and statistics. Several commonly used statistics are covered in the book that are linked to the normal distribution, including: (1) one-way analysis of variance, (2) repeated-measures analysis of variance, (3) factorial analysis of variance, (4) analysis of covariance, and (5) correlation coefficient and multiple regression analysis. Nonparametric statistics are covered later in the book that have less distribution requirements and are referred to as distribution-free statistics. The nonparametric statistics that are covered are Kruskal-Wallis one-way analysis of variance, Mann-Whitney U statistic, Friedman's rank test for k

correlated samples, and the Wilcoxon's matched-pairs signed-ranks test. Each statistic is demonstrated using the hypothesis-testing process that is the subject of the next chapter.

PROBLEM ASSIGNMENT

Review information was presented in this chapter related to measures of central tendency, variability, visual representations of data, and the normal distribution. Moreover, applications of descriptive and inferential statistics of the normal distribution were illustrated. Review problems are presented on the companion website for you to practice on. Use the examples presented in this chapter to guide you as you complete the assignment. Your instructor will evaluate your completed worksheet when it is finished.

KEY TERMS

abscissa	critical value
active independent variable	degrees of freedom (df)
alpha level	dependent t-test
alternative hypothesis	dependent variable (DV)
attribute independent variable	discrete scale
bar chart	discrete-nominal scale
bimodal	discrete-ordinal scale
categorical variable	extraneous variable (EV)
central limit theorem	frequency distribution
classification variable	histogram
coefficient of variation (C)	independent t-test
continuous scale	independent variable (IV)
continuous-interval scale	inferential statistics
continuous-ratio scale	mean ($\overline{X}$)
criterion variable (CV)	mean deviation scores

measures of central tendency

measures of variability (dispersion)
of scores

median (M_{dn})

mode (M_o)

negative side

nondirectional

normal distribution

null hypothesis

one-sample t-test (Student's t-test)

operational definition (OD)

ordinate

parameters

peak

percentile rank

positive side

predictor variable (PV)

Q-Q (quantile-quantile) plot

range

residuals

sampling distribution
of the mean

sampling error

shoulders

standard deviation of the
sample (s)

standard error of the mean

statistics

sum of squares

symmetry

tails

two-tailed test

unbiased estimate

unimodal

variance of the sample (s^2)

x-axis

y-axis

z-score

Chapter 2

LOGICAL STEPS

OF CONDUCTING

QUANTITATIVE RESEARCH:

HYPOTHESIS-TESTING

PROCESS

LEARNING OBJECTIVES

- Understand the logic and purpose of the hypothesis-testing process in scientific research.

- Identify the components and application of alternative and null hypotheses.

- Examine the meaning of alpha level and commonly used criterion levels of alpha (α) used in research.

- Explore the elements used to choose an appropriate statistic for use to test a null hypothesis.

o Understand decision rules associated with rejecting and failing to reject a null hypothesis.

o Realize the importance of including effect size and confidence interval information to further clarify making a decision concerning the null hypothesis.

The hypothesis-testing process is a logical sequence of steps to conduct the statistical analyses in a quantitative research study. Indeed, hypothesis testing is the most widely used statistical tool in scientific research (Salsburg, 2001, p. 114). However, we must remember that no method, including obtaining statistical results from hypothesis testing, is the absolute final answer to a research problem. As Snedecor and Cochran (1967) stated, "But the basic ideas in statistics assist us in thinking clearly about the problem, provide some guidance about the conditions that must be satisfied if sound inferences are to be made, and enable us to detect many inferences that have not good logical foundation" (p. 3).

HYPOTHESIS-TESTING PROCESS

There are six steps of the hypothesis-testing process that provide the procedure for conducting the statistical analyses used in this book. Descriptions and key concepts are discussed for each hypothesis step.

1. **Establish the alternative (research) hypothesis (H_a).**

An *alternative (research) hypothesis (H_a)* is a speculative statement about the relations between two or more variables used in a quantitative research study (Kerlinger & Lee, 2000). A researcher initially develops one or more research hypotheses about the direction and expected results of a study. In experimental and quasi-experimental research, the variables stated in an alternative hypothesis reflect the changes in an outcome (*dependent variable*) that can be attributed to a cause (*independent variable*) (Martin & Bridgmon,

2009). Researchers focusing on the predictive relationships among variables often use the terms *predictor variable* (independent) and *criterion variable* (dependent).

An alternative hypothesis can be conceptualized as either a *nondirectional hypothesis* or a *directional hypothesis*. A researcher does not have a clear expectation about what direction the results of study will likely take when a nondirectional hypothesis is used. Typically, there is little or no previous evidence to inform the researcher as to what the results have been in the past represented by similar studies when a nondirectional alternative hypothesis is used. For example, if a researcher is studying the effects of cognitive-behavioral therapy (CBT) and interpersonal therapy (IPT) on weight gain among women with bulimia, a researcher might state a narrative nondirectional alternative hypothesis (H_a) as:

H_a: There will be significant differences in weight gain among women with bulimia when comparing the effects of cognitive-behavioral therapy to the effects of interpersonal therapy.

This nondirectional alternative hypothesis does not declare a direction as to whether the one therapy condition will produce more effects than the other therapy condition. We can also write this nondirectional hypothesis in the following symbolic format:

$$H_a: \mu_{1\ (CBT)} \neq \mu_{2\ (IBT)}$$

The symbol μ *(mu)* represents a population mean that we estimate using a sample mean ($\overline{X}$) when conducting inferential statistics to assess mean differences. In this case, we are hypothesizing that the population mean of weight gain resulting from CBT will be different from (not less than or greater than) the population mean of weight gain produced by IPT. We analyze sample means as estimates of the population means and might choose to use an independent *t*-test in this example.

A directional alternative hypothesis does state an expectation for the outcome of the study. Researchers usually design their studies using previous research to guide them. Since a major purpose of research is to integrate study results with related previous and ongoing studies and theory, directional hypotheses are commonly used by researchers.

The following directional alternative hypothesis could be written based on previous research studies showing cognitive-behavioral therapy to be more effective than interpersonal therapy in reducing weight gain among women with bulimia.

H_a: Cognitive-behavioral therapy will produce significantly higher weight gain among women with bulimia when compared to the effects of weight gain produced by interpersonal therapy.

This directional alternative hypothesis is a declaration that cognitive-behavioral therapy will produce more weight gain than interpersonal therapy among women with bulimia. Symbolically, the directional alternative hypothesis can be written as:

$$H_a : \mu_{1 \, (CBT)} > \mu_{2 \, (IBT)}$$

This symbolic alternative hypothesis states that the population mean of weight gain resulting from CBT will be larger (greater) than the effects of IPT on the population mean of weight gain.

2. **Establish the null hypothesis (H_0). This is the hypothesis that is tested statistically.**

The *null hypothesis* (H_0) can be viewed as: (1) the hypothesis whose *nullification*, statistically, would be taken as evidence in support of a specified alternative hypothesis, or (2) the hypothesis that there is "no difference between two sets of data with respect to some parameter, usually their means, or of no effect of an experimental manipulation on the dependent variable of interest" (Nickerson, 2000, p. 242); the latter is most commonly used in psychological research. The "no difference" approach is often referred to as a *nil null hypothesis* or a nil hypothesis.

We will be combining both approaches in the statistical nullification of the null hypothesis in support of a specified alternative hypothesis. Also, we will be testing no difference nulls and *suspending judgment* when we fail to reject nulls. A null hypothesis related to our previous alternative hypothesis example can be stated as:

H_0: There will be no difference in weight gain among women with bulimia when comparing the effects of cognitive-behavioral therapy to the effects of interpersonal therapy.

A "no difference in effects" approach is taken in testing the null hypothesis. Also, a statistical nullification of the null would provide evidence in support of the specified alternative hypothesis. The null can be stated symbolically as:

$$H_0: \mu_{1\,(CBT)} = \mu_{2\,(IBT)}$$

The null hypothesis states that the population means of weight gain resulting from CBT and IPT will be equal. There will be no difference between the means resulting from either treatment condition.

When the null hypothesis is rejected, a significant difference is found between the sample means of weight gain (estimating the population means) produced by the treatment conditions. Moreover, we will conclude that this nullification provides evidence in support of the alternative hypothesis. If the sample means are not significantly different from each other, we have an inconclusive decision when we fail to reject the null hypothesis. We cannot say that there is absolutely no difference between the two means in this case. We instead suspend judgment as to the relation between the two means that are not significantly different from each other.

3. **Decide on the risk that one is willing to take for being wrong if one rejects a true H_0, thus making a Type I (alpha [α]) error. Also, make a decision about the risk one is willing to take for being wrong if one fails to reject a false H_0, thus making a Type II (beta [β] error).**

A researcher chooses (sets) an *alpha level (α)* prior to data analysis. Common alpha levels used in research are .001, .01, .05, and .10, with the two most common being $\alpha = .05$ and $\alpha = .01$. One of the founders of statistics, Sir Ronald A. Fisher, suggested using $\alpha = .05$ in the early 1900s (Fisher, 1925). His practice evolved into the four most used alpha levels ranging from .001 to .10. As Nickerson (2000) states, "If α is set at .05, say, and a significance test yields a value of p equal to or less than .05, the null hypothesis is rejected and the result is said to be statistically significant at that level" (p. 243).

We also need to consider the chances associated with making a *beta error (Type II error)* when we select an alpha level for a particular study. We do this by conducting an *a priori power analysis*, which tells us the probability in a proposed study of correctly rejecting the false null hypothesis in favor of an alternative hypothesis. The power analysis is conducted before a study begins using an estimated alpha level, sample size, and effect size. Power analysis is discussed further in Chapter 3.

4. **Decide on the appropriate statistic to be used to test the H_0 and the associated sampling distribution to be used (e.g., z, t, F, r, R, χ^2) on the assumption that H_0 is true.**

The next step in the hypothesis-testing process is to identify the appropriate statistic and associated *sampling distribution* to use to test the null hypothesis. The sampling distribution is a theoretical probability distribution that provides the foundation for testing hypotheses statistically.

Several issues are examined to determine whether a certain statistic is appropriate to use for a particular analysis (testing of an H_0) in a study. The choice of a statistic is based on elements related to: (1) the focus of the interplay among variables (e.g., relationships or differences), (2) the number of independent and dependent variables used in an analysis, (3) the scales of measurements of the dependent variables, (4) the number and relationships (dependent vs. independent) of participant groups being compared, and (5) the extent that underlying assumptions of the statistic are met. A statistical design process integrating these elements is presented in Chapter 4.

5. **Draw a sample of size N; screen the data for accuracy, missing values, and outliers; and assess whether the underlying assumptions of the statistic being used are met.**

It may be necessary to change a decision about the statistic chosen or to modify the data set based on your data screening results. Compute the sample statistic and compare the result to the critical value (CV) (e.g., $z_{.95}$, $t_{.99}$, $F_{.999}$) of the sampling distribution. More commonly, a comparison is made between the exact probability value obtained from the computer generated statistical result and the chosen alpha level to determine significance.

Initially in the *data screening process*, it is important to conduct data cleaning once the data is collected. Study data may be entered into a computerized statistical program by hand or imported or downloaded from another source. All methods of data compilation have the potential for varying degrees of imprecision. It is therefore important to use various methods to check the accuracy of data before conducting statistical analyses.

The extent and pattern of missing data are another focus of data screening. Missing data can occur from data handling error, from study participants failing to respond to items, or from participants discontinuing their involvement in a study. Missing data can make it difficult to interpret and generalize the results of statistical analyses to the population from which the study sample was drawn.

Data diagnostic procedures are undertaken after the data are determined to be accurate. Many statistical procedures, known as *parametric statistics*, require that certain underlying assumptions are met in order to use a given statistic with a data set. A parametric statistical process is undertaken when sample characteristics are used to estimate population parameters such as those from the known normal distribution, *t*-distribution, and *F*-distribution. For example, a one-way analysis of variance requires that the scores of the dependent variable approximate a normal distribution, their variances across groups are homogeneous or constant, and there is independence of observations. If the underlying assumptions are not found to be met, then a researcher may need to use a nonparametric statistic that does not require the same strict underlying assumptions. Another common alternative is to transform the data to minimize the effects of outliers, nonnormal distributions, heterogeneous variances, and dependence of observations.

Once the data are readied from data screening and diagnostics, the testing of the null hypothesis can be conducted using the statistical analysis. The statistical analysis significance probability (generated from the probabilities of the sampling distribution used) is compared to the selected alpha level. The researcher makes a decision to reject or fail to reject the null hypothesis.

6. **Make a decision regarding the H_0; either reject the H_0 in favor of the H_a or fail to reject H_0. Additionally, provide effects sizes and confidence intervals.**

If the statistical significance probability is equal to or less than the alpha level, the null hypothesis is rejected. The decision of failing to reject the H_0 is made if the statistical significance probability is greater than α. For example, in rejecting the null hypothesis when $\alpha = .05$, we will make a Type I error no more than five times in 100. There is only a 5 percent or less chance that we reject a true H_0. This statistical decision making can be illustrated using the null hypothesis stated earlier.

(Narrative Null)

H_0: There will be no difference in weight gain among women with bulimia when comparing the effects of cognitive-behavioral therapy to the effects of interpersonal therapy.

(Symbolic Null)

$$H_0: \mu_{1\,(CBT)} = \mu_{2\,(IBT)}$$

We will say that we found a statistical significance probability of $p = .003$ and the alpha level of significance is $\alpha = .05$. The $p = .003$ is less than the alpha criterion of $\alpha = .05$ so the rule is to reject the H_0. We can conclude that there was a significant difference in weight gain resulting from a comparison of the CBT and IBT conditions. There is a less than 5 percent chance that we reject a true H_0 ($p < .05$). We expect that fewer than five times in 100 would there be no difference between the two means. There is another way to state this statistical decision of rejecting the null hypothesis by linking to sampling distribution theory. It could be said that if one repeatedly took two random samples from the same population and tested the differences between their means, one would expect to get a difference that was significant at the .05 level about five times in 100 (Nickerson, 2000).

Now, let's say that that we found a statistical significance probability of $p = .11$ and the alpha level of significance is still $\alpha = .05$. The obtained $p = .11$ is greater than the alpha criterion of $\alpha = .05$, so the rule is to fail to reject the H_0 ($p > .05$). We can conclude that it is inconclusive that CBT and IPT have a differing effect on weight gain among participants. When we fail to reject the null hypothesis, we cannot conclude that there is an absolute noneffect or no difference. We would not say that CBT and IPT were equal in their effects on weight gain. A nonsignificant result is an inconclusive result or indefinite decision.

Making a decision about the null hypothesis is not enough. Additional information is needed to help draw accurate conclusions about one's study data. Cohen (1994) provided three recommendations to improve the null hypothesis significance testing (NHST) process. First, understand that there is no magic alternative to NHST. Second, before generalizing from your data, understand and improve the data using "detective work" methods such as data screening or exploratory data analysis (EDA). Third, routinely report *effect sizes* and report data in the form of confidence limits. Jones and Tukey (2000) proposed using *confidence intervals* when they are available and recognizing the limitations with traditional NHST.

Jones and Tukey (2000) also proposed another conclusion-making process, emphasizing that a researcher should assess the sample data and entertain one of three conclusions: "(a) act as if $\mu_A - \mu_B > 0$; (b) act as if $\mu_A - \mu_B < 0$; or (c) act as if the sign of $\mu_A - \mu_B$ is indefinite, that is, is not (yet) determined" (p. 412). Again, using our previous example, the first possible conclusion following statistical analysis is that $\mu_{CBT} - \mu_{IPT} > 0$, which reflects that CBT produces a higher weight gain than the IPT condition. The second possible conclusion is that $\mu_{CBT} - \mu_{IPT} < 0$ resulted in CBT producing less weight gain than the IPT condition. The final possible conclusion is that $\mu_{CBT} - \mu_{IPT}$ is indefinite—that is, inconclusive.

It is important to remember that *replication studies* provide the tenability of scientific findings. Scientific conclusions result from a stream of well-designed studies in which data are compared across studies to formulate theory. There is no final scientific truth, but, instead, there is evolving scientific theory.

SUMMARY

The six steps of the hypothesis-testing process were discussed in this chapter. The hypothesis-testing process is the model or template that is used to learn the statistical analyses covered in the book. The hypothesis-testing process is the most widely used tool in science; however, there are limitations to be aware of.

PROBLEM ASSIGNMENT

The components of the hypothesis-testing process were presented in this chapter, including a rationale for decision making regarding the rejecting or failing to reject the null hypothesis. Examples are available on the companion website for you to practice your understanding of the hypothesis-testing process.

KEY TERMS

alpha level (α)

alternative (research) hypothesis (H_a)

a priori power analysis

beta error (Type II error)

confidence intervals

criterion variable

data screening process

dependent variable

directional hypothesis

effect sizes

independent variable

nil null hypothesis

nondirectional hypothesis

null hypothesis (H_O)

nullification

parametric statistics

predictor variable

replication studies

sampling distribution

suspending judgment

μ (mu)

Chapter 3

MAXIMIZING HYPOTHESIS

DECISIONS USING

POWER ANALYSIS

LEARNING OBJECTIVES

○ Understand the balancing considerations to avoid making Type I and Type II errors in choosing an alpha level for a study.

○ Explore illustrations of study examples to avoid making Type I and Type II errors.

○ Understand the difference between a priori power analysis and post hoc power analysis.

○ Examine the three elements used in conducting an a priori power analysis: alpha level, estimated effect size, and sample size.

○ Understand the three classes of effect sizes.

○ Conduct and interpret an a priori power analysis using G*Power.

Making a correct decision about rejecting or failing to reject a null hypothesis relates to probability, not certainty. The null hypothesis statistical testing process balances between avoiding making either a Type I or Type II error. An a priori power analysis can be conducted to help a researcher maximize correctly rejecting a false null hypothesis in favor of the alternative hypothesis in a study.

The third step in the hypothesis testing process focuses on identifying an alpha level as a criterion for making a decision about rejecting or failing to reject a null hypothesis in a study. Choosing an alpha level involves considering avoiding making both a *Type I error (alpha [α] error)* and a *Type II error (beta [β] error)* when making a decision to either reject or fail to reject a null hypothesis (H_0). The correctness of rejecting or failing to reject an H_0 relates to a balance between avoiding making a Type I error and avoiding making a Type II error. Refer to Table 3.1 as we discuss this statistical decision process of rejecting or failing to reject a null hypothesis, balancing the avoidance of making a Type I or Type II error.

The heading called Possible Study Decision in Table 3.1 refers to the decisions facing a researcher to reject or fail to reject a null hypothesis related to a particular study. Foundational to the statistical hypothesis testing process is an understanding that when we reject or fail to reject a null hypothesis we never know absolutely if our decision was correct, because we are using probability as the basis of our decision. We want to make a tenable decision based on a high degree of probability that our decision is correct. We can conceptualize the correctness of our decision by comparing the possible study decisions about the null to the hypothetical actual truth (theoretical) about the null in our study.

We will use the previous example null of H_0: $\mu_{1\,(\text{CBT})} = \mu_{2\,(\text{IPT})}$ with $\alpha = .05$ to illustrate the possible statistical decisions using Table 3.1. We can conceptualize a true H_0 using our study example as meaning that there is no significant difference between means and a false H_0 as there is a significant difference between means.

TABLE 3.1 Decision Balance between Type I and Type II Errors

Possible Study Decision	Actual Truth about H_0	
	H_0 True	H_0 False
Reject H_0	Type I (α) error	Correct decision $p = 1 - \beta$ = Power
Fail to reject H_0	Correct decision	Type II error $p = \beta$

If we reject the H_0 ($p < .05$), we decided that there is a significant difference in weight gain of women with bulimia who received cognitive-behavioral therapy (CBT) compared to those who were provided the interpersonal therapy (IPT) condition. However, if in actual truth (theoretical) the null hypothesis is true—that is, there is no difference in weight gain comparing the mean of the CBT group to the mean of the IPT group of participants—then we made a Type I (α) error by rejecting a null hypothesis when we thought there was a difference in weight gain between the groups but in actuality there was no difference.

We make a correct decision if we reject the H_0 and in actuality the H_0 is false. The decision that there is a difference in mean weight gain between the groups is correct because in actual truth the H_0 is false.

We make a Type II (beta) error if we fail to reject the H_0 and in actual truth the null hypothesis is false. We declare there is no significant difference between group means when in actuality there is a significant difference in weight gain produced by the two conditions of CBT and IPT.

If we fail to reject the H_0 in our study and in actual truth the null hypothesis is true, we make a correct decision. We decided that there is no significant difference in weight gain produced by the CBT compared to the IPT conditions and in actuality there is no difference in weight gain between the two condition groups. As we discussed in Chapter 2, it is better to say that we suspend judgment on a difference when we fail to reject a null hypothesis.

BALANCE BETWEEN AVOIDING TYPE I AND TYPE II ERRORS

There is a give-and-take relationship between avoiding making either a Type I error or a Type II error when trying to make a correct decision about rejecting or failing to reject a null hypothesis. The alpha, beta, and the *a priori power* levels chosen by a researcher can influence the correctness of a significance decision about the null hypothesis. The influence of alpha related to making Type I and II errors is illustrated first.

Illustration of Avoiding Making a Type I (Alpha) Error

Suppose that administrators of a large school district have learned about a new curriculum that has demonstrated effectiveness in improving reading scores in elementary schools in two other large school districts in their state. The administrators have not concluded that they have a problem in their district, but the other districts have shown an increase in student reading achievement when they adopted the new curriculum. The school district administrators have estimated that to implement the new reading curriculum it would cost the district $900,000 in new materials and teacher training. The administrators plan a study to assess the effectiveness of the new reading curriculum compared to the old curriculum before making a decision. The school district research and development director creates and implements a randomized design comparing two treatments (old curriculum, new curriculum) on standardized reading achievement scores. We present the null and alternative hypotheses for this hypothetical study and go through possible decisions in Table 3.1 to discuss the reciprocal relationship between Type I and II errors in possible decisions about the null hypothesis.

$$H_0: \mu_{\text{OLD CURRICULUM}} = \mu_{\text{NEW CURRICULUM}}$$
$$H_a: \mu_{\text{old curriculum}} < \mu_{\text{new curriculum}}$$

Would it be of more concern for the researcher to avoid making a Type I error or a Type II error in this example? If a Type I error is made, the H_0 is rejected when in the true state of the world H_0 is true. The decision is made that there is significantly higher reading achievement scores of students who received the new curriculum versus the old curriculum; however, there really is no significant difference between the two curricula to improve reading achievement scores.

A Type II error would suggest that the researcher failed to reject the H_0 when the actual truth is that the H_0 is false. The researcher declared that there is no significant difference in reading achievement between the two curricula when in fact the new curriculum is more effective than the old curriculum.

It is always a balancing act between avoiding either a Type I or a Type II error, so there is no one absolutely true answer to the question posed earlier. The situational factors related to the research study contribute to the importance of avoiding Type I and II errors.

It could be argued in this situation that the researcher might be most concerned about avoiding making a Type I error, deciding there is a difference in the effect of the new curriculum compared to the old curriculum when in truth there is no difference. In making this error the school district might spend $900,000 and put forth a great deal of effort in training teachers to use the new curriculum when the new curriculum is no better than the old curriculum in increasing reading scores.

Selected alpha levels can affect the balance to avoid making either a Type I or a Type II error. You recall that the four most common alpha levels used in research as the criterion for rejecting or failing to reject an H_0 are:

	More Stringent		Less Stringent	
Alpha levels	.001	.01	.05	.10

More stringent signifies that is more difficult to reject the null hypothesis and less stringent means that it is less difficult to reject the null hypothesis. The choice of a more stringent alpha level (.001 or .01) reduces the chances of making a Type I error. For example, if the H_0 is rejected at the $\alpha = .01$ level, then there is a less than 1 percent chance that a true H_0 was rejected. In contrast, choosing an $\alpha = .10$ would result in a 10 percent chance of rejecting a true H_0. Choosing a more stringent alpha level in this example would reduce the probability of making a Type I error, which would increase the researcher's confidence that there is a real difference between the two curriculums on improving reading achievement. However, making the alpha level more stringent increases the chances of making a Type II error of failing to reject the H_0 when there may be an important difference between the two curricula on reading achievement but at a less stringent alpha level.

Illustration of Avoiding Making a Type II (Alpha) Error

Officials at a state department of public transportation want to determine from a series of studies how blood alcohol intake affects driving skills. The officials want to obtain evidence to consider whether driving under the influence (DUI) laws should be changed relative to blood alcohol concentration (BAC) levels. In one study, a sample of participants are randomly assigned to one of four alcohol consumption conditions that produce BAC levels of either .03, .06, .08, or .10. The participants are asked to drive automobiles through a driving skills course after reaching their designated BAC levels. The mean driving skill levels are compared across the BAC condition groups. A lower mean score reflects lower-skill performance during driving. The null and alternative hypotheses are stated as:

$$H_0: \mu_{BAC.03} = \mu_{BAC.06} = \mu_{BAC.08} = \mu_{BAC.10}$$
$$H_0: \mu_{BAC.03} > \mu_{BAC.06} > \mu_{BAC.08} > \mu_{BAC.10}$$

Would it be of more concern for the researcher to avoid making a Type I error or a Type II error in this example? There may be more reason in this example to emphasize the avoidance of making a Type II error. If the researcher fails to reject the H_0 that there is no difference in driving skills across the BAC levels when in the truth there is a difference, making this Type II error could result in decisions by the department of public transportation to allow more unsafe drivers on the road. The researcher may want to choose a less stringent alpha level (.05 or .10) to improve the chances of finding a difference if it exists. This decision, though, would increase the chances of making a Type I error. The researcher may declare differences in driving skills when in fact differences in BAC levels have no effect on driving skills.

A Priori Power Analysis

We have shown that the selection of alpha levels can influence the balance between making either a Type I or a Type II error. Another important ingredient to consider in the balancing process is *a priori power* (see Table 3.1). While beta (β) is incorrectly retaining a false H_0 (Type II error), power is the probability of correctly rejecting a false null hypothesis in favor of the stated alternative hypothesis. Just as a researcher develops a rationale for selection of an alpha level before (a priori) the study begins, the researcher also wants to conduct an a priori power analysis. A researcher also analyzes *post hoc (observed) power* after the study is conducted.

An a priori power probability is calculated before the study begins; its value ranges from 0 to 1.0, and we want it to be as large as possible. A priori power is an estimate of the probability of correctly rejecting a false null hypothesis in favor of an alternative hypothesis when important elements in a study are combined. The three important elements that comprise power are the (1) selected alpha level, (2) planned study sample size, and (3) estimated *a priori effect size*.

A researcher chooses an alpha level for a study following a process as illustrated in the earlier discussion. The researcher plans a study sample size based on practical issues such as availability and cost and also increasing the power of the study. Moreover, larger sample sizes are important in being able to generalize study findings to a target population and maximize the likelihood of finding a treatment effect if it exists in a study.

An *effect size (ES)* is used as either an a priori estimator in power analysis or a post hoc (after the study) measure of the magnitude of an effect or relationship. An effect size provides information about practical importance of a null hypothesis statistical finding.

There are several types of effect sizes that are organized into three classes: (1) *standardized differences effect sizes,* (2) *variance-accounted-for effect sizes,* and (3) *corrected effect sizes* (Vacha-Haase & Thompson, 2004). The standardized differences effect sizes are standardized scores (z-scores). A commonly used standardized difference ES is *Cohen's d statistic* as defined by $d = \overline{X}_{\text{Treatment}} - \overline{X}_{\text{Control}}/SD_{\text{Pooled}}$. The $\overline{X}_{\text{Treatment}}$ is the sample mean of the treatment group on a dependent variable, and the $\overline{X}_{\text{Control}}$ is the mean of the control group. The SD_{Pooled} is the pooled (weighted average) standard deviation of the standard deviations of both groups combined. Let's say that an antidepressant medication is compared to a placebo condition to improve mood symptoms as measured by a standardized test of mood where high scores reflect better mood. The sample means of mood scores and the pooled standard deviation are $\overline{X}_{\text{AntidepressantMedication}} = 45$, $\overline{X}_{\text{Placebo}} = 27$, and the $SD_{\text{Pooled}} = 8$. Then, $d = (45 - 27)/8 = 18/8 = 2.25$. We can say that the study results show that the mean score of mood was 2¼ standard deviations higher for the participants receiving antidepressant medication than for the participants who were in the placebo condition. Cohen (1988) also developed guidelines for identifying whether an effect size is small, medium, or large (see Table 3.2).

A $d = 2.25$ is well beyond the cutoff criterion ($>.80$) for being a large effect size. Effect sizes are best interpreted in the context of the variables being studied and in relation to findings from similar previous studies (Vacha-Haase & Thompson, 2004). Cohen's strength of effect size guidelines can be used for approximate general interpretations. These guidelines for d are most useful with the results of an independent

TABLE 3.2 Cohen's Strength of d Effect Sizes

Effect Size	d
Small	.20
Medium	.50
Large	.80

t-test. Cohen has also developed guidelines for other statistics (see Cohen, 2008). *Glass's Δ (delta) statistic* is another example of a standardized difference effect size. It is similar to the *d* statistic except that the denominator is the standard deviation of the control condition, so $\Delta = \overline{X}_{\text{Treatment}} - \overline{X}_{\text{Control}} / SD_{\text{ControlGroup}}$.

A second class is variance-accounted-for effect sizes. These effect sizes are interpreted differently than standardized differences effect sizes. Variance-accounted-for effect size values range from 0 to +1.0, whereas the standardized differences effect sizes are based on standard deviation units and can be plus or minus and be well over ±1.0.

Eta-squared (η^2) is a commonly used variance-accounted-for effect size. It is defined as $SS_{\text{Treatment}}/(SS_{\text{Treatment}} + SS_{\text{Error}})$ when using analysis of variance. Sum of squares treatment (also called SS_{Between}) is a calculated value that reflects systematic variation due to the treatment effect. Sum of squares error (also called SS_{Within}) is a value reflecting deviations of individual scores from its group mean that are difficult to explain. When dividing $SS_{\text{Treatment}}$ by itself and another value SS_{Error} it is clear that the resulting value will be less than 1.0. So, if a study comparing two relaxation techniques and a no-treatment control condition on reducing stress produces a $SS_{\text{Treatment}} = 356.633$, and a $SS_{\text{Error}} = 1,672.350$, then $\eta^2 = 356.633/(356.633 + 1,672.350) = .176$.

Cohen's guidelines for strength of η^2 effect sizes are presented in Table 3.3. An $\eta^2 = .176$ would fall beyond the minimum level ($>.14$) for being a large effect.

An effect size for a Pearson product-moment bivariate correlation coefficient (*r*) or a multiple correlation coefficient (*R*) is achieved by squaring the correlation coefficients, resulting in r^2 and R^2 respectively. If a correlation coefficient between the amount of marijuana use and the number of hours watching television is $r = .44$, the $r^2 = (.44)^2 = .194$. The $r^2 = .194$ would fall between a small and a medium effect size according to Table 3.4.

The last class of effect sizes is corrected effect sizes. The effect size of sample has its own uniqueness (sampling error variance) that may not easily generalize to the population it was sampled from. Additionally, the unique aspects of a sample

TABLE 3.3 Cohen's Strength of η^2 Effect Sizes

Effect Size	η^2
Small	.01–.06
Medium	>.06–.14
Large	>.14

TABLE 3.4   Cohen's Strength of r Effect Sizes

Effect Size	r
Small	.10
Medium	.30
Large	.50

may not be readily replicated in other samples. Therefore, some effect sizes have corrections or adjustments to better estimate population parameters and enhance reliability across replication studies.

Omega squared (ω^2) is an effect size used in analysis of variance that is a more conservative estimate of effect size. This is evident using the same data from the previous η^2 calculation, where K (number of groups) = 3, $SS_{\text{Treatment}}$ = 356.633, SS_{Error} = 1,672.350, and SS_{Total} = ($SS_{\text{Treatment}}$ = 356.633 + SS_{Error} = 1,672.350) = 2,028.983, and MS_{Error} = 29.339.

$$\omega^2 = \frac{SS_{\text{Treatment}} - (K-1)MS_{\text{Error}}}{SS_{\text{Total}} + MS_{\text{Error}}}$$

$$= \frac{356.633 - (2)29.339}{2,028.983 + 29.339}$$

$$= \frac{297.955}{2,058.322}$$

$$\omega^2 = .145$$

A comparison of $\eta^2 = .176$ and $\omega^2 = .145$ demonstrates the conservative strength of a corrected effect size.

An adjusted r^2 is another common corrected effect size that is also a more conservative estimate. The $r^2 = .194$ we used to illustrate a variance-accounted-for effect size might result in an adjusted $r^2 = .167$.

The interpretations associated with standardized differences and variance-accounted-for effect sizes are quite different. It is important for a researcher to connect an effect size with the correct interpretation and be careful about cross-interpretation from one effect size to another.

An effect size used in an a priori power analysis is an estimate of what is likely to be the treatment effect of the planned study. Ways to estimate an effect size used for a study include using prior research, deciding on what size effect is important, and choosing a value based on professional judgment (for a further discussion see Howell, 2010). It is preferred to select an estimated effect size that resulted from a similar previous study or series of such studies.

The three ingredients necessary to conduct an a priori power analysis are α, sample size, and a priori effect size. A priori power analysis occurs prior to conducting a study for the purpose of assessing whether the study is worth conducting with the given planned alpha level, sample size, and estimated effect size. The researcher wants to know, when given these elements, the likelihood of finding a treatment effect if it exists. In other words, the researcher wants to identify the probability of correctly rejecting a false null hypothesis (power) in favor of the alternative hypothesis. The researcher would like to be assured with a 1.0 power (100 percent chance); however, that can be difficult to achieve and may not be necessary. A commonly used power value criterion to aim for in *power analysis* is power $= .80$, reflecting an 80 percent chance of correctly rejecting a false null hypothesis in favor of the stated alternative hypothesis. A researcher combines and analyzes the three a priori power elements and hopes that the resulting value is equal to or greater than the power criterion of .80.

For example, a researcher of a pharmaceutical company wants to study the effects of a new pain medication in reducing headache pain when compared to a placebo (inactive) medication (H_0: $\mu_{PainMedication} = \mu_{Placebo}$). The average effect size from three similar previous studies was a $d = .65$, and it will be used as the estimated effect size in the a priori power analysis. The researchers in the previous study used an $\alpha = .01$ because they were more concerned with avoiding making a Type I error. There are similar drugs that are effective for reducing headaches, and it will be expensive to mass-produce and market the new drug. If the new medication has a similar effect to other similar drugs then there may be no reason to develop it. The researcher is planning to use 60 participants ($N_1 = 30$, $N_2 = 30$) for the study. A useful online power analysis program called G*Power 3.1 (Faul, Erdfelder, Lang, & Buchner, 2007) is used for this example and other examples in the book.

Power Analysis Using G*Power 3.1.2

Conduct the following steps.

1. Create a folder on your desktop called *gpower*.

2. Google **G*Power**.

3. Click on **G*Power3 is now available**.

4. Then, click on **Download and register** and click on the download and save to your folder.

5. Double click on a created folder called **GPower3**.

6. Then, double click on a box or icon called **GPower 3.1.2**.

The first page you see is found in Figure 3.1. Follow these nine steps to conduct a power analysis for the example.

1. Under **Test family** > **t tests** should be selected. The analysis will compare two means, so a *t*-test is appropriate.

2. Under **Statistical test** > select **Means: Difference between two independent means (two groups)**. This is an independent *t*-test because two independent groups of participants are being compared on pain reduction.

3. Under **Type of power analysis** > select **A priori: Compute required sample size—given α, power, and effect size**.

4. Beside **Tail(s)**, **One** should be selected. We expect that the group of participants receiving the pain medication will experience a significantly reduced headache pain when compared to the placebo group (H_a: $\mu_{1PainMedication} < \mu_{2Placebo}$).

5. Type in beside **Effect size d** the example estimated effect size = 0.65, which is an average effect size from three similar previous studies.

6. Type next to **α err prob** the selected example alpha = 0.01.

7. Type next to **Power (1−β err prob)** the selected power criterion = 0.80.

8. The number 1 should be typed next to **Allocation ratio N2/N1**. For the example, there are 60 participants with 30 participants in each group, so the allocation ratio would be 30/30 = 1.

9. Click **Calculate** at the bottom right of the page.

The results of the a priori power analysis are shown in Figure 3.2. The example elements were entered into G*Power: α = .01, estimated effect size = .65, and power criterion = .80 for a one-tailed test using an equal number of 30 participants in each of two groups for a total sample of $N = 60$. The results

FIGURE 3.1 G*Power First Page

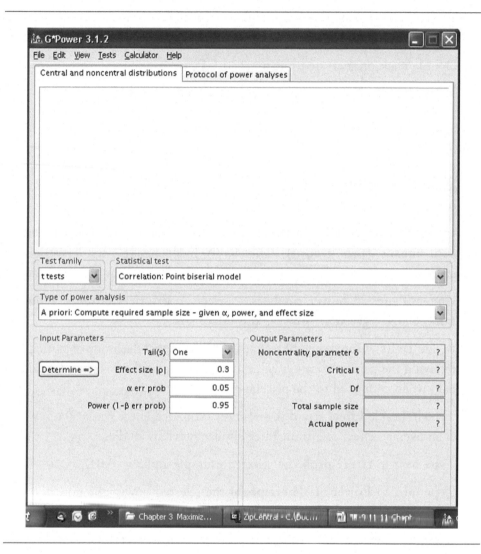

show that to reach an actual power of .8010789 using the planned α and esti-mated effect size, a total sample size of $N = 98$ with 49 participants in each of the two groups is required. Therefore, it would be advisable for the researcher to plan on increasing the total sample size to ≥98 participants before conducting the study to reach a power of .80.

Lowering the alpha level would reduce the sample size of participants needed to reach an a priori power = .80. However, that is not the reason to select an

FIGURE 3.2 A Priori Power Analysis for the Example

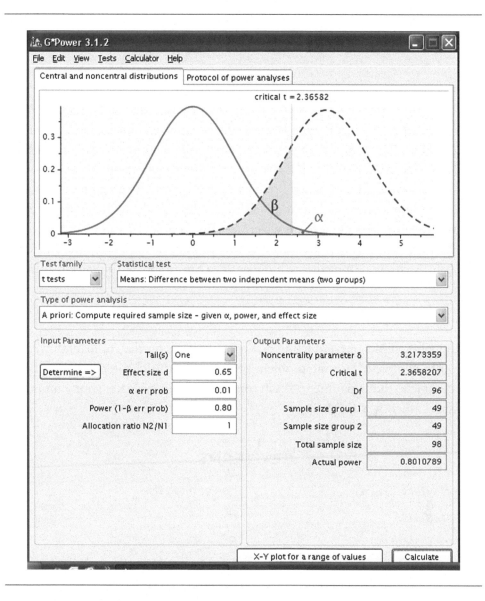

alpha level. The alpha was selected to choose the right balance between avoiding either a Type I or a Type II error related to the particular context of the study. Increasing the estimated effect size would also increase the a priori power. The estimated effect size was based on previous studies' findings, and one cannot change the results of previous studies. Increasing sample size is a legitimate way to increase a priori power, and it should be done in this example to maximize finding a significant difference, if it exists, between the effects of a new medication compared to a placebo in reducing headache pain.

SUMMARY

The correctness of rejecting or failing to reject an H_0 is a balance between avoiding making either a Type I or Type II error. There is no absolutely correct decision that can be made. However, a researcher can conceptualize the level of alpha most relevant to the context of the study. Moreover, the magnitude of treatment effects from previous research can be used to help estimate the likely outcomes of a study. Finally, it is important to select a sample size that will be conducive to finding an effect in a study. Alpha level, an a priori effect size, and sample size can be combined to estimate the probability of finding a real effect in a study. An a priori power analysis is used before a study is implemented to identify a probability of finding a real effect.

PROBLEM ASSIGNMENT

Additional examples of conducting power analysis are on the companion website for you to complete. Use the problem presented in this chapter to guide you as you complete the assignment. Your instructor will evaluate your completed worksheet when it is finished.

KEY TERMS

a priori effect size

a priori power

Cohen's d statistic

corrected effect sizes

effect size (ES)

eta-squared (η^2)

Glass's Δ (delta) statistic

omega squared (ω^2)

post hoc (observed) power

power analysis

r^2

R^2

standardized differences
    effect sizes

Type I error (alpha [α] error)

Type II error (beta [β] error)

variance-accounted-for effect sizes

Chapter 4

RESEARCH AND

STATISTICAL DESIGNS

LEARNING OBJECTIVES

○ Understand the importance of carefully formulating experimental conditions and procedures, reducing the imprecision in measurement, and controlling extraneous experimental influences.

○ Explore methods to control for extraneous variables.

○ Understand the threats to internal validity of experimental and quasi-experimental designs.

○ Examine commonly used experimental and quasi-experimental designs and examples of statistical methods that can be used in the designs.

○ Understand basic models used in correlation methods.

○ Understand issues to consider in choosing statistics to use in different research problems.

The purpose of this chapter is to identify important components of establishing experimental and quasi-experimental research by examining various designs. Correlational research models are also discussed.

Statistical designs are essentially linked to research designs. Research designs provide the blueprint for researchers to find answers to research questions. The choice and interpretation of statistics used in a particular study is dependent upon the research design selected by a researcher. A class of research designs called experimental designs has the purpose to assess outcomes of cause and effect among variables. Generally, the purpose of experimental research is to manage and understand the change among variables by *maximizing experimental variance*, *minimizing error variance*, and *controlling extraneous variance (MaxMinCon)* (Kerlinger & Lee, 2000).

A researcher maximizes experimental variance by carefully formulating experimental conditions and procedures. A researcher minimizes error variance by strategically reducing the imprecision in measurement and random error fluctuations. Controlling extraneous variance is dealt with by identifying and reducing the effects of unwanted variables through the identification of well-suited design, experimental procedures, and statistics (Martin & Bridgmon, 2009). A researcher considers several issues when choosing statistics to use for varying research problems.

FORMULATING EXPERIMENTAL CONDITIONS

Experimental research is initiated based on well-developed research questions, with alternative and null hypotheses usually connected to theory and previous research. *Independent (cause) variables* and *dependent (outcome) variables* are *operationally defined*. Operation definitions entail describing the variables in detail, especially as to how they function and are measured.

For example, suppose a treatment method for seasonal affect disorder (SAD) is an independent variable in a study and there are three treatment conditions (light therapy, cognitive-behavioral therapy (CBT), and a minimal contact-delayed treatment control condition). The dependent variable is the intensity of symptoms of a current SAD episode.

The independent variable is assessed as to whether it was implemented as planned, which is known as *treatment integrity (treatment fidelity)*. A researcher operationally defines every aspect of the experimental conditions to ensure an accurate and consistent implementation of the independent variable (*treatment delivery*). Equally important is defining how to assess whether the participants received (*treatment receipt*) and followed through with (*treatment adherence*) the intended treatment (Shadish, Cook, & Campbell, 2002).

The dependent variable of intensity of symptoms of the current SAD episode also needs to be operationally defined to know what the variable is and how it will be measured. The dependent variable might be operationally defined as the scores on a psychometrically validated instrument such as the Structured Interview Guide for the Hamilton Rating Scale of Depression and SAD subscale (SIGH-SAD). The researcher comprehensively identifies research that substantiates the validity and reliability of the SIGH-SAD.

Operationalism is vital to understanding research and maintaining objectivity. Moreover, clearly defined experimental procedures and measurements make it easier for researchers to replicate studies to confirm or repudiate important findings.

REDUCING THE IMPRECISION IN MEASUREMENT

All research includes fluctuations between an observed quantity and its true quantity. These fluctuations or differences are referred to as *errors* that represent imprecision in measurement. Two important sources of error are sampling error and error of measurement.

Sampling Error

A sample selected for study is intended to represent a population. Inferences about sample statistics such as a mean and standard deviation are used to estimate population parameters. It is highly unlikely that sample statistics will be exactly the same as population parameters. The difference between a sample mean and a population mean is referred to as *sampling error*. Indexes representing sampling error are available to help researchers understand the differences between sample statistics and population parameters. All parametric statistical procedures have sampling error terms to account for sampling error. For example, the sampling error index for the difference between a sample and a population mean (one-sample *t*-test) is called the *standard error of the mean*. The standard error terms associated with some other statistics include independent *t*-test (standard error of difference), analysis of variance *F*-test (mean square error), correlation coefficient-*r* (standard error of estimate), and multiple regression (standard error of regression coefficient).

The use of *random sampling* is the best way to reduce sampling error. Random sampling involves taking a random sample from a larger population by selecting cases by chance to represent the population. This probabilistic approach will result in the most representative sample if it is done correctly. For example, the first step for a researcher who wants to study third graders in a school district is to obtain a complete list of all third graders. The researcher would choose a desired sample size and then use a random number generator to select the number for the sample from the complete list of third graders (population).

Ideally, the two-step process of first randomly selecting a sample of participants and then *randomly assigning* them to a treatment condition is used in research for generalized causal inference. However, it is uncommon for participants to be randomly selected to participate in experimental studies (Shadish, Cook, & Campbell, 2002). Random assignment of participants to treatment conditions is required for a study to be considered experimental. The distinguishing characteristic of *quasi-experimental* research is that random assignment is not used.

Shadish et al. articulate an alternative selection method to random selection used by experimental researchers known as *purposive sampling*. Purposive sampling is a deliberate process by a researcher to identify population characteristics, including participants, treatments, outcomes, and settings, and then select a sample that embodies the desired population characteristics.

Error of Measurement

A second source of error is *error of measurement*. When using measures from participants to assess the dependent variables in a study, there are differences between the participants' observed scores and their true scores. An *observed score* is the actual measured score of a participant, and a *true score* is the actual score (theoretical) on the measure. Conceptually, an observed score is similar to a sample characteristic, and a true score is similar to a population parameter.

Error of measurement can be attributed to both *random error* and *systematic error*. Random error includes fluctuations is the characteristics of individuals, such as the motivation levels of participants changing randomly from one assessment to the next.

A novice examiner may depart from standardized assessment procedures in scoring or use an unreliable test in a study; these are examples of sources of random error. Measurement reliability is especially affected by random error.

Systematic error is represented by a decrease or an increase of scores on a dependent measure in a predictable way. This type of systematic error often relates to procedural irregularities in the research process. A weight scale calibrated incorrectly and consistently measuring three pounds heavier than it should represents systematic error. Systematic error most adversely affects measurement validity.

Measurement error exists in all studies. We cannot eliminate errors in measurement, but we can minimize their effects.

CONTROLLING EXTRANEOUS EXPERIMENTAL INFLUENCES

Experimental research strives to accurately and consistently measure whether changes in a dependent variable can be attributed to a specified independent variable. *Extraneous variables (nuisance variables)* confuse the assessment of the real effects of the independent variable on the dependent variable. Extraneous variables are first identified and then efforts are made to control their confounding effects.

For example, a researcher wants to compare the effects of a hypnosis treatment program to a nicotine gum therapy among smokers to see which program is more effective in producing smoking abstinence. It is discovered that the group of participants receiving the hypnosis treatment have a significantly lower average number of years smoking compared to the nicotine gum therapy participants. Prior number of years smoking is an extraneous variable that is salient in its potential impact on the dependent variable of smoking abstinence. This extraneous variable needs to be accounted for and controlled to accurately understand the cause-and-effect relationship between treatment and outcome.

Methods of Controlling Extraneous Variables

There are several general ways to control for extraneous variables. One way is to *eliminate an extraneous variable*. For example, a researcher is concerned about the extraneous effects of below-average and above-average IQ scores among individuals on correct responses in completing a task based on three methods of instruction. So the researcher decides to select participants with IQ scores between ± one standard deviation from the mean.

Another way to account for extraneous variance is to *build the extraneous variable into the design*. Prior evidence suggests that gender may confound the results of interventions on math achievement. Gender can be included as an independent variable in a design where its main and interaction effects can be assessed with the primary independent variable of interest.

The effects of extraneous variance also can be *statistically controlled* using techniques such as analysis of covariance and multiple regression. The extraneous variable needs to be measured and then the dependent variable is adjusted to account for its influence.

Matching participants across condition groups based on one or more extraneous variables can be used to rule out or hold constant their confounding effects. A researcher might match participants in a treatment and control condition based on gender, height, and age. A woman 5′ 0″ to 5′ 2″ in height who is between the ages of 20 and 25 years is matched to participant with similar characteristics in the other group. All participants would be matched on homogeneous characteristics. Sophisticated propensity score matching methods have been refined in recent years, which have enhanced the rigor of quasi-experimental designs (see Cook & Steiner, 2010).

The most important way to control extraneous variance is using *random assignment*. Each participant is assigned to experimental and control group conditions totally by chance. Tables of random numbers or computerized random number generators are used to accomplish random assignment. Random assignment makes groups randomly similar to each other. It is less likely that one group of participants will have more or less extraneous variance than another group when groups are randomly assigned from the same sample. Shadish, Cook, and Campbell (2002) reported the benefits of random assignment to generalized causal inference as: "equating groups before treatment begins, by making alternative explanations implausible, by creating error terms that are uncorrelated with treatment variables, and by allowing valid estimates of error terms" (p. 252).

Another method of controlling extraneous variables is to use *blinded procedures*. Participants are not informed about the nature or purpose of a study in a *single-blind procedure* to minimize participants behaving in reaction to the purpose of the study. In a *double-blind procedure* neither the participants nor the researchers are informed of the treatment conditions that the participants receive. This procedure helps minimize experimenter expectancy effects and participant reaction (demand) effects. This procedure usually requires that other people select groups, administer treatment, and record results. In a *triple-blind procedure* neither the participants nor the persons administering the treatment nor those evaluating the response to treatment know which participants are receiving a given treatment. A *partial-blind procedure* is used when the researcher finds out which treatment conditions are administered just before administering the treatment conditions.

Deception can be used to shift the participants' attention away from the actual purpose of a study so they do not react to the perceived purpose in a certain way. The use of deception requires careful consideration of ethical standards and approval from an Institutional Review Board (IRB). There are several other procedures to control for extraneous variables (see Kirk, 1995; Shadish, Cook, & Campbell, 2002).

INTERNAL VALIDITY AND EXPERIMENTAL DESIGNS

For over 50 years, Campbell (1957); Campbell and Stanley (1963); Cook and Campbell (1979); Shadish, Cook, and Campbell (2002); Shadish and Cook (2009); and Cook and Steiner (2010) have developed sophisticated methods in experimental and quasi-experimental research. Two of many experimental methodological areas that have evolved are internal validity and research designs.

Internal Validity

Determining *internal validity* is assessing whether the A (cause) → B (outcome) relationship is indeed causal based on the manipulations and measures of the variables used in a study. This assessment process includes knowing which variable is the cause and which is the effect, which is referred to as *ambiguous temporal precedence* (Shadish, Cook, and Campbell, 2002).

An important part of assessing for internal validity is ruling out threats to internal validity. Thirteen threats to internal validity are presented in Table 4.1. The first eight threats (*THIS MESS*) can be assessed and ruled out through the use of experimental designs, and the last five threats (*DREAD*) are corrected using

TABLE 4.1 Threats to Internal Validity: THIS MESS DREAD

Testing effect	The treatment effect may be confounded when changes in posttest scores of participants are influenced by their experience from taking a pretest.
History	An external but concurrent event to the experiment (e.g., a hurricane) may affect scores on a dependent measure that are unrelated to the treatment.
Instrumentation	Pretest and posttest scores may change because of a faulty measurement instrument, irrespective of the treatment.
Selection (differential)	Differences in characteristics of participants assigned (usually not random) to treatment conditions may confound attributing the changes in the dependent variable to the treatment.
Maturation	Psychological and physical changes within participants may occur in an experiment, especially over time. These participant maturational changes may have an extraneous effect on the dependent measure.
Experimental mortality (attrition)	The loss of participants to treatment or measurement of the dependent variable can produce unbalanced attribution of the effects of the treatment on the dependent variable.
Statistical regression	This is the phenomenon that extremely high or low group scores on a variable tend to regress to the mean (get lower or higher) on a second measurement of the variable, confounding the treatment effect.
Selection-maturation Interaction	This is a combination of two threats to internal validity. For example, some participants in one assigned treatment condition group may have matured in math self-efficacy more than participants in another treatment condition group, and the purpose of the study is to increase math achievement. Additionally, other combinations of threats could interact to confound the treatment effect.
Diffusion of experimental effect	The treatment may diffuse to the control group over time because the control group may seek access to the more desirable treatment.
Rivalry (compensatory)	The control group participants may perform beyond their usual level because they perceive that they are in competition with the experimental group.

Equalization of treatments (compensatory)	A treatment group may receive experimental rewards that appear more desirable than those received by the control group participants. Efforts are made by individuals outside of the experiment to compensate the control group participants with similar desirable goods. This would obscure the results of the treatment.
Ambiguous temporal precedence	A lack of clarity is provided by the researchers as to which variable occurred first, leading to a question of which variable is the cause and which is the effect.
Demoralization (resentfulness)	Lower performance of control group participants on the dependent measures may result from their belief that the treatment group is receiving a desirable treatment.

Source: Reprinted by permission from W. E. Martin Jr. & K. D. Bridgmon. (2009). Essential elements of experimental and quasi-experimental research. In S. Lapan & M. Quartaroli (Eds.), *Research essentials: An introduction to designs and practices* (pp. 35–58). San Francisco, CA: Jossey-Bass.

experimental procedures. Next, we will discuss how experimental designs are used to rule out threats to internal validity.

Experimental Designs

There are many *experimental designs*, *quasi-experimental designs*, and *correlation designs* available for use by researchers to execute their studies. Two fundamental and commonly used experimental designs are discussed first. Explanations are provided as to how the designs reduce the effects of THIS MESS. Examples of statistical designs that can be used with the designs are identified. The other five threats to internal validity (DREAD) are also discussed.

A few rules and symbols are used to describe experimental designs. Each row represents a group of participants receiving a different experimental condition. An R designates that the participants were randomly assigned to an experimental condition (treatment or control). All O's (observations) represent assessments of one or more dependent variables. An O before an experimental condition is a preexperimental condition assessment, and an O after the experimental condition is a postexperimental condition assessment. An X stands for a treatment condition and C symbolizes a control condition.

Randomized Multiple Treatments and Control with Posttest-Only Design

$$R \qquad\qquad X_1 \qquad\qquad O$$
$$R \qquad\qquad X_2 \qquad\qquad O$$
$$R \qquad\qquad C \qquad\qquad O$$

This design is used in the one-way analysis of variance (ANOVA) example in Chapter 7. The purpose of the study is to compare the effects of psychotherapeutic treatment (independent variable) on changes in depressive symptoms (dependent variable). Psychotherapeutic treatment has three experimental conditions: (1) cognitive-behavioral therapy (CBT), (2) interpersonal therapy (IPT), and (3) control group. Each line in the diagram represents one of the three groups. The R symbolizes random assignment to each group condition, which represents a study sample of participants being randomly assigned equally to each condition. The conditions by groups are represented by X_1 (CBT), X_2 (IPT), and C (Control). The O (observation) is the posttest following eight weeks of treatment implementation using the Center for Epidemiological Studies Depression Scale (CES-D) to measure differential change in depressive symptoms resulting from the different treatment conditions.

This *randomized multiple treatments and control with posttest-only design* strongly benefits from the essential elements of experimental research: (1) random assignment, (2) control groups, and (3) a manipulated independent variable. The design does reduce the threats of THIS MES but a concern arises with the last S (interaction of two threats). For example, more participants may be lost (attrition) from one or more randomly assigned groups (selection) during the course of an experiment. This affects the expected outcome of random assignment to make groups randomly similar to each other at the onset of the study. If there were a pretest in the design, information could be derived to help explain how the participants dropping out of the experiment affected changes in the dependent variable. The interaction effect of attrition and selection would not be an issue if there were no loss of participants using this design. Without a pretest, it is impossible to know the causal effects of the independent variable on the dependent variable because of the disproportionate loss of participants from one condition compared to the other condition.

A one-way ANOVA can be used in this design to compare the means of CES-D scores across the three psychotherapeutic conditions for significant differences. A post hoc analysis can be used to assess the differences between the three pairs of means.

Randomized Multiple Treatments and Control with Pretest and Posttest Design

R	O	X_1	O
R	O	X_2	O
R	O	C	O

The *randomized multiple treatments and control with pretest and posttest design* adds a pretest to the previous design. So, the participants could be measured on their depressive symptoms using an equivalent form of the CES-D before administering the experimental conditions. This reduces the concern about understanding the effects of interaction between attrition and selection. The pretest scores on depressive symptoms of people lost during the research process can be used to assist in controlling differences in participants by group on the posttest scores. The design helps control for all of the threats associated with THIS MESS.

A statistical design that could be used with this design is a 3 × 2 repeated-measures ANOVA. The 3 represents the independent variable (factor) of *psychotherapeutic treatment* with three conditions of CBT, IPT, and control. The 2 represents a second independent variable of *time* with two conditions (pretest and posttest). This statistical design allows for a comparison of the differences among the means of CES-D scores across the three experimental conditions. A post hoc analysis can be used to assess the differences between the three pairs of means.

Also, differences between the means at pretest and posttest can be analyzed. Finally, the interaction effects of psychotherapeutic treatment and time can be compared to see if the CES-D average scores differ at conditions of psychotherapeutic treatment when compared to pretest and posttest conditions. The interaction effect analysis could be followed by a simple effects analysis to determine which levels of the first independent variable interact with which levels of the second independent variable to produce significant effects on the dependent variable.

Effective experimental designs are used to reduce the threats to internal validity of THIS MESS. Seven recommended *experimental research procedures* that aid to reduce the threats of DREAD (see Table 4.1) are identified next.

1. Use different persons to implement each treatment condition.

2. Arrange treatment conditions so that contact between experimental and control group participants is minimized.

3. Use single-blind, double-blind, or triple-blind procedures to remove participant or experimenter bias.

4. Debrief participants using interviews to assess their experiences and expectations of the treatment conditions.

5. Consider not using experimental rewards.

6. Clearly define treatment conditions.

7. Use past research and theory to guide the evidence of an A (independent variable) → B (dependent variable) causal relationship.

Quasi-Experimental Designs

The purpose of using quasi-experimental designs is to discover causal relationships similar to using experimental designs. However, quasi-experimental designs are considered compromise designs because random assignment is not used. It is important for researchers using quasi-experimental designs to provide carefully detailed, logical arguments in ruling out alternative explanations (rival hypotheses) to account for their findings of a causal relationship.

Quasi-experimental designs are improved by (1) adding control or comparison groups, (2) adding pretests and posttests, (3) removing and reinstituting treatments, (4) adding replications, (5) reversing treatment, and (6) case matching (Shadish, Cook, & Campbell, 2002). Various statistical procedures also have been developed that have improved quasi-experimental designs. *Propensity scores* are used in case matching to equate individual cases from different populations to reduce selection bias. Propensity scores are a weighted composite of measured covariates that correlate with treatment (Cook & Steiner, 2010; Rosenbaum & Rubin, 1983). *Regression discontinuity designs* use cutoff scores to assign participants to conditions. The cutoff score is a measure obtained before treatment is undertaken. Then, posttest scores are analyzed with ordinary least squares regression using the cutoff scores (Shadish, Cook, & Campbell, 2002). Two commonly used quasi-experimental designs are presented next.

Repeated-Treatment Design with One Group

$$O_{\text{Baseline}} \qquad X_1 O_1 \qquad X_{2\text{Removed}} O_2 \qquad X_3 O_3 \qquad X_4 O_4$$

The focus of the research example of *repeated-treatment design with one group* is to assess whether the use of friends (support partners) in behavioral weight control treatment (BWCT) can improve the weight loss outcomes of persons who are overweight (this example is used in Chapter 8). A randomly selected group of participants who are overweight are weighed at baseline before treatment (O_{Baseline}). Then, each participant's weight loss is measured and recorded after three months of treatment with partner support ($X_1 O_1$ at 3 months), after three months when partner support is removed ($X_{2\text{Removed}} O_2$ at 6 months), after three months when partner support is added back to treatment ($X_3 O_3$ at 9 months), and after the treatment with partner support is continued for three months ($X_4 O_4$ at 12 months).

The most important result of this design to demonstrate some degree of causal relationship is measuring the change of weight loss when the treatment is removed and reinstated. External events (history) and physical/psychological changes affecting participants may confound the understanding of weight loss as it relates to the treatment. It would be difficult to tease out confounding without using a control group and random assignment. Moreover, participants' awareness of the cycle of treatment, treatment removal, and observations might behave uncharacteristically in reaction to the study cycle. Since the same participants are measured repeatedly over time under various conditions, a repeated-measures ANOVA would be an appropriate statistic to use in this study. The changes in mean weight and covariances at baseline, three months, six months, and 12 months would be assessed for differences.

Nonequivalent No-Treatment Control Group Time-Series Design

$$NR \quad O_1 \quad O_2 \quad O_3 \quad X \quad O_4 \quad O_5 \quad O_6$$
$$NR \quad O_1 \quad O_2 \quad O_3 \quad C \quad O_4 \quad O_5 \quad O_6$$

There is a control group in the *nonequivalent no-treatment control group time-series design* and no removal of treatment. The *NR* stands for nonrandom assignment. This design controls for most of the threats to internal validity, THIS MES. However, an interaction (S) between selection and history may be a concern. It is possible that one group of participants is affected differently by external events (history) that influence their scores more on a dependent variable than the other group. The control group and multiple pretests and posttests in this design provide valuable information to rule out threats to internal validity. Visual analyses of graphs are useful for understanding the results. Other statistics that can be used include repeated-measures ANOVA, randomization tests, and bootstrapping methods.

Correlational Research Methods

Correlations methods are used in experimental and quasi-experimental designs, but the primary purpose of correlation research is to explore *bivariate relationships*, *multiple relationships*, and predictions among variables. Variables in correlational research are often referred to as X and Y variables. The X variable is called either an independent or a *predictor variable*, and the Y variable is identified as either a dependent or a *criterion variable*. A bivariate correlation (r) assesses the relationship between two variables, and a multiple correlation (R) assesses the relationship among more than two variables. A *simple linear regression* uses a bivariate correlation to predict the dependent variable (Y) from the independent variable (X). A *multiple linear regression* uses a multiple correlation to predict a dependent variable (Y) from two or more independent variables (Xs).

In Chapter 12, an example is presented about a researcher who assessed whether lower interest in scientific activities is a better predictor of higher dissertation stress reported by counseling and clinical psychology doctoral students when compared to their interests in practitioner activities.

The first independent variable in the study is doctoral students' interest in scientific activities as measured by the Scientist Scale of the Scientist Practitioner

Inventory (SPI). The Scientist Scale measures student interests in activities related to research, statistics and design, teaching/guiding/editing, and academic ideas.

The second independent variable used in the study is students' interest in practitioner activities measured using the Practitioner Scale of the SPI. The Practitioner Scale assesses interests in activities involving therapy, clinical expertise and consultation, and testing and interpretation. Higher scores on the Practitioner Scale reflect higher interests.

First, we consider only one independent variable (scientific activities) and its prediction of dissertation stress. An analysis of the extent that students' interest in participating in scientific activities (X) relates and predicts dissertation stress (Y) could be answered using a bivariate correlation and simple linear regression model. The model could be written symbolically as $Yf(X)$, where Y (dissertation stress) is a function of X (scientific interests). A prediction model can be written as $Y' = A + B_1X_1$, where Y' is the predicted value on the dependent variable (dissertation stress), A is the intercept, the value of Y when all the X values are zero, B is the unstandardized regression coefficient assigned to each X value, and X is the measured value of the independent variable (scientific interests).

A multiple correlation and multiple regression analysis can be used to analyze the two independent variables with the dependent variable. It can be written symbolically as $Yf(X_1, X_2)$. The prediction model would be $Y' = A + B_1X_1 + B_2X_2$.

CHOOSING A STATISTIC TO USE FOR AN ANALYSIS

The consideration of five issues can be useful in deciding on a statistic to use in a particular analysis: (1) the focus of the interplay among variables (e.g., relationships or differences), (2) the number of independent and dependent variables used in an analysis, (3) the scales of measurements of the dependent variables, (4) the number and relationships (dependent vs. independent) of participant groups being compared, and (5) the extent that underlying assumptions of the statistic are met. These issues are illustrated in relation to statistics covered in this book (also see Figure 4.1).

One-Way Analysis of Variance

1. *Focus of analysis.* The purpose of a one-way ANOVA is to compare mean differences of a dependent variable among groups.

FIGURE 4.1 Issues in Choosing a Statistic to Use for an Analysis

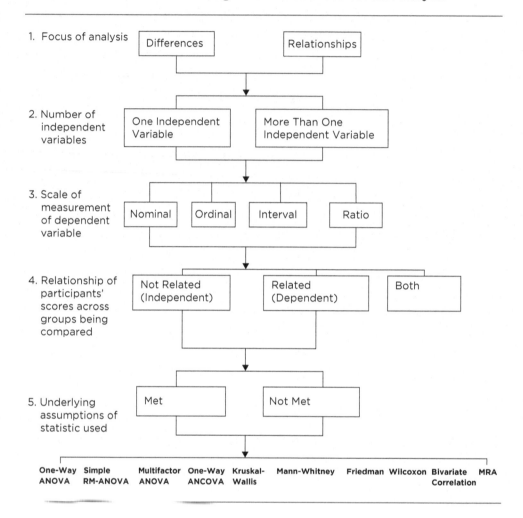

2. *Number of independent variables.* The descriptor *one-way* indicates that there is one independent variable.

3. *Scale of measurement of dependent variable.* A continuously scaled (interval or ratio) dependent variable is used in a one-way ANOVA.

4. *Relationship of participants' scores across groups being compared.* There are different participants in the groups being compared and their scores are not

related (independent) in a one-way ANOVA. This is also referred to as a between-group design.

5. *Underlying assumptions of the statistic being used.* The underlying assumptions of normality, homogeneity of variance, and independence of scores related to the dependent variable must be met. This applies to original dependent variables or dependent variables that have been successfully transformed.

Simple Repeated Measures Analysis of Variance

1. *Focus of analysis.* The purpose of simple RM-ANOVA is to compare mean differences across groups, conditions, or testing times (i.e., pretest-posttest).

2. *Number of independent variables.* There is one independent variable used in a simple RM-ANOVA.

3. *Scale of measurement of dependent variable.* A continuously scaled (interval or ratio) dependent variable is used in a simple one-way ANOVA.

4. *Relationship of participants' scores across groups being compared.* Scores are related to (dependent on) each other. Scores on the same or matched participants are obtained two or more times. This is also called a within-group design.

5. *Underlying assumptions of the statistic being used.* The underlying assumptions of normality, homogeneity of variance and covariance related to the dependent variable must be met. These assumptions apply to original dependent variables or dependent variables that have been successfully transformed.

Multifactor Analysis of Variance

1. *Focus of analysis.* The purpose of factorial ANOVA is to assess mean differences across main effects, interaction effects, and simple effects.

2. *Number of independent variables.* *Factor* is another word used for independent variables, so *multifactor* denotes that more than one independent variable is used in the analysis.

3. *Scale of measurement of dependent variable.* A continuously scaled (interval or ratio) dependent variable is used in a multifactor ANOVA.

4. *Relationship of participants' scores across groups being compared.* A multifactor ANOVA can include both scores that are not related (between groups) and scores that are related (within groups).

5. *Underlying assumptions of the statistic being used.* Normality, homogeneity of variance-covariance, and independence of scores related to the dependent variable must be met. This applies to original dependent variables or dependent variables that have been successfully transformed.

One-Way Analysis of Covariance

1. *Focus of analysis.* The purpose of a one-way ANCOVA is to compare mean differences among groups when the dependent variable has been adjusted for by one or more covariates.

2. *Number of independent variables.* The descriptor *one-way* indicates that there is one independent variable used in a one-way analysis of covariance.

3. *Scale of measurement of dependent variable.* A continuously scaled (interval or ratio) dependent variable is used in a one-way ANCOVA.

4. *Relationship of participants' scores across groups being compared.* There are different participants in the groups being compared, and their dependent variable scores are not related (independent). This is also referred to as a between-group design. If a covariate used is a pretest-posttest score, then there are elements of both between-group and within-group designs.

5. *Underlying assumptions of the statistic being used.* The underlying assumptions of normality, homogeneity of variance, and independence of scores related to the dependent variable must be met. This applies to original dependent variables or dependent variables that have been successfully transformed.

Kruskal-Wallis One-Way Analysis of Variance

1. *Focus of analysis.* The purpose of the Kruskal-Wallis (K-W) test is to compare mean rank differences among two or more groups. The K-W test is a nonparametric alternative to the one-way ANOVA.

2. *Number of independent variables.* There is one independent variable used in a K-W analysis.

3. *Scale of measurement of dependent variable.* A discrete-ordinal dependent variable is used in a K-W analysis. Continuous dependent variables can be used; however, the observed continuous scores are converted to ranks in the K-W analysis.

4. *Relationship of participants' scores across groups being compared.* There are different participants in the groups being compared, and their scores are not related (are independent) in a K-W analysis. This is also referred to as a between-group design.

5. *Underlying assumptions of the statistic being used.* The K-W test is a nonparametric statistical test and is considered distribution-free; therefore, the assumptions of normality and homogeneity of variance are not necessary. However, it is important that observations are independent from each other and there is some degree of continuity of the variable used.

Mann-Whitney *U* Test

1. *Focus of analysis.* The purpose of the Mann-Whitney *U* (MWU) test is to compare mean rank differences between two groups. The MWU test is the nonparametric alternative to the independent *t*-test.

2. *Number of independent variables.* There is one independent variable used in a MWU analysis.

3. *Scale of measurement of dependent variable.* A discrete-ordinal dependent variable is used in a MWU analysis. Continuous dependent variables can be used, and the observed continuous scores are converted to ranks in the MWU analysis.

4. *Relationship of participants' scores across groups being compared.* There are different participants in the groups being compared, and their scores are not related (are independent). This is also referred to as a between-group design.

5. *Underlying assumptions of the statistic being used.* The MWU test is a nonparametric statistical test and is considered distribution-free; therefore, the assumptions of normality and homogeneity of variance are not necessary. However, it is important that observations are independent from each other and there is some degree of continuity of the variable used.

Friedman Repeated Measures Analysis of Variance

1. *Focus of analysis.* The purpose of the Friedman RM-ANOVA is to compare mean rank differences among two or more groups with related scores. The Friedman RM-ANOVA is the nonparametric alternative to the RM-ANOVA.

2. *Number of independent variables.* There is one independent variable used in the Friedman RM-ANOVA analysis.

3. *Scale of measurement of dependent variable.* A discrete-ordinal dependent variable is used in a Friedman analysis. Continuous dependent variables can be used, but the observed continuous scores are converted to ranks in the Friedman RM-ANOVA analysis.

4. *Relationship of participants' scores across groups being compared.* Scores are related to (dependent on) each other. Scores on the same or matched participants are obtained two or more times. This is also referred to as a within-group statistical design.

5. *Underlying assumptions of the statistic being used.* The Friedman RM-ANOVA test is a nonparametric statistical test and is considered distribution-free; therefore, the assumptions of normality and homogeneity of variance are not necessary. However, it is important that observations are independent from each other and there is some degree of continuity of the variable used.

Wilcoxon Matched-Pairs Signed-Ranks Test

1. *Focus of analysis.* The purpose of the Wilcoxon test is to compare mean rank differences between two groups with related scores. The Wilcoxon test is the nonparametric alternative to the dependent *t*-test.

2. *Number of independent variables.* There is one independent variable used in the Wilcoxon test analysis.

3. *Scale of measurement of dependent variable.* A discrete-ordinal dependent variable is used in a Friedman analysis. Continuous dependent variables can be used, but the observed continuous scores are converted to ranks in the Wilcoxon test analysis.

4. *Relationship of participants' scores across groups being compared.* Scores are related to (dependent on) each other. Scores on the same or matched

participants are obtained two times. This is also referred to as a within-group statistical design.

5. *Underlying assumptions of the statistic being used.* The Wilcoxon test is a nonparametric statistical test and is considered distribution-free; therefore, the assumptions of normality and homogeneity of variance are not necessary. However, it is important that observations are independent from each other and there is some degree of continuity of the variable used.

Pearson's Product Moment Coefficient of Correlation (r)

1. *Focus of analysis.* The purpose of the Pearson correlation coefficient is to analyze the relationship between two variables.

2. *Number of independent variables.* There are two variables used in the analysis. It is not necessary, but one variable may be called an independent variable (X) or predictor variable and the other variable may be called a dependent variable (Y) or criterion variable.

3. *Scale of measurement of dependent variable.* The two variables used in the Pearson correlation coefficient analysis are continuously scaled (interval or ratio).

4. *Relationship of participants' scores across groups being compared.* Scores on the two variables are paired on the same participants, and therefore the scores are related to (dependent on) each other.

5. *Underlying assumptions of the statistic being used.* The Pearson correlation coefficient requires meeting normality and homogeneity in arrays that are the residual variance of a Y conditional to a specific X.

Multiple Regression Analysis

1. *Focus of analysis.* The purpose of a multiple regression analysis (MRA) is to analyze the extent that two or more independent variables relate to a dependent variable.

2. *Number of independent variables.* There are two or more continuously scaled independent (predictor) variables used in the analysis.

3. *Scale of measurement of dependent variable.* The dependent variable is also continuously scaled (interval or ratio) in an MRA analysis.

4. *Relationship of participants' scores across groups being compared.* Participants have scores on all of the variables used in the MRA, and therefore the scores are related to (dependent on) each other.

5. *Underlying assumptions of the statistic being used.* The underlying assumptions and other issues of an MRA to assess include normality, homoscedasticity, linearity, independence of errors, and multicollinearity.

SUMMARY

Research and statistical designs can be conceptualized as having the purpose to maximize treatment variance, minimize error variance, and control extraneous variance. The basic components of experimental, quasi-experimental, and correlational research designs were discussed in this chapter. Statistical methods used with various research designs were covered. Threats to internal validity were identified with examples of experimental and quasi-experimental designs. Finally, issues to consider in choosing statistics for research problems were presented.

PROBLEM ASSIGNMENT

Go to the companion website for additional examples of formulating experimental conditions and procedures, reducing imprecision in measurement, and controlling extraneous experimental influences. Use the information presented in this chapter to guide you as you complete the assignment.

KEY TERMS

ambiguous temporal precedence

bivariate relationships

blinded procedures

build the extraneous variable into
   the design

controlling extraneous variance

correlation designs

criterion variable

deception

dependent (outcome) variables

double-blind procedure

DREAD

eliminate an extraneous variable

error of measurement

errors

experimental designs

experimental research procedures

extraneous variables (nuisance variables)

independent (cause) variables

internal validity

matching participants

maximizing experimental variance

MaxMinCon

minimizing error variance

multiple linear regression

multiple relationships

nonequivalent no-treatment control group time-series design

observed score

operationally defined

partial-blind procedure

predictor variable

propensity scores

psychotherapeutic treatment

purposive sampling

quasi-experimental

quasi-experimental designs

random assignment

random error

random sampling

randomized multiple treatments and control with posttest-only design

randomized multiple treatments and control with pretest and posttest design

randomly assigning

regression discontinuity designs

repeated-treatment design with one group

rival hypotheses

sampling error

simple linear regression

single-blind procedure

standard error of the mean

statistically controlled

systematic error

THIS MESS

time

treatment adherence

treatment delivery

treatment integrity (treatment fidelity)

treatment receipt

triple-blind procedure

true score

Chapter 5

INTRODUCTION TO

IBM SPSS 20

LEARNING OBJECTIVES

- o Become familiar with the start-up procedures of IBM SPSS 20.

- o Learn navigational skills in the IBM SPSS 20 program.

- o Learn to name and define variables.

- o Practice entering data.

- o Execute basic computational procedures using IBM SPSS 20.

he focus of this chapter is to introduce you to the basic steps of setting up and manipulating *data* in *IBM SPSS 20*. It is important to follow the steps and take your time in setting up your data. It takes more time to set up your data than it does to run the analyses. The accuracy of the results is highly dependent upon the exactness of the data entered.

Data analysis commands used in this book are for use in IBM SPSS 20 for Windows. Most SPSS analysis commands have remained consistent across SPSS versions; however, students using older versions of SPSS may need to make modifications to the commands. IBM SPSS 20 can be operated both through pull-down menus and by syntax commands. Syntax commands are based on SPSS language that is written commands made by a user to generate statistical results. The pull-down menu is similar to many Windows applications; therefore, it is user friendly. If you select a particular option and then determine it is not what you were looking for, you can use the cancel feature. Basic applications for IBM SPSS 20 are described in this chapter, but you will learn more advanced applications as they are applied to statistics presented in the following chapters of the book.

When entering data or manipulating existing data sets in IBM SPSS 20, make sure to save often and use titles for the data that make sense for the data set. For example, you may wish to date the data set and include descriptive comments that will allow you to know what each data set is for future use. IBM SPSS 20 includes a Help feature that will assist users to obtain more information about commands and output. Next, we will go step-by-step in naming and defining variables in a data set (Variable View), enter data (Data View), and conduct some basic analyses.

Start-Up Procedures in IBM SPSS

1. Click on the **Start** button (bottom left of your screen) > click on **Programs** > click on IBM SPSS 20 or the version you are using. This start-up procedure may vary with computers based on how the program manager configured the program files.

2. When opening the IBM SPSS 20 program, the initial screen will provide several options (see Figure 5.1). The **Type in data** feature is the icon used to enter data for the first time. (After data has been saved, the default option of **Open an existing data source** is used to retrieve data. Also, you can click twice on a saved data set and open it.) Click on **Type in data** > click **OK**. This produces a *spreadsheet* (**Data View**) with the title at the top left, **Untitled1 [DataSet0] - IBM SPSS Statistics Data Editor** (see Figure 5.2). The **Data View** spreadsheet is where you will enter data.

FIGURE 5.1 IBM SPSS 20 Initial Screen

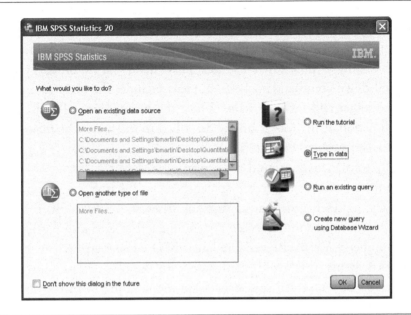

FIGURE 5.2 Data View Screen of IBM SPSS 20

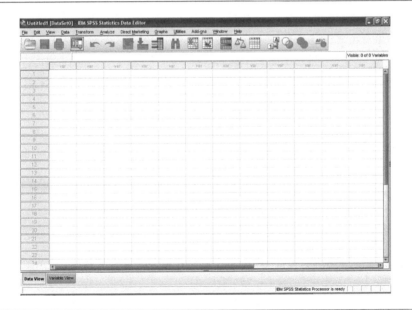

THE IBM SPSS 20 DATA VIEW SCREEN

The **Data View** screen has various options. The first line on the toolbar is the name of your data set. This is what the data set is named when the **Save As** feature is used. The next line is called the menu bar. This menu bar offers several options that offer a pull-down feature. This menu bar is primarily used for making pull-down command analyses, but also includes the Help tool. The third line is the toolbar and includes icons. Once the mouse curser is placed over an icon, the function of the tool is briefly described to the user. The majority of the screen is the spreadsheet for entering data. Scroll bars are available vertically and horizontally to maneuver around the screen.

Along the left side of the screen spreadsheet are the row (case) numbers. The rows usually represent the participants or cases in a study. It is important to remember that these numbers are not numbers that stay with participants but are row numbers. A separate variable labeled **ID** can be created to consistently identify participants; that avoids confusion with the row or case number.

At the top of the screen spreadsheet are the columns with the abbreviation *var* that stands for variable. Typically, the study variables are represented as columns in a data set.

At the bottom left-hand corner of the **Data View** screen are two tabs. One tab is titled **Data View** where the data is entered. The other tab is called **Variable View** and is used to name and define variables. Click on the **Variable View** tab and we will name and define variables before entering data (see Figure 5.3).

NAMING AND DEFINING VARIABLES IN VARIABLE VIEW

Naming and defining variables is important for entering data, analyzing data, and interpreting output after conducting an analysis. We will first name and define the variables used in this chapter. There are 10 variables that you will be naming and defining.

Entering Variables

Variable *ID*

1. In the **Variable View** screen, click on Row 1 of the **Name** column. The box will be highlighted once it is clicked.

2. In the cell under **Name** in Row 1, type in the variable's name, *ID*.

FIGURE 5.3   Variable View Screen of IBM SPSS 20

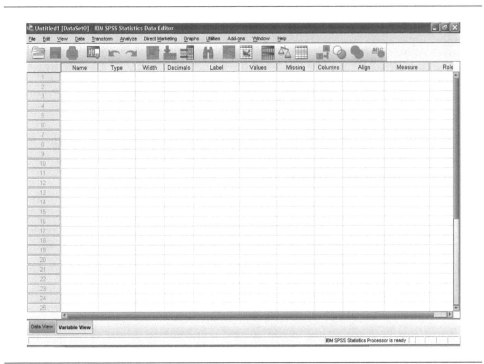

3. Press the *Tab* key. This is the **Type** column. Now there are three blue dots in this cell. The pull-down menu for TYPE can be used by clicking on the three dots to specify the type of variable. For this variable (ID numbers of participants), use the default (Numeric). You see that there are several options for Variable Type. If you click on the Help button, the Variable Types will be explained. We use primarily Numeric and String (variable values that are not numeric) Variable Types in this book. However, the Variable Type Date will be used in this introduction to IBM SPSS 20 chapter.

4. Press the *Tab* key again. This is the **Width** column. IBM SPSS 20 defaults to 8; however, in the cell, arrows are provided to increase or decrease the width of the variable's name. The desired width can also be entered by keying in the number. Obviously, the default width of 8 is sufficient for the two-letter name *ID*.

5. Press the *Tab* key. This is the **Decimals** column. SPSS 20 defaults to 2 decimal places. Again, this can be changed with the arrows or keying in the desired number of decimal places. If working with data that do not

include decimal places, decrease the Decimals cell to zero, as this will eliminate unneeded zeros in the decimal places. Change this to zero since the *ID* number does not need zeros.

6. Press the *Tab* key. This is the **Label** column that shows the identity of the variable in data output. Keep labels short but understandable so you can recognize a variable in the output. We will not use a label for the *ID* variable.

7. Press the *Tab* key. This is the **Values** column. Some variables will be categorized for analyses. For example, if Gender is used as a variable, this is the place when male and female would be labeled. Leave this blank since we are not categorizing the variable *ID*.

8. Press the *Tab* key. This is the **Missing** Values column that allows a user to enter values or ranges of values defined as missing data. IBM SPSS 20 defaults at none. By selecting none for this column, it allows missing data to be identified when conducting analyses. Leave the **Missing** Values cell blank for the *ID* variable.

9. Press the *Tab* key. This is the **Columns** column. IBM SPSS 20 defaults at an 8 character width for each column. This may be changed by using the arrow keys or keying in the desired column size. Leave the width at the default of the *ID* variable.

10. Press the *Tab* key. This is the **Align** column. IBM SPSS 20 will default to right. However, left, right, or center are all options. Leave the default of right for this variable.

11. Press the *Tab* key. This is the **Measure** column. The scale of measurement for each variable is selected here. The options of *Scale* (default), *Ordinal*, or *Nominal* are available. The Scale option is used for continuous-scaled variables, including either ratio- or interval-scaled variables such as time (ratio) or standardized achievement test score (interval). The Ordinal scale option is used for ranked variables such as a Likert scale. The Nominal scale is for data used as counts in mutually exclusive categories such as religious affiliation. Leave this variable as the default of Scale.

12. Press the *Tab* key. This is the **Role** column. IBM SPSS 20 defaults at Input. An Input variable is usually used as an independent or predictor variable. A Target variable is used as a dependent or criterion variable. The Both option means it may be used as either an Input or a Target variable in analyses.

Partition means that the variable will be used to partition data into separate samples for training, testing, and validation. Role assignment is used only when analyses support the role assignment and otherwise does not affect analyses. We will not need to use role assignments for the analyses in this book. However, it is recommended that you use the role assignment of Input for independent or predictor variables and Target for dependent or criterion variables. Use Input for all other variables. Leave the default of Input for the variable *ID*.

13. Press the *Tab* key. The curser is now back at NAME and is ready for the next variable.

Variable *returndate*

1. In the cell under **Name** in row 2, type in *returndate* (not in italics).

2. Click on **Type**; choose Date on the left, and to the right click on *mm/dd/yy* and click **OK**. Remember you must enter the data dates in the same format as *mm/dd/yy*.

3. Use the default definitions in the rest of the row.

Variable *status*

1. In the cell under **Name** in row 3, type in *status*.

2. **Type** is Numeric, **Width** should be 8, and **Decimals** should be 0.

3. Under the column **Label** in row 3, type in *counseling students and counseling professionals*.

4. Click on the cell under the column **Values**. You are going to type in the categories for the variable status that will tell the SPSS program what values represent. Beside Value type in 1, and beside Label type in *student*; then click on the Add button. Then, click on Value again; type in 2 and beside Label type in *professionals* and click on the Add button and then the **OK** button.

5. Leave as is (the default values) for **Missing**, **Columns**, and **Align**.

6. In the **Measure** column, choose nominal. Nominal-scaled variables have categories that have no intrinsic order.

7. In the **Role** column, select Input since *status* will be used as an independent variable in some analyses.

Variable *gender*

1. In the cell under **Name** in row 4, type in *gender*.

2. **Type** is Numeric, **Width** should be 8, and **Decimals** is 0.

3. In the **Label** column, label the variable as *sex*.

4. In the **Values** column, assign the following values for gender in the blue box: Value = 1; Label = Male > Click *Add*. Repeat for Female gender with Value = 2; Label = Female > Click *Add* > Click **OK**.

5. **Missing** is None, **Columns** = 8, and **Align** = Right.

6. In the **Measure** column, change the level of measurement to Nominal, and the **Role** column is Input.

Variable *age*

1. In the cell under **Name** in row 5, type in *age*.

2. Leave **Type** = Numeric, **Width** = 8, and change the **Decimals** cell to zero.

3. Keep all other columns to default except for **Measure** (change to Scale).

Variable *ethn*

1. In the cell under **Name** in row 6, type in *ethn*.

2. **Width** = 8 and change the **Decimals** column to zero.

3. In the **Label** column, label the variable as *ethnicity*.

4. In the **Values** column, assign the following values for Ethnicity: Value = 1; Label = af amer > Click *Add*. Value = 2; Label = as amer > Click *Add*. Value = 3; Label = eur amer > Click *Add*. Value = 4; Label = hisp amer > Click *Add*. Value = 5; Label = nat amer > Click *Add*. Value = 6; Label = Other > Click *Add* > Click **OK**.

5. **Missing** = None, **Columns** = 8, **Align** = Right, **Measure** = Nominal, and **Role** = Input.

Variable *ethnicother*

1. The variable *ethnicother* in row 7 has responses that are words, so select String under **Type**.

2. Since the responses are words, there is a need to expand the characters for this variable, so type in 25 in the cell under the column **Width**.

3. For **Decimals** the cell should be zero, and under **Label** type in *other ethnicity description.*

4. The other columns should be: **Values** = None, **Missing** = None, **Columns** = 8, **Align** = Left, **Measure** = Nominal, and **Role** = Input.

Variable *counconfid*

1. In the cell under **Name** in row 8, type in *counconfid*.

2. The cell under **Type** = Numeric, **Width** = 8, and change the **Decimals** column to zero.

3. In the **Label** column, label the variable as *confidence as a counselor.*

4. In the **Values** column, assign the following values for counseling confidence. Value = 1; Label = Strongly Disagree > Click *Add*. Value = 2; Label = Disagree > Click *Add*. Value = 3; Label = Somewhat Agree > Click *Add*. Value = 4; Label = Agree > Click *Add*. Value = 5; Label = Strongly Agree > Click *Add* > Click **OK**.

5. The other columns should be: **Missing** = None, **Columns** = 8, **Align** = Right, **Measure** = Ordinal, and **Role** = Target. Target is used because the variable (*counconfid*) is a dependent variable in the analyses.

Variable *micskill*

1. Type in the name *micskill* in the cell in row 9 under the column **Name**. This is a subscale called Micro Counseling Skills of the Counseling Self-Estimate Inventory (COSE).

2. The columns **Type** = Numeric, **Width** = 8, **Decimal** = 0, and under **Label** type in *COSE Confidence in Executing Microskills.*

3. The other columns should be: **Values** = None, **Missing** = None, **Columns** = 8, **Align** = Right, **Measure** = Scale, and **Role** = Target.

Variable *dealdiff*

1. Type in the name *dealdiff* in the cell in row 10 under the column **Name**. This is a subscale called Dealing with Difficult Clients of the Counseling Self-Estimate Inventory (COSE).

FIGURE 5.4   Variables Named and Defined in Variable View

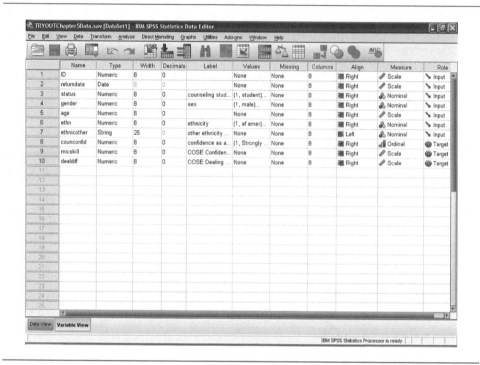

2. The columns **Type** = Numeric, **Width** = 8, **Decimal** = 0, and under **Label** type in *COSE Dealing with Difficult Client Behaviors.*

3. The other columns should be: **Values** = None, **Missing** = None, **Columns** = 8, **Align** = Right, **Measure** = Scale, and **Role** = Target.

4. Check the accuracy of the variables entered. Also check your work with Figure 5.4.

ENTERING DATA

Once variables have been correctly named and defined in **Variable View**, click on the **Data View** tab at the bottom left of the **Variable View** screen. You will see the variable names that you created at the top of the columns in the **Data View** screen. You will now be able to enter data for the variables created using the data in Figure 5.5. Consider these recommendations when entering data.

FIGURE 5.5   Example Data in Data View

1. The return key moves the curser down the spreadsheet. The tab key moves the curser across the spreadsheet.

2. If you make an error, click on the cell, delete, and retype the correct value.

3. Check your entered data for correctness and **Save As** *Chapter5Data.*

EXAMPLES OF BASIC ANALYSES

Commands are provided next using the pull-down menus for basic statistical analyses with output produced.

1. *Frequency Analysis* (good for ungrouped data).
   - Go to the top of the window and click on ***Analyze > Descriptive Statistics > Frequencies***.

TABLE 5.1 Frequencies Table of Ethnicity

	Frequencies Statistics	
	ethnicity	
N	Valid	20
	Missing	0

		Frequency	Percent	Valid Percent	Cumulative Percent
			ethnicity		
Valid	af amer	1	5.0	5.0	5.0
	as amer	2	10.0	10.0	15.0
	eur amer	11	55.0	55.0	70.0
	hisp amer	2	10.0	10.0	80.0
	other	4	20.0	20.0	100.0
	Total	20	100.0	100.0	

- In the box on the left, click on and highlight *ethnicity* [*ethn*] and then, using the arrow to the right, click it over to the space under *Variable(s)*. (If you want to stretch the Frequencies screen out, you can place your cursor to the left side of the box, left click, and move the end of the box left. This will allow you to see the fuller description of the variables. Another way is to place your cursor on the variable and it will show the full name of the variable.)

- Now click on the button called **Charts**. Select **Bar charts** as the type of *chart* and **Percentages** as the chart value > **Continue** > **OK**. This will produce a frequency table and bar chart for the variable (see Table 5.1 and Figure 5.6).

2. *Explore Analysis* (useful for grouped data and univariate data screening).

- Go to the top of the window and click on ***Analyze*** > ***Descriptive Statistics*** > ***Explore***.

- Click over the *Confidence in Executing Microskills* [*micskill*] into the **Dependent List**.

- Click over *Counseling Students and Counseling Professionals* [*status*] to the **Factor List**.

FIGURE 5.6   Bar Chart of Ethnicity

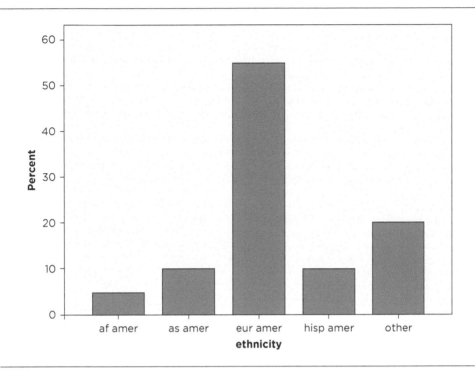

- Under *Display* keep the default at **Both**.

- To the upper right of the window are three buttons called **Statistics**, **Plots**, and **Options**. Click on **Plots** and choose **Stem-and-leaf** and **Histogram** under **Descriptive**. Also, choose **Normality plots with tests**, click **Continue**, and then click **OK**. This produces valuable output that is used for univariate data screening. The output provides results by grouping since we used *status* as a grouping variable. There are several plots and a table of information in the Explore output. The *descriptive statistics* table only is presented in Table 5.2.

3. *Independent t-test.* An analysis will be conducted to see if there is a significant difference ($\alpha = 01$) in the means of dealing with difficult client behaviors between the counseling students and counseling professionals. A high score on the dependent variable *dealdiff* means more confidence in dealing with difficult client behaviors.

TABLE 5.2 Descriptive Statistics of Status

Descriptives				Statistic	Std. Error
counseling students and counseling professionals					
student	COSE Confidence in Executing Microskills	Mean		55.27	2.435
		95% Confidence Interval for Mean	Lower Bound	49.85	
			Upper Bound	60.70	
		5% Trimmed Mean		55.58	
		Median		57.00	
		Variance		65.218	
		Std. Deviation		8.076	
		Minimum		40	
		Maximum		65	
		Range		25	
		Interquartile Range		13	
		Skewness		−.753	.661
		Kurtosis		−.311	1.279
professional		Mean		61.33	2.369
		95% Confidence Interval for Mean	Lower Bound	55.87	
			Upper Bound	66.80	
		5% Trimmed Mean		61.76	
		Median		61.00	
		Variance		50.500	
		Std. Deviation		7.106	
		Minimum		46	
		Maximum		69	
		Range		23	
		Interquartile Range		9	
		Skewness		−1.195	.717
		Kurtosis		2.053	1.400

- Go to the top of the window and click on **Analyze** > **Compare Means** > **Independent-Samples T Test**.

- Click over *counseling students and counseling professions* [*status*] under **Grouping Variable** (independent variable). Click on button called **Define Groups**. Type the number 1 (which represents counseling students) beside **Group 1**, and type the number 2 (which represents counseling professionals) beside **Group 2**; click **Continue**.

- Then click over *COSE Dealing with Difficult Client Behaviors* [*dealdiff*] under **Test Variables(s)** (dependent variables). Click **OK** and the output is produced.

(It is also possible to click over several variables under **Test Variable(s)** and it will run a separate independent *t*-test on each dependent variable.)

The output (Table 5.3) shows that $t = -4.406$ with a significant probability (Sig. [2-tailed]) equal to $p = .000$. Since $p = .000$ is less than the alpha criterion of .01, the rule is to reject the null hypothesis of no difference, so there is a significant difference. The mean of dealing with difficult client behaviors $\overline{X} = 24.64$ is for students and $\overline{X} = 34.78$ for professionals. Thus, the counseling professionals showed more confidence in dealing with difficult client behaviors than did the counseling students.

4. *Bivariate correlational matrix.* Next we look at creating a matrix of correlation coefficients among three continuously scaled variables: age, confidence in executing counseling microskills, and confidence in dealing with difficult client behaviors. We want to determine if age is significantly correlated ($\alpha = .05$) to the other two variables.

- Click **Analyze** > **Correlate** > **Bivariate**.

- Click over *age*, *micskill*, and *dealdiff* to **Variables**.

- Click on **Pearson** and click **OK**.

You can see that the correlation and significance between age and *COSE Confidence in Executing Microskills* is $r = .420, p = .065$, and age and *COSE Dealing with Difficult Client Behaviors* is $r = .663, p = .001$ (see Table 5.4). Age is significantly correlated to *COSE Dealing with Difficult Client Behaviors* since the $p = .001$ is less than the $\alpha = .05$ and the rule is to reject the null of no relationship when the computed probability is less than the chosen α criterion.

TABLE 5.3 An Independent t-Test Analysis

Group Statistics

	counseling students and counseling professionals	N	Mean	Std. Deviation	Std. Error Mean
COSE Dealing with Difficult Client Behaviors	student	11	24.64	5.334	1.608
	professional	9	34.78	4.842	1.614

Independent Samples Test

		Levene's Test for Equality of Variances		t-test for Equality of Means					95% Confidence Interval of the Difference	
		F	Sig.	t	df	Sig. (2-tailed)	Mean Difference	Std. Error Difference	Lower	Upper
COSE Dealing with Difficult Client Behaviors	Equal variances assumed	.025	.877	-4.406	18	.000	-10.141	2.302	-14.977	-5.305
	Equal variances not assumed			-4.451	17.764	.000	-10.141	2.279	-14.933	-5.350

TABLE 5.4   Correlation Matrix of Age, COSE Confidence in Executing Microskills, and COSE Dealing with Difficult Client Behaviors

		age	COSE Confidence in Executing Microskills	COSE Dealing with Difficult Client Behaviors
		Correlations		
age	Pearson Correlation	1	.420	.663*
	Sig. (2-tailed)		.065	.001
	N	20	20	20
COSE Confidence in Executing Microskills	Pearson Correlation	.420	1	.419
	Sig. (2-tailed)	.065		.066
	N	20	20	20
COSE Dealing with Difficult Client Behaviors	Pearson Correlation	.663**	.419	1
	Sig. (2-tailed)	.001	.066	
	N	20	20	20

*Correlation is significant at the 0.01 level (2-tailed).

5. *Simple scatter plot.* We now look at a *scatter plot* showing graphically the relationship between *age* and *COSE Dealing with Difficult Client Behaviors* (see Figure 5.7).

- Click **Graphs** > **Legacy Dialogs** > **Scatter/Dot**.

- Click on the chart to the left of **Simple Scatter** and click on the **Define** button.

- Click over *age* to the **Y Axis** and *COSE Dealing with Difficult Client Behaviors* to the **X Axis** and click **OK**.

   The scatter points are forming somewhat of an oval around a straight line that can be visualized starting at the bottom left corner of the rectangle and extending to the upper right corner of the rectangle.

Creating a Composite Summed Variable of Two Variables

1. Often researchers combine variables by summing them into a composite variable. We are going to add together the scores of *COSE Confidence in*

FIGURE 5.7 **Scatter Plot of *Age* and *COSE Dealing with Difficult Client Behaviors***

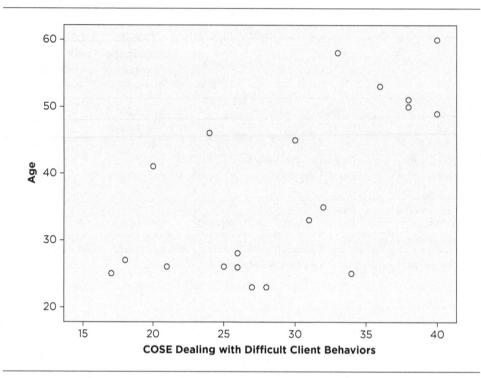

Executing Microskills and *COSE Dealing with Difficult Client Behaviors* and create a combined variable (composite) from the two variables.

- Click **Transform > Compute Variable >** under **Target Variable** type *COSEComposite*.

- Click over the variable *COSE Confidence in Executing Microskills* under **Numeric Expression** and click on the button that is a plus sign (+).

- Click over the variable *COSE Dealing with Difficult Client Behaviors* under **Numeric Expression**.

- Click the **OK** button and click out of the output created; look at the end of the columns on **Data View** and you will see a new column created called *COSEComposite*. This column represents the sum of the two variables (see Figure 5.8).

FIGURE 5.8 COSE Composite Sum Variable

Creating a Composite Mean Variable of Two Variables

1. Sometimes it is useful to create a composite variable of the averages (means) of several variables. We will create the composite mean of the scores of *COSE Confidence in Executing Microskills* and *COSE Dealing with Difficult Client Behaviors.*

2. Click **Transform > Compute Variable** > under **Target Variable** type *COSECompositeMean.* (If you information on the page from the previous analysis, press the **Reset** button.)

3. Under **Function group:**, click on **All >**, then under **Functions and Special Variables**, scroll down until you find **Mean** and click on it.

4. Using the arrow pointing up, click **Mean** to the **Numeric Expression** box. Under **Numeric Expression**, you will see **MEAN(?,?)**.

5. Click over *COSE Confidence in Executing Microskills* under **Numeric Expression** > click to the right of the comma (that has to be in the expression)

FIGURE 5.9 COSE Composite Mean Variable

and delete the question mark > then click over the variable *COSE Dealing with Difficult Client Behaviors* to **Numeric Expression**.

6. Click the **OK** button and click out of the output created; look at the end of the columns on **Data View** and you will see a new column created called *COSECompositeMean*. This column represents the mean of the scores of two variables (see Figure 5.9).

EXAMPLES OF MODIFYING DATA PROCEDURES

1. Inserting a new variable into **Data View**. (This can also be done in Variable View.)

   • In **Data View**, right click on the column where you want to insert the new variable to its left.

   • Click **Insert Variable**.

   • The new variable will be located to the left of the column you right clicked on.

2. Inserting a case in **Data View**.

- Click on **Data View**.

- Right click on the row you want a new row (case) to be above.

- Click **Insert Cases**.

- The new case will be above the highlighted row.

3. Sorting cases in *ascending* or *descending* order by a variable.

- Click **Data > Sort Cases** > Click over the variable to wish to sort and click on **Ascending** > click **OK**.

- To return the rows in the original order, click **Data > Sort Cases** > Deselect the variable you sorted and click over *ID* under **Sort By** and click on **Ascending**; click **OK**.

- Another option to sort data is to right click on the variable column in **Data View**, and click on either **Sort Ascending** or **Sort Descending**. To return the data set to its original order, sort the *ID* back to **Ascending**.

4. Square-root transformation of a variable.

- Click **Transform** > *Compute* **Variable**. Under the **Target Variable**, type the variable's name preceded by *sq* in the title for easy identification in your data set that you wish to transform, such as *sqcounconfid*.

- Go to **Function group:** and select **Arithmetic**.

- Under **Functions and Special Variables:**, click **Sqrt** under **Numeric Expression** and will look like **SQRT(?)** > click over variable *counconfid*; click **OK**. The new variable *sqconfidence* will show up on **Data View** as the last column.

SUMMARY

Data in IBM SPSS 20 can be entered and manipulated in various ways. Following the procedural steps outlined in this chapter provides a starting point for you to familiarize yourself with the program. You will be enhancing your knowledge and use of IBM SPSS 20 as you learn about various statistical procedures presented in this book through problem applications.

PROBLEM ASSIGNMENT

Go to the companion website for review questions on using IBM SPSS 20. Use the information presented in this chapter to guide you as you complete the assignment.

KEY TERMS

ascending	IBM SPSS 20
bivariate correlational matrix	independent t-test
chart	nominal
data	ordinal
descending	scale
descriptive statistics	scatter plot
Explore Analysis	spreadsheet
Frequency Analysis	variables

Chapter 6

DIAGNOSING STUDY DATA

FOR INACCURACIES

AND ASSUMPTIONS

LEARNING OBJECTIVES

- ○ Understand the reasons for diagnosing a data set for accuracy of data, missing data, univariate outliers, and underlying assumptions related to parametric statistics.

- ○ Examine the methods used to diagnose study data for inaccuracies and assumptions.

- ○ Execute procedures using IBM SPSS to conduct an assessment of data accuracy, missing data, univariate outliers, and underlying assumptions.

- ○ Conduct procedures to modify a data set using data diagnostic results, and interpret the outcomes.

The **purpose** of this chapter is to explore and implement methods for data screening a data set before conducting the main analyses related to the research hypotheses. Data diagnosis concepts, methods, and procedures are implemented to prepare a data set for analyses.

The purpose of *data diagnostics* (also called exploratory data analysis, data screening, or data preparation) is to protect the integrity of inferential statistical tests (Tabachnick & Fidell, 2007). Researchers want their data to be accurate, complete, and in compliance with the underlying assumptions of the statistics being used. This screening procedure is part of step 5 of the hypothesis-testing process and involves preparing one's data for statistical analyses to accurately answer questions about the research questions and hypotheses. Data diagnostics methods will be examined by analyzing data related to a hypothetical research example. The data to be entered into IBM SPSS are at the end of this chapter.

RESEARCH EXAMPLE

A researcher wants to implement a new and unique mindfulness training program to see if it is more effective in increasing mindfulness attention awareness when compared to a traditional mindfulness training program. The dependent variable mindfulness attention awareness is defined as the presence or absence of attention to and awareness of what is occurring in the present (Brown & Ryan, 2003). The dependent variable is measured using the Mindfulness Attention and Awareness Scale (MAAS). The norm group mean and standard deviation on the MAAS is $\overline{X} = 64$, and SD $= 9.9$. Forty participants are randomly assigned equally to each of the two conditions. Participant information related to various potential extraneous variables was obtained prior to assignment to a condition. The participants were compared by group on this information to verify that randomization did produce similar groups on key extraneous variables. All participants received six weeks of training and were compared between groups at the end of treatment using the MAAS scores following the development of a randomized posttest-only control group design.

Detecting Erroneous Data Entries

Obviously, the integrity of your data analyses can be significantly compromised by entering wrong data. It is most desirable to enter and check your own data by comparing the original data to the data in the computer program spreadsheet. Having a trusted colleague replicate your data entry and checking procedures is ideal.

When someone else is entering your data, you need to train and trust them as well as monitor their data entry. If you cannot check all of their data entry, then, at the minimum, check one or more random subsets of the data set.

Data that are downloaded, imported, or mined from another data source also need to be reviewed carefully compared to the original source of data. It is not uncommon to have data accuracy problems arise from different formats used by various software programs or even computer platforms.

After the data have been inputted or imported, one can conduct some screening analyses to assess whether scores on variables are in the expected ranges. Additionally, a determination can be made as to whether the frequencies, means, and standard deviations seem plausible.

Go to the **Data View** in the example data set you created and follow the these three commands:

1. At the top of the screen, choose **Analyze** > **Descriptive Statistics** > **Frequencies**.

2. Click over *TotalMAAS* and *Condition* to under **Variable(s)**:

3. Click on the **Statistics** button > click on **Mean** and **Std.deviation** > click on **Continue** and click **OK**.

A review of the output table called Statistics (Table 6.1) shows there is an unusually high standard deviation of 72.26442 (the group norm standard

TABLE 6.1 Mean and Standard Deviation of MAAS Scores

	Statistics TotalMAAS	
N	Valid	39
	Missing	1
Mean		64.4359
Std. Deviation		72.26442

TABLE 6.2 Frequencies of MAAS Scores

			TotalMAAS		
		Frequency	Percent	Valid Percent	Cumulative Percent
Valid	37.00	1	2.5	2.6	2.6
	38.00	1	2.5	2.6	5.1
	40.00	1	2.5	2.6	7.7
	43.00	2	5.0	5.1	12.8
	44.00	1	2.5	2.6	15.4
	46.00	4	10.0	10.3	25.6
	47.00	2	5.0	5.1	30.8
	48.00	1	2.5	2.6	33.3
	50.00	1	2.5	2.6	35.9
	51.00	2	5.0	5.1	41.0
	52.00	5	12.5	12.8	53.8
	53.00	1	2.5	2.6	56.4
	54.00	2	5.0	5.1	61.5
	56.00	2	5.0	5.1	66.7
	57.00	5	12.5	12.8	79.5
	58.00	1	2.5	2.6	82.1
	59.00	1	2.5	2.6	84.6
	60.00	1	2.5	2.6	87.2
	61.00	1	2.5	2.6	89.7
	63.00	1	2.5	2.6	92.3
	85.00	1	2.5	2.6	94.9
	86.00	1	2.5	2.6	97.4
	500.00	1	2.5	2.6	100.0
	Total	39	97.5	100.0	
Missing	System	1	2.5		
Total		40	100.0		

deviation is 9.9). Also, it is unusual to have a standard deviation value higher than the mean.

Looking at the Frequency Table (Table 6.2) also in the output, we see there is a number listed that is 500, which is considerably higher than the next-highest number of 86. Suppose that a review of the original data set shows that the 500 was inputted inaccurately and should be 50. The incorrect number of 500 also inflated the standard deviation out of the realm of plausibility.

Click out of the frequency table output (don't save the output unless you want to). Go to **Data View** and correct the incorrect value accordingly; save the corrected data set as anew data file, called **Data after data correction**.

ID #	Incorrect Value	New Corrected Value
	500	50

Identifying and Dealing with Missing Data

Missing data is a rather common and annoying phenomenon. When data is missing from a data set, there is a potential bias in your data that statistical analyses may ignore because of hidden causes of the missing data. For example, if persons aged 60 to 65 consistently refused to provide their age in a community survey, the results could be biased.

Reasons missing values exist in a data set include participants who don't respond to some items or sections of items, participants who discontinue their participation in a study (attrition), and data management mistakes. A researcher does not want any missing data, but the best type of the bad to have is *missing completely at random (MCAR)*. The MCAR missing data is unpredictable with no systematic pattern. The worst type of missing data to have in a data set is *missing not at random (MNAR)*. There is a systematic cause for MNAR missing data, such as patterns of not answered questions for a reason (e.g., purposeful avoidance of embarrassing questions) or a consistent error in data collection or recording methods. MNAR missing data creates hidden rival explanations in interpreting a data set.

One way to determine the impact of missing data is to create dummy variables. For example, a *dummy variable* might be created for variable A by applying the code 0 to represent each case with no missing data on variable A and using the code 1 to represent all cases with missing data on variable A. This dummy variable has two groups of cases: (1) those cases with no missing data, and (2) those cases with missing data. This variable can be used as an independent variable on variable B to see if there is a significant difference on variable B comparing the no missing data group to the missing data group using an independent *t*-test or one-way ANOVA and assessing the effect size of η^2. Other variables (C, D, E, etc.) could also be analyzed for significant differences using the dummy variable as the independent variable. Significant differences on the variables between the no missing data group and the missing data group would suggest there is a systematic effect of the missing data. A software program called IBM SPSS Missing Values diagnoses the missing values in a data set and estimates new values to replace the missing values. Another program, IBM SPSS AMOS (Analysis of Moment Structures), computes maximum likelihood statistics in the presence of random missing data.

There are several ways of handling missing data. Stevens (1996) states, "Probably the 'best' solution is to make every attempt to minimize the problem before and during the study" (p. 33).

Deleting cases that have a large number of missing data is one option. Hair, Black, Babin, Anderson, and Tatham (2006) offer the guideline that "missing data under 10% for an individual case or observation can generally be ignored, except when the missing data occurs in a specific nonrandom fashion" (p. 55). The deletion of cases may be more attractive when only a small subsample of random cases of a large sample of cases has missing data (Tabachnick & Fidell, 2007).

Deleting variables with substantial missing data is another option. Again, deletion of variables is more appealing if the missing data are random and the variables being deleted are not critical to the analysis.

Deletion of cases or variables is not the ideal solution. Deleting cases means smaller samples and potentially a less representative sample of the population they were drawn from. Deleting variables eliminates important information from a study that a researcher planned to examine.

More acceptable options for improving a data set with missing data include using various approaches to estimate (*impute*) the missing data. A popular approach has been *replacing missing values with a mean* of the available data on a target set of scores, such as a column that often represents a variable. For example, the mean may be from the variable of completed scores where the missing value(s) reside(s). Mean substitution is attractive because it is a conservative estimate since the mean of the scores on the variable does not change. However, the variance of the variable is reduced compared to another score that may have been the missing value, because one is replacing the missing value with its distribution mean. Correlations with other variables are also lowered because of the reduced variance. Mean substitution is less frequently used because other more accurate methods of imputation have been developed.

Another method is using regression analysis. Regression analysis takes completed case values from a data set and generates a regression equation to predict the missing values. This approach may be more sophisticated than mean substitutions, but it has limitations. If the variables used to predict the missing values are not good predictors of the missing values, then the outcome is not optimal.

A sophisticated imputation method called *expectation maximization (EM)* involves creating a distribution of partially missing data and making inferences about missing data under the likelihood of that created distribution (see Little & Rubin, 2002). As mentioned earlier, specialized statistical software programs have been developed to handle missing data, such as IBM SPSS Missing Values.

Repeating analyses with and without (imputed) missing data is highly recommended following any of the methods of handling missing data. You will be comparing the results for similarities and differences. If the results of the two analyses are similar, then this provides the researcher with self-assurance as to interpretation of the results. Further data investigation is needed if the results are different. It is good practice to report results from both a missing data set and an imputed missing data set.

We now look at an illustration of assessing and imputing a missing data point in the example data. We use an imputation technique available in IBM SPSS known as *linear trend at point*, which replaces missing values with a linear trend for that point. There is a regression on the existing series on an index variable scaled from 1 to *n*. This linear trend point estimates the missing values.

Initiate **Analyze > Descriptive Statistics > Frequencies**. If there are any variables still under the **Variable(s)** column, click on the **Reset** button at the bottom of the screen.

1. Click over *TotalMAAS* under **Variable(s):** and click **OK**.

    The output in the TotalMAAS Statistics Table (Table 6.3) shows that there are 39 cases and 1 case with a missing value. The ID for the missing case is #11 as seen on the **DataView**. There is a blank cell for ID #11 in the column for the dependent variable TotalMAAS.

    We will impute the missing value using a linear trend at point analysis.

2. To replace the missing value for *ID #11* on the variable *TotalMAAS*, initiate **Transform > Replace Missing Values >** first beside **Method:** choose **Linear trend at point >** then click over *TotalMAAS* under **New Variable(s): >** click **OK >** click out of the output produced and go to the **DataView**, where a new column is produced called *TotalMAAS_1*. Save a new data file named **Data**

TABLE 6.3 Missing Case for TotalMAAS

	Statistics TotalMAAS	
N	Valid	39
	Missing	1

after imputed value & data correction so you know that it contains an imputed value added to the corrected value completed previously.

You will notice that all of the values in the new column are the same except for the value that was imputed, and it is 53.76, which is the estimated value for the missing data. We will be using this changed data file (corrected value and imputed value) for several other analyses.

Identifying and Assessing Univariate Outliers

Next, we examine how to screen for *univariate outliers* and the underlying assumptions of the statistic used. We will also modify the data based on our findings. We are preparing our data to answer one simple question based on our study problem: Will there be a significant difference in mindfulness attention awareness resulting from a new and unique mindfulness training program compared to a traditional mindfulness training program? We will be testing the null hypothesis that there will be no difference in mindfulness attention awareness between the new and traditional mindfulness training programs (H_0: $\mu_{1New} =$ $\mu_{2Traditional}$). We will eventually run a one-way ANOVA (*F*-test) to see if there are significant differences (we could also run an independent *t*-test). We screened and corrected the data set for data entry problems and missing data. We will continue the data screening process to prepare our data for analysis to protect the integrity of the inferential statistical test (*F*-test).

Identifying and Assessing Univariate Outliers

Many statistical methods are sensitive to the impact of scores that are outliers, so it is important to identify and make decisions about what to do with them. The reason is, according to Stevens (1996): "Because we want the results of our statistical analysis to reflect most of the data, and not to be highly influenced by just 1 or 2 errant data points" (p. 13). The results of a data set with outliers do not generalize well to other samples unless they also have similar outliers.

Outliers can be univariate or multivariate. Univariate outliers are extreme scores by cases on one variable. Multivariate outliers are extreme score combinations by cases on two or more variables. There are many possible reasons for the existence of outliers (Tabachnick & Fidell, 2007). Outliers can be caused by errors in data entry and mismanagement of a data file. The participant with an outlying score on a dependent variable may not be a member of the population that you intended to sample. For example, you may be studying persons with obsessive-compulsive disorders (OCDs); a participant got into the sample who does not have an OCD disorder, and this person's score on a dependent variable is extreme compared to the OCD participants' scores. It is also possible that participants have outlying scores and they do represent the population you wanted to sample. The population may have more extreme scores than is expected in a normal curve.

Tabachnick and Fidell (2007) identified a guideline for determining if a participant's score on a continuously scaled dependent variable is a univariate outlier. If any z-score is in excess of $z = \pm 3.29$ ($p < .001$, two-tailed test), then it is declared to be a univariate outlier. This guideline is two-tailed, meaning it applies to extreme negative (left tail) scores and extreme positive (right tail) scores.

The raw scores on dependent variables are transformed to z-scores. If any z-score is greater than ± 3.29, it is considered a univariate outlier. Such a score would clearly be an extreme score using the ± 3.29 on the normal curve to make the determination. Next, we compute z-scores for the dependent variable (*TotalMAAS_1*) raw scores using the changed data file (corrected value and imputed value).

1. Select **Analyze** > **Descriptive Statistics** > **Descriptives**.

2. Click over *TotalMAAS_1* (the longer variable name is TREND(TotalMAAS) [*TotalMAAS_1*]) under **Variable(s):** > click on the box at the bottom of the screen that says **Save standardized values as variables** and then click **OK**.

3. Click out of the **Descriptives** output and see the new variable at the end of the **DataView** spreadsheet called *ZTotalMAAS_1*. These are the z-scores for each raw score. Save this file as a new data set called **Data after z-score, imputed value, & entry correction**.

Our task is to identify any value that is greater than ±3.29 in each cell under *ZTotalMAAS_1*. The value of $z = 3.37707$ for participant ID #32 in the control group is greater than $+3.29$, so the raw score of 86 is an outlier. The z-score $=$ 3.27498 (ID #8) in the treatment condition group is close to being an outlier using our criterion of ±3.29 but it does not reach the criterion level. However, it's near outlying (using our criterion) effects will be detected in additional analyses that will be conducted.

There are various approaches for minimizing the effects of outliers. Less desirable methods are to delete the case or variable with the outlier(s) based on an assessment of whether the case is representative of the population that the sample was drawn from. Another approach is using *trimmed means* by discarding 5 percent of the largest scores and doing the same for 5 percent of the smallest scores.

Conducting a *data transformation* of the original raw scores also is used to reduce the influence of extreme scores by bringing the outliers closer to the majority of scores in the distribution. The procedure to transform data is very common in the use of statistics. Data transformations are used when raw scores are converted to z-scores or *T*-scores. Several advanced statistics have natural logarithms in their formulas, including logistic regression and log-linear analysis.

Obtaining additional data screening information will be useful to assess before making a decision on how to handle the univariate outlier that we discovered in the data set. We will next screen the data to establish whether the data meet the underlying *univariate assumptions* of the one-way ANOVA statistic.

Screening and Making Decisions about Univariate Assumptions

Many statistical analyses "require that all groups come from normal populations with the same variance" (Norusis, 1994, p. 89). Statistics like the one-way ANOVA use sampling distributions to test whether a statistic is significant. The *central limit theorem* tells us that regardless of the shape of the population distribution, the sampling distribution of means, drawn from a population with variance σ^2 and mean μ, will approach a normal distribution with σ^2/N as sample size N increases. So, we want our sample distribution on the dependent variable to reflect *normality* and the *sample variances to be approximately equal* (same population) so that we can test whether two sample means come from the same populations or different populations. As such, we will assess whether all the group variances are equal and that samples come from normal populations. If these assumptions are violated then we will identify strategies to rectify the violations. More specifically, for normality we will assess histograms, normal Q-Q plots, skewness, kurtosis, and the Shapiro-Wilk statistic. We will examine the variance ratio (F_{max}) and the Levene's test to make a decision about the assumption of homogeneity of variance. Evidence is combined from all of the sources of information to make decisions about whether the dependent variable is normal and reflecting homogeneity of variance across the two conditions. The decisions made are based on the preponderance of evidence.

We begin by analyzing the dependent variable, mindfulness attention awareness, for normality using the modified variable *TotalMAAS_1*. We have discovered in the screening for unvariate outliers screening that dependent variable had one univariate outlier. We have postponed a decision on what to do with the univariate outlier until after our screening for normality and homogeneity of variance. Univariate outliers do have detrimental effects on both normality and homogeneity of variance. Conduct the following data analysis on *TotalMAAS_1*.

1. **Analyze > Descriptive Statistics > Explore**

2. Click over dependent variable TREND(TotalMAAS)[*TotalMAAS_1*]) to the **Dependent List**.

3. Click over independent variable (*Condition*) to *Factor List*.

4. Do not change **Display** choices; leave on *Both*.

5. In the upper right corner of the screen there are three buttons. Click on **Plots**. Then select **Histogram** and **Normality plots with tests**.

6. Click on **Continue**.

7. Click on **OK**.

Skewness and Kurtosis

Much of the data from the output provides information about the *skewness* and *kurtosis* of the sample distribution of scores. A distribution where scores are not balanced (*asymmetrical*) with extreme scores in either tail of the distribution is skewed. Outliers produce skewed distributions. If most of the scores are on the left but there are extreme scores on the right side of the curve, it is *positively skewed.* When the extreme scores are on the left side of the curve and most of the scores are on the right side, it is *negatively skewed.*

Kurtosis is the relative concentration of scores in the center, the upper and lower ends (tails), and the shoulders (between the center and the tails) of a distribution (Norusis, 1994). *Mesokurtic* refers to a curve as being more symmetrical and normal (bell) shaped. A curve that is more narrow and peaked is *leptokurtic.* *Platykurtic* reflects a shape of a curve that has scores more widely dispersed and flat.

Histograms

Histograms provide a general visual description of the distribution of data values. The inspection of histograms is a good place to start in understanding your study data distribution, but they are often difficult to interpret. Histograms show the extent that a distribution of values is symmetrical (mesokurtic) and whether cases cluster around a central value. You can see if the shape of the distribution is more peaked or narrow (high in the middle—leptokurtic) or more flat (dispersed—platykurtic). You can also tell if there are values far removed from the other values, such as values far to the right of the distribution (positive skew) or values far to the left of the distribution (negative skew).

Refer to the computer output and scroll down until you find the histograms of the mindfulness attention awareness (*TotalMAAS_1*) scores for both the treatment and control groups. The abscissa of the histograms represents the scores and the ordinate represents the frequency that participants generated the scores.

The treatment group scores appear somewhat symmetrical in Figure 6.1, but the score distribution is positively skewed with an extreme score on the right side of the curve. This is the near outlying score for participant ID #8. The peak of the curve seems to be higher than we might expect (leptokurtic) compared to the peak of a normal curve, but we won't find out for sure until we have conducted more analyses.

The histogram of mindfulness awareness scores for the control group (Figure 6.2) is positively skewed with a univariate outlier discovered earlier, score 86, participant ID #32. The curve is somewhat symmetrical and possibly leptokurtic.

Skewness Screening

A more accurate way to assess whether the distribution of scores on the dependent variable in each group is significantly skewed is done by creating *z*-scores. The

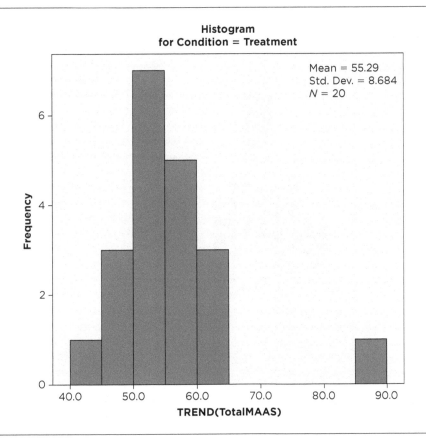

output table called **Descriptives** contains the information that we will be using for our analyses (see Table 6.4). We will examine skewness values and calculate skewness z-scores. The signs ($+$ or $-$) of skewness values and z-scores indicate the direction of the skew but not whether it is a significant skew. A positive skewness value and z-score indicate that the score distribution is in the direction of the right side of the curve, and a negative skewness value and z-score indicate the direction in the left size of the curve. A skewness value and z-score at or near 0 indicate there is no skewness.

The skewness value for the treatment condition group is 2.071 (positive skew direction), and the standard error value next to it is .512 (see Table 6.4). When the skewness value is divided by its standard error the result is a z-score.

FIGURE 6.2 Histogram of Mindfulness Attention Awareness Scores for the Control Group

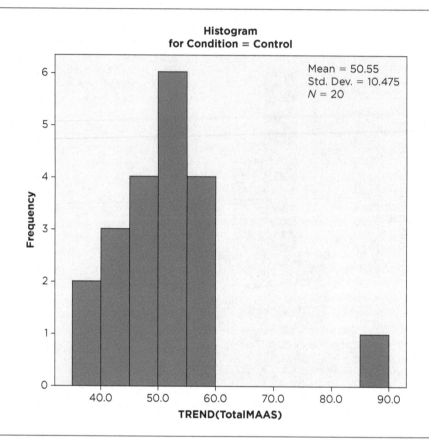

So, 2.071/.512 equals a $z_{Skew} = 4.045$. This value can be compared to the criterion that we used for univariate outliers, $z = \pm 3.29$ ($p < .001$, two-tailed test). The $z_{Skew} = 4.045$ is greater than $z = \pm 3.29$, so we conclude that the distribution of scores of the treatment condition group is significantly positively skewed ($p < .001$) and departs from being a normal distribution.

The skewness value (1.995, positive skew direction) and its standard error (.512) for the control group score distribution generate a $z_{Skew} = 1.995/.512 = 3.896$. Again, the control group distribution of scores is not normally distributed because it is significantly positively skewed since the $z_{Skew} = 3.896$ is greater than our criterion of $z = \pm 3.29$.

TABLE 6.4   Skewness and Kurtosis Values with Standard Errors of the Dependent Variable for Both Conditions

Descriptives			Statistic	Std. Error
Condition				
TREND (TotalMAAS)	Treatment	Mean	55.288	1.9418
		95% Confidence Interval for Mean — Lower Bound	51.224	
		95% Confidence Interval for Mean — Upper Bound	59.352	
		5% Trimmed Mean	54.320	
		Median	53.881	
		Variance	75.414	
		Std. Deviation	8.6841	
		Minimum	43.0	
		Maximum	85.0	
		Range	42.0	
		Interquartile Range	6.5	
		Skewness	2.071	.512
		Kurtosis	6.915	.992
	Control	Mean	50.550	2.3424
		95% Confidence Interval for Mean — Lower Bound	45.647	
		95% Confidence Interval for Mean — Upper Bound	55.453	
		5% Trimmed Mean	49.333	
		Median	50.000	
		Variance	109.734	
		Std. Deviation	10.4754	
		Minimum	37.0	
		Maximum	86.0	
		Range	49.0	
		Interquartile Range	11.0	
		Skewness	1.995	.512
		Kurtosis	6.457	.992

Kurtosis Screening

We conduct the same process obtaining kurtosis z-scores and compare them to the criterion of ± 3.29. A positive kurtosis value and z-score indicate that the distribution of scores is in the direction of a leptokurtic (more peaked) distribution, and a negative kurtosis value or z-score designates the direction of a platykurtic (more flat) distribution. A kurtosis value or z-score close to 0 signifies a mesokurtic (normal and symmetrical) distribution.

The kurtosis value for the treatment group is 6.915, the standard error is .992, and the $z_{Kurtosis} = 6.915/.992 = 6.971$ (see Table 6.4). The $z_{Kurtosis} = 6.971$ is greater than ± 3.29, so it reflects a significant leptokurtic distribution of scores, which is not a normal distribution.

The control group has a kurtosis value $= 6.457$ and standard error $= .992$, so the $z_{Kurtosis} = 6.457/.992 = 6.509 > \pm 3.29$, $p < .001$. The control group has a significant leptokurtic distribution of scores, thus departing from a normal distribution.

Shapiro-Wilk Statistic

The *Shapiro-Wilk (S-W) test* and the Kolmogorov-Smirnov test with Lilliefors correction are statistical tests that assess the hypothesis that the data are from a normal distribution. It is important to remember that whenever the sample size is large, almost any goodness-of-fit test will result in rejection of the null hypothesis since it is almost impossible to find data that are exactly normally distributed. For most statistical tests, it is sufficient that the data are approximately normally distributed (Norusis, 1994).

We will obtain additional evidence about the normality of the distributions of dependent variable scores in the two groups by testing the null hypothesis, H_0: sample distribution of scores = normal. If we fail to reject (retain) the H_0 in this analysis, this finding provides support for the sample scores being normally distributed. If we reject the H_0, then the finding suggests that sample scores are not normally distributed. Therefore, we are hoping to retain the null when using the Shapiro-Wilk (S-W) statistic. We will use an alpha (α) level of .05.

The significance probability of the S-W statistic for the treatment group is $p = .002$ (see Table 6.5). The rule for rejecting an H_0 is: if the significance probability of the statistic is equal to or less than the alpha level, then the H_0 is rejected. The null is rejected for the treatment group since $p = .002 < \alpha = .05$. This suggests that the sample distribution of scores for the treatment group is not normally distributed. The control group also had a significance probability of $p = .002$, which is less than $\alpha = .05$, so the null hypothesis is rejected. The control group distribution of scores is not normally distributed.

Assessing Normal Q-Q Plots for Normality

Each observed value in a distribution of scores is paired with its expected value from the normal distribution in a *normal probability plot (Q-Q plot)*. The expected values

TABLE 6.5   Shapiro-Wilk Statistic Results to Assess Normality

		Kolmogorov-Smirnov[a]			Shapiro-Wilk		
	Condition	Statistic	df	Sig.	Statistic	df	Sig.
TREND(TotalMAAS)	Treatment	.177	20	.099	.820	20	.002
	Control	.169	20	.136	.827	20	.002

Tests of Normality

[a] Lilliefors significance correction.

from the normal distribution are based on the number of cases in the sample and the rank order of the case in the sample. If the sample is from a normal distribution, we expect that the points will fall more or less on a straight line.

The Q-Q plots of distributions of scores for both conditions are in Figures 6.3 and 6.4. For the most part, the points are on or near the line. However, there is one point in each graph that is substantially off the line. Each point in the first and second Q-Q plots represents the extreme score in the treatment and control condition groups that we have identified earlier.

Summary of Our Screening Results for the Underlying Assumption of Normality

A significant univariate outlier was identified in the control group and an extreme score was also found in the treatment group but it was not significant. All the skewness and kurtosis z-scores and Shapiro-Wilk statistics were significant, indicating that the score distributions in both groups departed from normality. Finally, the Q-Q plots reflected outliers in the distributions of scores. The preponderance of evidence strongly suggests that the sample data do not meet the underlying assumptions of normality. Next, we assess whether the underlying assumption of homogeneity of variance is met.

Screening for Homogeneity of Variance

The variance ratio (F_{max}) and Levene's test will be used to assess homogeneity of variance. A *variance ratio analysis* can be obtained by dividing the highest group variance by the lowest variance of a group in an analysis. Norusis (2005) provided

FIGURE 6.3 Q-Q Plot to Assess Normality of Treatment Condition Scores

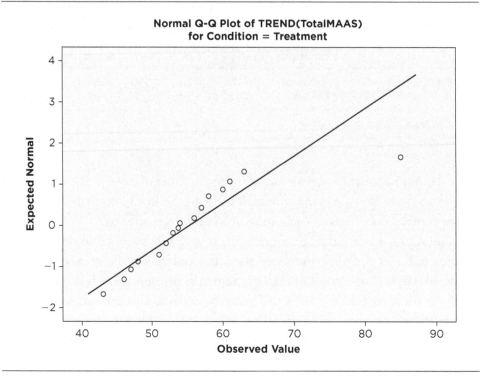

a guideline that the homogeneity is acceptable if the ratio of the largest variance to the smallest variance is less than 4:1. Tabachnick and Fidell (2007) suggested that if the group or cell sizes (participants per cell) are relatively equal, such as 4 to 1 for largest to smallest participants per cell, then a variance ratio as high as 10 is acceptable. However, if the largest to smallest number of participants per group (or cell) are as large as 9 to 1, then, a variance ratio (F_{max}) as low as 3 can be associated with inflated Type I error.

The participants per group are equal in size ($n_1 = 20$ and $n_2 = 20$). The variances of the two groups are found in Table 6.4. The control group had the highest variance of $s^2_{Control} = 109.734$ and $s^2_{Treatment} = 75.414$. The variance ratio is $F_{max} = 109.734/75.414 = 1.455$. The variance of the control group is 1.455 larger than the variance of the treatment group. This ratio is lower than the criterion of 4 times larger or 10 times larger. There appears to be homogeneity of variance across the two groups according to the variance ratio. We will verify this finding with the Levene's test.

FIGURE 6.4   Q-Q Plot to Assess Normality of Control Condition Scores

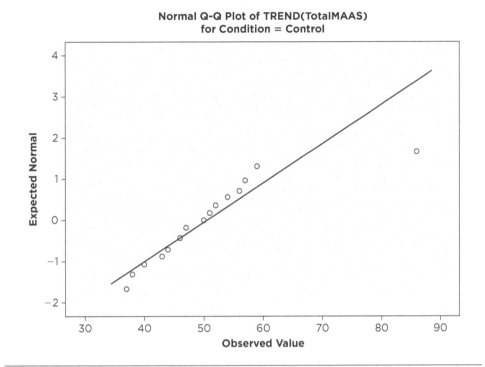

Normal Q-Q Plot of TREND(TotalMAAS)
for Condition = Control

Levene's Test

The *Levene's test* is a test of homogeneity of variance that is less dependent on the assumption of normality than most tests and thus is particularly useful with analysis of variance. It is obtained by computing, for each case, the absolute differences from its cell mean and performing a one-way analysis of variance on these differences. If the Levene's test statistic is significant, then the groups are not homogeneous and we may need to consider transforming the original data or using a nonparametric statistic (Norusis, 1994). The Levene's test results are provided with the one-way ANOVA results, allowing us to review both results at the same time.

1. **Analyze > General Linear Model > Univariate.**

2. Click over dependent variable TREND(TotalMAAS)[*TotalMAAS_1*] to **Dependent Variable:.**

3. Click over independent variable (*Condition*) to **Fixed Factor(s).**

4. Click on the **Options** button, then select **Descriptive statistics**, **Estimates of effect size**, **Observed power**, and **Homogeneity tests** in the Display box.

5. Click on **Continue**.

6. Click on **OK**.

The output results of the Levene's test are found in the table titled Levene's Test of Equality of Error Variances (Table 6.6). We are testing the null hypothesis that the variances and error variances of the dependent variable are equal across the two condition groups, H_0: $\sigma^2_{Error(Treatment)} = \sigma^2_{Error(Control)}$. We are using an $\alpha = .05$ to test the null hypothesis. The significance probability of the Levene's test result is $p = .578$, which is greater than $\alpha = .05$ so we fail to reject the H_0. We can conclude from the Levene's test that the variances and error variance are equal across the conditions, and we met the underlying assumption of homogeneity of variance. Both the Levene's test and the variance ratio support the presence of homogeneity of variance across the two sample distributions of scores. Next, we discuss the results of the one-way ANOVA that are also on the output following the Levene's test information.

One-Way Analysis of Variance Results

We did meet the underlying assumption of homogeneity of variance, but we did not meet the assumption requirement that dependent variable scores are normally distributed. We are therefore going to correct for the violation of normality by *transforming the dependent variable* to minimize the influence of the outlying scores that are causing the distribution of scores to be positively skewed and leptokurtic rather than normal. Both the nontransformed and transformed analyses are conducted and presented following good practice.

TABLE 6.6   Results of Levene's Test of Homogeneity of Variance

Levene's Test of Equality of Error Variances[a] Dependent Variable: TREND(TotalMAAS)			
F	*df1*	*df2*	Sig.
.315	1	38	.578

Tests the null hypothesis that the error variance of the dependent variable is equal across groups.

[a] Design: Intercept + Condition

Nontransformed One-Way ANOVA Results

The output results of the one-way ANOVA are in the table called Tests of Between-Subjects Effects (see Table 6.7). The research problem is a comparison between the effects a new and unique mindfulness training program and a traditional mindfulness training program on increasing mindfulness attention awareness. The null to be tested is H_0: $\mu_{1Treatment} = \mu_{1Control}$ using $\alpha = .05$. The results on the row labeled Condition under Source show that the significance probability is $p = .128$. The $p = .128$ is greater than the alpha criterion of .05, so we retain the null hypothesis that there are no mean differences between the two conditions on mindfulness attention awareness, $F(1, 38) = 2.425$, $p > .05$. We will see if the results are similar after we transform the dependent variable.

Transformed Screening and One-Way ANOVA Results

Especially if cases with extreme scores are considered part of the population you sampled, then a way to reduce the influence of a univariate outlier is to transform the variable to change the shape of the distribution to be more normal. Tabachnick and Fidell (2007) and Stevens (1996) provide guides on what type of transformation to use depending on the shape of the distribution you are planning to transform. For example, a square root or a log10 transformation can be used for positively skewed distributions to try to normalize them. For negatively skewed distributions, reflecting the negative distribution (reversing it to positive) and then using a square root or a log transformation may normalize the distribution. All transformations, changes of scores, and deletions should be reported in the findings of a study. Since we have a substantial positively skewed dependent variable, we are going to employ a *log10 transformation*. Please run the following analysis after clicking out of the output we have been using.

1. Select **Transform > Compute**.

2. Under **Target Variable** type *LTotalMAAS_1*. This command will create a new column of transformed scores on the **DataView**, so the *L* (for Logarithm) is used for clarity of what each column of scores represents.

3. Under **Functions group:** click on **All** > then under **Functions and Special Variables:** scroll down until you find **LG10**, then click on it and click on the arrow button to the left point up. This places **LG10** under **Numeric Expression:**.

TABLE 6.7 One-Way ANOVA Results before Log10 Data Transformation

Tests of Between-Subjects Effects
Dependent Variable: TREND(TotalMAAS)

Source	Type III Sum of Squares	df	Mean Square	F	Sig.	Partial Eta Squared	Noncent. Parameter	Observed Power[b]
Corrected model	224.499[a]	1	224.499	2.425	.128	.060	2.425	.329
Intercept	112,017.093	1	112,017.093	1,210.025	.000	.970	1,210.025	1.000
Condition	224.499	1	224.499	2.425	.128	.060	2.425	.329
Error	3,517.821	38	92.574					
Total	115,759.413	40						
Corrected total	3,742.319	39						

[a] R-squared = .060 (adjusted R-squared = .035)

[b] Computed using alpha = .05

4. Next go to variables under **Type and Label** and click on TREND(Total-MAAS)[TotalMAAS_1] and then click on the arrow to the right of the box of variables. It will show up in the place under **Numeric Expression** where the **?** was. So, the **Numeric Expression** should look like **LG10(TotalMAAS_1)**.

5. Then, click **OK** and the log10 transformed variable will be on your **Data-View** spreadsheet.

Now, we will see if the log10 transformation was successful in normalizing the distribution of the dependent variable. We will repeat the exploration commands to assess the measures of normality on the transformed dependent variable.

1. **Analyze > Descriptive Statistics > Explore**.

2. Click on **Reset** and then click over the transformed dependent variable (*LTotalMAAS_1*) to **Dependent List**.

3. Click over independent variable (*Condition*) to **Factor List**.

4. Do not change **Display** choices—leave on **Both**.

5. To the upper right there are three buttons. Click on **Plots**. Then, select **Histogram** and **Normality plots with tests**.

6. Click on **Continue**.

7. Click on OK.

The output of the histograms (Figures 6.5a and 6.5b) after Log10 transformation shows that the extreme scores have moved closer to the other scores in the distributions. However, they still are apart for the majority of scores in the distributions.

The output skewness and kurtosis values of the transformed data are in the Descriptives table (Table 6.8). The $z_{SkewTreatment} = 1.310/.512 = 2.559$ and the $z_{SkewControl} = 1.064/.512 = 2.078$. The z_{Skew} scores for both groups are below ± 3.29; thus the sample distribution scores are no longer significantly positively skewed. The log10 transformation was successful on skewness.

The $z_{KurtosisTreatment} = 4.061/.992 = 4.094$ and the $z_{KurtosisControl} = 3.006/.992 = 3.030$. The $z_{KurtosisTreatment} = 4.094 > \pm 3.29$, so it remains significantly leptokurtic; but the $z_{KurtosisControl} = 3.030 < \pm 3.29$, so it is no longer significantly leptokurtic.

FIGURE 6.5A AND B Histograms of the Dependent Variable by Condition Groups after Log10 Data Transformation

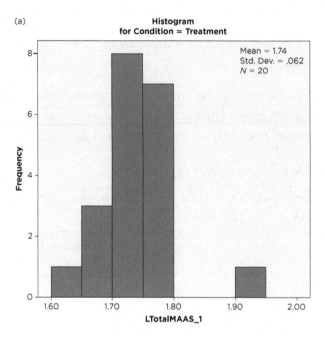

(a)

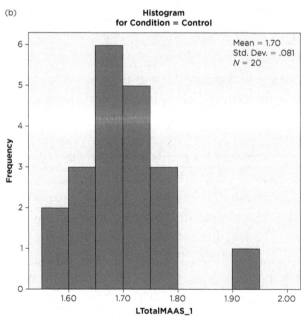

(b)

TABLE 6.8 **Skewness and Kurtosis Values after Log10 Transformation**

	Condition			Statistic	Std. Error
			Descriptives		
LTotalMAAS_1	Treatment	Mean		1.7382	.01384
		95% Confidence	Lower Bound	1.7092	
		Interval for Mean	Upper Bound	1.7672	
		5% Trimmed Mean		1.7334	
		Median		1.7314	
		Variance		.004	
		Std. Deviation		.06189	
		Minimum		1.63	
		Maximum		1.93	
		Range		.30	
		Interquartile Range		.05	
		Skewness		1.310	.512
		Kurtosis		4.061	.992
	Control	Mean		1.6961	.01806
		95% Confidence	Lower Bound	1.6583	
		Interval for Mean	Upper Bound	1.7339	
		5% Trimmed Mean		1.6900	
		Median		1.6990	
		Variance		.007	
		Std. Deviation		.08074	
		Minimum		1.57	
		Maximum		1.93	
		Range		.37	
		Interquartile Range		.10	
		Skewness		1.064	.512
		Kurtosis		3.006	.992

The Shapiro-Wilk statistics in the Tests of Normality output table (Table 6.9) show that the treatment group score distribution is still significant since the $p = .040$ is less than $\alpha = .05$, but the control group is no longer significant, $p = .094 > \alpha = .05$.

The output of the normal Q-Q plots (Table 6.10) shows that the log10 transformation was successful in bringing the points closer to the line, including the extreme scores (see Figures 6.6a and 6.6b). This reflects more congruence between observed and estimated normal scores.

TABLE 6.9   Shapiro-Wilk Statistics after Log10 Transformation

		Kolmogorov-Smirnov[a]			Shapiro-Wilk		
	Condition	Statistic	df	Sig.	Statistic	df	Sig.
LTotalMAAS_1	Treatment	.142	20	.200*	.900	20	.040
	Control	.130	20	.200*	.919	20	.094

[a] Lilliefors significance correction.
* This is a lower bound of the true significance.

TABLE 6.10   Levene's Test of Homogeneity of Variance after Log10 Transformation

Levene's Test of Equality of Error Variances[a]
Dependent Variable: LTotalMAAS_1

F	df1	df2	Sig.
.917	1	38	.344

Tests the null hypothesis that the error variance of the dependent variable is equal across groups.
[a] Design: Intercept + Condition

The preponderance of the evidence of the log10 transformed data suggests that the transformed dependent variable scores of both condition groups more closely approximate normal distributions. We will conduct a one-way ANOVA on the transformed data to see if there is a significant difference in mindfulness attention awareness between the new and tradition mindfulness training programs, H_0: $\mu_{1\text{Treatment}} = \mu_{1\text{Control}}$ using $\alpha = .05$.

1. **Analyze > General Linear Model > Univariate.**

2. Click over the log10 transformed dependent variable (*LTotalMAAS_1*) to **Dependent Variable**.

3. Click over independent variable (*Condition*) to **Fixed Factor(s)**.

FIGURE 6.6A AND B   Normal Q-Q Plots after Log10 Data Transformation

(a)

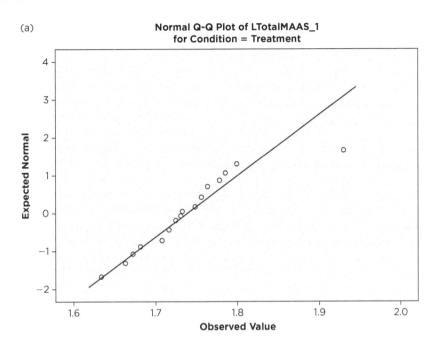

(b)

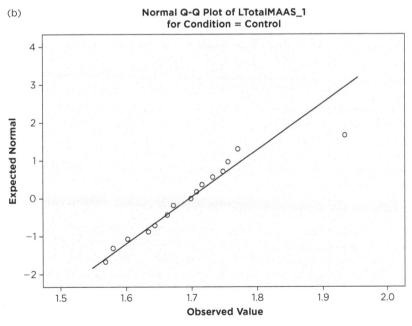

4. Click on the **Options** button, then select **Descriptive statistics**, **Estimates of effect size**, **Observed power**, and **Homogeneity tests** in the Display box.

5. Click on **Continue**.

6. Click on **OK**.

The Levene's test results are under the output table called Levene's Test of Equality of Error Variances (Table 6.10). The Levene's test significance probability is $p = .344 > \alpha = .05$. There is homogeneity of variance as before the transformation.

The one-way ANOVA results of the log10 transformed data are in the output table named Tests of Between-Subjects Effects (Table 6.11). The significance probability is $p = .072$ and is greater than $\alpha = .05$, so we fail to reject the null hypothesis, $F(1, 38) = 3.419$, $p > .05$. This is a similar to our finding using the nontransformed data. This result reinforces the original conclusion that there appears to be no significant difference in mindfulness attention awareness between the new and tradition mindfulness training programs that were implemented with this study sample.

The data we used for all of the previous analyses is in Table 6.12.

TABLE 6.11   One-Way ANOVA Results for the Log10 Transformed Data

Tests of Between-Subjects Effects
Dependent Variable: LTotalMAAS_1

Source	Type III Sum of Squares	df	Mean Square	F	Sig.	Partial Eta Squared	Noncent. Parameter	Observed Power[b]
Corrected model	.018[a]	1	.018	3.419	.072	.083	3.419	.437
Intercept	117.945	1	117.945	22,791.796	.000	.998	22,791.796	1.000
Condition	.018	1	.018	3.419	.072	.083	3.419	.437
Error	.197	38	.005					
Total	118.160	40						
Corrected total	.214	39						

[a] R-squared = .083 (adjusted R-squared = .058)
[b] Computed using alpha = .05

TABLE 6.12 Data Diagnostics Study Example

ID#	TotalMAAS	Condition
1	52	Treatment**
2	43	Treatment
3	57	Treatment
4	46	Treatment
5	52	Treatment
6	47	Treatment
7	53	Treatment
8	85	Treatment
9	52	Treatment
10	54	Treatment
11*		Treatment
12	51	Treatment
13	48	Treatment
14	56	Treatment
15	57	Treatment
16	58	Treatment
17	57	Treatment
18	63	Treatment
19	60	Treatment
20	61	Treatment
21	46	Control
22	500	Control
23	40	Control
24	50	Control
25	37	Control
26	59	Control
27	44	Control
28	51	Control
29	46	Control
30	56	Control
31	54	Control
32	86	Control
33	46	Control
34	57	Control
35	52	Control
36	57	Control
37	47	Control
38	38	Control
39	43	Control
40	52	Control

** Designed missing data cell for data screening.

SUMMARY

Assessing the integrity of data used in statistical analyses is essential to enhance the validity of study findings. Data diagnostics are used to screen for data accuracy, data representativeness, and data meeting the underlying assumptions of the statistics being used.

PROBLEM ASSIGNMENT

Go to the companion website for additional examples of diagnosing study data for inaccuracies and assumptions. Use the information presented in this chapter to guide you as you complete the assignment.

KEY TERMS

asymmetrical

central limit theorem

data diagnostics

data transformation

dummy variable

expectation maximization (EM)

histograms

impute

kurtosis

leptokurtic

Levene's test

linear trend at point

log10 transformation

mesokurtic

missing completely at random (MCAR)

missing data

missing not at random (MNAR)

negatively skewed

normal probability plot (Q-Q plot)

normality

platykurtic

positively skewed

repeating analyses

replacing missing values with a mean

sample variances to be approximately equal

Shapiro-Wilk (S-W) test

skewness

transforming the dependent variable

trimmed means

univariate assumptions

univariate outliers

variance ratio analysis

RANDOMIZED DESIGN

COMPARING TWO

TREATMENTS AND A

CONTROL USING A ONE-WAY

ANALYSIS OF VARIANCE

LEARNING OBJECTIVES

○ Demonstrate how to develop research questions and hypotheses as they relate to a research problem incorporating independent and dependent variables.

○ Identify the components and application of a randomized posttest-only control group design.

○ Examine Type I and II error considerations and a priori power analysis in establishing alpha (α).

- Conduct data diagnostics to assess for normality, homogeneity of variance, and independence of observations.

- Execute a one-way analysis of variance (ANOVA) and Tukey honestly significant difference (HSD) using IBM SPSS and formulas.

- Interpret post hoc analyses using eta-squared (η^2), omega-squared (ω^2), and confidence intervals.

- Understand the study findings combining the various analyses.

A one-way analysis of variance (ANOVA) is used to evaluate the effects of treatment programs to reduce depression among adolescents. A research question and hypotheses are developed postulating that cognitive-behavioral therapy and interpersonal therapy will produce significantly lower depressive symptoms among adolescents when compared to a no-treatment control. A randomized experimental research design comparing two treatments and a control is used. A data set is presented that is used for both IBM SPSS software and formula analyses.

An a priori power analysis is conducted to determine if the sample size, estimated effect size, and alpha level are adequate to proceed with the study. A one-way analysis of variance (ANOVA) is applied to test the overall (omnibus) null hypothesis. The magnitudes of treatment effects are assessed using both eta-squared and omega-squared effect size measures. A post hoc analysis is conducted using the Tukey honestly significant difference (HSD) statistic. The .95 confidence intervals are interpreted for the mean differences between group means. Finally, the overall results are presented.

RESEARCH PROBLEM

The purpose of this research is to determine how effective treatment programs are in reducing symptoms associated with depression among adolescents. Previous research has demonstrated the effectiveness of cognitive-behavioral therapy (CBT) and interpersonal therapy (IPT) for both treatment (Weisz et al., 2009; Rossello, Bernal, & Rivera-Medina, 2008) and prevention (Horowitz, Garber, Ciesla, Young, & Mufson, 2007).

Initially, 160 eighth and ninth grade participants comprised the sample. Prior to random assignment to condition, 10 participants were identified as not eligible for the study because they met exclusion criteria related to having a co-occurring medical or physical condition, receiving psychological treatment, or using medication for a behavioral or neurological disorder. The remaining 150 participants in the sample were randomly assigned to receive one of three treatment conditions: (1) cognitive-behavioral therapy (CBT), (2) interpersonal therapy (IPT), or (3) no-treatment control (Control). Following assignment to condition, two persons in the CBT condition and three persons in the IPT chose to discontinue before the study began. This resulted in 145 participants distributed in the treatment condition groups: CBT ($n_1 = 48$), IPT ($n_2 = 47$), and Control ($n_3 = 50$). The participants' average age was $M = 14.55$ ($SD = .68$) in this simulated example. Females and males were approximately equal in number in the sample, 75 (52 percent) females and 70 (48 percent) males. The adolescents lived in suburban, middle-class communities.

Depressive symptoms were measured using a self-report measure called the Center for Epidemiological Studies Depression Scale (CES-D). Higher scores on the CES-D reflect more depressive symptoms. The CES-D was administered to all participants in the study prior to treatment and following treatment. We will be analyzing the posttreatment scores only.

STUDY VARIABLES

The independent variable, depression treatment program, and how it was operationally defined in this study are described next. In addition, the dependent variable and its operational definition are identified.

Independent Variable

The *independent variable (IV)* designed to have an effect on the *dependent variable* (*DV*) (symptoms of depression) in this study is depression treatment program. Depression treatment program is *operationally defined (OD)* as having three conditions in this study: (1) cognitive-behavioral therapy (CBT), (2) interpersonal therapy (IPT), and (3) no-treatment control (Control). These three conditions will likely, based on previous research, show variability in their effects on symptoms of depression. Researchers of a different study might use more, fewer, or other conditions to operationally define the IV—depression treatment program. More specific operational definition information about the three conditions of the IV—depression treatment program is presented next.

The *cognitive-behavioral therapy* condition was developed from a specific psycho-educational program used for depression among adolescents. The program teaches adolescents how to (1) monitor daily moods, (2) identify causes of their moods, (3) discover and change personal negative beliefs, and (4) understand how negative beliefs affect mood and behavior. The manualized CBT will be delivered to the randomly assigned group of 48 adolescents in 90-minute sessions once a week over eight weeks.

The second treatment condition, *interpersonal therapy*, will be administered to a different group of 47 adolescents using the same session and time line format as used for the CBT condition. IPT prevents depression by teaching communication and social skills to maintain positive relations. IPT focuses on interpersonal improvement related to life changes, interpersonal conflicts, and interpersonal skill deficits.

The 50 adolescents participating in the *no-treatment, waiting-list control* condition will receive the treatment (CBT or IPT) that demonstrates more effectiveness when the study is completed. Additionally, the control group participants will be monitored weekly as to their functioning and will have immediate access to psychological assistance on their request.

The IV-depression treatment program is an active IV since it can be actively manipulated by the research. The scale of measurement of the IV is discrete-nominal (or categorical) as the conditions are designed to be mutually exclusive from each other with no intended order.

Dependent Variable

The dependent variable (DV) is represented by symptoms of depression and is expected to change as a result of the impact of the IV—depression treatment program. The DV, symptoms of depression, in this study is operationally defined as scores on the Center for Epidemiological Studies Depression Scale (CES-D). The CES-D is a self-report measure comprised of 20 items. Each item measures a depressive symptom on a 4-point frequency scale over the prior week. For example, an item is "I felt lonely" and the response format ranges from "Rarely or none of the time (<1 day)" through "Most or all of the time (5–7 days)." Higher scores on the CES-D represent higher depressive symptoms.

The CES-D scaled items are added together to form a composite scale that is treated as a continuous-interval scale. The CES-D was administered to all participants in the study prior to treatment and following treatment; however, we will be analyzing the posttreatment scores only.

RESEARCH DESIGN

The research design used for this research example is a *randomized posttest-only control group design* (Campbell & Stanley, 1963), also known as a randomized design comparing two treatments and a control (Shadish, Cook, & Campbell, 2002), comparing the dependent variable results of two groups of adolescents receiving different treatments and one group getting a *no-treatment control condition*. This is an experimental group design involving random assignment of participants to conditions, a manipulated independent variable, and use of a no-treatment, waiting-list control condition. The design can be diagrammed as follows:

$$
\begin{array}{ccc}
R & X_1 & O \\
R & X_2 & O \\
R & C & O \\
\end{array}
$$

Each line in the diagram represents a group (three groups), and the R symbolizes random assignment to each group condition. The conditions by groups are represented by X_1 (CBT), X_2 (IPT), and C (Control). The observation (O) is the posttest following eight weeks of treatment implementation using the CES-D to measure differential change in depressive symptoms resulting from the different treatment conditions.

Statistical Analysis: One-Way Analysis of Variance (ANOVA)

A one-way ANOVA (also called a simple ANOVA) tests for significant differences between two or more means. Theoretically, one-way ANOVA assesses mean differences among groups (samples) drawn from different populations, one population, or several identical populations. The one-way ANOVA is a mathematical extension of the independent *t*-test, and any number of means can be tested for differences. In a one-way ANOVA there is one independent variable (with two or more levels or conditions) and one dependent variable. The dependent variable used in a one-way ANOVA must be continuously scaled at the levels of interval or ratio. The following three underlying assumptions need to be met in order to use the one-way ANOVA.

1. *Normality.* The scores on the dependent variable for each condition are normally distributed around their mean.

2. *Homogeneity of variance.* The variances of the scores of the dependent variable across the conditions should be constant.

3. *Independence of observations.* The observations are independent from one another and not correlated with each other.

The one-way ANOVA is the basic statistic in the ANOVA family of statistics that is the most used group of statistics in research. The term *F*-test is used to denote the statistic in the ANOVA family. The symbol *F* was designated for ANOVA statistics by Snedecor (1934) in honor of the founder of the ANOVA, Sir Ronald Fisher.

There are several commonly used ANOVA family statistics. The *multifactor ANOVA (factorial ANOVA)* analyzes the effects of two or more independent variables on one dependent variable. The ANOVA statistic is referred to as a two-way ANOVA if there are two independent variables used in the analysis and a three-way ANOVA when there are three independent variables.

A *repeated-measures ANOVA (RM-ANOVA)* is used when there are two or more measures obtained on the same participants or matched participants. A RM-ANOVA can have one or more independent and dependent variables.

A *multivariate ANOVA* has one or more independent variables but more than one dependent variable. *Analysis of covariance (ANCOVA)* is used to assess mean differences using a covariate to control for an extraneous variable.

PROGRESS REVIEW

1. The research problem that is focused on in this chapter relates to comparing the effects of depression treatment program (independent variable) operationally defined as cognitive-behavioral therapy, interpersonal therapy, and a waiting-list control condition on reducing depressive symptoms (dependent variable) among adolescents.

2. The 145 adolescent participants are randomly assigned to the three treatment conditions using a randomized posttest-only control group design.

3. The changes in depressive symptoms as operationally defined as scores on the Center for Epidemiological Studies Depression Scale (CES-D) will be assessed across the three conditions (CBT, IPT, and Control) using a one-way analysis of variance statistic.

4. Next, the research question is stated and we begin completing the steps of the hypothesis-testing process.

STATING THE OMNIBUS (COMPREHENSIVE) RESEARCH QUESTION

The research question is typically stated before developing the alternative (research) and null hypotheses. A research question needs to be succinct and clearly stated so that people reading the research know what is being studied. Moreover, the variables used in a research study should be identified in the research question and suggest that they can be operational defined for the purposes of measurement and analysis. The steps of the hypothesis-testing process related to this research problem will be presented following the statement of the research question.

Omnibus Research Question (RQ)

Will there be significant mean differences in depressive symptoms (CES-D scores) across the depression treatment programs (CBT, IPT, Control) following treatment implementation?

HYPOTHESIS TESTING STEP 1: ESTABLISH THE ALTERNATIVE (RESEARCH) HYPOTHESIS (H_a)

The omnibus (comprehensive) *alternative hypothesis* for our research problem is stated next in both narrative and symbolic formats. We also will be addressing subquestions and subhypotheses following the overall analysis.

Omnibus Narrative Alternative Hypothesis (H_a)

There will be significant lower mean depressive symptoms (CES-D scores) between the depression treatment programs of CBT and IPT when compared to the control condition following treatment implementation.

Symbolic H_a

$$H_a: (\mu_1 \neq \mu_2) < \mu_3$$

where μ_1 = population mean of depressive symptoms (CES-D) of participants in the *CBT condition* being estimated by the sample mean

μ_2 = population mean of depressive symptoms (CES-D) of participants in the *IPT condition* being estimated by the sample mean

μ_3 = population mean of depressive symptoms (CES-D) of participants in the *Control condition* being estimated by the sample mean

This is a directional alternative hypothesis because it is expected that both the CBT and IPT treatments will significantly reduce depressive symptoms when compared to the no-treatment control condition. However, there is no direction hypothesized as to whether CBT or IPT will be more effective when compared to each other in reducing depressive symptoms. In this study, we are taking the position that there is nonconclusive previous evidence to hypothesize that either CBT or IPT will be superior to the other in reducing depressive symptoms. However, there is evidence from the literature allowing us to state a direction regarding the effectiveness of both CBT and IPT in reducing depressive symptoms compared to the control condition.

An alternative process to reach conclusions in analyzing one's sample data is following the recommendations of Jones and Tukey (2000). Act as if: (1) $(\mu_1 - \mu_2) > 0$, $(\mu_1 - \mu_3) > 0$, $(\mu_2 - \mu_3) > 0$; (2) $(\mu_1 - \mu_2) < 0$, $(\mu_1 - \mu_3) < 0$, $(\mu_2 - \mu_3) < 0$; or (3) the sign (< 0 or > 0) of $(\mu_1 - \mu_2)$, $(\mu_1 - \mu_3)$, $(\mu_2 - \mu_3)$ is indefinite. Using this approach, we will be making conclusions about whether omnibus and paired-mean differences are greater than zero or less than zero, or that the findings are inconclusive about the whether one mean is greater or less than zero. In this study, we are expecting that the CBT and IPT conditions will produce lower scores on depressive symptoms compared to the control condition, so we expect these conclusions to be that $(\mu_1 - \mu_3) < 0$ and $(\mu_2 - \mu_3) < 0$. We do not have enough previous evidence to hypothesize whether CBT and IPT will produce lower depressive symptoms when compared to each other, so we will state that $(\mu_1 - \mu_2)$ is indefinite.

HYPOTHESIS TESTING STEP 2: ESTABLISH THE NULL HYPOTHESIS (H_0)

The omnibus *null hypothesis* is stated in narrative and symbolic formats in the second step of the hypothesis-testing process.

Omnibus Narrative Null Hypothesis (H_0)

H_0: There will be no significant mean differences in depressive symptoms (CES-D scores) across the depression treatment programs (CBT, IPT, Control) following treatment implementation.

Symbolic H_0

$$H_0: \mu_1 = \mu_2 = \mu_3$$

HYPOTHESIS TESTING STEP 3: DECIDE ON A RISK LEVEL (ALPHA) OF REJECTING THE TRUE H_0 CONSIDERING TYPE I AND II ERRORS AND POWER

During this step of the hypothesis-testing process, we choose an *alpha criterion (α)* that we will use to make a decision about whether to reject a true null hypothesis (H_0). In choosing α, we will consider *Type I (alpha) error*, which is the probability of rejecting H_0 (mean differences) when in fact (theoretically) it is true (no mean differences). To balance making a Type I error, we need to also consider the making a *Type II (beta) error*, which is the probability of failing to reject H_0 (no mean differences) when it is in fact (theoretically) false (mean differences).

Then, we will use our chosen α level and combine it with anticipated sample size and an estimated (*a priori*) effect size and determine if we have enough *power* to conduct the study. Power is the probability of correctly rejecting a false null hypothesis.

Selecting Alpha (α) Considering Type I and Type II Errors

One decision we need to make before collecting and analyzing data to test the omnibus null hypothesis (H_0) is to choose a risk level we are willing to take in rejecting an H_0 (identifying a difference in means) when the H_0 is true (there is no difference in means). This decision is referred to as setting the alpha level (α). This decision is also called establishing a level of significance or setting the alpha criterion.

We will choose a level for α from .001, .01, .05, or .10, following common practice. The closer the chosen alpha is to .000, the stricter it is because the H_0 is more difficult to reject. Thus, an alpha of .001 (1 time in a thousand) is very strict, and $\alpha = .01$ (1 time in 100) can be viewed as strict. In contrast, an $\alpha = .05$ (5 times in 100) is somewhat strict and $\alpha = .10$ is less strict as risk levels in rejecting the null hypothesis.

There have been a few previous studies (see Horowitz & Garber, 2006) showing that CBT and IPT are effective in reducing depressive symptoms among adolescents when compared to a no-treatment control, but neither treatment has demonstrated superior effectiveness over the other.

A somewhat strict alpha of .05 will be used in this study to test the H_0, since there have been a limited number of previous studies conducted demonstrating the effectiveness of CBT and IPT on depressive symptoms in adolescents. There is not enough evidence yet concerning the pattern of mean differences in studies comparing CBT and IPT to each other and to a control condition. Thus, we will not use a stricter (.001 or .01) alpha level since we do not want, at this point, a criterion level that more closely differentiates a decision about the degree of differences between conditions on depressive symptoms.

An alpha of .05 provides a reasonable balance between avoiding rejecting the H_0 when there really is no significant difference in the means (Type I [alpha] error) and not rejecting the H_0 when there really is a significant difference in means (Type II [beta] error).

A Priori Power Analysis

It is important to assess if key elements are in place to find a significant difference in means on the dependent variable across the conditions if it exists before we conduct the study (a priori) or data analysis. Therefore, we will conduct an *a priori power analysis* that is the probability associated with correctly rejecting a false null hypothesis (see Figure 3.1 from previous Chapter 3). Initially, the a priori power analysis is conducted before participants are selected and assigned to conditions so that decisions can be made about study modifications such as increasing sample size before the study actually begins. If the selected number of participants is lower than the number of participants planned prior to selection, then power analysis is conducted again to see if it is acceptable. In our example, we are going to conduct an a priori power analysis after participant selection and assignment to condition before the data are analyzed.

The three key elements used to conduct an a priori power analysis are alpha, sample size, and *estimated (a priori) effect size*. We can combine these three elements together mathematically and determine if our planned alpha, sample size, and estimated effect size for our proposed study converge into an acceptable probability (power) necessary to find a significant difference in means if it exists. It is not in a researcher's best interest to go ahead and conduct the study if these three elements combined do not create a probability that maximizes the emergence of treatment effects in a study if they exist. This could result in making a Type II error, which is the probability of not finding a significant difference when there really is a difference—in other words, failing to reject the H_0 when it is false.

We have decided to use an alpha of .05 and we are planning on using a sample size of 145. Now we need to estimate an effect size and then we can combine the three elements to identify the probability of correctly rejecting a false null hypothesis (power). An effective method for estimating an effect size for the a priori power analysis is to use effect sizes resulting from previous studies that use variables and designs similar to the ones we will use in our study.

We are going to use findings obtained from four previous studies that focused on assessing the effects of either CBT or a combination of CBT and IPT on depression improvement among adolescents. The four studies produced the following post hoc effects sizes using *eta-squared* (η^2): $\eta^2 = .11$ ($N = 21$), $\eta^2 = .13$ ($N = 94$), $\eta^2 = .32$ ($N = 41$), and $\eta^2 = .61$ ($N = 59$). We can get an accurate measure of central tendency (mean) of the four effects sizes by weighting them by their sample sizes (i.e., *weighted by sample size*).

Weighted by Sample Size Average η^2

Next, we will calculate a weighted average η^2 that we will combine with our sample size and alpha for use in calculating power.

$$\overline{\eta^2} = \frac{21(.11) + 94(.13) + 41(.32) + 59(.61)}{215}$$

$$= \frac{2.310 + 12.220 + 13.120 + 35.990}{215}$$

$$= \frac{63.640}{215}$$

$$\overline{\eta^2} = .296 \text{ (This is the weighted by sample average } \eta^2$$
$$\text{from four previous studies.)}$$

Conversion to Cohen's Effect Size (*f*)

So, we now have an estimated effect size ($\eta^2 = .296$). We will next convert the average η^2 to another effect size *f* using the formula identified by Cohen (1988). This conversion will allow us to use several procedures developed by Cohen for analysis and interpretation.

$$f = \sqrt{\eta^{2*}/1 - \eta^2}$$
$$= \sqrt{.296/1 - .296}$$
$$= \sqrt{.296/.704}$$
$$= \sqrt{.420}$$
$$f = .648$$

*In our problem, η^2 is the average η^2 of four previous studies.

Power Analysis Using G*Power 3.1.2

A useful method to conduct a power analysis is to use a computer program called G*Power 3.1.2, developed by Erdfelder, Faul, & Buchner (2010). Conduct the following steps (see Figure 7.1).

1. Create a folder on your desktop called *gpower*.

2. Google **G*Power**.

3. Click on **G*Power3 is now available**.

4. Then, click on **Download and register**; click on the download and save to your folder.

5. Double click on a created folder called **GPower3**.

6. Double click **GPOWER 3.1.2** link.

7. Under **Test family** > select **F tests**.

8. Under **Statistical test** > select **ANOVA: Fixed effects, omnibus, one-way**.

9. Under **Type of Power Analysis** > select **A priori: Compute required sample size—given α, power, and effect size**.

10. Type in beside **Effect size f** 0.648.

11. Type next to **α err prob** 0.05.

12. Type next to **Power (1−β err prob)** 0.80.

13. Type next to **Number of groups** 3.

14. Click on the **Calculate** button and you will see that we need a total sample size = 27 to reach an actual power of 0.8145419.

FIGURE 7.1 A Priori Power Analysis of ANOVA Problem

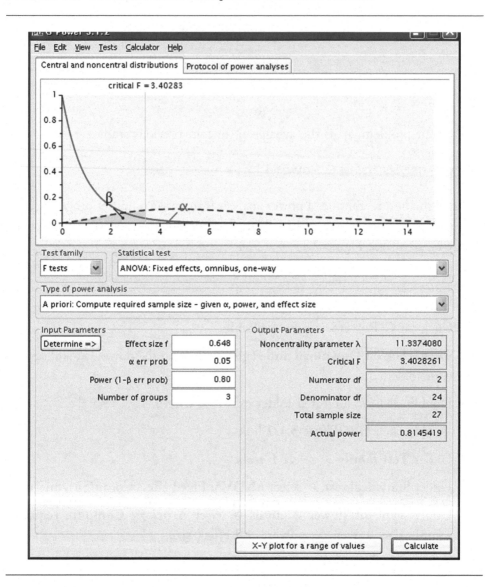

Our total sample of 145 far exceeds a needed sample size of 27. Considering the combined elements in our study of total sample size of 145, $f = .648$, and $\alpha = .05$, a power greater than .80 should be achieved. Therefore, we should be confident in correctly rejecting a false H_0 in our study and thus avoid making a Type II error.

PROGRESS REVIEW

1. We stated the research question for the study problem.

2. We completed the first two steps of the hypothesis-testing process by stating the alternative and null hypotheses in narrative and symbolic formats.

3. Next, we decided on the risk we are willing to take when rejecting a true null hypothesis by choosing alpha (α). We chose $\alpha = .05$, which we believed was a reasonable criterion in our study to avoid making a Type I or Type II error.

4. We conducted a power analysis to make sure that our probability of correctly rejecting a false null hypothesis in favor of an alternative hypothesis was adequate (power = .80) before moving ahead with the study. We found that we had adequate a priori power using an online power analysis program (G*Power). This provided information necessary to continue on with the study.

HYPOTHESIS TESTING STEP 4: CHOOSE APPROPRIATE STATISTIC AND ITS SAMPLING DISTRIBUTION TO TEST THE H_0 ASSUMING H_0 IS TRUE

We will be using a one-way ANOVA to test the null hypothesis: H_0: $\mu_1 = \mu_2 = \mu_3$. We are going to compare the means of depressive symptoms across the conditions (CBT, IPT, and Control) for significant differences using the F-distribution. The one-way ANOVA is appropriate to use because: (1) there is one independent variable, (2) there are different participants in each independent condition group, (3) there is one dependent variable, and (4) the dependent variable is continuously scaled.

HYPOTHESIS TESTING STEP 5: SELECT SAMPLE, COLLECT DATA, SCREEN DATA, COMPUTE STATISTIC, AND DETERMINE PROBABILITY ESTIMATES

Data are collected from a sample of participants during Step 5 of the hypothesis-testing process. The data are assessed for data accuracy, missing values, and univariate outliers, and to determine if the underlying assumptions of the statistic are met. If needed, data modifications are made. Then the omnibus null hypothesis is tested using statistical analyses.

Sample Selection and Assignment

The sample in this study is selected using *purposive sampling of typical instances* (Shadish, Cook, & Campbell, 2002). In purposive sampling of typical instances, we define the characteristics that reflect the persons, settings, times, independent variables, and dependent variables we intend to generalize in our findings. We then select participants who match the targeted characteristics. We can also use *inclusion criteria* and *exclusion criteria* to assist in the matching process for congruence to the targeted characteristics. Moreover, the use of exclusion criteria can help us assess whether the participants are appropriate and safe as they engage in the study conditions.

Adolescents with symptoms of mild depression in eighth and ninth grades living in suburban, middle-class communities in the Southwest United States during the 2012 fall semester were targeted for this study. Following necessary Institutional Review Board (IRB) approvals, school district professionals referred students for participation in the study.

The students were interviewed and assessed prior to being selected for the study. They needed to meet the inclusion criteria of: (1) being an eighth or ninth grade student in the school district, (2) having mild symptoms of depression as measured by having a score between 14 and 19 on the Beck Depression Inventory II (BDI-II), (3) assenting or agreeing to participate in the study, and (4) having parental consent to participate.

Students were excluded from participating in the study if they: (1) had a co-occurring medical or physical condition, (2) were currently receiving psychological treatment, (3) were currently using medication for a behavioral or neurological disorder, (4) had current thoughts or past history of suicide ideation, or (5) were currently involved in substance abuse. The school district professionals referred 160 eighth and ninth grade students for participation in the study. Before random assignment to condition, 10 participants were determined to be not eligible for the study because they met exclusion criteria related to having a co-occurring medical or physical condition, receiving psychological treatment, or using medication for a behavioral or neurological disorder. The remaining 150 participants in the sample were *randomly assigned* to three groups using a table of random numbers to receive one of three treatment conditions. Following assignment to condition, two persons in the CBT condition and three persons in the IPT chose to discontinue before the study began, leaving a sample of 145. This resulted in the following number of participants in each treatment condition group: CBT ($n_1 = 48$), IPT ($n_2 = 47$), and Control ($n_3 = 50$).

Study Data Diagnostics

Diagnostic assessments are conducted on the sample data after it has been collected but before the primary study hypothesis is tested. The purposes of *data diagnostics* (also called exploratory data analysis, data screening, or data preparation for analysis) are to: (1) check accuracy of data entries, (2) identify and deal with missing data (*missing data analysis*), (3) detect and make decisions about univariate (one dependent variable) *outliers*, and (4) screen and make decisions about *univariate parametric assumptions*. The underlying assumptions of a one-way ANOVA are that the dependent variable is normally distributed (normal enough), the group variances and error variances of the dependent variable are equal (not exactly equal but equal enough), and all observations are independent from each other. There are several measures to assess normality, homogeneity of variance, and independence. Screening measures have limitations as to their usefulness given various conditions of a study. We will therefore look at several screening measures to assess underlying assumptions and use a preponderance of evidence to make a decision about whether the underlying assumptions were met.

Accuracy of Data Entry

The original data were compared to the entered data by two members of the research team. The accuracy of the data was corroborated by the two researchers. Moreover, the variable scores were in the expected range, and the means and standard deviations appeared plausible.

Missing Data Analysis

There were no missing data in the original data set.

Means, Standard Deviations, Variances, and Assessing for Univariate Outliers IBM SPSS Commands

Enter the data from the One-Way Analysis of Variance Data table at the end of this chapter into IBM SPSS. Enter the data into three columns just as it appears in the table.

1. Click on **Data > Split File** > click on circle beside **Organize output by groups** > click on *Condition* and click the arrow so that *Condition* is under **Groups Based on** > click on **OK** and don't save command output. You have told the program to provide output by the three groups (**Condition**). You will need to change this command back later.

2. Click on **Analyze > Descriptive Statistics > Descriptives** > click over *DepSymptoms* to **Variable(s)** > click on **Save standardized values as variables** > click on **Options** and check **Minimum, Maximum, Mean, Std. deviation**, and **Variance** > click on **OK** > save the output as *ANOVA Descriptives*.

The Descriptive Statistics table (Table 7.1) lists the sample size of each group followed by the lowest (minimum) and highest (maximum) scores in each group. Valid *N* refers to the number of participant scores that do not having missing data. The average scores (means) by groups on the CES-D following treatment are provided. Measures of variability designate how the scores in each group distribution deviate from their group mean. The standard deviation is an average measure of score deviations from the mean, whereas the square of s is the variance (s^2) or general spread of scores from the mean. Higher scores reflect more deviation of scores from the mean for both s and s^2. As you can see, there is a higher deviation of scores from the mean for the control group followed by the CBT and IPT groups.

The standard values (z-scores) requested for the analysis to assess for univariate outliers are produced in a new column on the **Data View** spreadsheet and named *ZDepSymptoms*. These values represent the z-scores corresponding to the

TABLE 7.1 Descriptive Statistics of Depressive Symptoms by Condition Group

			Condition = CBT			
			Descriptive Statistics[a]			
	N	Minimum	Maximum	Mean	Std. Deviation	Variance
DepSymptoms	48	7.00	33.00	17.3333	6.22737	38.780
Valid N (listwise)	48					

			Condition = IPT			
			Descriptive Statistics[b]			
	N	Minimum	Maximum	Mean	Std. Deviation	Variance
DepSymptoms	47	5.00	32.00	17.0213	5.99452	35.934
Valid N (listwise)	47					

			Condition = Control			
			Descriptive Statistics[c]			
	N	Minimum	Maximum	Mean	Std. Deviation	Variance
DepSymptoms	50	10.00	35.00	21.6800	7.14697	51.079
Valid N (listwise)	50					

[a] Condition = CBT
[b] Condition = IPT
[c] Condition = Control

TABLE 7.2 Highest ±z-Scores by Condition Group

Condition	Highest +z	Outlier? > ±3.29	Highest −z	Outlier? > ±3.29
CBT	2.516*	No	−1.659	No
IPT	2.499	No	−2.005	No
Control	1.864	No	−1.634	No

* This number is rounded to three decimals.

raw scores in each group : CBT(rows 1−48), IPT(rows 49−95), and Control (rows 96−145). The three highest positive and negative z-scores for each group are reported in Table 7.2. For example, the highest +z score for CBT is 2.516 (rounded up to three decimal places) and is obtained by subtracting the raw score (33) from the CBT group mean (17.333) and dividing by the CBT group standard deviation (6.227).

$$Z = \frac{33 - 17.333}{6.227} = \frac{+15.667}{6.227} = +2.516$$

We are going to use as a criterion ±3.29 ($<.001$, two-tailed) to compare our z-scores, following a recommendation by Tabachnick and Fidell (2007). On the normal curve, only .001 (1 one-thousandth) of the curve remains beyond a z-score of ±3.29, and for a two-tailed test, only .0005 remains in either tail. So, any z-score representing a raw score from a group on the dependent variable of depressive symptoms greater than ±3.29 is indeed an extreme score (univariate outlier). Since the highest positive and negative z-scores for each group are less than ±3.29, there are no univariate outliers within any of the three groups using the $p < .001$, two-tailed test criterion. No individual score within a group is too far removed from the rest of the group's scores, given the criterion that we have selected.

At this point, remove the **Split File** filter. **Data > Split File** > click on the **Reset** button and then click **OK**; click out of the output and don't save it.

Assessing for Underlying Assumptions

Certain underlying assumptions must be present in order to apply various statistical analyses to data sets. Two important underlying assumptions for many parametric statistics are that the dependent variable is normally distributed and that there are equal variances and error variances across groups. We are going to use several measures to assess both normality and homogeneity of variance and evaluate the preponderance of evidence to determine if we have met these underlying assumptions. First, we will evaluate the dependent variable (depressive symptoms) for normality by assessing histograms, skewness, kurtosis, the Shapiro-Wilk statistic, and normal Q-Q plots.

Normality IBM SPSS Commands
1. **Analyze > Descriptive Statistics > Explore**.

2. Click over dependent variable *DepSymptoms* to **Dependent List**.

3. Click over independent variable (*Condition*) to **Factor List**. Factor is another term for independent variable.

4. Do not change **Display choices**—leave on **Both**.

5. To the upper right of Display are three buttons. Click on **Plots**. Then, select **Normality plots with tests**.

6. Under **Spread vs. Level with Levene Test** click on **Untransformed**.

7. Click on **Continue**.

8. Click on **OK**.

9. Save the output as *assumptionscreen*.

First, look at the information under Descriptives on the output (see Table 7.3), you will notice that there are several descriptive statistics provided relative to depressive symptoms for each of the three condition groups. For example, means, standard deviations, and variances are provided for each group, and these match the values that you identified in a previous analysis.

You also see values for skewness and "Std. Error" for each group. When you divide the skewness statistic value by its standard error value, the resulting value is a z-score. The skewness and standard error and their resulting skewness z-scores are presented in Table 7.4.

A *positively skewed (right-skewed) curve* has most of the scores at the lower values of the horizontal axis, and the curve tails off toward the higher end. Thus, more extreme scores relative to most of the scores in the distribution are in the positive (right) end of the distribution.

A *negatively skewed (left-skewed) distribution* has most of the scores at the higher values, and the curve tails off toward the lower end of the horizontal axis. Thus, more extreme scores relative to most of the scores in the distribution are in the negative (left) end of the distribution.

If a skewness z-score value is at or near 0, the distribution is symmetrical and considered normal or near normal. When the skewness z-score value is positive, there is some degree of skew in the positive (right) side of the curve but not necessarily a significant skew. A negative skewness z-score value suggests some degree of skew in the negative (left) side of the curve but again not necessarily a significant skew.

The skewness z-scores are compared to the same criterion that we used to determine univariate outliers, ± 3.29 ($p < .001$, two-tailed test). The distribution of raw scores on the dependent variable (depressive symptoms) for each condition group (CBT, IPT, and Control) does not significantly depart from normality using our criterion, as is evident when you compare the calculated

TABLE 7.3   Skewness, Kurtosis, and Standard Error Values by Group

	Condition			Statistic	Std. Error
DV	CogBehav	Mean		17.3333	.89884
		95% Confidence	Lower Bound	15.5251	
		Interval for Mean	Upper Bound	19.1416	
		5% Trimmed Mean		17.0648	
		Median		16.5000	
		Variance		38.780	
		Std. Deviation		6.22737	
		Minimum		7.00	
		Maximum		33.00	
		Range		26.00	
		Interquartile Range		9.50	
		Skewness		.613	.343
		Kurtosis		−.022	.674
	IPI-AST	Mean		17.0213	.87439
		95% Confidence	Lower Bound	15.2612	
		Interval for Mean	Upper Bound	18.7813	
		5% Trimmed Mean		16.8570	
		Median		16.0000	
		Variance		35.934	
		Std. Deviation		5.99452	
		Minimum		5.00	
		Maximum		32.00	
		Range		27.00	
		Interquartile Range		8.00	
		Skewness		.524	.347
		Kurtosis		.014	.681
	Control	Mean		21.6800	1.01073
		95% Confidence	Lower Bound	19.6489	
		Interval for Mean	Upper Bound	23.7111	
		5% Trimmed Mean		21.6556	
		Median		21.0000	
		Variance		51.079	
		Std. Deviation		7.14697	
		Minimum		10.00	
		Maximum		35.00	
		Range		25.00	
		Interquartile Range		12.25	
		Skewness		.093	.337
		Kurtosis		−1.143	.662

TABLE 7.4 Skewness z-Scores by Condition Group

Condition	Skewness z (Stat./ Std. Error = Z)	Skewness Direction	Sig. Departure? (> ±3.29)
CBT	.613/.343 = 1.787	Positive	No
IPT	.524/.347 = 1.510	Positive	No
Control	.093/.337 = .276	Positive	No

TABLE 7.5 Kurtosis z-Scores by Condition Group

Condition	Kurtosis z (Stat./ Std. Error = Z)	Kurtosis Direction	Sig. Departure? (> ±3.29)
CBT	−.022/.674 = −.033	Platykurtic	No
IPT	.014/.681 = .021	Leptokurtic	No
Control	−1.143/.662 = −1.727	Platykurtic	No

skewness z-score values from Table 7.4 to the criterion of ±3.29. For example, we found the highest skewness z-score to be +1.787, which is considerable lower than our criterion of ±3.29.

Below the skewness and standard error values in output reported in Table 7.3 are the "Kurtosis" and "Std. Error" values. We will divide the kurtosis statistic by its standard error and compare the z-score resultant to a ±3.29 to see if any group distribution significantly departs from normality. (See Table 7.5.)

Kurtosis is the clustering of scores in the center, the upper and lower ends (tails), and the shoulders (between the center and the tails) of a distribution (Norusis, 1994). A distribution that is symmetrical and normal is *mesokurtic* and will have a z-score around 0. A positive z-score indicates that the distribution is more *leptokurtic* with a shape that is more narrow and peaked. However, just having a positive z-score does not mean that the distribution is significantly departing from normality. A *platykurtic* shape generates a negative z-score and the distribution is more broad and flat, but it is not necessarily significantly departing from normality. None of the three condition group distributions have kurtosis z-scores that are greater than ±3.29, so they do not depart significantly from normality.

The *Shapiro-Wilk (S-W) statistic* is another source of evidence to use to determine if the distribution of the group conditions are normally distributed.

TABLE 7.6 Shapiro-Wilk Statistics by Condition Group

| | | Tests of Normality | | | | | |
| | | Kolmogorov-Smirnov[a] | | | Shapiro-Wilk | | |
	Condition	Statistic	df	Sig.	Statistic	df	Sig.
DV	CogBehav	.145	48	.013	.961	48	.107
	IPI	.159	47	.005	.967	47	.196
	Control	.092	50	.200*	.952	50	.043

[a] Lilliefors significance correction.
* This is a lower bound of the true significance.

The S-W statistic is found in the output under *Tests of Normality* (see Table 7.6). First, we are going to state a null hypothesis to test using the S-W with an alpha of .05.

$$H_0 : \text{The Sample Distribution} = \text{Normal}$$

More often than not, when we test a null hypothesis we want to reject it to demonstrate a significant difference or relationship. Interpreting the results of the S-W statistic is an example of when we want to retain the null hypothesis, which says that the sample distribution that we are testing is not deviating significantly from being normal.

In the output table called *Tests of Normality*, you see values associated with the Shapiro-Wilk statistic, *df*, and "Sig." We fail to reject the null hypotheses for the condition group distributions of the CBT and IPT groups since the significant probability levels ("Sig.") of the Shapiro-Wilk statistic are .107 and .196, which are greater than $\alpha = .05$. The rule is to reject a null hypothesis if the probability level of the calculated statistic is less than our stated alpha level and we fail to reject the null if our significance probability is greater than our alpha. Thus, we conclude that these two group distributions are not deviating significantly from being normal. However, the significant probability value of .043 for the Control group is lower than $\alpha = .05$; therefore, the null is rejected, suggesting that the distribution is not normally distributed.

The final evidence of normality that we will interpret is the normal Q-Q plot for each distribution. A plot for each group is located in the output under the

FIGURE 7.2 Normal Q-Q Plot of Depressive Symptoms for CBT Group

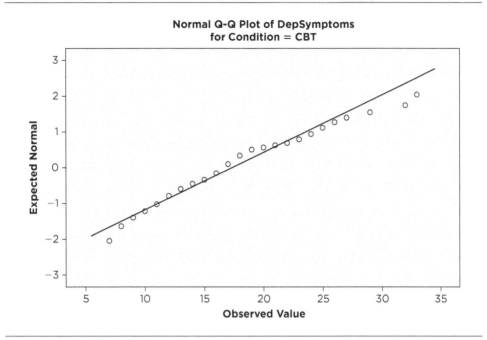

heading *Normal Q-Q Plots*. An observed value in the distribution is paired with its expected value from the normal distribution to form the *normal Q-Q plots*. The number of cases in the sample and the rank order of the cases in the sample are used to generate the expected values for the normal distribution. If the sample is from a normal distribution, we expect that the points will fall more or less on a straight line (see Figures 7.2, 7.3, and 7.4).

The vast majority of points on the Q-Q plots in all three condition group distributions fall on or near the straight line, providing further evidence that each group is normally distributed.

Summary of the Normality Evidence

There were no univariate outliers identified within the distributions of the three condition groups. The skewness *z*-scores, kurtosis *z*-scores, and Q-Q plots provided support that the three distributions are not deviating significantly from

FIGURE 7.3 **Normal Q-Q Plot of Depressive Symptoms for IPT Group**

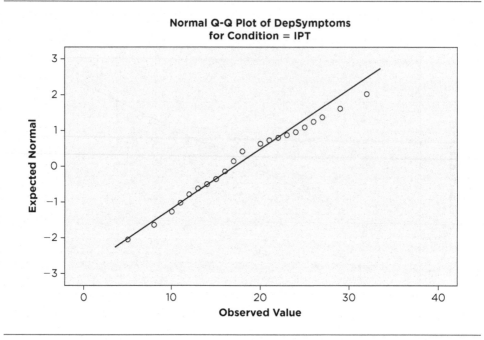

normality. The S-W statistic was satisfactory for the CBT and IPT distributions but less than satisfactory for the Control group distribution. Despite the S-W statistic finding for the Control group, the preponderance of evidence suggests that the three distributions are normal enough to clearly meet the underlying assumption of normality.

Homogeneity of Variance

In this study we are expecting that the independent variable (depression treatment program) will affect the means of the dependent variable (symptoms of depression) but not the variances of the groups. We want the variances of the three groups (CBT, IPT, and Control) on the dependent variable to be relatively constant. We are going to look at two methods to assess whether the variances are equal enough across the condition groups. The first method is called the variance ratio (F_{max}), which is the ratio of the largest group variance to the smallest group

FIGURE 7.4 Normal Q-Q Plot of Depressive Symptoms for Control Group

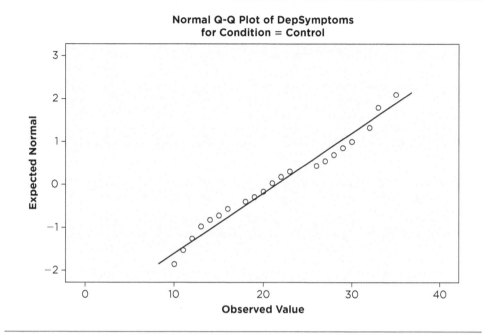

variance within the three condition groups. This provides a simple descriptive statistic for initial screening. If the ratio of group sizes is less than 4.0, then an F_{max} as high as 10.0 is acceptable. When the ratio of group sizes goes to 9.0, then an F_{max} of 3.0 is acceptable (Tabachnick & Fidell, 2007).

The Control group had the largest number of participants at 50, and the IBT had the smallest group size of 47 (see Table 7.1). The group size ratio is $50/47 = 1.064$; this is well below a group size ratio of 4.0, so we can apply the $F_{max} = 10.0$ guideline.

The Control group had the highest variance of 51.079, and the IPT group showed the lowest variance of 35.934. The $F_{max} = 51.079/35.934 = 1.421$ and is well below 10.0. The low variance ratio supports homogeneity of variance across the groups. We will next corroborate this finding with another measure of homogeneity of variance known as Levene's test.

We will test the following null hypothesis of equality of the error variances across the three groups when using Levene's test of homogeneity of variance.

TABLE 7.7 Levene's Test of Homogeneity of Variance

Test of Homogeneity of Variance		Levene's Statistic	*df1*	*df2*	Sig.
DepSymptoms	Based on mean	2.034	2	142	.135
	Based on median	1.826	2	142	.165
	Based on median and with adjusted *df*	1.826	2	141.911	.165
	Based on trimmed mean	2.060	2	142	.131

We want to retain the null hypothesis concluding that the variances across the three groups are equal enough using an alpha criterion of .05.

$$H_0: \sigma^2_{e\,\text{CBT}} = \sigma^2_{e\,\text{IPT}} = \sigma^2_{e\,\text{Control}}$$

The *Levene's statistic* is found in the "assumptionscreen" output under the heading *Test of Homogeneity of Variance* (see Table 7.7) on the line called "Based on the Mean."

We fail to reject the H_0 that the error variances are equal since the probability value of .135 is greater than the $\alpha = .05$. The underlying assumption of homogeneity of variance has been met using Levene's statistic.

Summary of the Homogeneity of Variance Evidence

The evidence from both the variance ratio (F_{max}) and Levene's statistic provide support that the variances and error variances are equal enough across the three condition groups. There is no alarming disparity in group sizes among the groups, so we will conclude that the underlying assumption of homogeneity of variance has been met.

Independence

There are different participants in each of the three groups, and each participant's score was produced independent of the other scores. If dependent variable test scores across condition groups are correlated with each other when the scores are collected in the same order, the significance level of the ANOVA can be smaller than it should be (Norusis, 2003). We are going to assess the independence of observations by graphing the responses of participants on the dependent variable by group condition based on the same order in which measurements (observations) were obtained. The data in the SPSS Data View spreadsheet are in a similar order by group based on when the data were collected. We will need to create three columns of data to complete the matrix scatter plot analysis to assess independence.

Matrix Scatter Plot IBM SPSS Commands

1. First, close all output that you have been working on. Under the column labeled *DepSymptoms* on the IBM SPSS **Data View** spreadsheet, left click and hold on the first cell, which is *16*, and drag down until you reach *row 48*, which happens to be another *16* and the last participant score in the *CBT group* (*condition 1*). All of the numbers should be in bold.

2. At the top of the screen, click on **Edit** and then **Copy**. This will copy the data for pasting to a new column.

3. Go to the first empty column (**var**), click on the first cell, and it will be bolded.

4. At the top of the screen, click on **Edit** and then click on **Paste** and the data from the *CBT group* will be copied to the new column.

5. At the bottom left of the spreadsheet, click on **Variable View** and then name the new column as *CBT* and change the **decimals** to 0.

6. Click on the **Data View** button and create a new column for the 47 *IPT* DepSymptoms scores (Condition 2) and a new column for the 50 *Control* scores (Condition 3) in the same way. Once you have completed the three new columns, **File** > **Save**.

7. At the top of the screen, click on **Graphs** > **Legacy Dialogs** > **Scatter/Dot** > **Matrix Scatter** > **Define**.

8. Click over the three new columns (*CBT*, *IPT*, and *Control*) to the space under **Matrix Variables** > **OK**.

The matrix scatter plot (Figure 7.5) shows the scores of each group compared to the other groups. The scores are in the order they were obtained and are paired

FIGURE 7.5 Matrix Scatterplot to Assess Independence

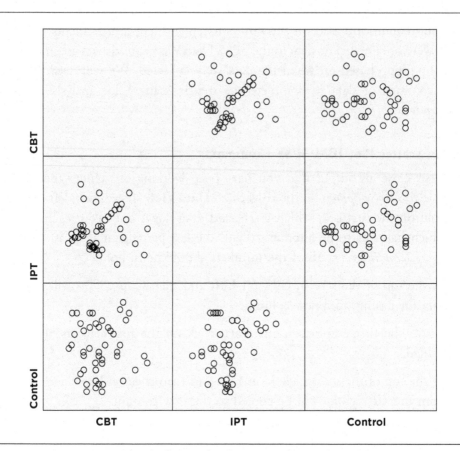

as circles in each graph representing two groups being compared. If the scores form a diagonal straight line when any two groups are compared, then the scores are correlated and not independent. There appear to be no serious linear trends between paired scores across the groups. The points scatter in many directions. Therefore, we will conclude that we have met the assumption of independence.

Summary of the Underlying Assumptions Findings

The preponderance of evidence assessed demonstrates that the distributions of scores on the dependent variable in the three condition groups did not deviate from normality. Both measures of homogeneity of variance supported fulfillment of the assumption of equality. Finally, the scatter plots suggest that independence of dependent variable scores was met. This information provides an endorsement to conduct the one-way analysis of variance statistic to test the omnibus null hypothesis in this study.

PROGRESS REVIEW

1. Data were collected from the study participants on the dependent variable (depressive symptoms) using the CES-D after the eight-week treatment of the 145 participants who were randomly assigned to one of the three condition groups (CBT, IPT, Control).

2. Problems with data accuracy and missing data were ruled out in the early steps of the data-screening process.

3. The distributions of CES-D scores of the condition groups were assessed for compliance to meeting the underlying assumptions of using the one-way ANOVA. The evidence showed that CES-D distributions of scores on the condition groups met normality, homogeneity of variance, and independence assumptions. The positive results of this screening assessment allow us to conduct the one-way ANOVA to determine the effects of the treatment conditions (CBT, IPT, Control) on depressive symptoms as measured by the CES-D.

One-Way Analysis of Variance of the Omnibus H_0

One-Way ANOVA IBM SPSS Commands

1. Click **Analyze** > click **General Linear Model** > click **Univariate** > click over *DepSymptoms* under **Dependent Variable** and *Condition* under **Fixed Factor(s)**.

2. Click on the **Plots** button > click *Condition* to **Horizontal Axis** > click the **Add** button > click **Continue**.

3. Click on **Post Hoc** button > click over *Condition* to **Post Hoc Tests for** > click on the box next to **Tukey** and then **Continue**.

4. Click on the **Options** button > click on the boxes for **Descriptive statistics, Estimates of effect size**, and **Observed power** > the **Significance level** should be .05 > click on **Continue** > click **OK**.

5. Save generated output as *ANOVA Results.*

The results of this analysis provide information to test the omnibus null hypothesis of the study:

H_0: There will be no significant mean differences in depressive symptoms (CES-D scores) across the depression treatment programs (CBT, IPT, Control) following treatment implementation.

$$H_0: \mu_1 = \mu_2 = \mu_3$$

The results of the one-way ANOVA are presented next. Additionally, interpretations are provided for the magnitude of treatment effects (effect sizes), post hoc power, post hoc multiple comparisons of means, and confidence intervals for the mean differences.

One-Way ANOVA Results

In the ANOVA output labeled *Tests of Between-Subjects Effects* you will see the name of the independent variable (*Condition*) under the heading *Source* that we created when the data were entered (see Table 7.8). We will be using the information in this row to make a decision about rejecting the null hypothesis.

The one-way ANOVA statistic is in the *F* column ($F = 7.909$) and the *F*-statistic is significant at the $p = .001$ probability level from the *Sig.* column. The criterion that we selected to make a decision about rejecting the null hypothesis was $\alpha = .05$. The significant statistic probability of .001 is less than $\alpha = .05$, so the decision is to reject the null hypothesis that the population's means that we are estimating with sample means are equal. There is a less than 5 percent chance that we rejected a true H_0 ($p < .05$). Only five times in 100

TABLE 7.8   One-Way Analysis Results

Tests of Between-Subjects Effects

Dependent Variable: DepSymptoms

Source	Type III Sum of Squares	df	Mean Square	F	Sig.	Partial Eta Squared	Noncent. Parameter	Observed Power[b]
Corrected model	665.985[a]	2	332.992	7.909	.001	.100	15.818	.951
Intercept	50,553.552	1	50,553.552	1,200.732	.000	.894	1,200.732	1.000
Condition	665.985	2	332.992	7.909	.001	.100	15.818	.951
Error	5,978.525	142	42.102					
Total	57,518.000	145						
Corrected total	6,644.510	144						

[a] R-squared = .100 (adjusted R-squared = .088)
[b] Computed using alpha = .05

would there be no difference between means. If one repeatedly took three random samples from the same population and tested the differences between their means, one would expect to get a difference that was significant at the .05 level about five times in 100 (Nickerson, 2000).

Thus, there is a significant difference among the means of the three groups (CBT, IPT, and Control) on depressive symptoms. We can write this finding of the omnibus hypothesis as $F(2, 142) = 7.909$, $p < .05$. The value 2 represents the *degrees of freedom* associated with the treatment (Condition) and the 142 reflects the degrees of freedom associated with error. The p symbol could also be stated as $p = .001$ since an $\alpha = .05$ was stated before the data were analyzed, which allows for a comparison between the alpha criterion and the derived statistic probability.

HYPOTHESIS TESTING STEP 6: MAKE DECISION REGARDING THE H_O AND INTERPRET POST HOC EFFECT SIZES AND CONFIDENCE INTERVALS

We can conclude, at this point, that there are mean differences in depressive symptoms somewhere across the condition groups. We will assess where the mean differences are among the three possible paired means after interpreting the magnitude of treatment effect and post hoc power.

Magnitude of Treatment Effect—Post Hoc Effect Size

Again refer to the *Tests of Between-Subject Effects* table of the ANOVA results output (see Table 7.8). You see an eta-squared value ($\eta^2 - .100$) on the *Condition* line next to the *Sig.* value. Eta-squared is a measure of practical significance and is referred to as a post hoc effect size or magnitude of treatment effect. Eta-squared values range from 0 (small) to 1.0 (large).

It is a ratio of the variance explained by the independent variable in relation to the total variance. The term *partial eta-squared* is most relevant when an ANOVA design results in analyses of several independent variables and interactions between the independent variables.

There are several different effect sizes, and η^2 is one that is commonly used.

We can interpret the $\eta^2 = .100$ by converting the fraction to a percentage by moving the decimal two spaces to the right, and can report that approximately 10 percent of the change in the dependent variable (depressive symptoms) can be attributed to the independent variable (depression treatment program). The $\eta^2 = .100$ has a medium strength effect according to Cohen's convention for η^2 where approximately 1 percent to 6 percent is small, >6 percent to 14 percent is medium, and >14 percent is large. There is clearly a meaningful magnitude of treatment effect of the depression treatment program on decreasing depressive symptoms.

Post Hoc Power

You remember that we estimated the probability of correctly rejecting a false null hypothesis prior to conducting the study resulting in a priori power results conducive to conducting the study. The observed post hoc power after the study was conducted is reported in the *Between-Subjects Effects* output under *Observed Power* for *Condition* (see Table 7.8). The post hoc power is .951, indicating that given a post hoc effect size of .100, an α of .05, and a sample size of 145, the probability is approximately 95 times in 100 that we correctly rejected a false null hypothesis. So, the a priori power analysis results were a good prediction and quite congruent with our post hoc power = .951 in the probability of correctly rejecting a false null hypothesis. The actual effect size (post hoc) generated in this study of .100 is lower than the estimated (a priori) effect size of .296. However, the a priori power was more than sufficient in this study.

Post Hoc Multiple Comparisons of Means

We have concluded that there is an overall significant difference among the group means of depressive symptoms resulting from the depression treatment program (CBT $M = 17.333$, IPT $M = 17.021$, Control $M = 21.680$). It also is useful to find out specifically which pairs of group means are different from each other. The results of a posthoc analysis of multiple mean comparisons are interpreted next using the *Tukey honestly significant difference (HSD) statistic*. The Tukey HSD is a commonly used post hoc analysis technique used for all pairwise comparisons of means (Norusis, 2005).

TABLE 7.9 HSD Post Hoc Analysis

		Multiple Comparisons				
		DepSymptoms Tukey HSD				
					95% Confidence Interval	
(I) Condition	(J) Condition	Mean Difference (I − J)	Std. Error	Sig.	Lower Bound	Upper Bound
CBT	IPT	.31	1.332	.970	−2.84	3.47
	Control	−4.35*	1.311	.003	−7.45	−1.24
IPT	CBT	−.31	1.332	.970	−3.47	2.84
	Control	−4.66*	1.318	.002	−7.78	−1.54
Control	CBT	4.35*	1.311	.003	1.24	7.45
	IPT	4.66*	1.318	.002	1.54	7.78

Based on observed means.
The error term is Mean Square(Error) = 42.102.
* The mean difference is significant at the .05 level.

You recall that the omnibus alternative hypothesis stated that there will be significant lower mean depressive symptoms (CES-D scores) between the depression treatment programs of CBT and IPT when compared to the Control condition following treatment implementation, H_A: $(\mu_1 \neq \mu_2) < \mu_3$. Thus, the focus of the post hoc analysis is to assess whether the CBT and IPT depression treatment programs significantly reduced depressive symptoms among the participants when compared to the control group. The extent that CBT and IPT produced a similar reduction in depressive symptoms also will be assessed.

The output called *Multiple Comparisons* shows the three possible multiple mean comparisons of CBT versus IPT, CBT versus Control, and IPT versus Control using the Tukey HSD statistic (see Table 7.9). The significance values are corrected for multiple comparisons being analyzed. The statistic probability for the mean difference between the CBT ($M = 17.333$) versus IPT ($M = 17.021$) is .970, which is greater than the alpha criterion of $\alpha = .05$, so we fail to reject the null ($p > .05$). The mean comparison of CBT ($M = 17.333$) and Control ($M = 21.680$) is significant ($p < .05$) since the statistic probability of .003 is less than $\alpha = .05$. Finally, the mean comparison of IPT ($M = 17.021$) and

Control ($M = 21.680$) is significant ($p < .05$) since the statistic probability of .002 is less than $\alpha = .05$.

The multiple mean comparisons support the directional alternative hypothesis that both the CBT and IPT depression treatment programs significantly reduce depressive symptoms among participants compared to a no-treatment control condition. Neither the CBT nor the IPT showed superiority in reducing depressive symptoms when they are compared with each other; CBT ($M = 17.333$) and IPT ($M = 17.021$), $p > .05$.

Applying Jones and Tukey's (2000) approach, we can conclude that the paired-means differences are ($\mu_1 - \mu_3$) < 0 ($p = .003$) and ($\mu_2 - \mu_3$) < 0 ($p = .002$). The difference in depressive symptoms comparing the CBT to IPT conditions ($\mu_1 - \mu_2$) is indefinite.

Confidence Intervals of Mean Differences

A confidence interval (CI) provides information about the probability that a given interval will encircle the true difference between the population means. The probability used for the confidence interval is .95 since $\alpha = .05$ in this study.

The .95 CI for each mean difference is provided in the output under the *Multiple Comparisons* table (see Table 7.9). These confidence intervals are corrected since we are making several (three) comparisons and have a wider range than would be expected if we were not adjusting for multiple comparisons. The interpretations of the mean difference confidence intervals for the two paired-mean comparisons that are significant (μ_1 vs. μ_3 and μ_2 vs. μ_3) are presented next. The .95 CI interval for the means difference in depressive symptoms for comparing the CBT and Control conditions is $(-7.45) - (-1.24)$. The probability is .95 that this interval will include the true mean differences between the population means of depressive symptoms between the CBT and control conditions for adolescents. The .95 confidence interval for the means difference in depressive symptoms comparing IPT to Control is $(-7.78) - (-1.54)$, and this interval will include the true means difference between the population means of depressive symptoms 95 times in 100. These mean differences are due to sampling from populations where the mean of the control group is not equal to the means of the CBT or IPT condition participants. It is important to note that the upper limit of both .95 intervals is a negative value that reflects a reduction in depressive symptoms.

PROGRESS REVIEW

1. The omnibus H_0: $\mu_1 = \mu_2 = \mu_3$ was rejected ($p < .05$), indicating the existence of significant mean differences.

2. The overall magnitude of treatment effect of the independent variable (depression treatment method) on the dependent variable (depressive symptoms) was a medium effect, $\eta_p^2 = .100$.

3. The post hoc power of .951 was considerably larger than the criterion of .80, which is consistent with our a priori power analysis results.

4. The post hoc paired-means comparisons using the Tukey HSD showed that CBT and IPT both produced significant lower ($p < .05$) depressive symptoms when compared to the Control condition. There was no significant difference between the CBT and IPT groups on reducing depressive symptoms.

5. The .95 confidence intervals for the mean differences reflected decreases in depressive symptoms of CBT versus Control and IPT versus Control.

FORMULA CALCULATIONS OF THE STUDY RESULTS

The formula calculations for the one-way ANOVA, Tukey HSD, post hoc effect sizes, and confidence intervals are presented next.

One-Way ANOVA Formula Calculations

The specifications for constructing an *ANOVA summary table* are presented first. The information in this table captures most of the important data needed to conduct the ANOVA. Additionally, the information in Table 7.10 will be useful for calculating the HSD, post hoc effect sizes, and confidence intervals. We will

TABLE 7.10   ANOVA Summary Table Specifications

Source of Variation	df	Sum of Squares (SS)	Mean Square (MS)	F
Treatment (T)	$K - 1$	$(df_T)(MS_T)$	Formula	$\dfrac{MS_T}{MS_E}$
Error (E)	$N_{TOT} - K$	$(df_E)(MS_E)$	Formula	—
Total (TOT)	$N_{TOT} - 1$	$(df_T)(MS_T) + (df_E)(MS_E)$	—	—

$df_T = K - 1$ is the treatment degrees of freedom where K is the number of treatments, groups, or means.

$df_E = N_{TOT} - K$ is the error degrees of freedom. The degrees of each group is $(n - 1\, df)$, which is summed across all treatments or groups.

$df_{TOT} = N_{TOT} - 1$ is the total degrees of freedom based on N scores with one score unable to vary.

complete the ANOVA summary table for this study after we calculate the necessary formulas.

ANOVA Formulas

There are several formulas that can be used to compute the ANOVA. We are using descriptive formulas to calculate *mean square treatment (MS$_T$)* and *mean square error (MSE)* terms. The means, group sizes, and variances that you will need to use for the formulas can be found in Table 7.1.

$$MS_T = \frac{n_1(M_1 - M_{tot})^2 + n_2(M_2 - M_{tot})^2 + n_3(M_3 - M_{tot})^2 + \cdots}{K - 1}$$

where

n_1, n_2, n_3 = number of participants in each condition group

M_1, M_2, M_3 = means of each condition group

M_{tot} = grand mean

Grand Mean

All of the values to complete the formulas are in the *Descriptive Statistics* table except for the *grand mean (M$_{TOT}$)*, which is calculated next using a weighted process since the group sizes are unequal.

$$M_{\text{tot}} = \frac{n_1(M_1) + n_2(M_2) + n_3(M_3)}{N}$$

$$= \frac{48(17.333) + 47(17.021) + 50(21.680)}{145}$$

$$= \frac{831.984 + 799.987 + 1084}{145}$$

$$= \frac{2715.971}{145}$$

$$M_{\text{tot}} = 18.731$$

Mean Square Treatment

Now, with the grand mean we can solve for the mean square treatment term.

$$MS_T = \frac{48(17.333 - 18.731)^2 + 47(17.021 - 18.731)^2 + 50(21.680 - 18.731)^2}{2}$$

$$= \frac{48(-1.398)^2 + 47(-1.710)^2 + 47(2.949)^2}{2}$$

$$= \frac{48(1.954) + 47(2.924) + 50(8.697)}{2}$$

$$= \frac{93.792 + 137.428 + 434.850}{2}$$

$$= \frac{666.07}{2}$$

$$MS_T = 333.035$$

Mean Square Error

Next, we will solve for the mean square error term.

$$MS_E = \frac{(n_1 - 1)S_1^2 + (n_2 - 1)S_2^2 + (n_3 - 1)S_3^2 + \cdots}{(n_1 - 1) + (n_2 - 1) + (n_3 - 1)\cdots}$$

$$= \frac{(48 - 1)38.780 + (47 - 1)35.934 + (50 - 1)51.079}{(48 - 1) + (47 - 1) + (50 - 1)}$$

$$= \frac{(47)38.780 + (46)35.934 + (49)51.079}{47 + 46 + 49}$$

$$= \frac{1,822.660 + 1,652.964 + 2,502.871}{142}$$

$$= \frac{5,978.495}{142}$$

$$MS_E = 42.102$$

ANOVA Summary Table

Refer to the specifications in Table 7.10 that were used to calculate MS_T and MS_E values in the ANOVA summary table (Table 7.11).

Graphical Representation of Findings

Figure 7.6 shows a visual representation of the findings. A critical value (CV) is obtained using an online calculator.

Go to www.danielsoper.com > select **Statistics Calculators** > select **F-Distribution** > select **Critical F-value Calculator** > type in 2 next to **Degrees of freedom 1:** > type 142 next to **Degrees of freedom 2:** > type 0.05 beside **Probability level:** > click on **Calculate!**

TABLE 7.11 ANOVA Summary Table

Source of Variation	df	Sum of Squares (SS)	Mean Square (MS)	F
Treatment (T)	2	666.070	333.035	$\frac{333.035}{42.102}$ $F = 7.910$
Error (E)	142	5,978.484	42.102	—
Total (TOT)	144	6,644.554	—	—

FIGURE 7.6   Hypothesis Testing Graph—One-Way ANOVA

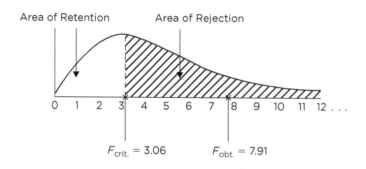

The F critical value is 3.05983069, rounded to 3.06. We place the F critical value on the abscissa (base of the curve) of the F-distribution curve. Then, we place the obtained omnibus ANOVA value of $F = 7.91$ on the curve. The area of rejection begins on the abscissa at the CV, and any obtained F to the right of the CV informs us to reject the null hypothesis. Our $F_{obtained} = 7.91$ falls in the area of rejection to the right of the $CV = 3.06$, so we reject the H_0, concluding that if the null hypothesis is true we would have obtained results like these less than 5 percent of the time. There is a difference in depressive symptoms across the three conditions at the .05 level of significance.

Tukey HSD Test for Multiple Comparisons

A calculation of the Tukey HSD is presented next. First, the HSD formulas for equal and unequal sample sized groups are presented. Since we have unequal samples, we will initially compute a weighted sample size value using the harmonic mean.

Tukey HSD with Equal Sample Sizes by Group

$$q_{.05} \sqrt{MS_E/n}$$

Tukey HSD with Unequal Sample Sizes by Group

$$q_{.05} \sqrt{MS_E/n_h}$$

where $q_{.05}$ is the Studentized range statistic that is a linear function of t, where $q = t\sqrt{2}$ (Howell, 2007). Using the q allows us to adjust the critical value (CV) of q for the number of means (three) involved in our post hoc analysis. To obtain a $q_{.05}$, go to the following online calculator.

> Google VassarStats > click on VassarStats : Statistical Computation Web Site > under Site Map click on Utilities > click on **Statistical Tables Calculator** > click on **critical values of Q** > under **K** type 3 and under **df** type 142 > click on **Calculate**. This results in $q_{.05} = 3.35$.

$$MS_E = 42.102,$$

$$n_h \text{ (harmonic mean of unequal n's)} = \frac{K}{1/n_1 + 1/n_2 + 1/n_3 \ldots}$$

$$= \frac{3}{1/48 + 1/47 + 1/50}$$

$$= \frac{3}{.021 + .021 + .020}$$

$$= \frac{3}{.062}$$

$$n_h = 48.39$$

Tukey HSD with Unequal-Sized Groups

$$HSD = 3.35\sqrt{42.102/48.39}$$
$$= 3.35\sqrt{.870}$$
$$= 3.35(.933)$$
$$HSD = 3.126$$

The mean differences of the three pairs of means are presented in Table 7.12. Any mean difference that is larger than our calculated HSD statistic of 3.126 is significantly different. Depressive symptoms are significantly lower ($p < .05$) following the CBT and IPT conditions when compared to the Control condition (see Table 7.9).

TABLE 7.12 Matrix of Mean Differences

Group Means[1]	$M_1 = 17.333$	$M_2 = 17.021$	$M_3 = 21.680$
CBT $M_1 = 17.333$	—	.312	−4.347*
IPT $M_2 = 17.021$	—	—	−4.659*
Control $M_3 = 21.680$	—	—	—

[1] Interpret these mean differences as absolute values ignoring the + or − signs.
* $p < .05$; these mean differences are greater than the HSD statistic = 3.126, so the differences are significantly different.

Post Hoc Effect Sizes

We are going to calculate the post hoc effect sizes that relate directly to the findings of the one-way ANOVA. The partial eta-squared is a descriptive measure of the magnitude of treatment effects that was reported in the IBM SPSS output. We will also calculate omega-squared (ω^2), which is a more conservative estimate of the population effect size and is not provided in the IBM SPSS output.

Eta-Squared (η^2)

Eta-squared is a measure of practical significance and is referred to as an effect size or magnitude of treatment effect. It is a ratio of the variance explained by the independent variable in relation to the total variance. ANOVA designs may result in analyses of several independent variables and interactions between the independent variables, and eta-squared statistics are computed for each, producing partial eta-squared values. Eta-squared values range from 0 (small) to 1.0 (large). There are several different effect sizes, and η^2 is commonly used. The $\eta^2_h = .100$ from the ANOVA output and is defined as:

$$\eta^2 = \frac{\text{Treatment (Condition) sum of squares (SS)}}{\text{Treatment SS} + \text{Error SS}}$$

$$= \frac{666.070}{666.070 + 5,978.484}$$

$$= \frac{666.070}{6,644.554}$$

$$\eta^2 = .100$$

We can interpret the $\eta^2 = .100$ by converting the fraction to a percentage by moving the decimal two spaces to the right, and report that approximately 10 percent of the change in the dependent variable (depressive symptoms) can be attributed to the independent variable (depression treatment program). The $\eta^2 = .100$ has a medium strength effect according to Cohen's convention where approximately 1 percent to 6 percent is low, >6 percent to 14 percent is medium, and >14 percent is large. There clearly is a meaningful magnitude of treatment effect of the depression treatment program on decreasing depressive symptoms.

Omega-Squared (ω^2)

Omega-squared is another useful effect size that is more conservative (lower) because it estimates effect size between the IV and the DV in the population (Tabachnick & Fidell, 2007). Eta-squared provides more of a descriptive effect size of the impact of the IV on the DV in a study. Omega-squared also ranges from 0 to 1.0.

$$\omega^2 = \frac{SS_{Treatment} - (K - 1)\,MS_{Error}}{SS_{Total} + MS_{Error}}$$

where $SS_{Treatment}$ = condition sum of squares

K = number of condition groups

MS_{Error} = error mean square

SS_{Total} = total sum of squares

Omega-squared is not reported in the Tests of Between-Subjects Effects output but it can be calculated using information from the table.

$$\omega^2 = \frac{666.070 - (3 - 1)42.102}{6{,}644.554 + 42.102}$$

$$= \frac{666.070 - 84.204}{6{,}686.656}$$

$$= \frac{581.866}{6{,}686.656}$$

$$\omega^2 = .087$$

The $\omega^2 = .087$ indicates that approximately 8.7 percent of the change in the dependent variable (depressive symptoms) in the population can be attributed to the independent variable (depression treatment program). The $\omega^2 = .087$ is lower than the $\eta^2 = .100$ as expected. However, both effect sizes provide similar perspectives of the magnitude of treatment effect.

Confidence Intervals (.95) for Mean Differences of Significant Pairs

The $CI_{.95}$ calculations for the mean differences within the three sets of paired means (CBT vs. IPT, CBT vs. Control, and IPT vs. Control) are presented next. The calculations closely approximate the confidence intervals displayed in Table 7.9 of the Multiple Comparisons table that were IBM SPSS generated. Minor differences are related to rounding differences.

$$\text{HSD CI}_{.95} = [q_{.05}/\sqrt{2}][\sqrt{\text{MS}_E(1/n_i + 1/n_j)}]$$

CBT versus IPT

$$[3.35/1.414][\sqrt{42.102(.021 + .021)}]$$
$$[2.369][\sqrt{42.102(.042)}]$$
$$[2.369][1.330]$$
$$3.151$$

$$(\text{CBT } M) - (\text{IPT } M) = (17.333 - 17.021) = +.312$$
$$CI_{.95} \text{ Lower limit} = +.312 - 3.151 = -2.839$$
$$CI_{.95} \text{ Upper limit} = +.312 + 3.151 = +3.463$$
$$CI_{.95} = (-2.839)\mu_{\text{Difference}}(+3.463)$$

CBT versus Control

$$[3.35/1.414][\sqrt{42.102(.021 + .020)}]$$
$$[2.369][\sqrt{42.102(.041)}]$$
$$[2.369][1.314]$$
$$3.113$$

$$(\text{CBT}\,M) - (\text{Control}\,M) = (17.333 - 21.680) = -4.347$$
$$CI_{.95}\ \text{Lower limit} = -4.347 - 3.113 = -7.460$$
$$CI_{.95}\ \text{Upper limit} = -4.347 + 3.113 = -1.234$$
$$CI_{.95} = (-7.460)\mu_{\text{Difference}}\,(-1.234)$$

IPT versus Control

$$[3.35/1.414][\sqrt{42.102(.021 + .020)}]$$
$$[2.369][\sqrt{42.102(.041)}]$$
$$[2.369][1.314]$$
$$3.113$$

$$(\text{IBT}\,M) - (\text{Control}\,M) = (17.021 - 21.680) = -4.659$$
$$CI_{.95}\ \text{Lower limit} = -4.659 - 3.113 = -7.772$$
$$CI_{.95}\ \text{Upper limit} = -4.659 + 3.113 = -1.546$$
$$CI_{.95} = (-7.772)\mu_{\text{Difference}}\,(-1.546)$$

ANOVA Study Results

It was hypothesized that two depression treatment programs, cognitive-behavioral therapy (CBT) and interpersonal therapy (IPT), would significantly reduce depressive symptoms among adolescents compared to a no-treatment control group (Control). It was expected that there would be no differences in the effects of cognitive-behavioral therapy versus interpersonal therapy on reducing depressive symptoms. The Center for Epidemiological Studies Depression Scale (CES-D) was used to measure depressive symptoms, and higher scores represent more self-reported depressive symptoms.

The sample consisted of 145 eighth and ninth grade participants who lived in suburban, middle-class communities. The average age of the participants was $M = 14.55$ ($SD = .68$), and there was a reasonable balance between females (52 percent) and males (48 percent).

An a priori power analysis was conducted to assess the probability of correctly rejecting a false null hypothesis. Using an alpha of .05, a sample size of 145, and an estimated effect size of $f = .65$, we found that we had adequate power ($>.80$) to correctly reject a false null hypothesis in favor of the alternative hypothesis.

The data were screened prior to testing the null hypothesis. The accuracy of the data set was checked and confirmed. The data set had no missing data or univariate outliers. The normality of the dependent variable (depressive symptoms) was assessed for each group. The distributions of depressive symptoms for the CBT and IPT groups fully met the underlying assumption of normality. The Control group did not meet the criteria of the Shapiro-Wilk normality statistic. However, the Control group distribution did meet the normality criteria of the Q-Q normality plots and the skewness and kurtosis standardized scores. Therefore, the decision was made to proceed with the analyses without modifying the Control group distribution since the preponderance of the evidence supported normality.

The underlying assumption of homogeneity of variance also was met across the three relatively equal-sized groups. The variance ratio (1.064 < 10.0) and Levene's test ($p > .05$) both demonstrated homogeneity of variance.

The depressive symptoms mean, standard deviation, and sample size for each condition in the study were: (1) CBT condition ($M = 17.333$, $SD = 6.227$, $n = 48$), (2) IPT condition ($M = 17.021$, $SD = 5.995$, $n = 47$), and (3) Control condition ($M = 21.680$, $SD = 7.147$, $n = 50$).

The adolescent participants across group conditions (CBT, IPT, Control) were tested for significant differences in depressive symptoms with a one-way ANOVA using an alpha criterion of $\alpha = .05$. The omnibus ANOVA analysis was significant, $F(2, 142) = 7.909$, $p = .001$ (or we can state this finding using the alpha level of the study as $p < .05$). If the null hypothesis is true, we would have obtained results like these less than 5 percent of the time. The $\eta^2 = .100$ ($\omega^2 = .870$) is a medium effect size, indicating that approximately 10 percent ($\omega^2 = 8.70\%$) of the variability in depressive symptoms can be explained by the depression treatment programs and control.

A post hoc analysis was conducted to compare all paired means using the Tukey HSD statistic. Two significant paired mean differences on reduced depressive symptoms were found between the CBT and the Control participants ($p < .05$, or $p = .003$) and the IPT versus Control participants ($p < .05$ or $p = .002$). The CBT and IPT conditions produced significantly lower depressive symptoms, whereas the CBT versus IPT participants showed similar results ($p > .05$ or $p = .970$). In other words, we can conclude that the paired-means differences were ($\mu_{CBT} - \mu_{Control}) < 0$ ($p = .003$) and ($\mu_{IPT} - \mu_{Control}) < 0$ ($p = .002$). The difference in depressive symptoms comparing the CBT to IPT conditions ($\mu_{CBT} - \mu_{IPT}$) is indefinite.

The .95 CI for the means difference between the two significant paired means were CBT versus Control $(-7.45) - (-1.24)$ and IPT versus Control $(-7.78) - (-1.54)$. The probability is .95 that these intervals will include the true mean differences between the population means of depressive symptoms between the CBT versus Control and the IPT versus Control, respectively. Decreases in depressive symptoms comprised the lower and upper limits of the .95 confidence intervals of CBT versus Control and IPT versus Control conditions.

In conclusion, the cognitive-behavioral therapy and interpersonal therapy depression treatment programs significantly reduced depressive symptoms among adolescents when compared to a no-treatment control condition. CBT and IPT were equally effective in reducing depressive symptoms.

SUMMARY

We have demonstrated how a randomized posttest-only control group design using a one-way analysis of variance statistic is applied to a research problem within the context of the hypothesis-testing process. Research questions and hypotheses were developed that incorporated independent and dependent variables. We established a criterion alpha level considering Type I and II errors. An a priori power analysis was conducted to assess the fidelity of the study.

Data were entered for computer analyses using the IBM SPSS statistical program (see data in Table 7.13). We conducted data diagnostics to make sure that data were accurate and that we met univariate underlying assumptions of normality, homogeneity of variance, and independence of scores. Confidence intervals of mean differences and magnitude of treatment effects were discussed. The one-way ANOVA, Tukey HSD, post hoc effect sizes, and confidence intervals also were presented using formulas. Finally, we presented a summary of the results.

PROBLEM ASSIGNMENT

The steps involved in conducting a one-way ANOVA using both IBM SPSS and formulas have been presented in this chapter. Now it is your turn to independently work through the steps of the hypothesis-testing process related to a one-way ANOVA using IBM SPSS. Go to the companion website and you will find a new one-way ANOVA research problem and data set along with a worksheet to

TABLE 7.13 One-Way Analysis of Variance Data

ID#	DepSymptoms	Condition*
1	16	1
2	26	1
3	24	1
4	25	1
5	22	1
6	21	1
7	20	1
8	19	1
9	18	1
10	17	1
11	23	1
12	27	1
13	11	1
14	12	1
15	14	1
16	15	1
17	14	1
18	8	1
19	10	1
20	12	1
21	7	1
22	14	1
23	9	1
24	17	1
25	16	1
26	16	1
27	18	1
28	25	1
29	23	1
30	32	1
31	29	1
32	24	1
33	33	1
34	18	1
35	18	1
36	18	1
37	16	1
38	16	1
39	10	1
40	13	1
41	12	1

42	13	1
43	11	1
44	8	1
45	12	1
46	17	1
47	17	1
48	16	1
49	26	2
50	20	2
51	24	2
52	25	2
53	23	2
54	22	2
55	21	2
56	20	2
57	18	2
58	29	2
59	25	2
60	29	2
61	32	2
62	27	2
63	10	2
64	11	2
65	12	2
66	13	2
67	14	2
68	15	2
69	12	2
70	11	2
71	14	2
72	8	2
73	10	2
74	12	2
75	10	2
76	14	2
77	5	2
78	8	2
79	12	2
80	17	2
81	17	2
82	17	2
83	17	2

(Continued)

TABLE 7.13 One-Way Analysis of Variance Data (Continued)

ID#	DepSymptoms	Condition*
84	17	2
85	16	2
86	16	2
87	16	2
88	16	2
89	16	2
90	16	2
91	18	2
92	15	2
93	18	2
94	18	2
95	18	2
96	29	3
97	30	3
98	33	3
99	35	3
100	26	3
101	27	3
102	28	3
103	23	3
104	30	3
105	28	3
106	21	3
107	32	3
108	29	3
109	27	3
110	28	3
111	32	3
112	32	3
113	32	3
114	32	3
115	21	3
116	22	3
117	22	3
118	26	3
119	21	3
120	16	3
121	18	3
122	12	3
123	13	3
124	20	3

125	20	3
126	16	3
127	23	3
128	18	3
129	19	3
130	18	3
131	10	3
132	13	3
133	11	3
134	13	3
135	10	3
136	20	3
137	12	3
138	15	3
139	23	3
140	16	3
141	12	3
142	20	3
143	14	3
144	21	3
145	15	3

*1 = CBT; 2 = IPT; 3 = Control

complete. Use the problem presented in this chapter to guide you as you complete the assignment. Your instructor will evaluate your completed worksheet when it is finished.

KEY TERMS

alpha criterion (α)

alternative hypothesis

analysis of covariance (ANCOVA)

ANOVA summary table specifications

a priori

a priori power analysis

confidence intervals for the mean
    differences

data diagnostics

degrees of freedom

dependent variable (DV)

estimated (a priori) effect size

eta-squared (η^2)

exclusion criteria

grand mean (M_{tot})

homogeneity of variance

inclusion criteria

independence of observations

independent variable (IV)

kurtosis

leptokurtic

Levene's statistic

magnitude of treatment effects
(effect sizes)

mean square error (MS_E)

mean square treatment (MS_T)

mesokurtic

missing data analysis

multifactor ANOVA (factorial ANOVA)

multivariate ANOVA

negatively skewed (left-skewed)
distribution

normality

normal Q-Q plots

no-treatment control condition

null hypothesis

omega-squared (ω^2)

operationally defined (OD)

outliers

platykurtic

positively skewed (right-skewed)
curve

post hoc multiple comparisons of
means

post hoc power

power

purposive sampling of typical
instances

randomized posttest-only control
group design

randomly assigned

repeated-measures ANOVA
(RM-ANOVA)

Shapiro-Wilk (S-W) statistic

Tukey honestly significant difference
(HSD) statistic

Type I (alpha) error

Type II (beta) error

univariate parametric assumptions

weighted by sample size

Chapter 8

REPEATED-TREATMENT

DESIGN USING A

REPEATED-MEASURES

ANALYSIS OF VARIANCE

LEARNING OBJECTIVES

○ Demonstrate how to develop research questions and hypotheses as they relate to a research problem incorporating independent and dependent variables.

○ Identify the components and application of a repeated-treatment research design.

○ Examine Type I and II error considerations and a priori power analysis in establishing alpha (α).

○ Conduct data diagnostics to assess for normality and sphericity.

- ○ Execute a repeated-measures analysis of variance (RM-ANOVA), profile plots, and Fisher's protected least significant differences (PLSD) pairwise mean analysis using SPSS and formulas.

- ○ Interpret post hoc analyses using eta-squared (η^2), trend analysis, and confidence intervals.

- ○ Understand the study findings combining the various analyses.

A repeated-measures analysis of variance (RM-ANOVA) is used to evaluate if support partners added to weight loss treatment can improve weight loss among persons who are overweight. Research questions and hypotheses are developed that anticipate that adding support partners to treatment will improve the outcome of weight loss. A repeated-treatment design is used with one group of persons who are overweight. A data set is presented that is used for both IBM SPSS and formula analyses.

An a priori power analysis is conducted to determine if the sample size, estimated effect size, and alpha level are adequate to proceed with the study. An RM-ANOVA is applied to test the overall (omnibus) null hypothesis. The magnitude of treatment effects is assessed using both eta-squared and omega-squared effect size measures. Post hoc analyses are conducted using profile plots, the Fisher's protected least significant differences (PLSD) statistic, and trend analysis. The .99 confidence intervals are interpreted for the mean differences between condition group means. Finally, the overall results are presented.

RESEARCH PROBLEM

The focus of this simulated research problem is to assess whether the use of friends (support partners) in behavioral weight control treatment (BWCT) can improve the weight loss outcomes of persons who are overweight. Gorin et al. (2005) found that support partners can improve the weight loss of individuals who are overweight if the support partners are also successfully losing weight during the treatment program.

There are 35 participants who are overweight in this study who were randomly selected from a large weight loss center in a metropolitan area in the United States. The participants' average age is 40 years old ($SD = 3.20$). Each participant has a support partner (friend) who is also participating in the behavioral weight control treatment, and the friends' average age is 41 ($SD = 5.23$).

The participants' weight is measured before the treatment begins. The treatment program begins with a behavioral weight control treatment including the support partners. After three months, the weight loss in pounds of the participants is measured and recorded. Next, the behavioral weight control treatment is continued for three months but without having the support partners participate. Again, the weight loss is assessed. The support partners are reinstituted to the behavioral weight control treatment for another three months, followed by a weight loss measurement. Finally, participants experience another three months of BWCT with support partners and the last assessment is made.

STUDY VARIABLES

The independent variable, *weight loss intervention*, and how it was operationally defined in this study are described next. Moreover, the dependent variable, *weight loss*, and its operational definition are identified.

Independent Variable

The independent variable (IV) in this study problem is *weight loss intervention*. The IV is operationally defined as a behavioral weight control treatment (BWCT) with the addition or removal of support partners. BWCT involves the daily self-monitoring of calories, fat, and activity. Goals are established to maintain 1,200 to 1,500 calories per day, 20 percent calories from fat, and 150 minutes of moderate activity each week. Individuals also participate in behavioral modification activities.

Support partners have several important roles to provide support and share the journey in the treatment of persons who are overweight. They establish cooperative, mutual goals toward weight loss. Support partners are counted on to reach the shared goals that work the best for both individuals. Support partners are available and willing to communicate consistently. Support partners must be able to determine what unique kinds of encouragement work best with a given individual. The format of the operationally defined conditions of the IV (*weight loss intervention*) are: (1) BWCT and support partners (three months), (2) BWCT with support partners removed (three months), (3) BWCT with support partners reinstituted (three months), and (4) BWCT with support partners continued (three months). The study extends over 12 months.

Dependent Variable

The dependent variable (DV) is *weight loss* in pounds from the baseline measured weight of the participants over the 12 months of the study. The operational definition of *weight loss* is the loss in pounds from their baseline weight before the treatment began. Weight loss is measured, recorded, and compared at three months, six months, nine months, and 12 months.

RESEARCH DESIGN

The research design used for this research example is a *repeated-treatment design* (Shadish, Cook, & Campbell, 2002). Initially, a randomly selected group of participants who are overweight are weighed at baseline before treatment. Then, each participant's weight loss is measured and recorded after three months of treatment with partner support (at three months), after three months when partner support is removed (at six months), after three months when partner support is added back to treatment (at nine months), and after the treatment with partner support is continued for three months (at 12 months). The repeated-treatment design with one group is diagrammed and explained in Figure 8.1.

Statistical Analysis: Repeated-Measures Analysis of Variance

The one-way ANOVA that we used previously was a between-subjects statistical design. Independent groups producing independent scores were compared for mean differences. In this study, a *repeated-measures ANOVA (RM-ANOVA)* is used, which is a *within-subjects design* in which participants experience more than one treatment condition and are measured more than once on a dependent

FIGURE 8.1 Repeated-Treatment Design with One Group for Study Example

$O_{Baseline}$ X_{1With} O_1 $X_{2Remove}$ O_2 X_{2Add} O_3 $X_{4Continue}$ O_4

$O_{Baseline}$	= Weight measurement of participants before treatment
X_{1With}	= Treatment with partner support for three months
O_1	= Weight loss measurement at three months
$X_{2Remove}$	= Treatment with removal of partner support for three months
O_2	= Weight loss measurement at six months
X_{3Add}	= Treatment with added partner support for three months
O_3	= Weight loss measurement at nine months
$X_{4Continue}$	= Treatment with continued partner support for three months
O_4	= Weight loss measurement at 12 months

FIGURE 8.2 Same Participants Measured Repeatedly over Time

Participants	SameMeasT1	SameMeasT2	SameMeasT3 ...
Person 1	1st score	2nd score	3rd score
Person 2	1st score	2nd score	3rd score
Person 3	1st score	2nd score	3rd score
Person 4	1st score	2nd score	3rd score
.	.	.	.
.	.	.	.
.	.	.	.

variable. The RM-ANOVA generalizes from the dependent *t*-test and allows for more than two measurements on the same individuals. In the next chapter, we conduct a factorial ANOVA that integrates a within-subjects IV and a between-subjects IV. However, a factorial ANOVA can also involve only between-subjects IVs. If the statistical design has both between-subjects effects and within-subjects effects, it is called a *mixed-subject ANOVA statistical design.*

Three common uses of repeated-measures ANOVA involve: (1) the same participants measured repeatedly over time (see Figure 8.2), (2) the same participants measured under different conditions (see Figure 8.3), and (3) matched pairs of participants measured under different conditions (see Figure 8.4).

In this study, we are studying the same participants measured repeatedly over time. The following three underlying assumptions need to be met in order to use the RM-ANOVA.

FIGURE 8.3 Same Participants Measured under Different Conditions

Participants	Condition 1	Condition 2	Condition 3 . . .
Person 1	1st score	2nd score	3rd score
Person 2	1st score	2nd score	3rd score
Person 3	1st score	2nd score	3rd score
Person 4	1st score	2nd score	3rd score
.	.	.	.
.	.	.	.
.	.	.	.

FIGURE 8.4 Matched Pairs of Participants Measured under Different Conditions

Participants	Condition 1	Matched Participants	Condition 2
Person 1	Score	Person matched	Score
Person 2	Score	Person matched	Score
Person 3	Score	Person matched	Score
Person 4	Score	Person matched	Score
.	.	.	.
.	.	.	.
.	.	.	.

1. The scores of participants are independent from the scores of all other participants, known as independence of scores.

2. Variables are assumed to be normally distributed around zero within each treatment.

3. The group variances and the covariances are assumed to be homogeneous across treatments, which is known as sphericity.

PROGRESS REVIEW

1. The research problem focuses on whether adding support partners to behavioral weight control treatment can increase

weight loss among persons who are overweight. A repeated-treatment research design is used.

2. The independent variable is weight loss intervention and is operationally defined as BWCT with the addition or removal of support partners: (1) BWCT and support partners (three months), (2) BWCT with support partners removed (three months), (3) BWCT with support partners reinstituted (three months), and (4) BWCT with support partners continued (three months). The dependent variable is weight loss and is operationally defined as number of pounds lost at three, six, nine, and 12 months.

3. Thirty-five persons who are overweight are randomly selected from a large weight loss center, and the same participants experience four treatment conditions and four weight loss measures.

4. The changes in weight loss of the participants across the conditions are assessed using the repeated-measures ANOVA statistic.

5. Next, the research question is stated and we begin completing the steps of the hypothesis-testing process.

STATING THE OMNIBUS (COMPREHENSIVE) RESEARCH QUESTION

The initial research question is stated. Then, the steps of the hypothesis-testing process related to this research problem will be presented following the statement of the research questions.

Omnibus Research Question (RQ)

Will there be significantly more weight loss (number of pounds) among persons who are overweight when support partners are included in a behavioral weight control treatment?

HYPOTHESIS TESTING STEP 1: ESTABLISH THE ALTERNATIVE (RESEARCH) HYPOTHESIS (H_a)

The omnibus (comprehensive) alternative hypothesis is stated next in both narrative and symbolic formats. Subquestions and subhypotheses follow the overall analysis.

Omnibus Narrative Alternative Hypothesis (H_a)

H_a: There will be significantly more weight loss (number of pounds) among persons who are overweight when support partners are included with BWCT compared to BWCT alone using the following schedule over 12 months: (1) BWCT and support partners (three months), (2) BWCT with support partners removed (three months), (3) BWCT with support partners reinstituted (three months), and (4) BWCT with support partners continued (three months).

Symbolic H_a

$$H_a: \mu_{1\,\text{Withsupport}} > \mu_{2\,\text{Removesupport}} < \left(\mu_{3\,\text{Addsupport}}, \mu_{4\,\text{Continuesupport}} \right)$$

where $\mu_{1\text{Withsupport}}$ is the population mean of weight loss of participants in the BWCT with support partners condition being estimated by the sample mean.

$\mu_{2\text{Removesupport}}$ is the population mean of weight loss of participants in the BWCT with support partners removed condition being estimated by the sample mean.

$\mu_{3\text{Addsupport}}$ is the population mean of weight loss of participants in the BWCT with support partners added back condition being estimated by the sample mean.

$\mu_{4\text{Continuesupport}}$ is the population mean of weight loss of participants in the BWCT with support partners continued condition being estimated by the sample mean.

This is a directional alternative hypothesis because it is expected that the three conditions that have support partners included with BWCT will produce more weight loss than when support partners are removed. It also is expected that the three conditions with support partners will not differ from each other in the amount of resulting weight loss.

An alternative process to reach conclusions in analyzing one's sample data is following the recommendations of Jones and Tukey (2000). Act as if: (1) $(\mu_{1\text{Withsupport}} - \mu_{2\text{Removesupport}}) > 0$, $(\mu_{3\text{Addsupport}} - \mu_{2\text{Removesupport}}) > 0$, $(\mu_{4\text{Continuesupport}} - \mu_{2\text{Removesupport}}) > 0$, or (2) $(\mu_{1\text{Withsupport}} - \mu_{2\text{Removesupport}}) < 0$, $(\mu_{3\text{Addsupport}} - \mu_{2\text{Removesupport}}) < 0$, $(\mu_{4\text{Continuesupport}} - \mu_{4\text{Continuesupport}}) < 0$; or (3) the sign ($< 0$ or > 0) of $(\mu_{1\text{Withsupport}} - \mu_{2\text{Removesupport}})$, $(\mu_{3\text{Addsupport}} - \mu_{2\text{Removesupport}})$, $(\mu_{4\text{Continuesupport}} - \mu_{2\text{Removesupport}})$ is indefinite. Using this approach, we will be making conclusions about whether omnibus and paired-mean differences are greater than zero or less than zero, or that the findings are inconclusive about whether one mean is greater or less than zero. In this study, we are expecting that the three conditions that combine BWCT with support partners will significantly increase weight loss when compared to the BWCT without support partners. Thus, we expect to make the following conclusions: $(\mu_{1\text{Withsupport}} - \mu_{2\text{Removesupport}}) > 0$, $(\mu_{3\text{Addsupport}} - \mu_{2\text{Removesupport}}) > 0$, $(\mu_{4\text{Continuesupport}} - \mu_{2\text{Removesupport}}) > 0$.

HYPOTHESIS TESTING STEP 2: ESTABLISH THE NULL HYPOTHESIS (H_0)

The omnibus null hypothesis is stated in narrative and symbolic formats in the second step of the hypothesis-testing process.

Omnibus Narrative Null Hypothesis (H_0)

There will be no significant weight loss (number of pounds) among persons who are overweight when support partners are included with BWCT compared to BWCT alone using the following schedule over 12 months: (1) BWCT and support partners (three months), (2) BWCT with support partners removed (three months), (3) BWCT with support partners reinstituted (three months), and (4) BWCT with support partners continued (three months).

Symbolic H_0

$$H_0: \mu_{1\,\text{Withsupport}} = \mu_{2\,\text{Removesupport}} = \mu_{3\,\text{Addsupport}} = \mu_{4\,\text{Continuesupport}}$$

HYPOTHESIS TESTING STEP 3: DECIDE ON A RISK LEVEL (ALPHA) OF REJECTING THE TRUE H_0 CONSIDERING TYPE I AND II ERRORS AND POWER

We will be choosing an alpha criterion (α) that we will use to make a decision about whether to reject a true null hypothesis (H_0) in this step of the hypothesis-testing process. We consider the balancing act between Type I (alpha) and Type II (beta) errors. Then, we will use our chosen α level and combine it with anticipated sample size and an estimated (a priori) effect size and determine whether we have enough power (a priori) to conduct the study. Power is the probability of correctly rejecting a false null hypothesis in favor of an alternative hypothesis.

Selecting Alpha (α) Considering Type I and Type II Errors

Previous studies have shown that including support partners with behavioral weight control treatment increases weight loss when compared to BWCT alone. We will use a stricter alpha criterion of $\alpha = .01$ for this study since we will be replicating past studies. This increases the probability of not making a Type I error, which is rejecting a true null (no mean differences). This will provide more confidence in our decision if the support partner conditions with BWCT significantly increase weight loss when compared to the BWCT condition alone (reject H_0). However, if we don't reject the null that there are differences, the $\alpha = .01$ increases the probability of making a Type II error of failing to reject H_0 when there are significant differences in means (false H_0).

A Priori Power Analysis

It is important to assess whether key elements are in place to find a significant difference in means on the dependent variable across the conditions if it exists before we conduct the study (a priori) or analyze data. Therefore, we will conduct an a priori power analysis that is the probability associated with correctly rejecting a false null hypothesis (see Figure 3.1 from previous Chapter 3). Initially, the a priori power analysis is conducted before participants are selected and assigned to conditions so that decisions can be made about study modifications such as increasing sample size before the study actually begins. If the selected number of participants is lower than the number of participants planned prior to selection, then power analysis is conducted again to see if the number is acceptable. In our example, we are going to conduct an a priori power analysis after participant selection and assignment to condition before the data are analyzed.

The three key elements used to conduct an a priori power analysis are alpha, sample size, and estimated effect size (a priori). For an RM-ANOVA, we also need an a priori value for the correlation between the repeated measures. In the previous study, *average correlation* across the repeated measures was $r_{average} = .55$. We have decided to use an alpha of .01 and we are planning on using a sample size of 35. Now we need to estimate an effect size and then we can combine the three elements to identify the probability of correctly rejecting a false null hypothesis (power). An effective method for estimating an effect size for the a priori power analysis is to use effect sizes resulting from previous studies that use similar variables and designs to those we will use in our study.

We are going to use findings obtained from a very similar previous study that resulted in a partial eta-squared: $\eta_p^2 = .35$. We now have the elements ($\alpha = .01$, $\eta_p^2 = .35$, $N = 35$, $r_{average} = .55$) necessary to conduct a power analysis for the RM-ANOVA. We will use G*Power 3.1 to determine if our key elements combined result in an acceptable power $\geq.80$ (see Figure 8.5).

Power Analysis Using G*Power 3.1.2

1. Open up the G*Power 3.1.2 program.

2. Select **F tests** under **Test family** > under **Statistical test**, select **ANOVA: Repeated measures, within factors** > under **Type of power analysis**, select **A priori: Compute required sample size - given α, power, and effect size**.

3. Click on the button called **Determine** to the left of **Effect size f** > a new window opens to the right > click on the **Direct** button > beside η_p^2 type in our partial eta-squared of .35 > click on the button that says **Calculate and transfer to main window** > and click on **Close**.

4. In the main window is the $f = .7337994$ that was calculated using the $\eta_p^2 = .35$ > beside α **err prob**, type .01 > beside **Power (1-β err prob)**, type 0.80 > beside **Number of groups**, type 1 > beside **Number of measurements**, type 4 > beside **Corr among rep measures**, type 0.55 > leave the 1 next to **Nonsphericity correction e** > click on the **Calculate** button.

FIGURE 8.5 Power Analysis for the RM-ANOVA Problem

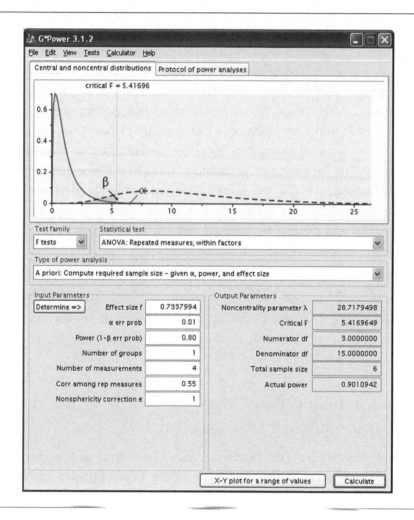

The power analysis results show that we would need only a total sample size = 6 participants to reach a power ≥.80; in the analysis the power was .901 (rounded). Our total sample of 35 far exceeds a needed sample size of 6. Considering the combined elements in our study of total sample size of 35, $f = .7337994$, and $\alpha = .01$, and an average correlation of measures = .55, a power greater than .80 should be achieved. We are therefore confident that we will correctly reject a false H_0 in our study and avoid making a Type II error.

PROGRESS REVIEW

1. The research question for the study problem was stated.

2. The first two steps of the hypothesis-testing process were completed by stating the alternative and null hypotheses in narrative and symbolic formats.

3. We decided on the risk we are willing to take when rejecting a true null hypothesis and chose $\alpha = .01$, which was believed to be a reasonable balance in our study to avoid making a Type I or Type II error.

4. We conducted a power analysis to make sure that our probability of correctly rejecting a false null hypothesis was adequate (power = .80) before continuing with the study as planned. A G*Power analysis confirmed that the a priori power was larger than .80, allowing us to continue the study with confidence.

HYPOTHESIS TESTING STEP 4: CHOOSE APPROPRIATE STATISTIC AND ITS SAMPLING DISTRIBUTION TO TEST THE H_0 ASSUMING H_0 IS TRUE

The RM-ANOVA will be used to test the null hypothesis:

$$H_0 : \mu_{1\,\text{Withsupport}} = \mu_{2\,\text{Removesupport}} = \mu_{3\,\text{Addsupport}} = \mu_{4\,\text{Continuesupport}}$$

We are comparing the means of weight loss across the four conditions for significant differences using the F-distribution. The RM-ANOVA is appropriate to use because: (1) the same participants are being measured more than two times, (2) there is one dependent variable, and (3) the dependent variable is continuously scaled.

HYPOTHESIS TESTING STEP 5: SELECT SAMPLE, COLLECT DATA, SCREEN DATA, COMPUTE STATISTIC, AND DETERMINE PROBABILITY ESTIMATES

Data are collected from a sample of participants during Step 5 of the hypothesis-testing process. The data are assessed for data accuracy, missing values, and univariate outliers, and to determine whether the underlying assumptions of the statistic are met. If needed, data modifications are made. Then the null hypothesis is tested using statistical analyses.

Sample Selection and Assignment

Thirty-five participants were randomly selected from a client population of a large weight loss center in a metropolitan area in the United States. The average age of the participants is 40 years old ($SD = 3.20$). Each participant has a support partner (friend) who is also participating in the behavioral weight control treatment, and the friends' average age is 41 ($SD = 5.23$).

Study Data Diagnostics

We will next screen the sample data after it has been collected but before the primary study hypothesis is tested. We are screening to: (1) check accuracy of data entries, (2) identify and deal with missing data, (3) detect and make decisions about univariate (one dependent variable) outliers, and (4) screen and make decisions about univariate parametric assumptions. The underlying assumptions of a repeated-measures ANOVA are that the dependent variable is assumed to be normally distributed around zero within each treatment, and the group variances and *covariances* are assumed to be homogeneous across treatments, which is known as *sphericity*. Sphericity refers to the variances being constant and the covariances being constant within the covariance matrix, which is also known as *compound symmetry*.

Accuracy of Data Entry

The original data were compared to the entered data by members of the research team. The data were determined to be accurate. The check of frequencies in the descriptive statistics analysis showed that the variable scores were in expected range and the means and standard deviations appeared plausible.

Missing Data Analysis

There were no missing data in the original data set.

Means, Standard Deviations, Variances, and Assessing for Univariate Outliers SPSS Commands

Enter the data found at the end of the chapter into IBM SPSS. Enter the data into five columns just as it appears in the table. There is one ID column and there are four data columns.

1. Click on **Analyze > Descriptive Statistics > Descriptives** > click over *Withsupport*, *Removesupport*, *Addsupport*, and *Continuesupport* to **Variable(s):**.

2. Click on **Options** button and check **Mean, Std. deviation**, and **Variance** and click on **Continue**.

3. Click on the box **Save standardized values as variables** and click **OK**.

4. Save the output as *RM-ANOVA Descriptives*.

The Descriptive Statistics Table 8.1 lists the sample size (N) of each group followed by the lowest (minimum) and highest (maximum) scores in each group. Valid N refers to the number of participant scores that do not having missing data. The average scores (means) of weight loss by conditions are provided. Measures of variability designate how the scores in each group distribution deviate from their group mean. The standard deviation is an average measure of score deviation from the mean, whereas the square of s is the variance (s^2) or

TABLE 8.1 Descriptive Statistics of Weight Loss by Condition Group

				Descriptive Statistics		
	N	Minimum	Maximum	Mean	Std. Deviation	Variance
Withsupport	35	7.00	15.00	10.3143	2.24619	5.045
Removesupport	35	1.00	7.00	4.1143	1.67633	2.810
Addsupport	35	8.00	16.00	10.6000	1.63059	2.659
Continuesupport	35	7.00	14.00	10.2571	1.82052	3.314
Valid N (listwise)	35					

TABLE 8.2   Highest ±z-Scores by Condition Group

Condition	Highest +z	Outlier? > ±3.29	Highest −z	Outlier? > ±3.29
Withsupport	2.086*	No	−1.476	No
Removesupport	1.721	No	−1.858	No
Addsupport	3.312	Yes	−1.595	No
Continuesupport	2.056	No	−1.789	No

* This number is rounded to three decimals.

general spread of scores from the mean. Higher scores reflect more deviation of scores from the mean for both s and s^2. As you can see, there is a higher standard deviation of scores from the mean for the *Withsupport* condition, and the standard deviations associated with the other conditions are closer together.

The standard values (z-scores) requested for the analysis to assess for univariate outliers are produced in a new column for each condition on the **Data View** spreadsheet and named *ZWithsupport, ZRemovesupport, ZAddsupport,* and *ZContinuesupport.* These values represent the z-scores corresponding to the raw scores in each condition. The highest positive and negative z-scores associated with the raw scores of weight loss for each condition are reported in Table 8.2. The z-scores are obtained by subtracting each condition's raw scores from that condition mean and dividing by its standard deviation ($z = [X_i − M]/SD$).

One participant (ID #24) has a weight loss of 16 pounds at the condition *Addsupport* that is a univariate outlier ($z = 3.312$) using the criterion of ±3.29 (<.001, two-tailed). No other weight loss scores are outliers in any of the four condition groups.

The outlying raw score of 16 is higher than the other 34 participants at the end of the *Addsupport* condition, with the condition group average weight loss being $M = 10.60$ ($SD = 1.631$). Looking at the other weight loss scores for #24 when the treatment included both the BWCT and support partners, the pounds lost are *Withsupport* (15 lbs.) and *Continuesupport* (14 lbs.) (see **Data View** to view these numbers for participant #24). The group outlying score of 16 for *Addsupport* is not an uncharacteristic score for participant #24 when compared to that individual's other scores.

Case study information relative to participant #24 is analyzed to determine if there are any personal characteristics, events during the study, or unique treatment or measurement conditions that would explain the outlying weight loss score at the nine-month weight measure for the *Addsupport* condition. No explanations for the outlying score were identified. The decision is to keep the outlying score and participant in the study since there is no reason to expect that this individual is not representative of the population that we have sampled from.

Assessing for Underlying Assumptions

Initially, we will evaluate the dependent variable (*weight loss*) for normality by assessing histograms, skewness, kurtosis, the Shapiro-Wilk statistic, and normal Q-Q plots.

Normality SPSS Commands

1. Click on **Data > Descriptive Statistics > Explore >** click over *Withsupport*, *Removesupport*, *Addsupport*, and *Continuesupport* to **Dependent List**.

2. **Both** should be clicked on under **Display**. In the upper right section, click on the **Plots** button and click on **Histogram** and **Normality plots with tests** and click **Continue** and **OK**.

3. Save the output as *RM-ANOVA-assumptionscreen*.

First, look at the histograms of the weight loss in the four conditions (see Figures 8.6a, 8.6b, 8.6c, and 8.6d). Notice that they appear to approximate being symmetrical. You will see the outlying score of 16 represented graphically by the *Addsupport* histogram. It is difficult to confirm that a distribution is normal enough for using a parametric statistic by viewing a histogram, so we will obtain more definitive information.

Next, we will use the output information under Descriptives in the output (see Table 8.3) to calculate skewness and kurtosis values.

We divide the skewness statistic value by its "Std. Error" value, and the resulting value is a z-score that we compare to the criterion ±3.29 ($p < .001$, two-tailed test). The skewness and standard error and their resulting skewness z-scores are presented in Table 8.4.

The distribution of raw scores on the dependent variable (*weight loss*) for each condition group (*Withsupport*, *Removesupport*, *Addsupport*, and *Continuesupport*) does not significantly depart from normality using our criterion, as is evident when you compare the calculated skewness z-score values from Table 8.4 to the

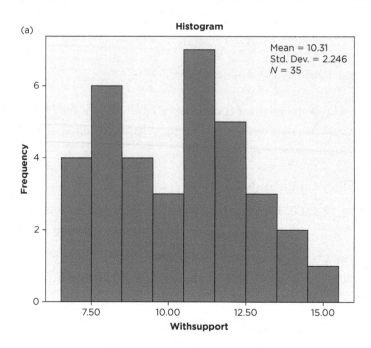

(a)

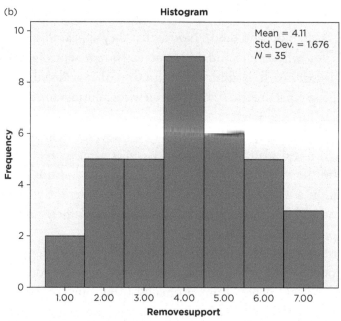

(b)

(c)

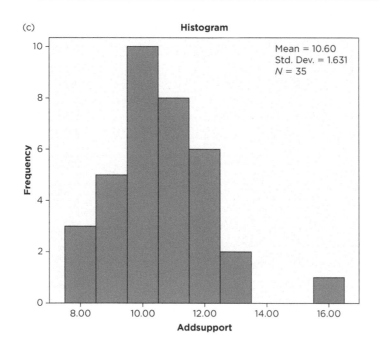

(d)

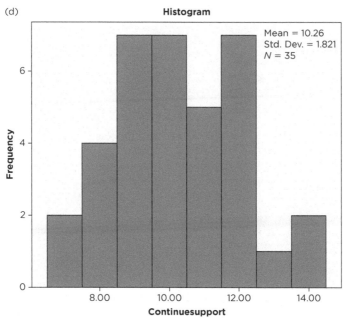

TABLE 8.3 Skewness, Kurtosis, and Standard Error Values by Condition Group

Descriptives			Statistic	Std. Error
Withsupport	Mean		10.3143	.37968
	95% Confidence	Lower Bound	9.5427	
	Interval for Mean	Upper Bound	11.0859	
	5% Trimmed Mean		10.2619	
	Median		11.0000	
	Variance		5.045	
	Std. Deviation		2.24619	
	Minimum		7.00	
	Maximum		15.00	
	Range		8.00	
	Interquartile Range		4.00	
	Skewness		.160	.398
	Kurtosis		−.919	.778
Removesupport	Mean		4.1143	.28335
	95% Confidence	Lower Bound	3.5384	
	Interval for Mean	Upper Bound	4.6901	
	5% Trimmed Mean		4.1270	
	Median		4.0000	
	Variance		2.810	
	Std. Deviation		1.67633	
	Minimum		1.00	
	Maximum		7.00	
	Range		6.00	
	Interquartile Range		2.00	
	Skewness		−.032	.398
	Kurtosis		−.748	.778
Addsupport	Mean		10.6000	.27562
	95% Confidence	Lower Bound	10.0399	
	Interval for Mean	Upper Bound	11.1601	
	5% Trimmed Mean		10.5159	
	Median		10.0000	
	Variance		2.659	
	Std. Deviation		1.63059	
	Minimum		8.00	
	Maximum		16.00	
	Range		8.00	
	Interquartile Range		2.00	

	Skewness		.912	.398
	Kurtosis		2.231	.778
Continuesupport	Mean		10.2571	.30772
	95% Confidence	Lower Bound	9.6318	
	Interval for Mean	Upper Bound	10.8825	
	5% Trimmed Mean		10.2302	
	Median		10.0000	
	Variance		3.314	
	Std. Deviation		1.82052	
	Minimum		7.00	
	Maximum		14.00	
	Range		7.00	
	Interquartile Range		3.00	
	Skewness		.183	.398
	Kurtosis		−.531	.778

TABLE 8.4 Skewness z-Scores by Condition Group

Condition	Skewness z (Stat./Std. Error = Z)	Skewness Direction	Sig. Departure? (> ±3.29)
Withsupport	.160/.398 = .402	Positive	No
Removesupport	−.032/.398 = −.080	Negative	No
Addsupport	.912/.398 = 2.291	Positive	No
Continuesupport	.183/.398 = .460	Positive	No

criterion of ±3.29. The degree of skewness is the highest in the positive direction of the Addsupport distribution ($Z = 2.291$), which is the result of the univariate outlier in the group. However, the outlier is not causing the group distribution to depart from normality.

We follow the same procedures to assess kurtosis (see values in the output in Table 8.3), which is the clustering of scores in the center, the upper and lower ends (tails), and the shoulders (between the center and the tails) of a distribution (Norusis, 1994).

None of the distribution kurtosis z-scores are considered problematic using the ±3.29 criterion (see Table 8.5). However, notice that the kurtosis of the

TABLE 8.5 Kurtosis z-Scores by Condition Group

Condition	Kurtosis z (Stat./Std. Error = Z)	Kurtosis Direction	Sig. Departure? (> ±3.29)
Withsupport	−.919/.778 = −1.181	Platykurtic	No
Removesupport	−.748/.778 = −.961	Platykurtic	No
Addsupport	2.231/.778 = 2.868	Leptokurtic	No
Continuesupport	−.531/.778 = −.683	Platykurtic	No

TABLE 8.6 Shapiro-Wilk Statistics by Condition Group

	Tests of Normality					
	Kolmogorov-Smirnov[a]			Shapiro-Wilk		
	Statistic	df	Sig.	Statistic	df	Sig.
Withsupport	.134	35	.112	.947	35	.093
Removesupport	.130	35	.143	.951	35	.125
Addsupport	.158	35	.027	.919	35	.014
Continuesupport	.128	35	.162	.958	35	.197

[a]Lilliefors significance correction

Addsupport condition group ($z = 2.868$) also is affected by the univariate outlier but not significantly departing from being a mesokurtic distribution.

The Shapiro-Wilk (S-W) statistic is assessed as another source of evidence to use to determine whether the distributions of the group conditions are normally distributed. The S-W statistic is found in the output under Tests of Normality (see Table 8.6). The null hypothesis to test the S-W with an alpha of .01 is presented next. We want to retain these hypotheses.

$$H_0: \text{The Sample Distribution} = \text{Normal}$$

We fail to reject the null hypotheses ($p > .01$) for all of the condition group distributions since the significant probability levels (Sig.) of the Shapiro-Wilk statistic are larger than $\alpha = .01$. We conclude that the four group distributions are not deviating significantly from being normal as indicated by the S-W statistic. As you can see, the Sig. of .014 of the *Addsupport* group is close to our criterion of $\alpha = .01$, but it is still above the criterion so we fail to reject the null hypothesis that the sample distribution is normal. Again, the univariate outlier in the *Addsupport* group is causing the S-W statistic to be close to reflecting nonnormality.

The final evidence of normality that we will interpret is the normal Q-Q plot for each distribution. A plot for each group is located in the output under the heading Normal Q-Q Plot of Withsupport, Removesupport, Addsupport, and Continuesupport (see Figures 8.7a, 8.7b, 8.7c, and 8.7d). An observed value in the distribution is paired with its expected value from the normal distribution to form the normal Q-Q plots. The number of cases in the sample and the rank order of the case in the sample are used to generate the expected values for the normal distribution. If the sample is from a normal distribution, we expect that the points will fall more or less on a straight line.

The Q-Q plots reflect acceptable normality, with the vast majority of points on the Q-Q plots in all condition group distributions falling on or near the straight line, providing further evidence that each group is normally distributed (see Figures 8.7a, 8.7b, 8.7c, and 8.7d). Again, you can see the univariate outlier in the *Addsupport* Q-Q plot.

Summary of the Normality Evidence

There was one univariate outlier identified within the *Addsupport* distribution. The effects of the univariate outlier were evident in all of the measures to assess normality. This demonstrates how one case outlier can have a substantial effect on the normal shape of a distribution. However, the skewness z-scores, kurtosis z-scores, S-W statistics, and Q-Q plots were all in the acceptable range for us to assume that the distributions were normal enough to conduct the RM-ANOVA.

Next, we assess the homogeneity of variances and covariances (sphericity) assumption. We will need to run the actual RM-ANOVA analysis to get information to assess this assumption.

Repeated-Measures Analysis of Variance of the Omnibus H_0

RM-ANOVA SPSS Commands

1. Click **Analyze** > click **General Linear Model** > click **Repeated Measures** > in the box that says **factor1**, type in *conditions* and in the box beside **Number of Levels:** type in the number *4* and click on the **Add** button and then click on the **Define** button.

FIGURE 8.7A, B, C, AND D Normal Q-Q Plots of Weight Loss by Weight Loss Intervention Conditions

(a)

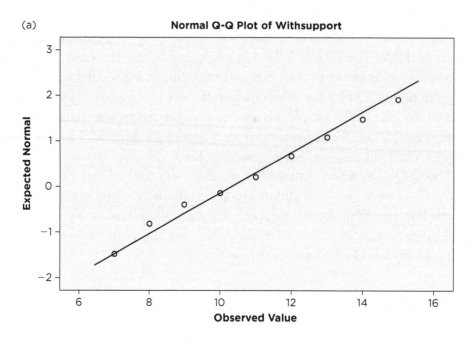

Normal Q-Q Plot of Withsupport

(b)

Normal Q-Q Plot of Removesupport

(c)

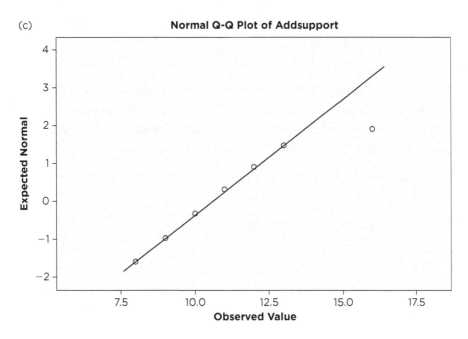

(d)

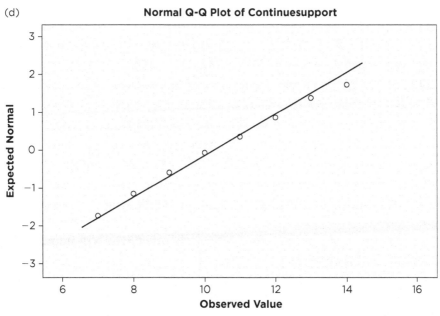

2. In a new window, click each of the four variables (*Withsupport*, *Remove-support*, *Addsupport*, and *Continuesupport*) to the section titled **Within-Subjects Variables (factor 1):**.

3. Click on the **Plots** button, then click over *conditions* to box under **Horizontal Axis:**, then click on the **Add** button and the **Continue** button.

4. Click on the **Options** button, click over **(OVERALL)** and *conditions* under the box title **Display means for:**, click on **Compare main effects** and select **LSD (none)** under **Confidence interval adjustment:**, click on **Descriptive statistics**, **Estimates of effect size**, and **Observed power**.

5. In the box next to **Significance level:**, type in .01 and click on the **Continue** button and click on **OK**.

6. Save the output as *RM-ANOVAResults*.

Sphericity

The assumption of sphericity means that there is a constant pattern of variances with each other and covariances with each other on the dependent variable weight loss across the four conditions. Remember that variance is the mean of the sum of the squared deviations from the mean score divided by the number of scores (minus 1), $S^2 = \Sigma(X - M)^2/N - 1$. Covariance is conveys the extent that two variables vary together, $\text{cov}_{XY} = \Sigma(X - M_x)(Y - M_y)/N - 1$.

Sphericity is similar to the assumption of homogeneity, but covariances are added, resulting in variance-covariance matrices that are assessed. Since there are four measures on the same dependent variable for each participant, the scores and means are dependent (related) to each other, producing covariances that need to be consistent with each other to accurately test the null hypothesis using RM-ANOVA.

We are using Mauchly's test to assess whether the variance-covariance matrix meets the assumption of sphericity by testing the following null hypothesis:

H_0: The variances are constant with each other, and covariances are constant with each other.

We want to retain the null hypothesis. If we reject the H_0, then we will have to make corrections to accurately interpret the *F*-test value produced from the RM-ANOVA.

TABLE 8.7 Mauchly's Test of Sphericity

Mauchly's Test of Sphericity[a]							
Measure: MEASURE_1							
Within-Subjects Effect	Mauchly's W	Approx. Chi-Square	df	Sig.	Epsilon[b]		
					Greenhouse-Geisser	Huynh-Feldt	Lower Bound
Conditions	.761	8.942	5	.112	.867	.945	.333

Tests the null hypothesis that the error covariance matrix of the orthonormalized transformed dependent variables is proportional to an identity matrix.

[a] Design: Intercept within Subjects.

[b] May be used to adjust the degrees of freedom for the averaged tests of significance. Corrected tests are displayed in the Tests of Within-Subjects Effects table (Table 8.8).

Design: Conditions.

On the output, refer to the table titled *Mauchly's Test of Sphericity* (see Table 8.7).

The significance level associated with Mauchly's W test is $p = .112$, which is larger than our $\alpha = .01$. We retain the H_0 that there is a constant pattern of variances and covariances. We have met the sphericity assumption. We will interpret the *F*-statistic results associated with the source *Sphericity Assumed*.

If we had rejected the H_0 that the variances and covariances are not constant, then we could use the df_t and df_e of the *Greenhouse-Geisser* or *Huynh-Feldt* to obtain a critical value to evaluate the significance of *F*. The adjusted degrees of freedom are obtained by taking the epsilons in the Mauchly table times the degrees of freedom of the *F*-test in the tests of the Within-Subjects Effects Table. The Greenhouse-Geisser is more conservative (especially with small samples) than the Huynh-Feldt to correct for problems with sphericity.

Summary of Underlying Assumptions Findings

The assumption of normality of the four distributions of *weight loss* is met based on the preponderance of evidence using several measures. The assumption of sphericity is also met.

PROGRESS REVIEW

1. The weight of participants was obtained at baseline. Then data were collected on the dependent variable (weight loss) in four three-month intervals over 12 months at the following conditions: (1) with support partners in treatment, (2) remove support partners in treatment, (3) add support partners in treatment, and (4) continue support partners in treatment.

2. Problems with data accuracy and missing data were ruled out in the early steps of the data-screening process.

3. The distributions of weight loss of the condition groups were assessed for compliance in meeting the underlying assumptions of using the RM-ANOVA. One participant had a weight loss score that was a univariate outlier. The decision was to keep the outlying score and participant in the study since the participant was found to be representative of the accessible population.

4. All other the measures of normality confirmed that the distributions met the underlying assumption of normality.

5. The underlying assumption of sphericity also was met.

6. The RM-ANOVA is conducted next.

RM-ANOVA Results

The following omnibus null hypothesis is tested next using the RM-ANOVA.

$$H_0: \mu_{1\text{Withsupport}} = \mu_{1\text{Removesupport}} = \mu_{1\text{Addsupport}} = \mu_{1\text{Continuesupport}}$$

Refer to the RM-ANOVA Results output reproduced in Table 8.8 as the table called *Tests of Within-Subjects Effects*.

See conditions under the column titled Source. We used the term *conditions* to reflect the independent variable in the study when we set up the data set. There are

TABLE 8.8 RM-ANOVA Results for the Omnibus Null Hypothesis

Tests of Within-Subjects Effects

Measure: MEASURE_1

Source		Type III Sum of Squares	df	Mean Square	F	Sig.	Partial Eta Squared	Noncent. Parameter	Observed Power[a]
Conditions	Sphericity assumed	1,036.364	3	345.455	110.325	.000	.764	330.976	1.000
	Greenhouse-Geisser	1,036.364	2.600	398.651	110.325	.000	.764	286.811	1.000
	Huynh-Feldt	1,036.364	2.834	365.689	110.325	.000	.764	312.663	1.000
	Lower bound	1,036.364	1.000	1,036.364	110.325	.000	.764	110.325	1.000
Error (conditions)	Sphericity assumed	319.386	102	3.131					
	Greenhouse-Geisser	319.386	88.389	3.613					
	Huynh-Feldt	319.386	96.356	3.315					
	Lower bound	319.386	34.000	9.394					

[a] Computed using alpha = .01

four rows under conditions, and we are going to use the row called "Sphericity assumed" since we previously found that are data met the underlying assumption of sphericity. We see that the Sig. value is .000 and that is less than our $\alpha = .01$, so we can reject the null hypothesis, $F(3, 102) = 110.325, p < .01$. There is a significant difference in means of weight loss pounds across the condition groups: (1) with support partners in treatment ($M = 10.314$, $SD = 2.246$), (2) remove support partners in treatment ($M = 4.114$, $SD = 1.676$), (3) add support partners in treatment ($M = 10.600$, $SD = 1.631$), and (4) continue support partners in treatment ($M = 10.257$, $SD = 1.821$).

We found that there are mean differences in weight loss among the four condition groups. Specifically, we will assess which pairs of means are significantly different from each other.

Post Hoc Multiple Comparisons of Pairs of Means

We rejected the omnibus null hypothesis, concluding that there was a significant difference in weight loss among the four condition groups. We also want to find which pairs of means are significantly different from each other. The Fisher's protected least significant differences (PLSD) *statistic* is used to make pairwise comparisons.

The results of comparing the pairs of means are in a table called Pairwise Comparisons in the RM-ANOVA results output (reproduced in Table 8.9).

The first column in Table 8.9 shows the mean pairs of condition group comparisons being made where 1 = with support partners in treatment ($M = 10.314$), 2 = remove support partners in treatment ($M = 4.114$), 3 = add support partners in treatment ($M = 10.600$), and 4 = continue support partners in treatment ($M = 10.257$).

The first row is comparing 1 (with support partners in treatment) ($M = 10.314$) to 2 (remove support partners in treatment) ($M = 4.114$). The Sig. value of the differences between the two means is .000, which reflects a significant difference ($p < .01$). The participants had significantly more weight loss with support partners in treatment than when the support partners were removed.

A review of the other rows shows that the mean weight loss of condition group 2 (remove support partners in treatment) ($M = 4.114$) is significantly lower than all of the other group means. And the other three groups are not

TABLE 8.9   Post Hoc Comparisons Using the Fisher's Protected Least Significant Differences (PLSD) Statistic

		Pairwise Comparisons				
		Measure: MEASURE_1				
					99% Confidence Interval for Difference[a]	
(I) Conditions	**(J) Conditions**	**Mean Difference (I − J)**	**Std. Error**	**Sig.**[a]	**Lower Bound**	**Upper Bound**
1	2	6.200*	.458	.000	4.950	7.450
	3	−.286	.435	.516	−1.472	.901
	4	.057	.494	.909	−1.289	1.404
2	1	−6.200*	.458	.000	−7.450	−4.950
	3	−6.486*	.379	.000	−7.519	−5.452
	4	−6.143*	.434	.000	−7.327	−4.958
3	1	.286	.435	.516	−.901	1.472
	2	6.486*	.379	.000	5.452	7.519
	4	.343	.315	.284	−.516	1.202
4	1	−.057	.494	.909	−1.404	1.289
	2	6.143*	.434	.000	4.958	7.327
	3	−.343	.315	.284	−1.202	.516

* Based on estimated marginal means.
* The mean difference is significant at the .01 level.
[a] Adjustment for multiple comparisons: least significant difference (equivalent to no adjustments).

significantly different from each other. We can conclude that when the support partners are included in the treatment of persons with weight problems, a significantly higher weight loss is experienced by the participants.

Trend Analysis

Trend analysis is another post hoc approach that is useful when the groups are defined by the independent variable ordered along a continuum (Howell, 2010). Trend analysis allows us to continue the analysis from the overall RM-ANOVA to an analysis of the characteristics of the shape of the relationship between the independent variable and the dependent variable. For example, one can mathematically model the form of the decline (or incline) of a dependent variable. Common shapes tested in

FIGURE 8.8 Profile Plot of Means of Weight Loss by Condition Groups

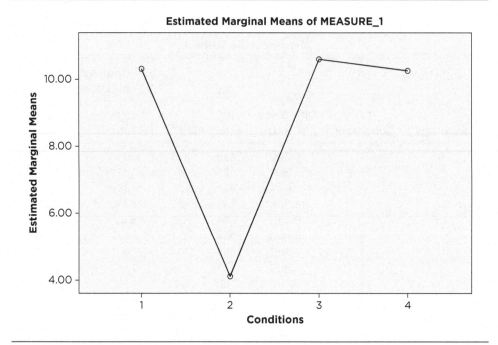

trend analysis are *linear trend* (straight line), *quadratic trend* (variation of a U or V shape), *cubic trend* (variation of an S shape), and *quartic trend* (similarities to previous shapes but including another bend in the shape).

In this study, we expect that the condition of removing the support partners from treatment for three months would decrease the weight loss of participants. When the support partners are added to treatment, there would be an increase in weight loss.

Looking at the profile plot of means of weight loss by condition groups from the RM-ANOVA results (see Figure 8.8), a V shape (quadratic trend) is evident. This graphical trend can be assessed for significance from information presented in the *Tests of Within-Subjects Contrasts* table in the RM-ANOVA output (see Table 8.10). The null we will be testing is H_0: Quadratic trend = 0. The row Conditions—Quadratic shows a Sig. value of .000, which is less than $\alpha = .01$ and therefore significant. There is a significant quadratic trend in the means of weight loss across the condition groups, $F(1, 34) = 114.583$, $p < .01$. The effect size of practical significance is substantial, $\eta_p^2 = .771$.

TABLE 8.10 Trends of Weight Loss Means Across the Condition Groups

Tests of Within-Subjects Contrasts

Measure: MEASURE_1

Source	Conditions	Type III Sum of Squares	df	Mean Square	F	Sig.	Partial Eta-Squared	Noncent. Parameter	Observed Power[a]
Conditions	Linear	69.773	1	69.773	15.682	.000	.316	15.682	.883
	Quadratic	300.179	1	300.179	114.583	.000	.771	114.583	1.000
	Cubic	666.413	1	666.413	286.676	.000	.894	286.676	1.000
Error	Linear	151.277	34	4.449					
(conditions)	Quadratic	89.071	34	2.620					
	Cubic	79.037	34	2.325					

[a] Computed using alpha = .01

HYPOTHESIS TESTING STEP 6: MAKE DECISION REGARDING THE H_0 AND INTERPRET POST HOC EFFECT SIZES AND CONFIDENCE INTERVALS

The results showed that there was an overall significant difference among the weight loss means across the four conditions. The post hoc analyses showed that when the partner support was removed, the resulting mean weight loss was significantly lower from all of the other three conditions of Withsupport, Addsupport, and Continuesupport. Moreover, we discovered a significant quadratic trend in the condition means that showed the dramatic effect on weight loss of removing the partner support (Removesupport). The magnitude of treatment effect, post hoc power, and confidence intervals are presented next to provide further clarification to the results.

Magnitude of Treatment Effect—Post Hoc Effect Size

Again refer to the *Tests of Within-Subjects Effects* table of the RM-ANOVA results output (see Table 8.8). You see a partial eta-squared value ($\eta_p^2 = .764$) on the "Conditions—Sphericity assumed" line next to the *Sig.* value. Eta-squared ranges from 0 (small) to 1.0 (large).

We can interpret the $\eta_p^2 = .764$ by converting the fraction to a percentage by moving the decimal two spaces to the right, and report that approximately 76.40 percent of the change in the dependent variable (weight loss) can be attributed to the independent variable (weight loss intervention). There is clearly a substantial magnitude of treatment effect of the weight loss program on weight loss.

Post Hoc Power

The actual power after the study was conducted is reported in the Tests of Within-Subjects Effects table of the RM-ANOVA results output (see Table 8.8). You see the observed power value (1.000) on the "Conditions—Sphericity assumed" line at the end of the row. We had a 100 percent chance of correctly rejecting a false null hypothesis in favor of the alternative hypothesis with a post hoc effect size of .764, a sample size of 35, and an alpha of .01. This post hoc power is consistently large as was the a priori power value of .901.

Confidence Intervals of Mean Differences

The .99 CI for each means difference is provided in the output under Multiple Comparisons Table (see Table 8.9). The interpretations of the mean difference confidence intervals for the three paired-mean comparisons that are significant ($\mu_{1Withsupport}$ vs. $\mu_{2Removesupport}$), ($\mu_{3Addsupport}$ vs. $\mu_{2Removesupport}$), and ($\mu_{4Continuesupport}$ vs. $\mu_{2Removesupport}$) are presented next. The .99 CI interval for the means difference in weight loss comparing 1 (with support partners in treatment) to 2 (remove support partners in treatment) is $(4.950) - (7.450)$. The probability is .99 that this interval will include the true means difference between the population means of weight loss between 1 (with support partners in treatment) and 2 (remove support partners in treatment) and conditions for persons who are overweight. The .99 confidence interval for the means difference in weight loss comparing 3 (add support partners in treatment) to 2 (remove support partners in treatment) is $(5.452) - (7.519)$, and this interval will include the true means difference between the population means of weight loss 99 times in 100. The $CI_{.99}$ for the difference between 4 (continue support partners in treatment) and 2 (remove support partners in treatment) is $(4.958) - (7.327)$. The lower and upper limits of all of the intervals are positive, which shows the high probability associated with having an increase in weight loss when support partners are involved in treatment.

PROGRESS REVIEW

1. After concluding that the group distributions met the sphericity assumption, the omnibus null hypothesis was rejected ($p < .01$), indicating the existence of significant mean differences.

2. The overall magnitude of treatment effect of the independent variable (weight loss intervention) on the dependent variable (weight loss) was substantial, $\eta_p^2 = .764$.

3. The post hoc power value (observed power = 1.0) showed that we had a 100 percent chance of correctly rejecting a false null hypothesis with a post hoc effect size of .764, a

sample size of 35, and an alpha of .01. This post hoc power is consistent with the a priori power value of .901.

4. The pairwise mean comparisons using the PLSD statistic showed that when the support partners are included in the treatment of persons with weight problems, a significantly higher weight loss is experienced by the participants.

5. The .99 confidence intervals for the mean differences show the high probability associated with having an increase in weight loss when support partners are involved in treatment.

6. The trend analysis demonstrated a significant quadratic trend, providing further evidence for the increase in weight loss when support partners are included in behavioral weight control treatment.

FORMULA CALCULATIONS OF THE STUDY RESULTS

The RM-ANOVA summary table specifications are found in Table 8.11. The column and row means by subject and condition that we will be using in the formula calculations are found in Table 8.12.

TABLE 8.11   RM-ANOVA Summary Table Specifications MS_T/MS_E

Source of Variation	df	Sum of Squares (SS)	Mean Square (MS)	F
Within subjects (S)	$N - 1$	$T\Sigma(M_S - M_{TOT})^2$	SS_S/df_S	—
Treatment (T)	$K - 1$	$N\Sigma(M_T - M_{TOT})^2$	SS_T/df_T	MS_T/MS_E
Error (E)	$(K - 1)(N - 1)$	$SS_{TOT} - SS_T - SS_S$	SS_E/df_E	—
Total (TOT)	$N_{TOT} - 1$	$N\Sigma(M_{all} - M_{TOT})^2$	—	—

$df_S = N - 1$ is the within-subjects degrees of freedom where N is the number of subjects.
$df_T = K - 1$ is the treatment degrees of freedom where K is the number of treatments.
$df_E = (K - 1)(N - 1)$ is the error degrees of freedom: the number of treatments minus 1 times the number of subjects minus 1.
$df_{TOT} = N_{TOT} - 1$ is the total degrees of freedom based on N scores with one score unable to vary. N_{TOT} is calculated by $[(K)(N) - 1]$.

TABLE 8.12   Study Data with Column and Row Means by Subject and Condition

Subject	With support	Remove support	Add support	Continue support	Subject Means
1	11	6	11	9	9.250
2	8	5	11	8	8.000
3	8	4	12	10	8.500
4	8	3	10	12	8.250
5	7	4	9	11	7.750
6	12	2	10	8	8.000
7	12	6	10	9	9.250
8	13	7	9	7	9.000
9	7	1	12	14	8.500
10	8	2	11	13	8.500
11	11	4	11	12	9.500
12	13	4	10	11	9.500
13	14	5	10	10	9.750
14	9	4	11	9	8.250
15	9	6	9	8	8.000
16	8	3	8	8	6.750
17	11	2	10	9	8.000
18	11	4	10	7	8.000
19	12	5	13	12	10.500
20	10	4	11	12	9.250
21	10	3	10	11	8.500
22	7	5	12	9	8.250
23	7	6	9	10	8.000
24	15	7	16	14	13.000
25	14	2	8	10	8.500
26	12	1	13	10	9.000
27	11	4	11	12	9.500
28	11	4	12	11	9.500
29	10	3	10	10	8.250
30	9	3	9	9	7.500
31	12	5	8	12	9.250
32	11	5	10	11	9.250
33	9	6	12	10	9.250
34	8	7	11	12	9.500
35	13	2	12	9	9.000
Treatment means	10.314	4.114	10.600	10.257	8.821

Calculation of Sums of Squares

The within, treatment, total, and error sum of squares are calculated with formulas using the row means, column means, and grand mean ($M_{TOT} = 8.821$) using the data from Table 8.12. The calculated results are then transferred to the RM-ANOVA summary table, Table 8.13.

$$SS_{Within} = T\Sigma(M_S - M_{tot})^2$$
$$= 4\Sigma(9.250 - 8.821)^2 + \cdots + (9.000 - 8.821)^2 = 150.730$$
$$SS_{Treatment} = N\Sigma(M_T - M_{tot})^2$$
$$= 35\Sigma(10.314 - 8.821)^2 + (4.114 - 8.821)^2 + (10.600 - 8.821)^2$$
$$+ (10.257 - 8.821)^2$$
$$= 35\Sigma(1.493)^2 + (-4.707)^2 + (1.779)^2 + (1.436)^2$$
$$= 35\Sigma 2.229 + 22.156 + 3.165 + 2.062$$
$$= 35(29.612)$$
$$= 1036.42$$

$$SS_{Total} = N\Sigma(M_{allscores} - M_{tot})^2$$
$$= \Sigma(11 - 8.821)^2 + (8 - 8.821)^2 + \cdots + (12 - 8.821)^2$$
$$+ (9 - 8.821)^2 = 1506.536$$
$$SS_{Error} = SS_{Total} - SS_{Treatment} - SS_{Subjects}$$
$$= 1506.536 - 1036.42 - 150.730$$
$$SS_{Error} = 319.386$$

TABLE 8.13 RM-ANOVA Summary Table Specifications

Source of Variation	df	Sum of Squares (SS)	Mean Square (MS)	F
Within Subjects (S)	34	150.73		
Treatment (T)	3	1,036.42	345.473	110.3
Error (E)	102	319.386	3.131	—
Total (TOT)	139	1,506.536	—	—

FIGURE 8.9 Hypothesis Testing Graph RM-ANOVA

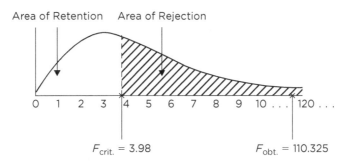

Figure 8.9 shows a visual representation of the findings. A critical value (CV) is obtained using an online calculator.

> Go to www.danielsoper.com > select **Statistics Calculators** > select **F-Distribution** > select **Critical F-value Calculator** > type in 3 next to **Degrees of freedom 1:** > type 102 next to **Degrees of freedom 2:** > type 0.01 beside **Probability level:** > click on **Calculate!**

The F critical value is 3.97960580, rounded to 3.98. We place the F critical value on the abscissa (base of the curve) of the F-distribution curve. Then, we place the obtained omnibus ANOVA value of $F = 110.3$ on the curve. The area of rejection begins on the abscissa at the CV, and any obtained F to the right of the CV informs us to reject the null hypothesis. Our $F_{obtained} = 110.3$ falls in the area of rejection to the right of the CV = 3.98, so we reject the H_0, concluding that if the null hypothesis is true we would have obtained results like these less than 1 percent of the time. There is a difference in weight loss across the four conditions at the .01 level of significance.

Post Hoc Effect Size—Partial Eta-Squared

The η_p^2 is calculated next, resulting in $\eta_p^2 = .764$; this has a large strength effect according to Cohen's convention, where approximately 1 percent to 6 percent is low, >6 percent to 14 percent is medium, and >14 percent is large. There clearly is a very large magnitude of treatment effect of the weight-loss intervention program on increasing weight loss.

$$\eta_p^2 = \frac{SS_{\text{WithinSubjects}}}{SS_{\text{WithinSubjects}} + SS_{\text{Error}}}$$

$$= \frac{1{,}036.42}{1{,}036.42 + 319.386}$$

$$= \frac{1{,}036.42}{1{,}355.806}$$

$$\eta_p^2 = .764$$

Post Hoc Paired-Means Comparisons

Fisher's Protected Least Significant Differences (PLSD)

Fisher's protected least significant differences (PLSD) is a multiple comparison procedure to assess for differences in pairs of means following a significant omnibus F statistic. It is considered a liberal approach since more mean differences are found with this procedure than with most other procedures. The mean square error term from the omnibus F analysis is used in the denominator of the PLSD formula and helps protect against making a Type I error. In this problem the MS_e is 3.131, which can be found in Table 8.13.

We start by obtaining a t critical value to compare to obtained t-values using an online calculator.

> Go to www.danielsoper.com > click on **Statistics Calculators** > scroll down and click on **t-Distribution** > click on **Student t-Value Calculator** > type in 34 beside **Degrees of freedom:** > click 0.01 next to **Probability level:** > click on **Calculate!** and the answer is **t-value (two-tailed):** ±2.72839437.

The rounded value is $t_{\text{CV}} = \pm 2.728$ using an $\alpha = .01$ with 34 df ($N_{\text{pairs}} - 1, 35 - 1 = 34$). The obtained PLSD values for mean pairs are calculated next, and the obtained t values are then compared to the $t_{\text{CV}} = \pm 2.728$. Obtained values greater than the $t_{\text{CV}} = \pm 2.728$ reflect significant differences ($p < .01$) between pairs of means.

Withsupport Mean versus Removesupport Mean

$$t_{PLSD} = \frac{\overline{X}_1 - \overline{X}_2}{\sqrt{MS_e \left(\frac{1}{n_1} + \frac{1}{n_2} \right)}}$$

$$= \frac{10.314 - 4.114}{\sqrt{3.131 \left(\frac{1}{35} + \frac{1}{35} \right)}}$$

$$= \frac{6.200}{\sqrt{3.131(.029 + .029)}}$$

$$= \frac{6.200}{\sqrt{3.131(.058)}}$$

$$= \frac{6.200}{\sqrt{.182}}$$

$$= \frac{6.200}{.427}$$

$$t_{PLSD} = 14.520, \ p < .01$$

Withsupport Mean versus Addsupport Mean

$$t_{PLSD} = \frac{\overline{X}_1 - \overline{X}_3}{\sqrt{MS_e \left(\frac{1}{n_1} + \frac{1}{n_2} \right)}}$$

$$= \frac{10.314 - 10.600}{\sqrt{3.131 \left(\frac{1}{35} + \frac{1}{35} \right)}}$$

$$= \frac{-.286}{\sqrt{3.131(.029 + .029)}}$$

$$= \frac{-.286}{\sqrt{3.131(.058)}}$$

$$= \frac{-.286}{\sqrt{.182}}$$

$$= \frac{-.286}{.427}$$

$$t_{\text{PLSD}} = -.670, \ p > .01$$

Withsupport Mean versus Continuesupport Mean

$$t_{\text{PLSD}} = \frac{\overline{X}_1 - \overline{X}_4}{\sqrt{MS_e \left(\frac{1}{n_1} + \frac{1}{n_2} \right)}}$$

$$= \frac{10.314 - 10.257}{\sqrt{3.131 \left(\frac{1}{35} + \frac{1}{35} \right)}}$$

$$= \frac{.057}{\sqrt{3.131(.029 + .029)}}$$

$$= \frac{.057}{\sqrt{3.131(.058)}}$$

$$= \frac{.057}{\sqrt{.182}}$$

$$= \frac{.057}{.427}$$

$$t_{\text{PLSD}} = .130, \ p > .01$$

Removesupport Mean versus Addsupport Mean

$$t_{PLSD} = \frac{\overline{X}_2 - \overline{X}_3}{\sqrt{MS_e\left(\dfrac{1}{n_1} + \dfrac{1}{n_2}\right)}}$$

$$= \frac{4.114 - 10.600}{\sqrt{3.131\left(\dfrac{1}{35} + \dfrac{1}{35}\right)}}$$

$$= \frac{-6.486}{\sqrt{3.131(.029 + .029)}}$$

$$= \frac{-6.486}{\sqrt{3.131(.058)}}$$

$$= \frac{-6.486}{\sqrt{.182}}$$

$$= \frac{-6.486}{.427}$$

$$t_{PLSD} = -15.190, \ p < .01$$

Removesupport Mean versus Continuesupport Mean

$$t_{PLSD} = \frac{\overline{X}_2 - \overline{X}_4}{\sqrt{MS_e\left(\dfrac{1}{n_1} + \dfrac{1}{n_2}\right)}}$$

$$= \frac{4.114 - 10.257}{\sqrt{3.131\left(\dfrac{1}{35} + \dfrac{1}{35}\right)}}$$

$$= \frac{-6.143}{\sqrt{3.131(.029 + .029)}}$$

$$= \frac{-6.143}{\sqrt{3.131(.058)}}$$

$$= \frac{-6.143}{\sqrt{.182}}$$

$$= \frac{-6.143}{.427}$$

$$t_{\text{PLSD}} = -14.386, \ p < .01$$

Addsupport Mean versus Continuesupport Mean

$$t_{\text{PLSD}} = \frac{\overline{X}_3 - \overline{X}_4}{\sqrt{MS_e \left(\frac{1}{n_1} + \frac{1}{n_2} \right)}}$$

$$= \frac{10.600 - 10.257}{\sqrt{3.131 \left(\frac{1}{35} + \frac{1}{35} \right)}}$$

$$= \frac{.343}{\sqrt{3.131(.029 + .029)}}$$

$$= \frac{.343}{\sqrt{3.131(.058)}}$$

$$= \frac{.343}{\sqrt{.182}}$$

$$= \frac{.343}{.427}$$

$$t_{\text{PLSD}} = .803, \ p > .01$$

The three condition means of with support, add support, and continue support are significantly different ($p < .01$) from the remove support mean;

however, the three condition means are not significantly different from each other. These results are the same as we found from the PLSD pairwise comparisons in the SPSS results (Table 8.9).

Study Results

The purpose of this study was to determine if support partners included in a behavioral weight control treatment (BWCT) program for persons who are overweight would increase their weight loss. A repeated-treatment design with a group of participants was used in the study. After obtaining a baseline weight from participants, they received three months of BWCT including support partners and their weight loss was measured. Then the BWCT continued, removing the support partners for three months, and the participants' weight loss was measured again. The support partners were added back to the BWCT for three months and the participants' weight loss was measured. Finally, the BWCT and support partners were continued for three more months and weight loss measurements were made one last time.

The sample consisted of 35 participants who were randomly selected from a client population of a large weight loss center in a metropolitan area in the United States. The average age of the participants was 40 years old ($SD = 3.20$). Each participant has a support partner (friend) who was also participating in the behavioral weight control treatment, and the friends' average age was 41 ($SD = 5.23$).

An a priori power analysis was conducted using $\alpha = .01$, $N = 35$, a priori effect size $f = .734$, and average correlation of measures $= .55$. The analysis showed a power $\geq.80$, so we were confident that we would correctly reject a false H_0 in our study and avoid making a Type II error.

The data were screened prior to testing the null hypothesis. The accuracy of the data set was checked and confirmed. The data set had no missing data. One participant's weight loss score was a univariate outlier ($z = 3.312 > 3.29$) but was determined to be representative of the target population. Additional measures were used to assess the normality of the data set, including skewness and kurtosis z-scores, Shapiro-Wilk statistics, and Q-Q plots. All normality measures reflected acceptable normality. Sphericity was assessed, and the variance and covariances of weight loss across the conditions were constant. The means and standard deviations of the sample at each condition were: (1) with support partners in treatment ($M = 10.314$, $SD = 2.246$), (2) remove support partners in treatment ($M = 4.114$,

$SD = 1.676$), (3) add support partners in treatment ($M = 10.600$, $SD = 1.631$), and (4) continue support partners in treatment ($M = 10.257$, $SD = 1.821$).

A significant difference in the four means was found using a RM-ANOVA, $F(3, 102) = 110.325$, $p < .01$. The magnitude of treatment effect was very large, $\eta_p^2 = .764$. The PLSD statistic was used to assess the pairs of means for significance. The mean of weight loss after removing support partners from BWCT was significantly lower ($p < .01$) than the means of all of the other conditions that included support partners with BWCT. No other pairs were significantly different among the three conditions that included support partners.

The $CI_{.99}$ intervals for the mean difference of significant pairs were 1 (with support partners in treatment) vs. 2 (remove support partners in treatment) $(4.950) - (7.450)$, 3 (add support partners in treatment) vs. 2 (remove support partners in treatment) $(5.452) - (7.519)$, 4 (continue support partners in treatment) vs. 2 (remove support partners in treatment) $(4.958) - (7.327)$. The lower and upper limits of all of the intervals were positive, which shows the high probability associated with having an increase in weight loss when support partners are involved in treatment. A trend analysis resulted in a significant quadratic trend ($p < .01$) reinforcing an increase in weight loss when support partners are included in behavioral weight control treatment.

In conclusion, the results of this study demonstrate that when support partners are included in behavioral weight control treatment for persons who are overweight, weight loss increases significantly when compared to BWCT without the use of support partners.

SUMMARY

We used an RM-ANOVA within a repeated-treatment design applied to a research problem within the context of the hypothesis-testing process. Research questions and hypotheses were developed that incorporated independent and dependent variables. We established a criterion alpha level considering Type I and II errors. An a priori power analysis using G*Power was conducted to assess the fidelity of the study.

Data were entered for computer analyses using the IBM SPSS statistical program (see Table 8.14). Data diagnostics were conducted to make sure that data were accurate and that we met univariate underlying assumptions of normality, sphericity, and independence of scores. Interpretations were discussed of

TABLE 8.14 Repeated-Measures Analysis of Variance Data

ID	With support	Remove support	Add support	Continue support
1	11	6	11	9
2	8	5	11	8
3	8	4	12	10
4	8	3	10	12
5	7	4	9	11
6	12	2	10	8
7	12	6	10	9
8	13	7	9	7
9	7	1	12	14
10	8	2	11	13
11	11	4	11	12
12	13	4	10	11
13	14	5	10	10
14	9	4	11	9
15	9	6	9	8
16	8	3	8	8
17	11	2	10	9
18	11	4	10	7
19	12	5	13	12
20	10	4	11	12
21	10	3	10	11
22	7	5	12	9
23	7	6	9	10
24	15	7	16	14
25	14	2	8	10
26	12	1	13	10
27	11	4	11	12
28	11	4	12	11
29	10	3	10	10
30	9	3	9	9
31	12	5	8	12
32	11	5	10	11
33	9	6	12	10
34	8	7	11	12
35	13	2	12	9

the omnibus RM-ANOVA results, pairwise mean comparisons, trend analysis, effect size, post hoc power, and confidence intervals. Formula calculations were conducted for the RM-ANOVA and pairwise mean comparisons. Finally, a summary of the results was presented.

PROBLEM ASSIGNMENT

Another RM-ANOVA problem with data set is found on the companion website. Use the worksheet that is provided along with the steps used in this chapter to complete the assignment.

KEY TERMS

average correlation

compound symmetry

covariances

cubic trend

Greenhouse-Geisser

Huynh-Feldt

linear trend

Mauchly's Test of Spericity

mixed-subject ANOVA statistical design

protected least significant differences (PLSD)

quadratic trend

quartic trend

repeated-measures ANOVA (RM-ANOVA)

repeated-treatment design

sphericity

Sphericity Assumed

Tests of Within-Subjects Effects

trend analysis

within-subjects design

Chapter 9

RANDOMIZED FACTORIAL

EXPERIMENTAL DESIGN

USING A FACTORIAL ANOVA

LEARNING OBJECTIVES

○ Demonstrate how to develop research questions and hypotheses as they relate to a research problem incorporating the effects of two independent variables on one dependent variable.

○ Identify the components and application of a randomized factorial experimental design.

○ Examine prestudy considerations, conduct data diagnostics, and execute a two-way analysis of variance (ANOVA) using IBM SPSS and formulas.

○ Perform post hoc analyses and understand the study findings by combining the various analyses.

A study example is presented assessing methods to retain cocaine abusers in treatment. A partially randomized factorial design using a two-way ANOVA is used to evaluate if a standard care plus contingency management intervention can improve the treatment completion rate of cocaine abusers. Also assessed is whether the number of prior treatment attempts has an effect on treatment retention.

An a priori power analysis is conducted prior to the factorial ANOVA. Specifically, a 2 × 2 ANOVA is executed resulting in F-tests for two main effects, one interaction, and simple effects. The results of the several analyses are presented.

RESEARCH PROBLEM

People with substance abuse disorders typically try several treatment attempts over the life course of their disorders. In fact, Dennis, Scott, Funk, and Foss (2005) reported that substance abusers attempt treatment three to four times over a median of nine years before reaching a minimum of one year of sustained abstinence. The purpose of this study is to assess whether a behavioral intervention known as contingency management (CM) can improve treatment retention compared across prior treatment attempts by cocaine abusers. This simulated example approximates findings of a study by Rash, Alessi, and Petry (2008).

A sample size of 125 participants was obtained. Two individuals met exclusion criteria and three persons dropped out of the study before it began, resulting in a study sample of 120 cocaine abusers who sought treatment. Fifty-four percent ($n = 65$) of the participants were males, while females comprised 46 percent ($n = 55$) of the sample. The average age of participants was 35, and on average they had abused cocaine for over 10 years ($M = 10.50$ years, $SD = 7.23$).

STUDY VARIABLES

The independent and dependent variables are identified next. Additionally, the operational definitions of the variables are described.

Independent Variables

Treatment condition is one independent variable (IV$_A$), and *treatment status* is a second independent variable (IV$_B$). Independent variables are also referred to as *factors*, and we will be using both terms synonymously in our discussion. *Treatment retention* is the dependent variable.

Treatment condition is operationally defined with two levels: (1) standard care (SC) of substance abuse outpatient treatment and (2) standard care + contingency management (CM). The SC level for participants with cocaine use disorders involved group therapy, psycho-education, skills-based instruction, 12-step treatment, and screening of breath and urine samples over 12 weeks. The participants in the SC + CM level condition received standard care as just described, with the added benefit of being given a financial reinforcement for verified abstinence and goal-related activity completion over the same time period. Participants' abstinence from cocaine during treatment was measured with 21 sets of breath and urine samples over the 12 weeks. Each time the participants gave a clean breath and urine sample they received a financial reinforcement. Moreover, each time the participants completed a goal-related activity they received money as a reinforcement. The scale of measurement of the IV_A is discrete-nominal (categorical) since the conditions are designed to be mutually exclusive from each other with no intended order.

Treatment status is the second independent variable (IV_B) and is used in this study to determine if the number of previous attempts by participants to treat their cocaine disorder affects treatment retention. Treatment status in the study example is operationally defined as (1) 0–1 prior treatment attempts and (2) ≥ 2 prior treatment attempts. The scale of measurement of the IV_B also is discrete-nominal (categorical).

Dependent Variable

The dependent variable (DV) is *treatment retention*, operationally defined as the number of successful weeks in treatment. Since there are 12 weeks of treatment, the possible range of scores for the dependent variable is 0–12 weeks. The DV is continuously scaled (ratio) variable with equal distances between number points and a true zero reference.

RESEARCH DESIGN

The research design used for this research example is a *factorial design* (Shadish, Cook, & Campbell, 2002) to assess the effects of two independent variables, *treatment condition* (X_A) and *treatment status* (X_B), on one dependent variable (*treatment retention*).

TABLE 9.1 2 × 2 Factorial Design Matrix

		X_B Treatment	Status
		0–1 Prior treatment attempts (1)	≥2 Prior treatment attempts (2)
X_A Treatment	SC (1)	Cell X_{A1B1}	Cell X_{A1B2}
Condition	SC + CM (2)	Cell X_{A2B1}	Cell X_{A2B2}

This is a 2 × 2 *factorial design* that is represented as a matrix in Table 9.1. It is a partially randomized design in which participants were randomly assigned to the standard condition and the standard condition + contingency management condition. However, the independent variable of Treatment Status is an attribute IV since participants bring with them prior treatment attempts, resulting in being classified as either 0–1 prior treatment attempts or ≥2 prior treatment attempts.

The two levels, SC (1) and SC + CM (2), of the independent variable X_A *Treatment Condition* are two rows in the matrix. The two levels, 0–1 Prior Treatment Attempts (1) and ≥2 Prior Treatment Attempts (2), of the second independent variable X_B *Treatment Status* are columns in the matrix. This 2 × 2 factorial design creates four cells. In this study, we are using a between 2 × 2 randomized factorial design in which the cells are *independent* or *orthogonal* from each other. There are different participants in each cell receiving a unique combination of one level of each independent variable. For example, participants in Cell X_{A1B1} will receive the SC treatment level condition and they will be individuals who have had 0–1 prior treatment attempts. A different group of participants who are in Cell X_{A2B2} will receive the SC + CM treatment level condition and they will have ≥2 prior treatment attempts.

The 2 × 2 factorial design can be diagrammed as follows:

$R\ X_{A1B1}\ O$

$R\ X_{A1B2}\ O$

$R\ X_{A2B1}\ O$

$R\ X_{A2B2}\ O$

Each line in the diagram represents an independent group (four groups [cells]), and the R symbolizes random assignment to each group condition. The combination of one level of each independent variable represents the unique treatment condition and treatment status of the participants in each independent group: (1) X_{A1B1} ([SC] and [0–1 prior treatment attempts]), (2) X_{A1B2} ([SC] and [≥2 prior treatment attempts]), (3) X_{A2B1} ([SC + CM] and [0–1 prior treatment attempts]), and (4) X_{A2B2} ([SC + CM] and [≥2 prior treatment attempts]). The observation (O) is the post measure following 12 weeks of treatment implementation reflecting the number of weeks completed successfully in treatment, which is the dependent variable, treatment retention.

Statistical Analysis: Factorial Analysis of Variance

A factorial ANOVA is used to test the effects of two (or more) independent variables (*main effects*) on the same dependent variable and also examine how the independent variables influence each other on the dependent variable (*interaction effects*). The term *factor* is synonymous with independent variable, and a factorial ANOVA also is referred to as a multifactor ANOVA, reflecting the fact that there is more than one independent variable used in the statistical design. We can also use the descriptor *two-way ANOVA* since there are two independent variables in this study.

In our example, a 2×2 ANOVA means that there are two independent variables (factors) with two levels to each independent variable (factor). The initial analyses test the null hypotheses associated with the effects of each independent variable (factor) on the dependent variable (two main effects), and a combination of effects on the dependent variable from certain levels of the first independent variable (factor) with certain levels of the second independent variable (factor) (one interaction effect). If the interaction effect is significant, we will conduct a *simple effects analysis* to determine which levels of the first independent variable with which levels of the second independent variable interact to produce significant effects on the dependent variable.

Any ANOVA can be classified as being a between-subjects, within-subjects, or mixed-subjects ANOVA design. A *between-subjects ANOVA design* compares participant scores across groups that are not dependent on each other. A *within-subjects ANOVA design* compares repeated-measured scores across participants. A *mixed-subjects ANOVA design* combines both analyses between scores of independent groups and within analyses of repeated measured scores of participants. In this study, the 2×2 factorial ANOVA is a between-subjects ANOVA design. We will be analyzing scores across independent groups, and there are no repeated measurements on participants.

Factorial ANOVA models can get more complex (higher orders) such as a $2 \times 3 \times 2$ ANOVA, which means the analysis would involved three independent variables, the first IV with two levels, the second IV with three levels, and a third IV with two levels. We can visualize this analysis with a three-dimensional cube (having 12 cells) where we are analyzing rows (first IV with levels), columns (second IV with levels), and layers (third IV with levels) and then the interactions between rows and columns, rows and layers, columns and layers, and rows, columns, and layers. So, in the first analysis there would be seven null hypotheses tested. Then the many possible post hoc and simple effects analyses would be conducted.

The following underlying assumptions need to be met in order to use a factorial ANOVA. Data screening will be conducted to assess whether the data set meets these three assumptions:

1. *Normality.* The scores on the dependent variable for each condition are normally distributed around their mean.

2. *Homogeneity of variance.* The variances of the scores of the dependent variable across the conditions should be constant.

3. *Independence of observations.* The observations are independent from one another and not correlated with each other.

PROGRESS REVIEW

1. The research problem was presented that focuses on whether a contingency management approach added to standard care for cocaine abusers can increase their completion rate in treatment. The independent variables are Treatment Condition (SC vs. SC + CM) and Treatment Status (0–1 prior treatment attempts vs. ≥2 prior treatment attempts), and their effects on the dependent variable (Treatment Retention) will be assessed.

2. The 120 participants are randomly assigned to the four treatment conditions using a 2×2 randomized factorial design.

3. The changes in the dependent variable, *Treatment Retention*, are operationally defined as successful weeks in treatment and will be assessed across the conditions using a two-way analysis of variance statistic.

4. Next, the research questions are stated and we begin completing the steps of the hypothesis-testing process.

STATING THE OMNIBUS (COMPREHENSIVE) RESEARCH QUESTIONS

The statistical results of a two-way ANOVA automatically generate three findings, which are two main effects and one interaction effect. Additional statistical findings can be created from these basic three analyses. We are going to start by identifying the three omnibus research questions that relate the basic analysis of the 2×2 ANOVA used in this problem. The steps of the hypothesis-testing process related to this research problem will be presented following the statement of the three research questions.

Omnibus Research Questions (RQs)

RQ_1 (Main Effect of Treatment Condition): To what extent will the standard care + contingency management condition produce significantly higher treatment retention (successful weeks in treatment) among participants when compared to the standard care condition?

RQ_2 (Main Effect of Treatment Status): To what extent will the ≥ 2 prior treatment attempts level result in higher treatment retention (successful weeks in treatment) among participants when compared to the 0–1 prior treatment attempts level?

RQ_3 (Interaction Effect of Treatment Condition & Treatment Status): To what extent will there be significant mean differences in treatment retention (successful weeks in treatment) across levels of treatment condition and treatment status? (Or it could be stated: To what extent will there be a significant inter-action effect between treatment condition and treatment status on treatment retention as measured by successful weeks in treatment?)

HYPOTHESIS TESTING STEP 1: ESTABLISH THE ALTERNATIVE (RESEARCH) HYPOTHESIS (H_a)

The three omnibus alternative hypotheses for our research problem are stated next in both narrative and symbolic formats. We also will be addressing sub-questions and subhypotheses following the overall analysis.

Omnibus Narrative Alternative Hypotheses (H_a)

H_{a1} (Main Effect of Treatment Condition): The standard care + contingency management condition will produce significantly higher treatment retention (successful weeks in treatment) among participants when compared to the standard care condition without the contingency management (CM) condition.

H_{a2} (Main Effect of Treatment Status): The ≥ 2 prior treatment attempts level will result in higher treatment retention (successful weeks in treatment) among participants when compared to the 0–1 prior treatment attempts level.

H_{a3} (Interaction Effect of Treatment Condition & Treatment Status): There will be significant mean differences in treatment retention (suc-cessful weeks in treatment) across levels of treatment condition and treatment status.

Symbolic Alternative Hypotheses (H_a)

$$H_{a1} : \text{(Main Effect of Treatment Condition): } \mu_1 < \mu_2$$

where μ_1 = population mean of treatment retention (successful weeks in treatment) of participants in the SC level of the *treatment condition* being estimated by the sample mean

μ_2 = population mean of treatment retention (successful weeks in treatment) of participants in the SC + CM level of the *treatment condition* being estimated by the sample mean

$$H_{a2}: \text{(Main Effect of Treatment Status): } \mu_1 < \mu_2$$

where μ_1 = population mean of treatment retention (successful weeks in treatment) of participants in the 0–1 prior treatment attempts level of the *treatment status* being estimated by the sample mean

μ_2 = population mean of treatment retention (successful weeks in treatment) of participants in the ≥ 2 prior treatment attempts level of the *treatment status* being estimated by the sample mean

$$H_{a3}: \text{(Interaction Effect of Treatment Condition \& Treatment Status)}$$
$$: \mu_1 \times \mu_2 > 0$$

where μ_1 = population means of *treatment retention* (successful weeks in treatment) of participants in both levels of the treatment condition (SC and SC + CM) estimated by the sample means

μ_2 = population means of *treatment retention* (successful weeks in treatment) of participants in both levels of *treatment status* (0–1 prior attempts and ≥ 2 prior treatment attempts) estimated by the sample means

The alternative hypotheses for the main effects are directional. The SC + CM level of treatment condition is expected to produce better treatment retention (successful weeks in treatment) when compared to the SC level. The ≥ 2 prior treatment attempts level of treatment status is expected to generate higher treatment retention when compared to 0–1 prior treatment attempts. The interaction alternative hypothesis is stated in a nondirectional format. The specific differences in treatment retention across levels of treatment condition and treatment status are not specified.

Jones and Tukey (2000) Recommended Process to Reach Conclusions

We have three possible decisions that can be made for each of the three hypotheses following the recommendations by Jones and Tukey (2000). For the first two main effects, there are three possible conclusions for each main effect: (1) the mean number of treatment completed weeks resulting from the SC (μ_1) condition is higher than for the SC + CM condition (μ_2), (2) the mean number of treatment completed weeks resulting from the SC (μ_1) condition is lower than for the SC + CM condition (μ_2), or (3) the conclusions are indefinite. The two possible conclusions for the interaction effect are that there is an interaction effect or that the presence of an interaction effect is indefinite.

(Main Effect of Treatment Condition). Act as if:

1. $(\mu_1 - \mu_2) > 0$, (2) $(\mu_1 - \mu_2) < 0$, or (3) the sign (<0 or >0) of $(\mu_1 - \mu_2)$ is indefinite.

(Main Effect of Treatment Status). Act as if:

2. $(\mu_1 - \mu_2) > 0$, (2) $(\mu_1 - \mu_2) < 0$, or (3) the sign (<0 or >0) of $(\mu_1 - \mu_2)$ is indefinite.

(Interaction Effect of Treatment Condition & Treatment Status). Act as if:

3. $(\mu_1 \times \mu_2) > 0$ or (2) the sign (>0) of $(\mu_1 \times \mu_2)$ is indefinite.

HYPOTHESIS TESTING STEP 2: ESTABLISH THE NULL HYPOTHESIS (H_0)

The omnibus null hypotheses are stated in narrative and symbolic formats in the second step of the hypothesis testing process.

Omnibus Narrative Null Hypotheses (H_0)

H_{01} (Main Effect of Treatment Condition): There will be no significant mean difference in treatment retention (successful weeks in treatment) when comparing the effects of the standard care (SC) condition to the standard care + contingency management (CM) condition.

H_{02} (Main Effect of Treatment Status): There will be no significant mean difference in treatment retention (successful weeks in treatment) when comparing the effects of 0–1 prior treatment attempts to ≥ 2 prior treatment attempts.

H_{03} (Interaction Effect of Treatment Condition & Treatment Status): There will be no significant mean differences in treatment retention (successful weeks in treatment) across levels of treatment condition and treatment status.

Symbolic Null Hypotheses (H_0)

H_{01}: (Main Effect of Treatment Condition): $\mu_1 = \mu_2$

H_{02}: (Main Effect of Treatment Status): $\mu_1 = \mu_2$

H_{03}: (Interaction Effect of Treatment Condition & Treatment Status): $\mu_1 \times \mu_2 = 0$

HYPOTHESIS TESTING STEP 3: DECIDE ON A RISK LEVEL (ALPHA) OF REJECTING THE TRUE H_0 CONSIDERING TYPE I AND II ERRORS AND POWER

We will choose an alpha criterion (α) that we will use to make a decision about whether to reject a true null hypothesis (H_0) in this step of the hypothesis-testing process. During this step of the hypothesis-testing process, we choose an alpha criterion (α) that we will use to make a decision about whether to reject a true null hypothesis (H_0). We consider the balancing act between Type I (alpha) and Type II (beta) errors. Then, we will use our chosen α level and combine it with anticipated sample size and an estimated (a priori) effect size and determine if we have enough power (a priori) to conduct the study. Power is the probability of correctly rejecting a false null hypothesis.

Selecting Alpha (α) Considering Type I and Type II Errors

As is customary, we will choose an α level of either .001, .01, .05, or .10. Several previous studies have shown that adding contingency management to standard care practices is effective in keeping cocaine abusers in treatment. Moreover, previous research has shown that persons with ≥ 2 prior treatment attempts have higher treatment retention than individuals with 0–1 prior attempts. This study has a goal to replicate findings from past studies. Therefore, a stricter alpha criterion of $\alpha = .01$ will be used in this study. This increases the probability of not making a Type I error, which is rejecting a true null. This will provide more confidence in our decision if the SC + CM condition and ≥ 2 prior treatment attempts level produces significantly higher treatment retention when compared to the SC condition and 0–1 prior attempts level (reject H_0). However, if we don't reject the null that there are differences, the $\alpha = .01$ increases the probability of making a Type II error of failing to reject H_0 when there are significant differences in means (false H_0).

A Priori Power Analysis

Next, we will conduct an a priori power analysis to determine the probability of correctly rejecting the false null hypotheses in our study. We have a sample size ($N = 120$) and alpha ($\alpha = .01$) but need estimated effect sizes for the two main effects and the interaction effect to conduct the power analysis. One might use different power analysis criteria for various effects. For example, previous literature may show that the estimated effect size of one main effect is lower than the other main effect. In that case, we would use different estimated effect sizes when conducting the power analyses for each main effect.

We are going to use the following a priori effect sizes based on average eta-squared effect sizes from several related studies: (1) Treatment Condition, $\eta^2 = .24$; (2) Treatment Status, $\eta^2 = .19$; (3) Treatment Condition $\times$ Treatment Status Interaction, $\eta^2 = .22$. We are going to use G*Power 3.2.1 to compute the power analyses.

Power Analysis Using G*Power 3.1

We also will conduct the power analysis using G*Power 3.1.2 for the two main effects and the interaction effect. The $\alpha = .01$, desired power of .80, and an estimated effect sizes of Treatment Condition ($\eta^2 = .24$), Treatment Status ($\eta^2 = .19$), and Treatment Condition X Treatment Status Interaction, $\eta^2 = .22$ are used.

Treatment Condition

1. Open up the G*Power 3.1.2 program.

2. Select **F tests** under **Test family** > under **Statistical test**, select **ANOVA: Fixed effects, special, main effects and interactions** > under **Type of power analysis**, select **A priori: Compute required sample size - given α, power, and effect size**.

3. To the left of **Effect size f**, click on the **Determine** button and a new attached window opens up that requests additional information. Click on the

Direct circle and beside **partial η^2** type in the first $\eta^2 = .24$ (Treatment Condition) and click on the **Calculate and transfer to the main window** button and click on the **Close** button.

4. You will notice that next to **Effect size f** is the number 0.5619515. Next, beside **α err prob** type 0.01 > beside **Power (1-β err prob)**, type 0.80 > beside **Numerator df**, type 1 > beside *Number of groups*, type 2 > click on **Calculate** button.

The analysis for Treatment Condition produced a required total sample size of 41 participants to reach a power of .8073356 using an $\alpha = .01$ and an estimated effect size of $\eta^2 = .24$. (See Figure 9.1.) Our study sample size of $N = 120$ exceeds the requirement.

Treatment Status   Follow the same procedures to conduct the power analysis for Treatment Status now using an $\eta^2 = .19$. (See Figure 9.2.) Click on the **Direct** circle and beside **partial η^2** type in the $\eta^2 = .19$ (Treatment Status) and click on the **Calculate and transfer to the main window** button and click on the **Close** button. This produces in the main window an effect size $f = 0.4843221$. Next, beside **α err prob** type 0.01 > beside **Power (1-β err prob)**, type 0.80 > beside **Numerator df**, type 1 > beside **Number of groups**, type 2 > click on **Calculate** button.

The analysis for Treatment Status produced a required total sample size of 54 participants to reach a power of .8075639 using an $\alpha = .01$ and an estimated effect size of $\eta^2 = .19$. Our study sample size of $N = 120$ exceeds the requirement.

Treatment Condition × Treatment Status Interaction   Follow the same procedures to conduct the power analysis for Treatment Condition × Treatment Status Interaction now using now an $\eta^2 = .22$. (See Figure 9.3.) Click on the **Direct** circle and beside **partial η^2** type in the $\eta^2 = .22$ (Treatment Condition × Treatment Status) and click on the **Calculate and transfer to the main window** button and click on the **Close** button. This produces in the main window an effect size $f = 0.5310850$. Next, beside **α err prob** type 0.01 > beside **Power (1-β err prob)**, type 0.80 > beside **Numerator df**, type 1 > beside **Number of groups**, type 4 (there are four groups or cells being compared) > click on **Calculate** button.

The analysis for Treatment Status produced a required total sample size of 46 participants to reach a power of .8113268 using an $\alpha = .01$ and an estimated effect size of $\eta^2 = .22$. Our study sample size of $N = 120$ exceeds the requirement.

FIGURE 9.1 Power Analysis for Treatment Condition of the Factorial ANOVA Problem

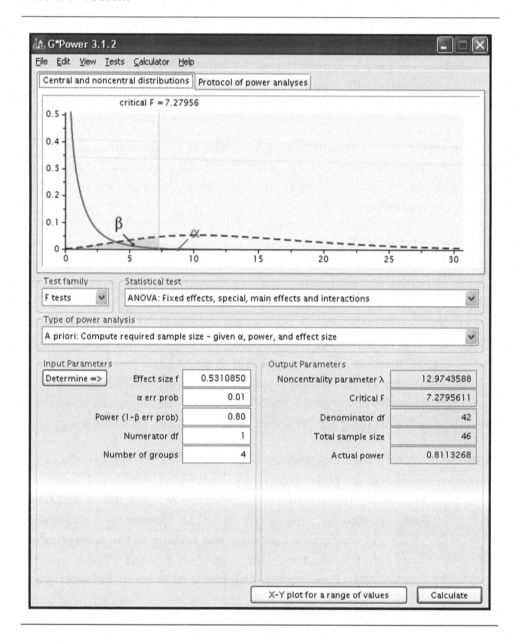

FIGURE 9.2   Power Analysis for Treatment Status of the Factorial ANOVA Problem

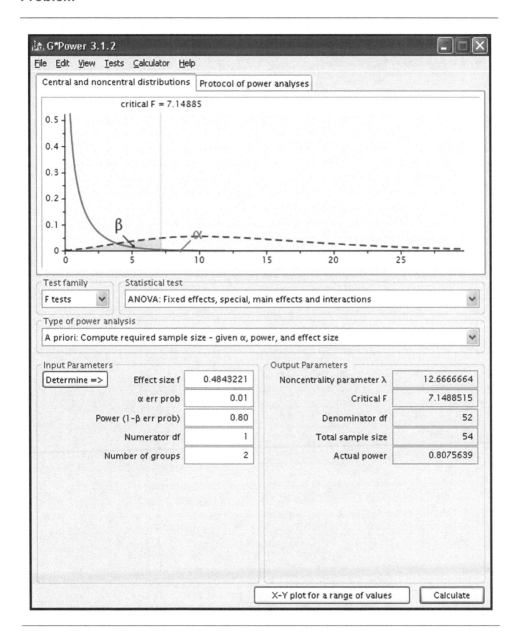

FIGURE 9.3 **Power Analysis for Treatment Condition × Treatment Status Interaction of the Factorial ANOVA Problem**

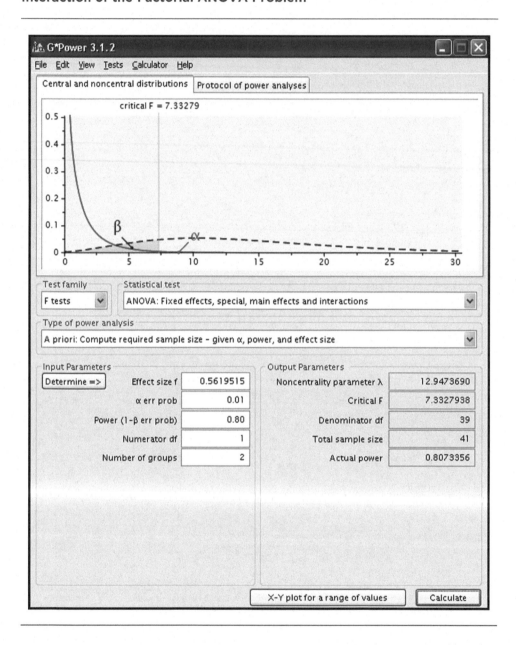

PROGRESS REVIEW

1. We stated the research questions for the study problem.

2. We completed the first two steps of the hypothesis-testing process by stating the alternative and null hypotheses in narrative and symbolic formats.

3. Next, we decided on the risk we are willing to take when rejecting a true null hypothesis by choosing alpha (α). We chose $\alpha = .01$, which we believed was a reasonable criterion in our study to avoid making a Type I or Type II error.

4. We conducted a power analysis to make sure that our probability of correctly rejecting a false null hypothesis was adequate (power $= .80$) before moving ahead with the study. Using G*Power 3.1.2, we found that we met the a priori power expectation of .80.

HYPOTHESIS TESTING STEP 4: CHOOSE APPROPRIATE STATISTIC AND ITS SAMPLING DISTRIBUTION TO TEST THE H_0 ASSUMING H_0 IS TRUE

We are using a two-way ANOVA to test the three null hypotheses in this study. We are going to compare the means of *Treatment Retention* (DV) for each main effect of *Treatment Condition* (IV_1) and *Treatment Status* (IV_2) and their interaction effect for significant differences using the *F* distribution. The two-way ANOVA is appropriate to use because: (1) there are two independent variables, (2) there are different participants in each of the four groups, (3) there is one dependent variable, and (4) the dependent variable is continuously scaled.

HYPOTHESIS TESTING STEP 5: SELECT SAMPLE, COLLECT DATA, SCREEN DATA, COMPUTE STATISTIC, AND DETERMINE PROBABILITY ESTIMATES

In Step 5 of the hypothesis-testing process, data are collected from a sample of participants. The data are assessed for data accuracy, missing values, and univariate outliers, and to determine if the underlying assumptions of the statistic are met. Data modifications are made if warranted by the data screening results. Then the null hypotheses are tested using the two-way ANOVA.

Sample Selection and Assignment

The sample of this study consisted of cocaine abusers seeking treatment in a substance use disorder clinic. Participants were included in the study if they were 18 years of age or older and had abused cocaine within the past year or longer. Also, they had to meet the *Diagnostic and Statistical Manual of Mental Disorders* criteria for dependency.

Potential participants were excluded if they had a psychosis diagnosis, suicidal ideation, or chronic gambling history. They also were excluded if they were unable to comprehend and follow the study procedures.

The independent variable of Treatment Status is an attribute IV where the participants either have 0–1 prior treatment attempts or equal to or greater than two (≥ 2) prior treatment attempts. Therefore, it was necessary to select a sample with an equal number of participants in the two categories of prior treatment attempts. The initial sample was 125 individuals; however, two individuals met exclusion criteria and three persons dropped out of the study before it began. The final study sample was 120 cocaine abusers who sought treatment. The participants encompass characteristics that reflect the persons, settings, times, independent variables, and dependent variables we intend to use to generalize our findings.

The 120 participants were assigned randomly to four groups as follows: (1) X_{A1B1} ([SC] and [0–1 prior treatment attempts]), (2) X_{A1B2} ([SC] and [≥ 2 prior treatment attempts]), (3) X_{A2B1} ([SC + CM] and [0–1 prior treatment attempts]), and (4) X_{A2B2} ([SC + CM] and [≥ 2 prior treatment attempts]). Whether a participant had either 0–1 prior treatment attempts or ≥ 2 prior treatment attempts was an attribute that participants brought with them to the study, so random assignment could not be used across the two conditions.

However, random assignment was used to group participants by Treatment Status into the two groups used for each condition.

Study Data Diagnostics

We are next going to conduct data diagnostics to assess for accuracy of data entries, missing data, univariate outliers, and compliance to the underlying assumptions of the two-way ANOVA. This is done after the data are collected and before the null hypotheses are tested.

Accuracy of Data Entry

The individual scores on the dependent variable were in expected range and the means and standard deviations were credible when compared to descriptive statistics from previous studies. All of the original data were compared and corroborated to the entered data by two members of the research team.

Missing Data Analysis

There were no missing data in the original data set.

Means, Standard Deviations, Variances, and Assessing for Univariate Outliers IBM SPSS Commands

Enter the data from the Two-Way Analysis of Variance Data table at the end of the chapter into IBM SPSS. Enter the participant ID numbers and three columns of data just as they appear in the table.

1. Click on **Data** > **Split File** > click on circles beside **Compare groups** and **Sort the file by grouping variables** > click on *TreatmentStatus* and *TreatmentCondition* and click the arrow so that *TreatmentStatus* and *TreatmentCondition* are under **Groups Based on** > click on **OK** and don't save command output. You have instructed the program to generate output by the four groups (*TreatmentStatus* × *TreatmentCondition*). You will need to change back this split file command later.

2. Click on **Analyze** > **Descriptive Statistics** > **Descriptives** > click over *TreatmentRetention* to **Variable(s)** > click on **Save standardized values as variables** > click on **Options** and check **Mean, Std. deviation,** and **Variance** > click on **OK** > save the output as *TwowayANOVA Descriptives*.

The Descriptive Statistics Table 9.2 lists the sample size of each group followed by the lowest (minimum) and highest (maximum) scores in each group. Valid N refers to the number of participant scores that do not having missing data. The average scores (means) by groups on the *Treatment Retention* (number of treatment weeks successfully completed) are provided. Measures of variability designate the extent that the scores in each group distribution deviate from their group mean. The standard deviation is an average measure of score deviation from the mean, whereas the square of s is the variance (s^2) or general spread of scores from the mean. Higher scores reflect more deviation of scores from the mean for both s and s^2. As you can see, the standard deviations and variances do not deviate highly from one another, which suggests we may have homogeneity of variance.

The standard values (z-scores) requested for the analysis to assess for univariate outliers are produced in a new column on the Data View IBM SPSS spreadsheet and named *ZTreatmentRetention*. These values represent the z-scores corresponding to the raw scores in each group. Since we used the "Split File" command, the z-scores for participant scores are produced separately for each of the four groups. The first group, ([SC] and [0–1 prior treatment attempts]), is represented by ID #s 1–30, group 2 ([SC] and [$\geq$2 prior treatment attempts]) = ID #s 31–60, group 3 ([SC + CM] and [0–1 prior treatment attempts]) = ID #s 61–90, and group 4 ([SC + CM] and [$\geq$ 2 prior treatment attempts]) = ID #s 91–120. The highest positive and negative z scores for each group are reported in Table 9.3.

None of the z-scores exceed the criterion of ± 3.29 ($<.001$, two-tailed), so we conclude that the raw scores of each group are not far removed from the rest of the scores in each group.

At this point, remove the **Split File** filter. **Data** > **Split File** > click on the **Reset** button and then click **OK**; click out of the output and don't save it.

Assessing for Underlying Assumptions

Initially, we will assess the dependent variable (treatment retention) by each group for normality by assessing histograms, skewness, kurtosis, the Shapiro-Wilk statistic, and normal Q-Q plots.

TABLE 9.2 Descriptive Statistics of Treatment Retention by Treatment Condition × Treatment Status Groups

TreatmentCondition	TreatmentStatus		N	Minimum	Maximum	Mean	Std. Deviation	Variance
Standard Care	0–1 Prior treatment attempts	TreatmentRetention	30	3.00	9.00	5.5667	1.50134	2.254
		Valid N (listwise)	30					
	≥2 Prior treatment attempts	TreatmentRetention	30	2.00	7.00	4.8000	1.42393	2.028
		Valid N (listwise)	30					
Standard Care + Contingency Management	0–1 Prior treatment attempts	TreatmentRetention	30	2.00	8.00	5.7000	1.57896	2.493
		Valid N (listwise)	30					
	≥2 Prior treatment attempts	TreatmentRetention	30	5.00	11.00	7.5333	1.35782	1.844
		Valid N (listwise)	30					

TABLE 9.3   Highest ±z-Scores by Group

Conditions Group	Highest +z	Outlier? > ±3.29	Highest −z	Outlier? > ±3.29
SC/0-1	2.287*	No	−1.710	No
SC/≥2	1.545	No	−1.966	No
SC + CM/0-1	1.457	No	−2.343	No
SC + CM/ 2	2.553	No	−1.866	No

*These numbers are rounded to three decimals.

Normality IBM SPSS Commands

1. **Analyze > Descriptive Statistics > Explore**.

2. Click over dependent variable *TreatmentRetention* to **Dependent List**.

3. Click over independent variables (*TreatmentCondition & TreatmentStatus*) to **Factor List**. Remember factor is another term for independent variable.

4. Do not change **Display choices**—leave on **Both**.

5. To the upper right of Display are three buttons. Click on **Plots**. Then, select **Histograms, Normality plots with tests**.

6. Under **Spread vs. Level with Levene Test** click on **Untransformed**. (If we wanted a .99 CI of the Mean, we would change at Statistics button.)

7. Click on **Continue**.

8. Click on **OK**.

9. Save the output as *TwowayANOVAassumptionscreen*.

First, look at the information under Descriptives on the output (see Table 9.4). There are two SPSS tables of descriptives. The first table shows means of the dependent variable (Treatment Retention) based on Treatment Condition and is followed by several other statistical tables of information that we will use. The second table of descriptives based on Treatment Status is in the second half of the SPSS output followed by several tables. Please note that these four means are row and column means that combined cell means of each of the two rows and two columns. The four means in Table 9.4 are the cell means that are used to compute the row and

TABLE 9.4 Skewness, Kurtosis, and Standard Error Values by Group

		Descriptives		Statistic	Std. Error
TreatmentRetention	Standard Care	Mean		5.1833	.19382
		95% Confidence Interval for Mean	Lower Bound	4.7955	
			Upper Bound	5.5712	
		5% Trimmed Mean		5.1667	
		Median		5.0000	
		Variance		2.254	
		Std. Deviation		1.50132	
		Minimum		2.00	
		Maximum		9.00	
		Range		7.00	
		Interquartile Range		2.00	
		Skewness		.049	.309
		Kurtosis		-.215	.608
	Standard Care + Contingency Management	Mean		6.6167	.22309
		95% Confidence Interval for Mean	Lower Bound	6.1703	
			Upper Bound	7.0631	
		5% Trimmed Mean		6.6481	
		Median		7.0000	
		Variance		2.986	
		Std. Deviation		1.72805	
		Minimum		2.00	
		Maximum		11.00	
		Range		9.00	
		Interquartile Range		2.75	
		Skewness		-.255	.309
		Kurtosis		.371	.608

(Continued)

TABLE 9.4 Skewness, Kurtosis, and Standard Error Values by Group (Continued)

Descriptives

TreatmentStatus			Statistic	Std. Error
TreatmentRetention	0–1 Prior treatment attempts	Mean	5.6333	.19739
		95% Confidence Interval for Mean Lower Bound	5.2383	
		Upper Bound	6.0283	
		5% Trimmed Mean	5.6481	
		Median	6.0000	
		Variance	2.338	
		Std. Deviation	1.52900	
		Minimum	2.00	
		Maximum	9.00	
		Range	7.00	
		Interquartile Range	2.00	
		Skewness	−.144	.309
		Kurtosis	−.348	.608
	≥2 Prior treatment attempts	Mean	6.1667	.25174
		95% Confidence Interval for Mean Lower Bound	5.6629	
		Upper Bound	6.6704	
		5% Trimmed Mean	6.1667	
		Median	6.0000	
		Variance	3.802	
		Std. Deviation	1.94994	
		Minimum	2.00	
		Maximum	11.00	
		Range	9.00	
		Interquartile Range	2.75	
		Skewness	−.029	.309
		Kurtosis	−.271	.608

column means. Later, we will combine the cell, row, and column means into one table to clarify the interpretation of the two-way ANOVA.

Skewness

Look at the values for skewness and "Std. Error" for each group in Table 9.4. Divide the skewness statistic value by its Std. Error value to obtain z-scores. The skewness and standard error and their resulting skewness z-scores are presented in Table 9.5.

There are no extreme scores relative to most of the scores in the distributions in the positive (right) end or negative (left) end of the distributions. The skewness z-scores are not even close to the criterion of ± 3.29 ($p < .001$, two-tailed test).

Below the skewness and standard error values in Table 9.4 are the "Kurtosis" and "Std. Error" values. We will divide the kurtosis statistic by its standard error and compare the resultant z-score to ± 3.29 to see if any group distribution significantly departs from normality (see Table 9.6).

None of the four condition group distributions have kurtosis z-scores that are greater than ± 3.29, so they do not depart significantly form normality.

TABLE 9.5   Skewness z-Scores by Condition Group

Condition	Skewness z (Stat./Std. Error = Z)	Skewness Direction	Sig. Departure? (> ±3.29)
SC	.049/.309 = .159	Positive	No
SC + CM	−.255/.309 = −.825	Negative	No
0–1 Prior visits	−.144/.309 = −.466	Negative	No
≥2 Prior visits	−.029/.309 = −094	Negative	No

TABLE 9.6   Kurtosis z-Scores by Condition Group

Condition	Kurtosis z (Stat./Std. Error = Z)	Kurtosis Direction	Sig. Departure? (> ±3.29)
SC	−.215/.608 = −.354	Platykurtic	No
SC + CM	.371/.608 = .610	Leptokurtic	No
0–1 Prior visits	−.348/.608 = −.572	Platykurtic	No
≥2 Prior visits	−.271/.608 = −.446	Platykurtic	No

Shapiro-Wilk (S-W) Statistic

The S-W statistic provides corroborating evidence to use to determine if the distribution of the group conditions are normally distributed. The S-W statistics are found in the output under *Tests of Normality* (see Table 9.7). The null hypothesis that we are testing ($\alpha = .01$) for each group with the S-W is:

$$H_0: \text{The Sample Distribution} = \text{Normal}$$

We want to retain the null hypothesis, which says that the sample distribution that we are testing is not deviating significantly from being normally distributed.

The significant probability levels (Sig.) of the Shapiro-Wilk statistic are .051 (SC), .075 (SC + CM), .042 (0–1 prior attempts), and .208 (≥ 2 prior attempts); all of these levels are greater than $\alpha = .01$. Our rule is to reject a null hypothesis if the probability level of the calculated statistic is less than our stated alpha level, and we fail to reject the null if our significance probability is greater than our alpha. Therefore, we conclude that these four group distributions are not deviating significantly from being normally distributed.

Normal Q-Q Plots

The final evidence of normality that we will interpret is the normal Q-Q plot for each distribution. A plot for each group is located in the output under the heading Normal Q-Q Plots. If the sample is from a normal distribution, we expect that the points will fall more or less on a straight line, reflecting congruence between observed values in the distribution paired with their expected values from the normal distribution (see Figures 9.4a, 9.4b, 9.4c, and 9.4d).

The points fall on or near the straight line of the Q-Q plots for all four groups, adding to the evidence that each group is normally distributed.

Summary of the Normality Evidence

No individual *Treatment Retention* scores were univariate outliers within the four groups represented by combinations of the two levels of the two

TABLE 9.7 Shapiro-Wilk Statistics by Condition Group

Tests of Normality

		Kolmogorov-Smirnova			Shapiro-Wilk		
	TreatmentCondition	Statistic	df	Sig.	Statistic	df	Sig.
TreatmentRetention	Standard Care	.140	60	.005	.961	60	.051
	Standard Care + Contingency Management	.154	60	.001	.964	60	.075

Tests of Normality

		Kolmogorov-Smirnovb			Shapiro-Wilk		
	TreatmentStatus	Statistic	df	Sig.	Statistic	df	Sig.
TreatmentRetention	0-1 Prior treatment attempts	.145	60	.003	.959	60	.042
	= ≥2 Prior treatment attempts	.132	60	.011	.973	60	.208

a,b Lilliefors significance correction.

FIGURE 9.4A, B, C, AND D   Normal Q-Q Plot by Condition Groups

(a)

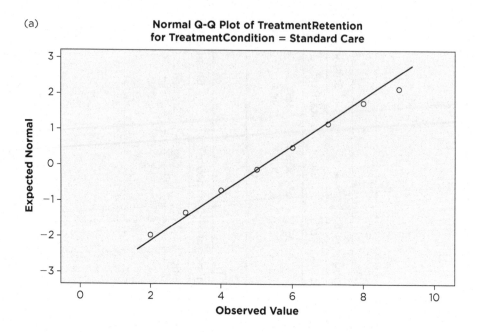

Normal Q-Q Plot of TreatmentRetention
for TreatmentCondition = Standard Care

(b)

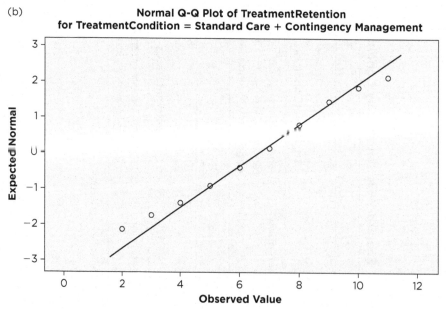

Normal Q-Q Plot of TreatmentRetention
for TreatmentCondition = Standard Care + Contingency Management

(c)

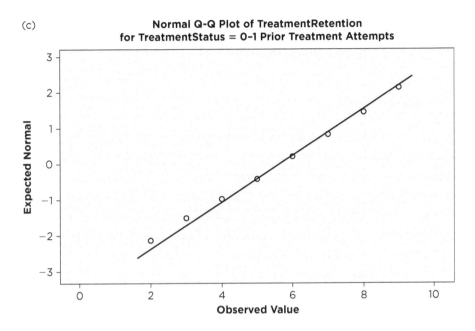

(d)

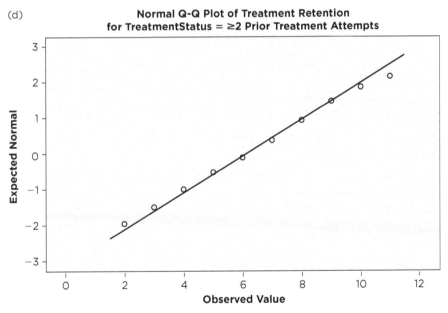

independent variables. The skewness z-scores, kurtosis z-scores, S-W statistics, and Q-Q plots demonstrated that the four distributions were not deviating significantly from normality. The consistency of the evidence supports that the Treatment Retention is normally distributed within the distributions of the groups, meeting the assumption of normality.

Homogeneity of Variance

We want the variability of the scores across groups to be constant. First we will calculate the variance ratio of the highest variance by the lowest variance of the four groups (see Table 9.4). The highest variance is 3.802 for the $=\geq 2$ Prior Treatment Attempts group, and the lowest variance is 2.254 for the Standard Care group. The variance ratio (F_{max}) is $3.802/2.254 = 1.687$. Since the groups are equal in size, we can use the criterion of an $F_{max} < 10$ being acceptable. Clearly, our F_{max} of 1.687 is less than 10.

Next, we will see if Levene's test of homogeneity of variances also supports meeting the underlying assumption. We are testing the null hypothesis of equality of the error variances across the four groups. We want to retain the null hypothesis concluding that the variances across the three groups are equal enough using an alpha criterion of .01.

$$H_0: \sigma^2_{e\,SC} = \sigma^2_{e\,SC+CM} = \sigma^2_{e\,0-1\,PriorAttempts} = \sigma^2_{e\geq 2\,PriorAttempts}$$

The Levene's statistic is found in the "assumptionscreen" output under the heading *Test of Homogeneity of Variance* (see Tables 9.8 and 9.9) on the line called "Based on mean."

We fail to reject the H_0 that the error variances are equal in both comparisons since the probability value of .365 (SC vs. SC + CM) and .068 (0–1 vs. ≥2) are greater than the $\alpha = .01$. The underlying assumption of homogeneity of variance has been met using the Levene's statistic.

Summary of the Homogeneity of Variance Evidence

The evidence from both the variance ratio (F_{max}) and the Levene's statistic support that the variances and error variances of the dependent variable are equal

TABLE 9.8 Levene's Test Comparing Variances of the Treatment Condition Groups (SC vs. SC + CM)

	Test of Homogeneity of Variance				
		Levene's Statistic	df1	df2	Sig.
TreatmentRetention	Based on mean	.828	1	118	.365
	Based on median	.477	1	118	.491
	Based on median and with adjusted df	.477	1	112.202	.491
	Based on trimmed mean	.800	1	118	.373

TABLE 9.9 Levene's Test Comparing Variances of the Treatment Status Groups (0–1 vs. ≥2)

	Test of Homogeneity of Variance				
		Levene's Statistic	df1	df2	Sig.
TreatmentRetention	Based on mean	3.400	1	118	.068
	Based on median	3.440	1	118	.066
	Based on median and with adjusted df	3.440	1	115.785	.066
	Based on trimmed mean	3.423	1	118	.067

across the two groups of each independent variable. These findings paired with the group sizes being equal allow us to conclude that the underlying assumption of homogeneity of variance has been met.

Independence

There are different participants in each of the four groups, and each participant's score was produced independent of the other scores. However, if dependent variable test scores across condition groups are correlated with each other when the scores are collected in the same order, the significance level of the ANOVA can be smaller than it should be (Norusis, 2003). We are going to assess the independence of observations by graphing the responses of participants on the dependent variable by group condition based on the same order in which measurements (observations) were obtained. The data in the SPSS Data View spreadsheet are in a similar order by group based on when the data were collected. We will need to create four columns of data to complete the analysis of matrix scatter plots to assess independence.

Matrix Scatter Plot SPSS Commands

1. First, close all output that you have been working on. Under the column labeled *TreatmentRetention* on the IBM SPSS **Data View** spreadsheet, left click and hold on the first cell, which is 6, and drag down until you reach *ID# 30*, which is the value 5 and the last participant score in the *Treatment Condition SC + Treatment Status 0–1* group. All of the numbers should be in bold.

2. At the top of the screen, click on **Edit** and then **Copy**. This will copy the data for pasting to a new column.

3. Go to the first empty column in the **Data View** and click on the first cell, and it will be bolded.

4. At the top of the screen, click on **Edit** and then click on **Paste**; the data from the *SC + 0–1* group will be copied to the new column.

5. At the bottom left of the spreadsheet, click on **Variable View** and name the new column as *sc01* and change the **decimals** to 0.

6. Click on **Data View** button and create a new column for the other three groups of 30 participants in the same way; call them *sc2*, *sccm01*, and *sccm2*. Once you have completed the four new columns, **File > Save**.

7. At the top of the screen, click on **Graphs > Legacy Dialogs > Scatter/Dot > Matrix Scatter > Define**.

8. Click over the four new columns you created to the space under **Matrix Variables > OK**.

The matrix scatter plot (Figure 9.5) shows the scores of each group compared to the other groups. The scores are in the order they were obtained and are paired as circles in each graph representing two groups being compared. If the scores form a diagonal straight line when any two groups are compared, then the scores are correlated and not independent. There appear to be no clear linear trends between paired scores across the groups. The points scatter in many directions. We therefore conclude that we have met the assumption of independence.

Summary of Underlying Assumptions Findings

The majority of evidence obtained shows that the distributions of scores on the dependent variable in the four groups did not deviate from normality. Both measures of homogeneity of variance supported fulfillment of the assumption of constancy of variance across the groups. Finally, the scatter plots suggest that independence of dependent variable scores was met. This information provides support for conducting the 2×2 ANOVA to test the omnibus null hypotheses in this study.

PROGRESS REVIEW

1. The reported data were collected from the sample participants on the dependent variable treatment retention as measured by the number of successful weeks in treatment.

2. Four groups were formed based on combinations of the independent variable treatment condition (SC and SCCM) and treatment status (0-1 and ≥ 2).

3. Data were screened and met the criteria for missing data and underlying assumptions.

Two-Way Analysis of Variance of the Omnibus H_0's

Two-Way ANOVA SPSS Commands

1. Click **Analyze** > click **General Linear Model** > click **Univariate** > click over *TreatmentRetention* under **Dependent Variable** and *TreatmentCondition* and *TreatmentStatus* under **Fixed Factor(s)**.

2. Click on the **Plots** button > click *TreatmentCondition* to **Horizontal Axis** and *TreatmentStatus* to **Separate Lines** > click the **Add** button > click **Continue**.

3. Click on the **Options** button > click on the boxes for **Descriptive statistics**, **Estimates of effect size**, **Observed power**, and **Homogeneity tests** > the **Significance level** should be .01 > click on **Continue** > click **OK**.

4. Save generated output as *Two-WayANOVA Results*.

The results of this analysis provide information to test the three omnibus null hypotheses of the study:

H_{01} (Main Effect of Treatment Condition): There will be no significant mean difference in treatment retention (successful weeks in treatment) when comparing the effects of the standard care (SC) condition to the standard care + contingency management (CM) condition (H_{01}: $\mu_1 = \mu_2$).

H_{02} (Main Effect of Treatment Status): There will be no significant mean difference in treatment retention (successful weeks in treatment) when comparing the effects of 0–1 prior treatment attempts to ≥ 2 prior treatment attempts (H_{02}: $\mu_1 = \mu_2$).

H_{03} (Interaction Effect of Treatment Condition & Treatment Status): There will be no significant mean differences in treatment retention (successful weeks in treatment) across levels of treatment condition and treatment status (H_{03}: $\mu_1 \times \mu_2 = 0$).

The results of the two-way ANOVA are presented next. Additionally, interpretations are provided for the magnitude of treatment effects (effect sizes), post hoc power, post hoc multiple comparisons of means, and confidence intervals for the mean differences.

Two-Way ANOVA Computer Analysis Results

Descriptive statistics are provided in the two-way ANOVA output (see Table 9.10) showing means, standard deviations, and sample sizes by combinations of conditions.

Previously, we assessed for homogeneity of variance of the treatment retention across the two groups for each condition and found there was constancy of variance. Table 9.11 shows the results of assessing the variances of all four groups together, and it shows that the significance is .822, which is greater than the $\alpha = .01$. Thus, we fail to reject the null that the variances are equal, and this result supports the previous finding of constancy of variance.

In the two-way ANOVA output (see Table 9.12) labeled *Tests of Between-Subjects Effects* you will see the name of the independent variables (*TreatmentCondition*, *TreatmentStatus*, and *TreatmentCondition* × *TreatmentStatus*) under the heading *Source* that we created when the data were entered. We will be using

TABLE 9.10 Descriptive Statistics by Conditions

	Descriptive Statistics			
	Dependent Variable: TreatmentRetention			
TreatmentCondition	TreatmentStatus	Mean	Std. Deviation	N
SC	0–1	5.567	1.501	30
	+2	4.800	1.424	30
	Total	5.183	1.501	60
SC + CM	0–1	5.700	1.579	30
	+2	7.533	1.358	30
	Total	6.617	1.728	60
Total	0–1	5.633	1.529	60
	+2	6.167	1.950	60
	Total	5.900	1.765	120

TABLE 9.11 Levene's Test of Equality of Error Variances[a]

Dependent Variable:TreatmentRetention			
F	df1	df2	Sig.
.305	3	116	.822

Tests the null hypothesis that the error variance of the dependent variable is equal across groups.
[a]Design: Intercept + TreatmentCondition + TreatmentStatus + Treatment-Condition × TreatmentStatus

the information in these rows to make decisions about rejecting or failing to reject the three null hypotheses.

The results of testing all three null hypotheses are in Table 9.12. The results of the first main effect of *Treatment Condition* (SC vs. SC + CM) on the dependent variable *Treatment Retention* (successful weeks in treatment) are under the column called Source across the row *TreatmentCondition*. The test of significance of the first main effect is in the *F* column ($F = 28.605$) and is significant at the $p = .000$, which is less than our $\alpha = .01$ and thus is significant, $F(1, 116) = 28.605, p < .01$. There was a significant difference between the row means (see Table 9.10) of the SC level ($M = 5.183, SD = 1.501$) versus the SC + CM level ($M = 6.617, SD = 1.728$). The standard condition + contingency management level increased significantly

TABLE 9.12 Two-Way Analysis of Variance Results

Tests of Between-Subjects Effects

Dependent Variable: TreatmentRetention

Source	Type III Sum of Squares	df	Mean Square	F	Sig.	Partial Eta-Squared	Noncent. Parameter	Observed Power[a]
Corrected model	120.867[b]	3	40.289	18.699	.000	.326	56.097	1.000
Intercept	4,177.200	1	4,177.200	1,938.738	.000	.944	1,938.738	1.000
TreatmentCondition	61.633	1	61.633	28.605	.000	.198	28.605	.996
TreatmentStatus	8.533	1	8.533	3.961	.049	.033	3.961	.270
TreatmentCondition × TreatmentStatus	50.700	1	50.700	23.531	.000	.169	23.531	.986
Error	249.933	116	2.155					
Total	4,548.000	120						
Corrected total	370.800	119						

[a]Computed using alpha = .01.
[b]R-squared = .326 (adjusted R-squared = .309).

($p < .01$) the number of successful weeks in treatment (*Treatment Retention*) of the participants with cocaine disorders when compared to the standard condition level.

The second null hypothesis related to the main effect of *Treatment Status* on *Treatment Retention* (successful weeks in treatment) generated a significant probability of $p = .049$, which is larger than the criterion $\alpha = .01$ so the effect is not significant, $F(1, 116) = 3.961, p > .01$. There was not a significant difference ($p > .01$) between the column means of successful weeks in treatment of the 0–1 prior treatment attempts level ($M = 5.633$, $SD = 1.529$) versus the ≥ 2 prior treatment attempts level ($M = 6.167$, $SD = 1.950$).

The third null hypothesis related to the interaction effect was significant, $F(1, 116) = 23.531, p < .01$. There were significant mean differences in *treatment retention* (successful weeks in treatment) across levels of *treatment condition* and *treatment status*.

The significant interaction is demonstrated in Figure 9.6 in relation to means on *treatment retention* (weeks successful treatment completed) produced by the independent variables. The two means of the *TreatmentCondition* (horizontal axis) are compared to the two means of the *TreatmentStatus* level. (These cell means are found in Table 9.10.) Parallel lines indicate no interaction, and nonparallel lines reflect interaction. The lines in Figure 9.6 cross each other, reflecting interaction (nonparallel lines) between the two independent variables on the dependent variable. The two means across the levels of the treatment condition for the treatment status level of 0–1 prior treatment attempts are similar (SC [$M = 5.567$] vs. SC + CM = [$M = 5.700$]. In contrast, the two means across the levels of the treatment condition for the treatment status level ≥ 2 prior treatment attempts are quite different. The SC + CM mean on *treatment retention* ($M = 7.533$) is considerably higher than the mean produced by the SC condition level ($M = 4.800$). These cell means being graphically compared can be statistically tested, which is called a simple effects analysis.

Simple Effects Analysis

A simple effect is the effect of one factor (IV) on the DV at one level of the other factor. We are going to conduct this because we have a significant interaction effect. We are going to use IBM SPSS syntax commands to obtain these results. Syntax commands are the instructions that you write to the program to initiate an action.

FIGURE 9.6   Estimated Marginal Means of Treatment Retention

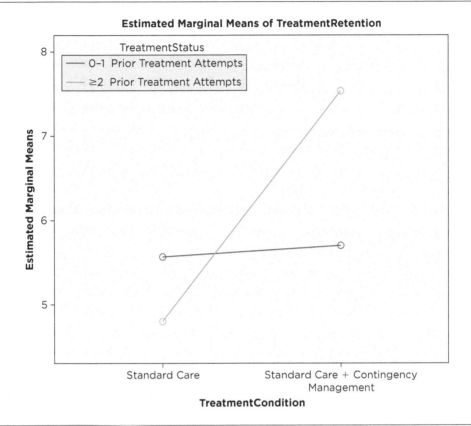

1. Go to **File** > **New** > **Syntax** > and type exactly the syntax for treatment condition at each treatment status level below.

2. When complete save as *sytax1*.

3. Select **Run** > click on **All** > and the results will be produced as an output; save as *output1*.

Syntax for Treatment Condition at Each Treatment Status Level Results

MANOVA

TreatmentRetention BY TreatmentCondition(1 2) TreatmentStatus(1 2)

/METHOD=UNIQUE

/ERROR WITHIN

/DESIGN=TreatmentCondition WITHIN TreatmentStatus(1) TreatmentCondition WITHIN TreatmentStatus(2).

After clicking out of the first syntax you wrote, follow the same commands as
previously to produce the results of syntax for treatment status at each level of
treatment condition and save as *syntax2* and *output2*.

Syntax for Obtaining Treatment Status at Each Level of Treatment Condition Results

MANOVA

TreatmentRetention BY TreatmentCondition(1 2) TreatmentStatus(1 2)

/METHOD=UNIQUE

/ERROR WITHIN

/DESIGN=TreatmentStatus WITHIN TreatmentCondition(1) TreatmentStatus WITHIN TreatmentCondition(2).

Table 9.13 shows the results of two comparisons for *Treatment Condition* (SC
and SC + CM) at each *Treatment Status* level (0–1 and ≥2). The first comparison is
between the cell means of Treatment Condition ($M_{SC} = 5.567$) compared to
($M_{SC+CM} = 5.700$) at the treatment status level of 0–1 prior treatment attempts
(see Table 9.10). There is no significant difference since the Sig. of *F* value is .726
($p > .01$). The second comparison is between the cell means of Treatment Condition ($M_{SC} = 4.800$) compared to ($M_{SC+CM} = 7.533$) at the treatment status level

TABLE 9.13 Treatment Condition at Each Treatment Status Level Results

Tests of Significance for TreatmentRetention using UNIQUE sums of squares					
Source of Variation	SS	DF	MS	*F*	Sig. of *F*
WITHIN Cells	249.93	116	2.15		
TreatmentCondition WITHIN TreatmentStatus(1)	.27	1	.27	.12	.726
TreatmentCondition WITHIN TreatmentStatus (2)	112.07	1	112.07	52.01	.000

TABLE 9.14 Treatment Status at Each Level of Treatment Condition Results

Tests of Significance for TreatmentRetention using UNIQUE sums of squares					
Source of Variation	SS	DF	MS	F	Sig of F
WITHIN Cells	249.93	116	2.15		
TreatmentStatus WITHIN TreatmentCondition(1)	8.82	1	8.82	4.09	.045
TreatmentStatus WITHIN TreatmentCondition(2)	50.42	1	50.42	23.40	.000

of ≥ 2 prior treatment attempts (see Table 9.10). Participants with ≥ 2 prior treatment attempts and who received the Standard Care + Contingency Management treatment showed a significantly higher number of successful weeks in treatment than those with ≥ 2 prior treatment attempts who received the standard care treatment, $F(1, 116) = 52.01$, $p < .01$.

In Table 9.14, the results of two comparisons for *Treatment Status* (0–1 and ≥ 2) at each *Treatment Condition* level (SC and SC + CM) are shown. The first analysis compares the means of ($M_{0-1} = 5.567$) compared to ($M_{\geq 2} = 4.800$) at SC, resulting in no significant difference ($p > .01$). Next, there was a significant difference between the means of the *treatment status* level 0–1 prior treatment attempts ($M = 5.70$) compared to the ≥ 2 prior treatment attempts level ($M = 7.533$) at the treatment condition level of SC + CM, $F(1, 116) = 23.40$, $p < .01$. Participants receiving SC + CM showed a significantly higher number of successful weeks in treatment if they had ≥ 2 prior treatment attempts when compared to those with 0–1 weeks of prior treatment. Overall, the group of participants who showed the most success had ≥ 2 prior treatment attempts and received the standard care plus contingency management treatment.

HYPOTHESIS TESTING STEP 6: MAKE DECISION REGARDING THE H_0 AND INTERPRET POST HOC EFFECT SIZES AND CONFIDENCE INTERVALS

The decisions regarding rejecting or failing to reject the omnibus null hypotheses of the main effects and interaction effect are presented in Table 9.15. Since we rejected the interaction effect, the decisions and conclusions regarding the simple effects analysis are in Table 9.16.

TABLE 9.15 Decisions and Conclusions Regarding Null Hypotheses of Main Effects and Interaction Effect

Effects	Null Hypotheses	Decision	Conclusion
Main effect of Treatment Condition (TC)	H_{01}: $\mu_{1SC} = \mu_{2\ SC+CM}$	Reject $P < .01$	Higher completed weeks in treatment for SC+CM vs. SC.
Main effect of Treatment Status (TS)	H_{02}: $\mu_{10-1} = \mu_{2\geq2}$	Fail to reject $P > .01$	Difference in completed weeks was not found.
Interaction effect of TC and TS	H_{03}: $\mu_{1TC} \times \mu_{2\ TS} = 0$	Reject $P < .01$	Difference in completed weeks across levels of TC and TS.

TABLE 9.16 Decisions and Conclusions Regarding Null Hypotheses of Simple Effects

Effects	Null Hypotheses	Decision	Conclusion
Treatment Condition at 0-1 prior treatment attempts	H_{01}: $\mu_{SC} = \mu_{SC+CM}$	Fail to reject $P > .01$	Difference in completed weeks was not found.
Treatment Condition at ≥ 2 prior treatment attempts	H_{02}: $\mu_{SC} = \mu_{SC+CM}$	Reject $P < .01$	Higher completed weeks in treatment for SC + CM at ≥ 2 prior treatment attempts.
Treatment Status at SC	H_{03}: $\mu_{0-1} = \mu_{\geq2}$	Fail to reject $P > .01$	Difference in completed weeks was not found.
Treatment Status at SC + CM	H_{04}: $\mu_{0-1} = \mu_{\geq2}$	Reject $P < .01$	Higher completed weeks in treatment for ≥ 2 prior treatment attempts at SC + CM.

Magnitude of Treatment Effect—Post Hoc Effect Sizes

Please refer to the *Tests of Between-Subject Effects* table of the ANOVA results output (see Table 9.12). First, find *TreatmentCondition* in the Source column and go across the row until you find the partial eta-squared value of $\eta_p^2 = .198$. Approximately

19.80 percent of the change in the dependent variable (*TreatmentRetention*) can be attributed to the first independent variable (*TreatmentCondition*). The $\eta_p^2 = .198$ has a large strength effect according to Cohen's convention for η^2 where approximately 1 percent to 6 percent is small, >6 percent to 14 percent is medium, and >14 percent is large.

Following the same procedure to find the effect size for the second main effect (*TreatmentStatus*), the $\eta_p^2 = .033$. Only 3.3 percent of the variability in *TreatmentRetention* can be explained by the effect of *TreatmentStatus*, which reflects a small effect. Finally, the interaction effect produced a large magnitude of treatment effect, $\eta_p^2 = .169$.

Post Hoc Power

Power is the probability of correctly rejecting a false null hypothesis. We conducted a priori power analysis to help us determine if a combination of our planned alpha level, estimated effect size, and sample size would be enough to detect a significant difference if it existed. The actual or post hoc power values obtained after the data were analyzed are found in the *Tests of Between-Subjects Effects* table (Table 9.12). The post hoc power for the *TreatmentCondition* main effect is .996, indicating that given a post hoc effect size of .198, $\alpha = .01$, and a sample size of 120, the probability was approximately 99.6 times in 100 that we would correctly reject a false null hypothesis in favor of the alternative hypothesis.

The post hoc power for the *TreatmentStatus* main effect is power $= .270$, indicating that the probability was approximately 27 times in 100 that we would correctly reject a false null hypothesis given a post hoc effect size of .033, α of .01, and a sample size of 120. Certainly, the lower than expected post hoc effect size affects the low power value. The power $= .986$ of the interaction effect represented a high probability of correctly rejecting a false null hypothesis in this study.

Confidence Intervals of Mean Differences

A confidence interval (CI) provides information about the probability that a given interval will encircle the true difference between the population means. The probability used for the confidence interval is .99 since $\alpha = .01$ in this study. Conduct the following SPSS analyses to obtain the $CI_{.99}$ for the *TreatmentRetention* mean differences of the main effects of *TreatmentCondition* and *TreatmentStatus*.

IBM SPSS Commands to Obtain $CI_{.99}$ of Mean Differences

1. **Analyze > Compare Means > Independent-Samples T Test.**

2. Click over *Treatment Retention* to **Test Variable(s):** and click over *Treatment Condition* to **Grouping Variable: >** click on the **Define Groups** button; type the number 1 next to **Group 1**, type the number 2 next to **Group 2**, and click on **Continue**.

3. Click on the **Options** button and type in 99%; click on **Continue** and click on **OK**. This produces the output for *Treatment Condition*. Keep the output open.

4. Now, follow the same procedures and replace *Treatment Condition* with *Treatment Status*. Add the resulting output to the output you have already produced. Then, save the output as *Confidence Interval Two-Way ANOVA*.

In Table 9.17, at the end of the row *Equal variances assumed* and under the column *99% Confidence Interval of the Difference*, the $CI_{.99}$ lower limit is -2.207 and the upper limit is $-.660$. The .99 CI interval for the means difference in *TreatmentRetention* comparing the SC and SC + CM conditions is $(-2.207) - (-.660)$. The probability is .99 that this interval will encircle the true mean difference between the population means of *TreatmentRetention* between the SC and SC + CM conditions for adults with cocaine abuse disorders.

The confidence interval for the means difference in *TreatmentRetention* comparing the 0–1 prior treatment attempts and ≥ 2 prior treatment attempts is $(-1.371) - (.304)$ (see Table 9.18). The probability is .99 that this interval will encircle the true mean difference between the population means of *Treatment Retention* between the levels of 0–1 prior treatment attempts and ≥ 2 prior treatment attempts for adults with cocaine abuse disorders.

TABLE 9.17 CI.99 for Mean Difference of Treatment Retention by Treatment Condition

Independent Samples Test

		Levene's Test for Equality of Variances		t-Test for Equality of Means					99% Confidence Interval of the Difference	
		F	Sig.	t	df	Sig. (2-tailed)	Mean Difference	Std. Error Difference	Lower	Upper
TreatmentRetention	Equal variances assumed	.828	.365	-4.850	118	.000	-1.43333	.29553	-2.20706	-.65961
	Equal variances not assumed			-4.850	115.740	.000	-1.43333	.29553	-2.20731	-.65936

TABLE 9.18 CI.₉₉ for Mean Difference of Treatment Retention by Treatment Status

Independent Samples Test

		Levene's Test for Equality of Variances		t-Test for Equality of Means					99% Confidence Interval of the Difference	
		F	Sig.	t	df	Sig. (2-tailed)	Mean Difference	Std. Error Difference	Lower	Upper
TreatmentRetention	Equal variances assumed	3.400	.068	-1.667	118	.098	-.53333	.31990	-1.37087	.30421
	Equal variances not assumed			-1.667	111.649	.098	-.53333	.31990	-1.37165	.30499

PROGRESS REVIEW

1. The omnibus *TreatmentCondition* main effect was significant, whereas the *TreatmentStatus* main effect was not significant. The interaction effect also was significant.

2. Two simple effects were found to be significant. There were higher completed weeks in treatment for participants who received the SC + CM treatment compared to the SC treatment at ≥2 prior treatment attempts. Moreover, those who received the SC + CM treatment and had ≥2 prior treatment attempts showed more completed weeks in treatment than participants who had 0–1 prior treatment attempts.

3. The *TreatmentCondition* main effect and the interaction effect were large, and the *TreatmentStatus* main effect was small.

4. The post hoc power values were larger than the criterion of .80 for the *TreatmentCondition* main effect and the interaction effect. However, the power value (.270) was considerably lower than expected, primarily influenced by the low post hoc effect size.

5. The upper and lower limit of the .99 confidence intervals for the mean difference of the SC versus SC + CM were negative values, suggesting that this interval encircling the true mean difference between the population means of *TreatmentRetention* would be higher for the SC + CM condition. In contrast, the CI.99 for the mean difference between 0–1 prior treatment attempts and ≥2 prior treatment attempts was inconclusive. The lower limit was a negative value and the upper limit was a positive value, suggesting that either level of *TreatmentStatus* could be higher in *TreatmentRetention.*

TABLE 9.19 Two-Way ANOVA Summary Table Specifications

Source of Variation	df	Sum of Squares (SS)	Mean Square (MS)	F
Treatment(1)$_{\text{MainEffect}}$	$K_{T1} - 1$	Formula	SS_{T1}/df_{T1}	MS_{T1}/MS_E
Treatment(2)$_{\text{MainEffect}}$	$K_{T2} - 1$	Formula	SS_{T2}/df_{T2}	MS_{T2}/MS_E
Treatment (3)$_{\text{Int.Effect}}$	$(df_{T1})(df_{T2})$	Formula	SS_{T3}/df_{T3}	MS_{T3}/MS_E
Error (E)	$(df_{Tot}) - (df_{T1}) - (df_{T2}) - (df_{T3})$	Formula	SS_E/df_E	—
Total (TOT)	$N_{TOT} - 1$	Add up the preceding cells	—	—

$df_{T1} = K_{T1} - 1$ is the first main effect degrees of freedom, where K_{T1} is the number of treatments, groups, or means of the first main effect.

$df_{T2} = K_{T2} - 1$ is the second main effect degrees of freedom, where K_{T2} is the number of treatments, groups, or means of the second main effect.

$df_{T3} = (df_{T1})(df_{T2})$ is the interaction effect degrees of freedom, where df_{T1} is multiplied by df_{T2}.

$df_E = (df_{Tot}) - (df_{T1}) - (df_{T2}) - (df_{T3})$ is the error degrees of freedom, where the three treatment dfs are substracted from the total degrees of freedom.

$df_{TOT} = N_{TOT} - 1$ is the total degrees of freedom based on N scores with one score unable to vary.

FORMULA CALCULATIONS OF THE STUDY RESULTS

The formula calculations for the two-way ANOVA, post hoc effect sizes, and confidence intervals are presented next. Calculated values are a little different from the computer values due to rounding differences.

Two-Way ANOVA Formula Calculations

The specifications for constructing a two-way ANOVA summary table are presented first (Table 9.19). The information in this table captures most of the important data needed to conduct the two-way ANOVA. Additionally, the information in Table 9.19 will be useful for calculating post hoc effect sizes and confidence intervals. We will complete the two-way ANOVA summary table for this study after we calculate the necessary formulas. The information in Table 9.20 will be useful in calculating the formulas.

Factorial ANOVA Formulas

We will be using treatment, error, and total sum of squares (SS) formulas to calculate the F-tests for the main effects, interaction effects, and simple effects.

TABLE 9.20 Study Data with Column and Row Means by Subject and Condition

	Standard Care	Standard Care + Contingency Management
Mean$_{Rows}$		
0–1 Prior Attempts		
	6	6
	9	7
	4	5
	5	4
	7	3
	7	4
	5	5
	4	6
	3	7
	6	8
	6	6
	3	5
	8	4
	5	7
	6	3
	7	8
	4	2
	5	6
	6	5
	6	7
	6	6
	3	8
	5	7
	4	5
	8	6
	6	5
	6	8
	5	7
	7	6
	5	5
Mean 5.567 [SC][0–1]	5.700 [SC + CM][0–1]	5.633 [M_{0-1}]
$n = 30$	$n = 30$	$n = 60$

(Continued)

TABLE 9.20   Study Data with Column and Row Means by Subject and Condition (Continued)

	Standard Care	Standard Care + Contingency Management
≥2 Prior Attempts		
	4	8
	6	10
	2	8
	4	7
	5	6
	7	7
	5	8
	3	9
	4	11
	5	8
	6	7
	3	9
	7	7
	6	6
	4	7
	4	8
	5	6
	3	5
	2	8
	6	8
	6	7
	5	8
	7	9
	4	6
	6	7
	5	5
	7	7
	4	8
	5	9
	4	7
Mean 4.800 [SC][≥2] 7.533 [SC + CM][≥2]		6.167 [$M_{≥2}$]
$n = 30$	$n = 30$	$n = 60$
Mean$_{Cols.}$ 5.183[M_{SC}]	6.617 [M_{SC+CM}]	5.900 [GM]
$n = 60$	$n = 60$	$n = 120$

Total (TOT)

$$SS_{Total} = \sum (X_i - GM \ldots)^2$$

where $\sum$ = sum up the resultants of the operations that follow:

X_i = individual score of the data set,

GM = grand mean (total mean weighted by group sample size)

$$= \sum (6 - 5.900)^2 + (9 - 5.900)^2 \ldots (9 - 5.900)^2 (7 - 5.900)^2$$
$$SS_{Total} = 370.800$$

Treatment(1)$_{MainEffect}$

$$
\begin{aligned}
SS_{TreatmentCondition} &= (n)\sum (M_i - GM \ldots)^2 \\
&= (60)[(5.183 - 5.900)^2 + (6.617 - 5.900)^2] \\
&= (60)[(-.717)^2 + (.717)^2] \\
&= (60)[(.514) + (.514)] \\
&= (60)(1.028) \\
SS_{TreatmentCondition} &= 61.680
\end{aligned}
$$

Treatment(2)$_{MainEffect}$

$$
\begin{aligned}
SS_{TreatmentStatus} &= (n)\sum (M_j - GM \ldots)^2 \\
&= (60)[(5.633 - 5.900)^2 + (6.167 - 5.900)^2] \\
&= (60)[(-.267)^2 + (.267)^2] \\
&= (60)[(.071) + (.071)] \\
&= (60)(.142) \\
&= 8.520
\end{aligned}
$$

$$
\begin{aligned}
SS_{CellMeans} &= (n)\sum (M_{ij} - GM \ldots)^2 \\
&= (30)[(5.567 - 5.900)^2 + (4.800 - 5.900)^2 + (5.700 - 5.900)^2 \\
&\quad + (7.533 - 5.900)^2] \\
&= (30)[(-.333)^2 + (-1.100)^2 + (-.200)^2 + (1.633)^2]
\end{aligned}
$$

$$= (30)[(.111) + (1.210) + (.040) + (2.667)]$$
$$= (30)(4.028)$$
$$= 120.840$$

Treatment $(3)_{\text{Int.Effect}}$

$$SS_{\text{Int.Effect}} = SS_{\text{Cell Means}} - SS_{\text{TreatmentCondition}} - SS_{\text{TreatmentStatus}}$$
$$= 120.840 - 61.680 - 8.520$$
$$= 50.640$$
$$SS_{\text{Error}} = SS_{\text{Tot.}} - SS_{\text{TreatmentCondition}} - SS_{\text{TreatmentStatus}} - SS_{\text{Int.Effect}}$$
$$= 370.830 - 61.680 - 8.520 - 50.640$$
$$= 249.990$$

The observed F-values for testing the null hypotheses of the main effect of Treatment Condition, the main effect of Treatment Status, and the interaction effect of Treatment Condition $\times$ Treatment Status are in Table 9.21. Critical values to compare the F-values to can be found using an online calculator.

1. Go to www.danielsoper.com > select **Statistics Calculators** > select **F-Distribution** > select **Critical F-value Calculator** > type in 1 next to **Degrees of freedom 1:** > type 116 next to **Degrees of freedom 2:** > type 0.01 beside **Probability level:** > click on **Calculate!**

The F critical value is 6.85852061, rounded to 6.86. We place the F critical value on the abscissa (base of the curve) of the F-distribution curve. Then, we place the obtained omnibus ANOVA values of $F = 28.6$ (Treatment Condition),

TABLE 9.21 Two-Way ANOVA Summary Table

Source of Variation	df	Sum of Squares (SS)	Mean Square (MS)	F
Treatment(1)$_{\text{MainEffect}}$	1	61.680	61.680	28.6
Treatment(2)$_{\text{MainEffect}}$	1	8.520	8.520	3.9
Treatment(3)$_{\text{Int.Effect}}$	1	50.640	50.640	23.5
Error (E)	116	249.990	2.155	—
Total (TOT)	119	370.830	—	—

FIGURE 9.7 Hypothesis Testing Graph Factorial ANOVA

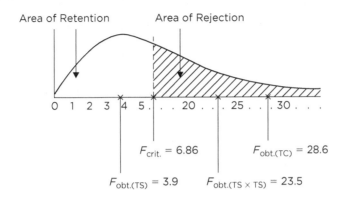

$F = 3.9$ (Treatment Status), and $F = 23.5$ (Treatment Condition $\times$ Treatment Status) on the curve. The area of rejection begins on the abscissa at the CV, and any obtained F to the right of the CV informs us to reject the null hypothesis (see Figure 9.7). The main effect of Treatment Condition and interaction effect of Treatment Condition $\times$ Treatment Status fall in the area of rejection.

Simple Effects Analysis

Since the interaction effect was significant, a simple effects analysis is conducted. A simple effect is the effect of one factor (IV) on the DV at one level of the other factor.

$SS_{\text{TreatmentCondition at 0-1 Prior Treatment Attempts}}$

$$(30)[(5.567 - 5.633)^2 + (5.700 - 5.633)^2]$$
$$(30)[(-.066)^2 + (.067)^2]$$
$$(30)[(.004) + (.004)]$$
$$(30)[(.008]$$
$$.24$$

$SS_{\text{TreatmentCondition at} \geq 2 \text{ Prior Treatment Attempts}}$

$$(30)[(4.800 - 6.167)^2 + (7.533 - 6.167)^2]$$
$$(30)[(-1.367)^2 + (1.366)^2]$$

$$(30)[(1.869) + (1.866)]$$
$$(30)[(3.735]$$
$$112.05$$

$SS_{\text{TreatmentStatus at SC Condition}}$

$$(30)[(5.567 - 5.183)^2 + (4.800 - 5.183)^2]$$
$$(30)[(.384)^2 + (-.383)^2]$$
$$(30)[(.147) + (.147)]$$
$$(30)[(.294]$$
$$8.82$$

$SS_{\text{TreatmentStatus at SC+CM Condition}}$

$$(30)[(5.700 - 6.617)^2 + (7.533 - 6.617)^2]$$
$$(30)[(-.917)^2 + (.916)^2]$$
$$(30)[(.841) + (.839)]$$
$$(30)[(1.680]$$
$$50.40$$

TABLE 9.22 Simple Effects Summary Table

Source of Variation	df	Sum of Squares (SS)	Mean Square (MS)	F
TreatmentCondition				
0–1 Prior treatment attempts	1	.24	.24	.111
≥2 Prior treatment attempts	1	112.05	112.05	51.995
TreatmentStatus				
SC condition	1	8.82	8.82	4.093
SC + CM condition	1	50.40	50.40	23.387
Error	116	249.990	2.155	

Post Hoc Effect Sizes

The magnitude of treatment effects are calculated next for the main effects and interaction effect using both eta-squared (η_p^2) and omega squared (ω^2).

Partial Eta-Squared (η^2)

Eta-squared is a measure of practical significance ranging from 0 (small) to 1.0 (large). The information needed to calculate the following formulas are found in Table 9.21.

$$\eta_p^2 = \frac{\text{Treatment (Effect) Sum of Squares (SS)}}{\text{Treatment SS} + \text{Error SS}}$$

$$\text{Treatment Condition Main Effect} = \frac{61.680}{61.680 + 249.990}$$

$$= \frac{61.680}{311.67}$$

$$\eta^2 = .198$$

Treatment Status Main Effect

$$= \frac{8.520}{8.520 + 249.990}$$

$$= \frac{8.520}{258.510}$$

$$\eta^2 = .033$$

Interaction Effect

$$= \frac{50.640}{50.640 + 249.990}$$

$$= \frac{50.640}{300.630}$$

$$\eta^2 = .168$$

Omega-Squared (ω^2)

Omega-squared is a more conservative (lower) because it estimates effect size between the IV and DV in the population (Tabachnick & Fidell, 2007) and also ranges from 0 to 1.0.

$$\omega^2 = \frac{\text{Treatment SS} - (K - 1)\text{Error MS}}{\text{Treatment SS} + \text{Error SS} + \text{Error MS}}$$

where   Treatment SS = condition sum of squares

   K = number of condition groups

   Error MS = error mean square

   Treatment SS = treatment sum of squares

   Error SS = error sum of squares

Omega-squared is not reported in the Tests of Between-Subjects Effects output, but it can be calculated using information from Table 9.12, Two-Way Analysis of Variance Results.

Treatment Condition Main Effect

$$\omega^2 = \frac{61.633 - (2-1)2.155}{61.633 + 249.933 + 2.155}$$

$$= \frac{61.633 - 2.155}{313.721}$$

$$= \frac{59.478}{313.721}$$

$$\omega^2 = .190$$

Treatment Status Main Effect

$$\omega^2 = \frac{8.533 - (2-1)2.155}{8.533 + 249.933 + 2.155}$$

$$= \frac{8.533 - 2.155}{260.621}$$

$$= \frac{6.378}{260.621}$$

$$\omega^2 = .024$$

Interaction Effect

$$\omega^2 = \frac{50.700 - (2 - 1)2.155}{50.700 + 249.933 + 2.155}$$

$$= \frac{50.700 - 2.155}{302.788}$$

$$= \frac{48.545}{302.788}$$

$$\omega^2 = .160$$

Confidence Intervals (.99) for Mean Differences

The $CI_{.99}$ calculations for the mean differences of Treatment Retention by Treatment Condition (SC vs. SC + CM) and Treatment Status (0–1 prior treatment attempts versus ≥ 2 prior treatment attempts) are presented next.

$CI_{.99}$ for Treatment Retention by Treatment Condition

1. $MSE = S_1^2 + S_2^2/2$

   where MSE = mean square error

   S_1^2 = variance of the SC group

   S_2^2 = variance of the SC + CM group

   $MSE = 2.254 + 2.986/2 = 5.236/2 = 2.618$

2. $SE_{meandiff} = \sqrt{2MSE/n}$

   where n = number of participants in a group

   $$SE_{meandiff} = \sqrt{2(2.618)/60} = \sqrt{5.236/60} = \sqrt{.087} = .295$$

3. $t_{(.99)(58df)} = 2.663$

4. $M_{1(SC)} - M_{2(SC+CM)} = 5.183 - 6.617 = -1.434$

5. $CI_{.99}$Lower Limit $= -1.434 - (2.663)(.295)$
$$= -1.434 - (.786)$$
$$= -2.220$$
$CI_{.99}$Upper Limit $= -1.434 + (2.663)(.295)$
$$= -1.434 + (.786)$$
$$= -.648$$
$CI_{.99}(-2.220) \quad \mu_{Difference}(-.648)$

$CI_{.99}$ for Treatment Retention by Treatment Status

1. $MSE = S_1^2 + S_2^2/2$
$MSE = 2.338 + 3.802/2 = 6.140/2 = 3.070$

2. $SE_{meandiff} = \sqrt{2MSE/n}$

where $\quad n =$ number of participants in a group

$$SE_{meandiff} = \sqrt{2(3.070)/60} = \sqrt{6.140/60} = \sqrt{.102} = .319$$

3. $t_{(.99)}(58df) = 2.663$

4. $M_{1(SC)} - M_{2(SC+CM)} = 5.633 - 6.167 = -.534$

5. $CI_{.99}$Lower Limit $= -.534 - (2.663)(.319)$
$$= -.534 - (.849)$$
$$= -1.383$$

$$\text{CI}_{.99}\text{Upper Limit} = -.534 + (2.663)(.319)$$
$$= -.534 + (.849)$$
$$= .315$$
$$\text{CI}_{.99}(-1.383) \quad \mu_{\text{Difference}}(.315)$$

Study Results

The purpose of this study was to assess whether a contingency management (CM) intervention when added to a standard care (SC) condition would increase the retention of cocaine abusers in treatment. The researchers also focused on whether the number of prior treatment attempts would produce an interaction effect with the contingency management treatment on treatment retention. It was expected that the addition of a contingency management treatment would increase the length of stay in treatment of the cocaine abusers.

One independent variable in the study was treatment condition (SC vs. SC + CM), and the second independent variable was treatment status (0–1 prior treatment attempts vs. ≥2 prior treatment attempts). Treatment retention was the dependent variable, and it is operationally defined as number of successful weeks in treatment.

The study sample consisted of 120 cocaine abusers who sought treatment in community programs. Fifty-four percent ($n = 65$) of the participants were males while females comprised 46 percent ($n = 55$) of the sample. The participants' average age was 35 and their average time abusing cocaine was over 10 years ($M = 10.50$ years, $SD = 7.23$).

The a priori power analyses were conducted to assess the probability of correctly rejecting false null hypotheses in favor of alternative hypotheses. Using an alpha of .01, a sample size of 120, and estimated effect sizes from previous research, the power analyses demonstrated that the a priori power was adequate to conduct the study. All of the a priori power values were higher than the threshold guideline of .80, which provided support for conducting the study.

The data were screened prior to testing the null hypotheses. The data set was checked for data entry accuracy and no missing data were identified. There were no univariate outliers related the treatment retention scores for the four groups. All measures of normality, homogeneity of variance, and independence were assessed as meeting the underlying assumptions.

There was a significant main effect of *TreatmentCondition* on *TreatmentRetention*, $F(1, 116) = 28.605, p < .01$. The mean number of completed weeks in treatment was significantly higher for the participants in the SC + CM condition ($M = 6.617$, $SD = 1.728$) compared to those in the SC condition ($M = 5.183$, $SD = 1.501$). The magnitude of treatment effect was large, $\eta_p^2 = .198$. The mean difference $CI_{.99}$ was $(-2.207) - (-.660)$.

There was not a significant main effect of *TreatmentStatus* on *TreatmentRetention*, $F(1, 116) = 3.961, p > .01$. The mean number of weeks completed in treatment was not significantly different comparing the participants who had 0–1 prior treatment attempts ($M = 5.633$, $SD = 1.529$) to those who had ≥ 2 prior treatment attempts ($M = 6.167$, $SD = 1.950$). Consistent with this finding was a small effect size, $\eta_p^2 = .033$. The $CI_{.99}$ of the mean difference was $(-1.371) - (.304)$.

Combining *TreatmentCondition* and *TreatmentStatus*, the interaction effect on *TreatmentRetention* was significant, $F(1, 116) = 23.531, p < .01$. The interaction effect generated a large magnitude of treatment effect, $\eta_p^2 = .169$.

Since the significant interaction effect showed differences in *TreatmentRetention* across the levels of *TreatmentCondition* and *TreatmentStatus*, a simple effect analysis was conducted to pinpoint the differences. The participants who had ≥ 2 prior treatment attempts showed a significantly higher number of completed weeks of treatment if they were in the SC + CM condition ($M = 7.53$) when compared to those in the SC condition ($M = 4.80$), $F(1, 116) = 52.01, p < .01$. A second significant simple effect was for participants who received the SC + CM condition; they had a higher number of completed weeks of treatment if they had ≥ 2 prior treatment attempts level ($M = 7.533$) compared to those who had 0–1 prior treatment attempts ($M = 5.70$), $F(1, 116) = 23.40, p < .01$.

In conclusion, the standard care plus contingency management intervention condition was more effective in increasing the number of weeks in treatment for cocaine abusers when compared standard care. The length of prior treatment attempts of the participants did not produce a significant effect on the number of weeks in treatment. However, there were significant differences between the levels of treatment condition and treatment status. Participants with ≥ 2 prior treatment attempts demonstrated more completed days in treatment if they were provided the standard care + contingency management condition. Overall, the group of participants who showed the most success had ≥ 2 prior treatment attempts and received the standard care plus contingency management treatment.

SUMMARY

A 2×2 ANOVA using a factorial research design was applied to a research problem to assess whether a behavioral intervention known as contingency management can improve treatment retention compared across prior treatment attempts by cocaine abusers.

We conducted a priori power analyses and determined that study specifications supported the threshold probability of correctly rejecting the false null hypotheses in favor of alternative hypotheses in our study. Data were screened and met criteria for conducting the statistical analyses.

A 2×2 ANOVA was conducted assessing the significance of two main effects and an interaction effect using data from Table 9.23. A simple effects analysis was used to determine the effect of one factor (IV) on the DV at one level of the other factor. The study results were presented.

PROBLEM ASSIGNMENT

Another 2×2 ANOVA problem with data set is found on the companion website. Use the worksheet that is provided along with the steps used in this chapter to complete the assignment.

TABLE 9.23 Two-Way Analysis of Variance Data

ID#	TreatmentRetention	TreatmentCondition*	TreatmentStatus**
1	6	1	1
2	9	1	1
3	4	1	1
4	5	1	1
5	7	1	1
6	7	1	1
7	5	1	1
8	4	1	1
9	3	1	1
10	6	1	1
11	6	1	1

(Continued)

TABLE 9.23 Two-Way Analysis of Variance Data (Continued)

ID#	TreatmentRetention	TreatmentCondition*	TreatmentStatus**
12	3	1	1
13	8	1	1
14	5	1	1
15	6	1	1
16	7	1	1
17	4	1	1
18	5	1	1
19	6	1	1
20	6	1	1
21	6	1	1
22	3	1	1
23	5	1	1
24	4	1	1
25	8	1	1
26	6	1	1
27	6	1	1
28	5	1	1
29	7	1	1
30	5	1	1
31	6	2	1
32	7	2	1
33	5	2	1
34	4	2	1
35	3	2	1
36	4	2	1
37	5	2	1
38	6	2	1
39	7	2	1
40	8	2	1
41	8	2	1
42	5	2	1
43	4	2	1
44	7	2	1
45	3	2	1
46	8	2	1
47	2	2	1
48	6	2	1
49	5	2	1
50	7	2	1

ID#	TreatmentRetention	TreatmentCondition*	TreatmentStatus**
51	6	2	1
52	8	2	1
53	7	2	1
54	5	2	1
55	6	2	1
56	5	2	1
57	8	2	1
58	7	2	1
59	6	2	1
60	5	2	1
61	4	1	2
62	6	1	2
63	2	1	2
64	4	1	2
65	5	1	2
66	7	1	2
67	5	1	2
68	3	1	2
69	4	1	2
70	5	1	2
71	6	1	2
72	3	1	2
73	7	1	2
74	6	1	2
75	4	1	2
76	4	1	2
77	5	1	2
78	3	1	2
79	2	1	2
80	6	1	2
81	6	1	2
82	5	1	2
83	7	1	2
84	4	1	2
85	6	1	2
86	5	1	2
87	7	1	2
88	4	1	2
89	5	1	2

(Continued)

TABLE 9.23   Two-Way Analysis of Variance Data (Continued)

ID#	TreatmentRetention	TreatmentCondition*	TreatmentStatus**
90	4	1	2
91	8	2	2
92	10	2	2
93	8	2	2
94	7	2	2
95	6	2	2
96	7	2	2
97	8	2	2
98	9	2	2
99	11	2	2
100	8	2	2
101	7	2	2
102	9	2	2
103	7	2	2
104	6	2	2
105	7	2	2
106	8	2	2
107	6	2	2
108	5	2	2
109	8	2	2
110	8	2	2
111	7	2	2
112	8	2	2
113	9	2	2
114	6	2	2
115	7	2	2
116	5	2	2
117	7	2	2
118	8	2	2
119	U	2	2
120	7	2	2

*1 = SC
*TreatmentCondition
1 = SC
2 = SC + CM
TreatmentStatus
1 = 0–1 Prior treatment attempts.
2 = ≥2 Prior treatment attempts.

KEY TERMS

between-subjects ANOVA design	mixed-subjects ANOVA design
factorial design	orthogonal
factors	simple effects analysis
independent	2×2 factorial design
interaction effects	within-subjects ANOVA design
main effects	

Chapter 10

ANALYSIS OF COVARIANCE

LEARNING OBJECTIVES

- Demonstrate how to develop research questions and hypotheses as they relate to a research problem incorporating an independent variable, a covariate, and a dependent variable.

- Conduct data diagnostics to assess underlying assumptions.

- Execute conducting a one-way analysis of covariance (ANCOVA) using IBM SPSS and by hand.

- Interpret post hoc effect size analyses using eta-squared (η^2) and confidence intervals.

- Understand the study findings combining the various analyses.

As stated in Chapter 7, a one-way analysis of variance (ANOVA) was used to evaluate the effects of treatment programs to reduce depression among adolescents. The independent variable was the treatment program. The dependent variable (DV) was the symptoms of depression and was expected to change as a result of the impact of the IV. Researchers may come to realize that *extraneous variables* at times interfere with the cause-and-effect relationship planned for a study. In order to discover the independent variable's effect on the dependent variable only, the effects of the extraneous variable(s) must be accounted for and extracted from the results. *Covariates* represent one or more other variables that are affecting the DV, but are not designated as IVs. They usually cause unwanted *variance*.

An analysis of covariance (*ANCOVA*) is a statistical method that uses both the analysis of variance and a *regression analysis*. An ANCOVA adjusts the posttest means to what they would be if all groups started out equally on the covariate.

The research problem presented in this chapter is similar to the problem in Chapter 9. One condition is standard care (SC), and the other condition is standard care with contingency management (SC + CM). The dependent variable is longest duration of abstinence (LDA), operationally defined as the number of weeks of the longest duration of objectively verified continuous abstinence achieved. Age is considered an extraneous variable in this study and treated as a covariate to be partialed out of the dependent variable. This example is simulated based on a study by Rash, Alessi, and Petry (2008).

RESEARCH PROBLEM

The purpose of this research is to examine whether substance abuse treatment condition controlling for age affects longest duration of abstinence from drugs. Older participants are expected to have more weeks of objectively verified continuous abstinence achieved. Older participants also are hypothesized to have more prior attempts at drug rehabilitation treatment programs and more coping skills for relapse prevention. Participants in drug rehabilitation treatment are randomly assigned to one of the two treatment conditions: (1) standard care and (2) standard care plus contingency management. This resulted in 114 participants randomly distributed in the treatment condition groups, standard care ($n_1 = 57$) or standard care plus contingency management ($n_2 = 57$).

STUDY VARIABLES

Independent Variable

The independent variable (IV) is a drug treatment program that is intended to influence the dependent variable (DV) (longest duration of abstinence) in this study. The drug treatment program is operationally defined (OD) as having two conditions in this study: (1) standard care and (2) standard care plus contingency management. The IV is active since the conditions can be manipulated. The scale of measurement of the IV is *discrete-nominal* (or categorical). Analysis of covariance can be used with several independent and dependent variables. Moreover, more than one covariate can be used at the same time. In this study, one independent variable, one dependent variable, and one covariate are used.

Dependent Variable

The dependent variable (DV) is the longest duration of abstinence (LDA). The DV in this study is operationally defined as the number of weeks of longest duration of objectively verified continuous abstinence. Participants were assessed on their longest duration of objectively verified continuous abstinence from zero to 12 weeks; therefore it represents a *continuous scale* of measurement.

Covariate

The covariate is age of the participants and is continuously scaled. The covariate is used to measure the extraneous variable of age that acts like an unwanted independent variable affecting the dependent variable. For example, if the participants in one of the groups (either SC or SC + CM) are older than the participants in the other group, age may confound an understanding of the effects of Treatment Condition (IV) on the DV (LDA). ANCOVA partials out the unwanted differential effects of age so that we have a more accurate understanding of the effects of the IV to the DV.

RESEARCH DESIGN

The research design used for this example is a *two-group posttest-only randomized experimental design with covariate*. We are comparing the dependent variable's results adjusted by the covariate age of the two groups of adults receiving different substance abuse treatment conditions. This is an experimental group design involving random assignment of participants to conditions, with a manipulated independent variable. The research design can be diagrammed as follows:

$$R \quad X_{SC} \quad\quad O_{adj.for.age}$$
$$R \quad X_{SC+CM} \quad O_{adj.for.age}$$

The R represents random assignment to the conditions. The conditions by groups are represented by X_{SC} (standard care) or X_{SC+CM} (standard care plus contingency management). The observation ($O_{adj.for.age}$) is the greatest number of consecutive weeks of objectively verified continuous abstinence achieved adjusted for the covariate age.

Statistical Analysis: Analysis of Covariance (ANCOVA)

Analysis of covariance (ANCOVA) is a statistical method that utilizes both analysis of variance and regression analysis. The introduction of the covariate represents some other variable that is affecting the DV. The researcher is interested in knowing what the outcome of the posttest would be if the covariate was not there. Covariates are usually measured unwanted, extraneous variables (EVs) that are correlated with the DV.

The following assumptions underlie the requirement to use the ANCOVA. The ANCOVA has similar assumptions that were assessed in the ANOVA research problem in Chapter 7, with a few exceptions. The underlying assumptions of the ANCOVA are normality, homogeneity of variance, independence, and *homogeneity of regression (slope)*.

PROGRESS REVIEW

1. The research problem relates to comparing the effects of substance abuse treatment condition (independent variable)

on the number of weeks of longest duration of objectively verified continuous abstinence achieved (dependent variable) when adjusted for the covariate age among adults. The independent variable is operationally defined as standard care, and standard care and contingency management.

2. The 114 adults with substance abuse problems are randomly assigned to the two treatment conditions.

3. The research method is a two-group posttest-only randomized experimental design using a covariate, and the statistical method is a one-way analysis of covariance.

STATING THE OMNIBUS (COMPREHENSIVE) RESEARCH QUESTION

Will there be significant mean differences in longest duration of abstinence across the substance abuse treatment conditions (standard care, and standard care plus contingency management) when adjusted for the covariate of age?

HYPOTHESIS TESTING STEP 1: ESTABLISH THE ALTERNATIVE (RESEARCH) HYPOTHESIS (H_a)

Omnibus Narrative Alternative Hypothesis (H_a)

H_a: There will be a significantly lower number of reported weeks of longest duration of abstinence when adjusted for the covariate of age for the standard care treatment group when compared to the standard care plus contingency management group.

Symbolic H_a

$$H_a : \mu_{SCadj} < \mu_{SC+CMadj}$$

where μ_{SC} is the population mean of the number of weeks of longest duration of objectively verified continuous abstinence of participants in the standard care condition being estimated by the *sample mean*, and μ_{SC+CM} is the *population mean* of the number of weeks of longest duration of objectively verified continuous abstinence for participants in the *standard care plus contingency management condition* being estimated by the sample mean. The reference to "adj." refers to the posttest means of the number of weeks of longest duration being adjusted using the covariate age.

This is a directional alternative hypothesis because it is expected that the standard care plus contingency management treatment condition will significantly increase the number of reported weeks of longest duration of abstinence when compared to the standard care treatment condition.

HYPOTHESIS TESTING STEP 2: ESTABLISH THE NULL HYPOTHESIS (H_0)

The omnibus null hypothesis is stated in both narrative and symbolic formats in the second step of the hypothesis-testing process.

Omnibus Narrative Null Hypothesis (H_0)

H_0: There will be no significant mean differences in longest duration of abstinence across the two substance abuse treatment conditions (standard care and standard care plus contingency management) with a covariate adjustment of age.

Symbolic H_0

$$H_0: \mu_{SCadj} = \mu_{SC+CMadj}$$

HYPOTHESIS TESTING STEP 3: DECIDE ON A RISK LEVEL (ALPHA) OF REJECTING THE TRUE H_0 CONSIDERING TYPE I AND II ERRORS AND POWER

During this step of the hypothesis-testing process, we choose an alpha criterion (α) that will take into consideration both Type I (alpha) and Type II (beta) errors. The decision is made to select an alpha level of .01 for this example to provide more rigor in assessing the difference on LDA between the two conditions.

A Priori Power Analysis

We use the chosen α level of .01 and combine it with anticipated sample size and an estimated (a priori) effect size and determine if we have enough power to conduct the study.

We will use alpha, sample size, and estimated effect size to conduct an a priori power analysis. We can combine these three elements together mathematically and determine if our planned alpha, sample size, and estimated effect size for our proposed study converge into an acceptable probability (power) necessary to find a significant difference in means if it exists.

We have decided to use an alpha of .01 and we are planning on using a sample size of 114. We will use an average $\eta^2 = .11$ from four previous studies. Now we can combine the three elements to identify the probability of correctly rejecting a false null hypothesis in favor of the alternative hypothesis (power).

Power Analysis Using G*Power 3.1.2

Using a computer program such as *G*Power 3.1* (Erdfelder, Faul, & Buchner, 2010), you can conduct the power analysis using G*Power 3.1 by following the steps presented next. The steps of downloading free G*Power 3.1 are located in Chapter 7.

1. Under **Test family**, click on **F tests** (see Figure 10.1A).

2. Under **Statistical test**, click on **ANCOVA: Fixed effects, main effects and interactions.**

3. Under **Type of power analysis**, click on **A priori: Compute required sample size - given α, power, and effect size**.

4. Click on the button called **Determine** to the left of **Effect size f**, and in the new attached window to the right, click on the **Direct** circle and type 0.11 in the box next to **Partial η^2**; then click on the button that says **Calculate and transfer to main window** and then click on the **Close** button.

5. For the next row, α **err prob**, type in our $\alpha = .01$.

6. For **Power** type in the criterion threshold we are using, which is 0.80.

7. The **Numerator df** in our study is 1.

8. There are two groups in our study, so type in 2.

9. There is one covariate in our study, so type in 1.

10. Click on **Calculate** and you will see that we need a total sample size $= 98$ to reach an actual power of .8005192 (see Figure 10.1B). Our total sample of 114 exceeds a needed sample size. Considering the combined elements in our study of total sample size of 114, $\eta^2 = .11$, and $\alpha = .01$, a power greater than .80 should be achieved. Therefore, we should be confident in correctly rejecting a false H_0 in our study and thus avoiding making a Type II error.

FIGURE 10.1A AND B   G*Power Screen Shots for ANCOVA Problem

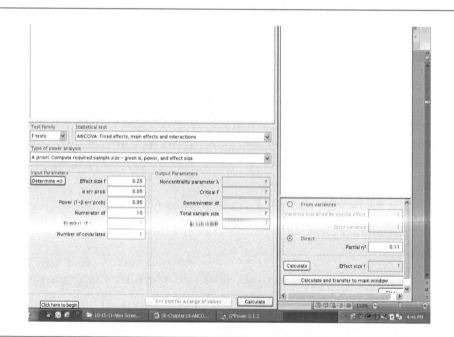

FIGURE 10.1A AND B (Continued)

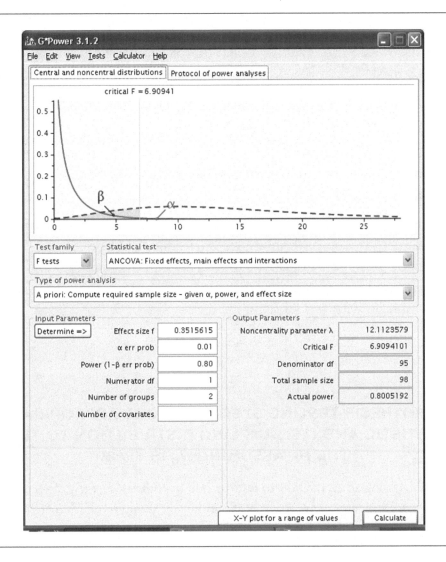

PROGRESS REVIEW

1. We stated the research question for the problem.

2. We completed the first two steps of the hypothesis-testing process by stating the alternative and null hypotheses in narrative and symbolic formats.

3. Next, we decided on the risk we are willing to take when rejecting a true null hypothesis by choosing alpha (α). We chose $\alpha = .01$.

4. We conducted a power analysis using G*Power to make sure that our probability of correctly rejecting a false null hypothesis was adequate (power $= .80$) before moving ahead with the study. This provided information necessary to continue on with the study.

HYPOTHESIS TESTING STEP 4: CHOOSE APPROPRIATE STATISTIC AND ITS SAMPLING DISTRIBUTION TO TEST THE H_0 ASSUMING H_0 IS TRUE

We will be using an ANCOVA to test the null hypothesis: $H_0: \mu_{1adi} = \mu_{2adi}$. We are going to compare the means of weeks of longest duration of abstinence across the conditions (standard care and standard care plus contingency management) for significant mean differences. The purpose of the ANCOVA is to increase the sensitivity of the test of main effects and interactions by reducing the *error term*; the error term is adjusted for, and it is hoped reduced by, the relationship between the DV and the covariate. Another purpose of the ANCOVA is to adjust the means of the DVs themselves to what they would be if all participants scored equally on the covariate.

HYPOTHESIS TESTING STEP 5: SELECT SAMPLE, COLLECT DATA, SCREEN DATA, COMPUTE STATISTIC, AND DETERMINE PROBABILITY ESTIMATES

The study sample participants are selected and data are collected from them. The data are assessed for data accuracy, missing values, and univariate outliers, and to determine if the underlying assumptions of the ANCOVA have been satisfied.

Sample Selection and Assignment

A sample for this study was selected using purposive sampling that involved the application of inclusion and exclusion criteria. The sample consisted of 114 treatment-seeking substance abusers who were randomly assigned to one of two treatment conditions. This resulted in the following number of participants in each treatment condition group: standard care ($n_1 = 57$) and standard care with contingency management ($n_3 = 57$).

Exploratory Data Analysis

The purposes of exploratory data analysis (data screening) are to ensure the data has been properly entered, extracted, or imported into the statistical spreadsheet; locate and address any missing data; handle potential outliers; and assess for univariate underlying assumptions. This process is essential to maintain data integrity.

The following IBM SPSS commands are used to gather descriptive statistics. To start, we assess the dependent variable of longest duration of abstinence (DVLDA) and the covariate (COVAge) for univariate outliers. Then, we evaluate COVAge and LDA by group for normality and homogeneity of variance by examining histograms, skewness, kurtosis, the Shapiro-Wilk statistic, normal Q-Q plots, and Levene statistics.

Data Screening IBM SPSS Commands

1. **Analyze > Descriptive Statistics > Descriptives**.

2. Click over *COVAge* and *DVLDA* to under **Variable(s):** and check the box called **Save standardized values as variables** and click **OK**. This command produces z-scores on the **Data View**.

3. **Analyze > Descriptive Statistics > Explore**. This command results in information used for assessing underlying assumptions.

4. Click over the covariate (*COVAge*) and the dependent variable (*DVLDA)* to **Dependent List**.

5. Click over independent variable *IVTreatment Condition* to **Factor List**.

6. Do not change **Display** choices—leave on **Both**.

7. Click on the **Plots** button in the upper right corner. Then, select **Normality plots with tests**.

8. Under **Spread vs. Level with Levene Test**, click on **Untransformed**.

9. Click on **Continue**.

10. Click on **OK**.

The highest and lowest postive z-scores for the covariate age and the dependent variable longest duration of abstinence are identified in Table 10.1. The z-scores were produced on the Data View spreadsheet as new columns. The z-scores are transformed scores of participants on COVAge and DVLDA. None of the z-scores are greater than a ± 3.29 ($P = .001$, two-tailed). As such, we conclude that there are no participant scores that represent univariate outliers on either the covariate or dependent variable.

The output of skewness, kurtosis, and standard errors for CovAge and DVLDA by group are presented in Table 10.2.

TABLE 10.1 Highest ±z-Scores for the Covariate Age and the Dependent Variable Longest Duration of Abstinence

Highest +z	Outlier? ≥ ±3.29	Highest −z	Outlier? ≥ ±3.29
CovAge 2.858*	No	−1.588	No
DVLDA 2.664	No	−2.119	No

*This number is rounded to three decimals.

TABLE 10.2 Skewness, Kurtosis, and Standard Error Values by Group

Descriptives

	IVTreatmentCondition			Statistic	Std. Error
CovAge	SC	Mean		31.82	1.171
		95% Confidence Interval for Mean	Lower Bound	29.48	
			Upper Bound	34.17	
		5% Trimmed Mean		31.31	
		Median		31.00	
		Variance		78.147	
		Std. Deviation		8.840	
		Minimum		19	
		Maximum		57	
		Range		38	
		Interquartile Range		15	
		Skewness		.681	.316
		Kurtosis		.039	.623
	SC + CM	Mean		34.75	1.191
		95% Confidence Interval for Mean	Lower Bound	32.37	
			Upper Bound	37.14	
		5% Trimmed Mean		34.37	
		Median		34.00	
		Variance		80.796	
		Std. Deviation		8.989	
		Minimum		20	
		Maximum		59	
		Range		39	
		Interquartile Range		15	
		Skewness		.461	.316
		Kurtosis		−.315	.623
DVLDA	SC	Mean		4.79	.245
		95% Confidence Interval for Mean	Lower Bound	4.30	
			Upper Bound	5.28	
		5% Trimmed Mean		4.80	
		Median		5.00	
		Variance		3.419	
		Std. Deviation		1.849	
		Minimum		1	
		Maximum		9	
		Range		8	
		Interquartile Range		3	

(Continued)

TABLE 10.2   Skewness, Kurtosis, and Standard Error Values by Group (Continued)

Descriptives			Statistic	Std. Error
IVTreatmentCondition				
	Skewness		−.189	.316
	Kurtosis		−.385	.623
SC + CM	Mean		6.07	.283
	95% Confidence Interval for Mean	Lower Bound	5.50	
		Upper Bound	6.64	
	5% Trimmed Mean		6.06	
	Median		6.00	
	Variance		4.566	
	Std. Deviation		2.137	
	Minimum		2	
	Maximum		11	
	Range		9	
	Interquartile Range		4	
	Skewness		.042	.316
	Kurtosis		−.649	.623

We divide the skewness statistics by the standard errors and examine if there is significant skewness by comparing the skewness z-scores to the critical value of ±3.29. Since the skewness z-score values are less than ±3.29, we conclude that the distributions are not significantly skewed (see Table 10.3).

We follow the same procedures to examine the kurtosis of the distributions of the groups. (See Table 10.4.) The researcher will divide the kurtosis statistic by its standard error and compare the z-score to the critical value of ±3.29 to see if a group distribution significantly departs from normality.

The kurtosis z-scores are all within acceptable standards of being normally distributed (< ±3.29).

The Shapiro-Wilk (S-W) statistic is the next statistic we will use to establish whether the distribution of the group conditions are normally distributed. (See Table 10.5.) Remember, we want to retain the null hypothesis, which indicates that the sample distribution that we are looking at is not deviating significantly from normal.

TABLE 10.3   Skewness z-Scores by Treatment Condition Group

Variable/Condition	Skewness z (Stat./Std. Error = Z)	Skewness Direction	Sig. Departure? (> ±3.29)
CovAge			
Standard Care	.681/.316 = 2.155	Positive	No
Standard Care + Contingency Management	.461/.316 = 1.459	Positive	No
DVLDA			
Standard Care	−.189/.316 = −.598	Negative	No
Standard Care + Contingency Management	.042/.316 = .133	Positive	No

TABLE 10.4   Kurtosis z-Scores by Substance Treatment Group

Variable/Condition	Kurtosis z (Stat./Std. Error = Z)	Kurtosis Direction	Sig. Departure? (> ±3.29)
CovAge			
Standard Care	.039/.623 = .063	Leptokurtic	No
Standard Care + Contingency Management	−.315/.623 = − .506	Platykurtic	No
DVLDA			
Standard Care	−.385/.623 = −.618	Platykurtic	No
Standard Care + Contingency Management	−.649/.623 = −1.042	Platykurtic	No

TABLE 10.5   Shapiro-Wilk Statistics by Substance Treatment Condition

		Tests of Normality					
		Kolmogorov-Smirnov[a]			Shapiro-Wilk		
	IVTreatment Condition	Statistic	df	Sig.	Statistic	df	Sig.
CovAge	SC	.111	57	.078	.947	57	.014
	SC + CM	.104	57	.192	.964	57	.084
DVLDA	SC	.147	57	.004	.963	57	.079
	SC + CM	.107	57	.161	.968	57	.131

[a]Lilliefors significance correction

Since the significant probability levels of the Shapiro-Wilk statistic are all larger than the set alpha level of .01, we conclude these group distributions on both CovAge and DVLDA are not deviating significantly from being normal.

Last, we will observe the Q-Q plot for each distribution (see Figure 10.2A and B). While the Q-Q plots look better for the DVLDA (see Figure 10.3A and B), the majority of points of all distributions for both variables fall on or near the line. Thus, the Q-Q plots support the normality of the distributions.

The integrated results of the analyses of univariate outliers, skewness z-scores, kurtosis z-scores, Shapiro-Wilk statistics, and the Q-Q plots support the normality of the distributions.

Homogeneity of Variance

In this study we are expecting that the independent variable (drug rehabilitation treatment conditions) will affect the means of the covariate age and the dependent

FIGURE 10.2A AND B Normal Q-Q Plots of CovAge by Groups

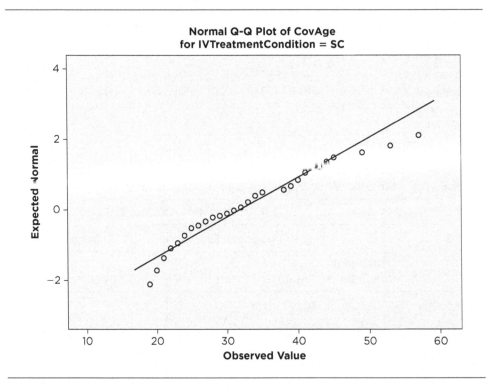

FIGURE 10.2A AND B (Continued)

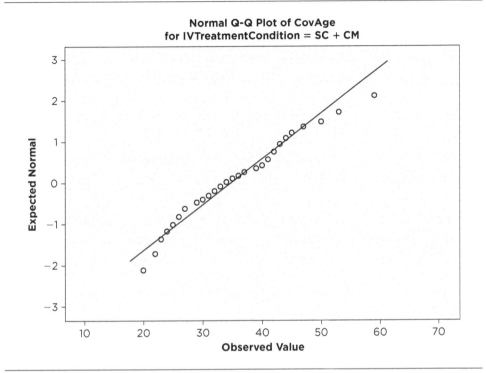

Normal Q-Q Plot of CovAge for IVTreatmentCondition = SC + CM

variable (longest duration of abstinence) but not the variances of the groups. We want the variances of the two groups (standard care and standard care plus contingency management) on the covariate and the dependent variable to be relatively constant. We are going to use the variance ratio (F_{max}), which is the ratio of the largest group variance to the smallest group variance between the two condition groups providing simple descriptive statistics for initial screening.

The two groups have the same number of participants, so the group size ratio is $57/57 = 1.00$; since this is well below a group size ratio of 4, we can apply the $F_{max} = 10$ guideline (Tabachnick & Fidell, 2007).

The SC + CM group had the highest variance on CovAge and the SC group variance had the lowest (see Table 10.2). The $F_{max} = 80.796/78.147 = 1.034$, and the ratio is well below 10.

Again for the DVLDA variable, the SC + CM group had the highest variance of 4.566 and the standard care group showed the lowest variance of 3.419. The $F_{max} = 4.566/3.419 = 1.335$ and is <10. The low variance ratios support homogeneity of variance across the two groups on both variables. We next confirm this finding with the results of the Levene's test.

We test the following null hypothesis of equality of the error variances between the two groups when using Levene's test of homogeneity of variance. We want to retain the null hypothesis concluding that the variances across the two groups on both variables are equal enough using an alpha criterion of .01.

$$H_0: \sigma^2_{e \text{ standard care}} = \sigma^2_{e \text{ standard care plus contingency management}}$$

The Levene's statistic is found in the "assumptionscreen" output under the heading *Test of Homogeneity of Variance* (see Table 10.6) on the line called "Based on mean."

We fail to reject the H_0 that the error variances are equal since the probability values (Sig.) based on the mean (CovAge $= .772$ and DVLDA $= .306$) are

FIGURE 10.3A AND B   Normal Q-Q Plots of DVLDA by Groups

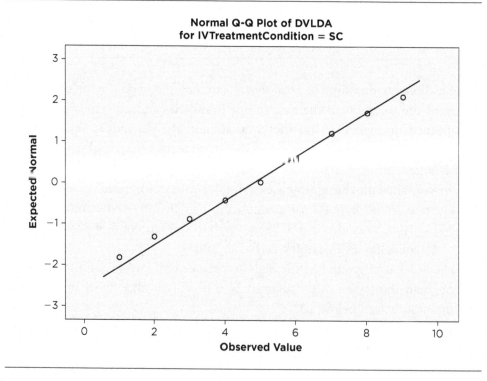

FIGURE 10.3A AND B   (Continued)

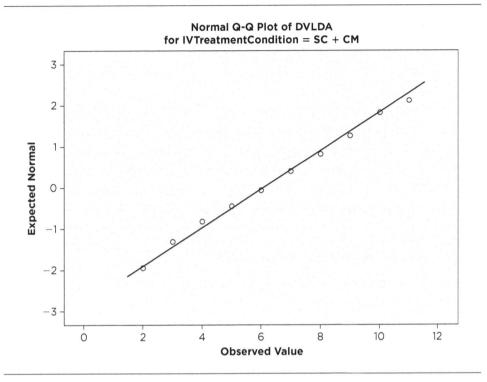

Normal Q-Q Plot of DVLDA
for IVTreatmentCondition = SC + CM

TABLE 10.6   Levene's Test of Homogeneity of Variance for CovAge and DVLDA

	Test of Homogeneity of Variance				
		Levene's Statistic	*df*1	*df*2	Sig.
CovAge	Based on mean	.084	1	112	.772
	Based on median	.066	1	112	.797
	Based on median and with adjusted *df*	.066	1	111.948	.797
	Based on trimmed mean	.076	1	112	.783
DVLDA	Based on mean	1.056	1	112	.306
	Based on median	1.221	1	112	.272
	Based on median and with adjusted *df*	1.221	1	110.669	.272
	Based on trimmed mean	1.057	1	112	.306

greater than $\alpha = .01$. The evidence from the variance ratios and the Levene's statistic suggests that the underlying assumption of homogeneity of variance has been met.

Independence

We are going to assess the independence of observations by graphing the responses of participants on the dependent variable by treatment condition based on the same order in which measurements (observations) were obtained. The data in the IBM SPSS Data View spreadsheet are in a similar order by group based on when the data were collected. We will need to create two columns of data to complete the matrix scatter plot analysis to assess independence.

Matrix Scatter Plot IBM SPSS Commands

1. Under the column labeled DV*LDA* on the IBM SPSS **Data View** spreadsheet, left click and hold on the first cell, which is score *3*, and drag down until you reach *row 57*, which is score 6 and is the last participant score in the *standard care group (treatment condition)*.

2. At the top of the screen, click on **Edit** and then **Copy**.

3. Go to the first empty column, click on the first cell, and it will be bolded.

4. At the top of the screen, click on **Edit** and then click on **Paste** and the data from the *standard care group* will be copied to the new column.

5. At the bottom left of the spreadsheet, click on **Variable View**; name the new column on the fifth row as *LDASC* and change the decimals to 0.

6. Click on **Data View** button and create a new column for the 57 *standard care plus contingency management* scores *(treatment condition 2)* in rows 58 through 114 in the same way. Name the new column as *LDASCCM*. Once you have completed the two new columns, click **File** > **Save**.

7. At the top of the screen, click on **Graphs** > **Legacy Dialogs** > **Scatter/Dot** > **Matrix Scatter** > **Define**.

8. Click over the two new columns (*SCLDA, LDASCCM*) to the space under **Matrix Variables** > **OK**.

FIGURE 10.4   Matrix Scatter Plot to Assess Independence

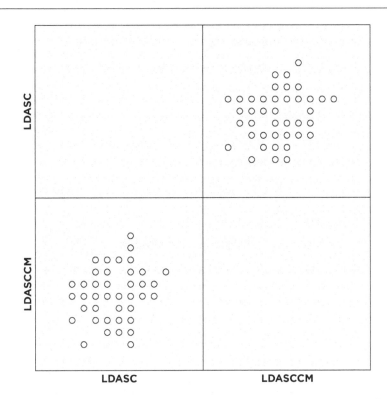

The matrix scatter plot (Figure 10.4) shows the scores of each group compared to the other groups. The scores are in the order they were obtained and are paired as circles in each graph. Since the points scatter in many directions, we conclude that we have met the assumption of independence.

Homogeneity of Regression (Slope) Assumption

In addition to testing the assumption of independence and the assumption of normality, we need to conduct a test of homogeneity of regression (slope) assumption. This test examines the interaction between the covariate (age) and the independent variable (treatment condition) in the prediction of the dependent variable (longest duration of abstinence). We do not want the interaction between the dependent variable and the covariate to be significant. A significant interaction indicates that the difference on the dependent variable (LDA) between the treatment conditions is different because of the covariate (age).

Homogeneity of Regression (Slope) IBM SPSS Commands

1. Click **Analyze**, click **General Linear Model**, and then click **Univariate**.

2. Click the dependent variable (*DVLDA*), click the arrow to move it to the **Dependent variable:** box.

3. Click the independent variable (*IVTreatmentCondition*), click the arrow to move it to the **Fixed Factor(s)** box.

4. Click the covariate (*COVAge*), click the arrow to move it the **Covariate(s):** box.

5. Click on the **Model** button.

6. Click the **Custom** circle under **Specify Model**.

7. Click over *IVTreatCond* and *COVAge* to the space under **Model**.

8. Next, holding down the Ctrl key, click both the *IVTreatmentCondition* and COVAge together in the **Factors & Covariates** box. Check to see that the default option **Interaction** is specified in the drop-down menu in the **Build Term(s)** box. If it is not, select it.

9. Click the arrow going right and COVAge * *IVTreatmentCondition* should now appear in the **Model** box along with IVTreatCond and CovAge.

10. Click **Continue**. This will bring you back to the Univariate screen.

11. Click **OK**.

In Table 10.7, find the interaction effect called *IVTreatCond*COVAge* under the column Source. The significance value (Sig.) is $P = .022$. The interaction is not significant ($P > .01$). We conclude that the assumption of homogeneity of regression is tenable and proceed with the ANCOVA.

Summary of Underlying Assumptions Findings

The evidence obtained demonstrates that the distributions of scores on the dependent variable for both condition groups did not deviate from normality. Both measures of homogeneity of variance supported the assumption of equality.

TABLE 10.7   Homogeneity of Regression (Slope)

Tests of Between-Subjects Effects

Dependent Variable: DVLDA

Source	Type III Sum of Squares	df	Mean Square	F	Sig.
Corrected model	169.178[a]	3	56.393	19.101	.000
Intercept	22.937	1	22.937	7.769	.006
IVTreatCond	6.416	1	6.416	2.173	.143
CovAge	105.161	1	105.161	35.619	.000
IVTreatCond*CovAge	15.876	1	15.876	5.377	.022
Error	324.761	110	2.952		
Total	3,855.000	114			
Corrected total	493.939	113			

[a]R-squared $= .343$ (adjusted R-squared $= .325$)

The scatter plots suggested that independence was met. The homogeneity of regression (slope) was not significant. This information provides support to conduct the ANCOVA statistic to test the omnibus null hypothesis in this study.

PROGRESS REVIEW

1. We collected the data on the dependent variable longest duration of abstinence from the 114 participants who were randomly assigned to one of two condition groups (standard care and standard care plus contingency management).

2. Problems with data accuracy and missing data were ruled out in the early steps of the data screening process.

3. The distributions of the covariate age and the dependent variable longest duration of abstinence (LDA) scores of two condition groups were assessed for compliance to meeting the underlying assumptions of using the ANCOVA. The positive results of this screening assessment allow us to conduct

(continued)

the ANCOVA to determine the effects of the substance abuse treatment conditions (standard care and standard care plus contingency management) on longest duration of abstinence with age as a covariate.

Analysis of Covariance of the Omnibus H_0

ANCOVA IBM SPSS Commands

1. Click **Analyze** > click **General Linear Model** > click **Univariate** > click over *LDA* under **Dependent Variable**, *TreatmentCondition* under **Fixed Factor(s)**, and *Age* over to **Covariate(s)**.

2. Click on the **Plots** button > click *TreatmentCondition* to **Horizontal Axis** > click the **Add** button > click **Continue**.

3. Click on the **Options** button > click *(Overall) and TreatmentCondition* to **Display Means for**. Select **Compare Main Effects**. Select **LSD(none)**.

4. Click on the boxes for **Descriptive statistics, Estimates of effect size, Observed power**, and **Homogeneity tests** > the **Significance level** should be .01 > click on **Continue** > click **OK**.

5. Save generated output as *ANCOVA with Age Results*.

The results of this analysis provide us with information to test the omnibus null hypothesis of the study:

H_0: There will be no significant mean differences in longest duration of abstinence across the two substance abuse treatment conditions (standard care and standard care plus contingency management) with a covariate adjustment for age.

$$H_0: \mu_{SCadj} = \mu_{SC+CMadj}$$

The results of the ANCOVA are presented next. Additionally, interpretations are provided for the magnitude of treatment effects (effect sizes), post hoc power, post hoc multiple comparisons of means, and confidence intervals for the mean differences.

ANCOVA Results

Previously, homogeneity of variance was assessed across groups for the dependent variable and covariate separately (see Table 10.6) and the assumption was met. Table 10.8 shows the test of homogeneity of variance of the dependent variable when the independent variable and covariate are combined. The significance value of .506 is greater than the $\alpha = .01$, so we retain the null hypothesis that the variances are equal and the assumption is met.

In the ANCOVA output labeled Tests of Between-Subjects Effects you will see the name of the independent variable (*IVTreatmentCondition*) under the heading Source that we created when the data were entered (see Table 10.9). We will be using the information in this row to make a decision about rejecting the null hypothesis.

The ANCOVA statistic is in the *F* column ($F = 8.332$) and the *F*-statistic is significant at the $p = .005$ probability level from the Sig. column (see Table 10.9). The criterion that we selected to make a decision about rejecting the null hypothesis was $\alpha = .01$. The significant statistic probability of .005 is less than $\alpha = .01$, so the decision is to reject the null hypothesis ($p < .01$). Hence, there is a significant difference among the two group (standard care and standard care plus contingency management) means on longest duration of abstinence when age is adjusted as the covariate. We can write this finding of the omnibus hypothesis as $F(1, 111) = 8.332$, $p < .01$.

TABLE 10.8 Test of Homogeneity of Variance of DVLDA Including CovAge and IVTreatmentCondition

Levene's Test of Equality of Error Variances[a]			
Dependent Variable: DVLDA			
F	df1	df2	Sig.
.445	1	112	.506

Tests the null hypothesis that the error variance of the dependent variable is equal across groups.
[a]Design: Intercept + CovAge + IVTreatmentCondition

TABLE 10.9 ANCOVA Results

Tests of Between-Subjects Effects

Dependent Variable: DVLDA

Source	Type III Sum of Squares	df	Mean Square	F	Sig.	Partial Eta Squared	Noncent. Parameter	Observed Power[a]
Corrected model	153.302[b]	2	76.651	24.978	.000	.310	49.955	1.000
Intercept	23.973	1	23.973	7.812	.006	.066	7.812	.570
CovAge	106.556	1	106.556	34.722	.000	.238	34.722	.999
IVTreatmentCondition	25.570	1	25.570	8.332	.005	.070	8.332	.605
Error	340.637	111	3.069					
Total	3,855.000	114						
Corrected total	493.939	113						

[a]Computed using alpha = .01
[b]R-squared = .310 (adjusted R-squared = .298)

You can see in Table 10.8 that the covarate age was significant ($p = .000$), indicating the two groups did differ in the average age. Thus, it was a good decision to use age as a covariate.

Estimated Marginal Means

The purpose of the ANCOVA was to control the effects of an extraneous variable, age, interacting differentially with the IV (Treatment Condition) on the DV (Longest Duration of Abstinence). In other words, what would the values of means of the DV be if the participants in the two condition groups (SC and SC + CM) had not differed on the covariate (age)? ANCOVA partials out the effects of the covariate (age) on the DV (Longest Duration of Abstinence) on the means produced by the SC and the SC + CM conditions. These adjusted means are then tested for significant differences. These adjusted (estimated) means are presented in the output (see Table 10.10). The estimated (adjusted) mean of the DV for the SC condition group is $M = 4.95$, and before the mean was adjusted for the covariate (age) it was $M = 4.79$ (see Table 10.2 earlier in the chapter). The estimated mean of the DV for the SC + CM condition group is $M = 5.91$, compared to the unadjusted mean of $M = 6.07$.

The plot of the two estimated marginal means is depicted in Figure 10.5. You can visually see the higher adjusted mean representing longer duration in treatment for the participants who received the SC + CM compared to the CM condition. We discovered previously that this difference is significant.

The mean comparisons support the directional alternative hypothesis that standard care plus contingency management treatment condition significantly increase the number of weeks of abstinence.

TABLE 10.10 Estimated Marginal Means

Estimates				
Dependent Variable: DVLDA				
			99% Confidence Interval	
IVTreatmentCondition	Mean	Std. Error	Lower Bound	Upper Bound
SC	4.950[a]	.234	4.337	5.562
SC + CM	5.910[a]	.234	5.298	6.522

[a]Covariates appearing in the model are evaluated at the following values: COVAge = 33.29.

FIGURE 10.5   Profile Plot

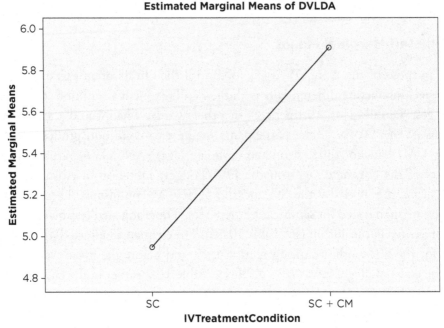

Estimated Marginal Means of DVLDA

Covariates appearing in the model are evaluated at the following values: COVAge = 33.29.

HYPOTHESIS TESTING STEP 6: MAKE DECISION REGARDING THE H_0 AND INTERPRET POST HOC EFFECT SIZES AND CONFIDENCE INTERVALS

We conclude there are mean differences in longest duration of abstinence across the two condition groups with age as a covariate. We next assess the magnitude of treatment effect, post hoc power, and the .99 confidence interval of the mean difference.

Magnitude of Treatment Effect—Post Hoc Effect Size

In the *Tests of Between-Subject Effects* table of the ANCOVA results output (see Table 10.9), the partial eta-squared value ($\eta^2 = .070$) is located on the *Condition* line next to the *Sig.* value. We will interpret the $\eta^2 = .070$ by converting the fraction to a percentage and reporting that approximately 7 percent of the change in the dependent variable (longest duration of abstinence) can be attributed to the independent variable (substance abuse treatment program) when age scores are used as the covariate. The $\eta^2 = .070$ has a medium strength effect according to Cohen's convention where approximately 1 percent to 6 percent is small, >6 percent to 14 percent is medium, and >14 percent is large. The substance abuse treatment program has a significant magnitude of treatment effect on the duration of abstinence.

Post Hoc Power

You remember that we estimated the probability of correctly rejecting a false null hypothesis prior to conducting the study resulting in an a priori power = .80. The actual power after the study was conducted is reported in the *Between-Subjects Effects* output under *Observed Power* for *Condition* (see Table 10.9). The post-hoc power is .605, indicating that given a post hoc effect size of .070, α .01, and a sample size of 114, the probability was approximately 60.5 times in 100 that we would correctly reject a false null hypothesis. The lower than desired post hoc power of .605 was likely due to overestimating the a priori effect size at $\eta^2 = .11$. The post hoc effect size was $\eta^2 = .070$. Fortunately, we were still able to identify a significant difference in longest duration of abstinence resulting from comparing the treatment effects of standard care to the treatment effects of standard care plus contingency management.

Confidence Intervals of Mean Differences

The probability used for the confidence interval is .99 since $\alpha = .01$ in this study. The $CI_{.99}$ was found by using the least significant difference (LSD) pairwise comparisons output (see Table 10.11). The pairwise mean comparisons do not need to be interpreted since there are only two groups (SC and SC + CM) and we already know that the two means are different from the ANCOVA analysis.

The .99 CI interval for the means difference in longest duration of abstinence for comparing the standard care and standard care plus contingency management conditions is $(.088) - (1.832)$. The probability is .99 that this interval will include the true mean difference between the population means of longest duration of abstinence between the standard care and standard care plus contingency management conditions. It is important to note that the upper and lower limits of the .99 interval are going in the same direction, indicating an interval that reflects a gain in duration of abstinence.

TABLE 10.11 Confidence Interval (.99) for the Mean Difference between SC and SC + CM

Pairwise Comparisons

Dependent Variable: DVLDA

(I) IVTreatmentCondition	(J) IVTreatmentCondition	Mean Difference (I − J)	Std. Error	Sig.[a]	99% Confidence Interval for Difference[a] Lower Bound	99% Confidence Interval for Difference[a] Upper Bound
SC	SC + CM	-.960*	.333	.005	-1.832	-.088
SC + CM	SC	.960*	.333	.005	.088	1.832

Based on estimated marginal means.

*The mean difference is significant at the .01 level.

[a]Adjustment for multiple comparisons: Least significant difference (equivalent to no adjustments).

PROGRESS REVIEW

1. The omnibus H_0: $\mu_{SCadj} = \mu_{SC+CMadj}$ was rejected ($p < .01$), indicating the existence of significant mean differences on the dependent variable (LDA).

2. The overall magnitude of treatment effect of the independent variable (substance abuse treatment condition) on the dependent variable (longest duration of abstinence) was a medium effect, $\eta^2 = .070$.

3. The post hoc power of .605 was smaller than the criterion of .80, but we still found a significant effect.

4. The probability is .99 that this interval $(.088) - (1.832)$ will include the true mean difference between the population means of longest duration of abstinence between the standard care and standard care plus contingency management conditions adjusted for age.

FORMULA ANCOVA CALCULATIONS OF THE STUDY RESULTS

The calculation of the ANCOVA problem data are presented in steps following the format of Lowry (2011).

Step 1: Calculations for the Dependent Variable LDA (Y)

The data for LDA (DV, Y) are presented by the groups SC and SC + CM. At the end of the Table 10.12, the N, sums of scores, sums of scores squared, sums of squares and means are provided by group and as totals. The summary statistics will be used in calculating SS_{Total}, $SS_{Between}$, and SS_{Within}. These SS values will be used in later analyses.

TABLE 10.12 Data and Summary Statistics for LDALDA DV (Y)

SC	SC + CM
3	7
2	2
5	4
2	6
3	6
6	5
1	4
4	8
1	7
3	4
1	6
4	3
2	5
5	9
6	3
8	6
3	4
5	3
2	7
8	7
3	5
6	8
7	8
5	5
5	9
7	7
7	6
6	1
5	5
4	7
6	6
7	7
6	3
4	3
6	2
5	6
7	7
5	6
6	3
3	8

SC			SC + CM
6			9
5			5
4			4
5			5
4			9
9			8
6			10
4			4
6			9
4			7
7			6
4			7
6			9
3			9
6			11
4			6
6			7

Totals

N	57	57	114
ΣY_i	273	346	619
ΣY_i^2	1,499	2,356	3,855
SS	215	279	494
M	4.79	6.07	5.43

$$SS_{Total} = \sum (X_{ij} - M_{Tot.})^2$$
$$= (3 - 5.43)^2 + (2 - 5.43)^2 \cdots (6 - 5.43)^2 + (7 - 5.43)^2$$
$$= 493.94$$
$$SS_{Between} = n_1(M_1 - M_{tot.})^2 + n_2(M_2 - M_{tot.})^2$$
$$= 57(4.79 - 5.43)^2 + 57(6.07 - 5.43)^2$$
$$= 57(-.64)^2 + 57(.64)^2$$
$$= 57(.410) + 57(.410)$$
$$= 23.37 + 23.37$$
$$= 46.74$$

$$SS_{Within} = SS_{Total} - SS_{Between}$$
$$= 493.94 - 46.74$$
$$= 447.20$$

Step 2: Calculations for the Covariate Age (X)

The data for Age (covariate, X) are presented in table 10.13 by groups SC and SC + CM. At the end of the table the N, sums of scores, sums of scores squared, sums of squares, and means are provided by group and as totals. The summary statistics are used in calculating SS_{Total}, $SS_{Between}$, and SS_{Within}, in later analyses.

TABLE 10.13   Data and Summary Statistics for Age

Age COV (X)	
SC	SC + CM
19	36
20	33
20	23
21	53
21	41
21	32
22	37
22	29
22	40
23	31
24	25
24	26
24	42
24	55
24	23
24	26
25	26
25	22
26	43
27	41
27	25
27	45
27	35
28	24
29	53

Age COV (X)

SC			SC + CM
30			43
30			44
31			23
31			41
32			34
32			37
33			40
33			39
33			22
33			25
33			34
34			32
34			31
34			27
35			37
38			35
38			31
39			29
39			30
40			41
40			47
40			42
40			20
41			33
41			27
43			27
43			45
44			42
45			50
49			59
53			27
57			43

Totals

N	57	57	
ΣX_i	1,814	1,981	3,795
ΣX_i^2	62,106	73,373	135,479
SS	4,499	4,647	9,146
M	31.825	34.754	33.289

$$SS_{Total} = \sum (X_{ij} - M_{Tot.})^2$$
$$= (19 - 33.29)^2 + (20 - 33.29)^2 (27 - 33.29)^2 + (43 - 33.29)^2$$
$$= 9{,}145.45$$
$$SS_{Between} = n_1 (M_1 - M_{tot.})^2 + n_2 (M_2 - M_{tot.})^2$$
$$= 57(31.825 - 33.289)^2 + 57(34.754 - 33.289)^2$$
$$= 57(-1.464)^2 + 57(1.465)^2$$
$$= 57(2.143) + 57(2.146)$$
$$= 122.151 + 122.322$$
$$= 244.473$$
$$SS_{Within} = SS_{Total} - SS_{Between}$$
$$= 9{,}145.45 - 244.47$$
$$= 8{,}900.98$$

Step 3: Calculations of Covariance of Age $\times$ LDA

Next, the covariance calculations of the covariate (Age) times the dependent variable (LDA) are conducted. These analyses result in sums of the cross product of Age and LDA for SC and SC + CM groups and a total. Then, the sums of squares total and within of the covariance are calculated.

SC		SC + CM	
Age	LDA	Age	LDA
19	3	36	7
20	2	33	2
20	5	23	4
21	2	53	6
21	3	41	6
21	6	32	5
22	1	37	4
22	4	29	8
22	1	40	7
23	3	31	4
24	1	25	6
24	4	26	3

SC		SC + CM	
Age	LDA	Age	LDA
24	2	42	5
24	5	33	9
24	6	23	3
24	8	26	6
25	3	26	4
25	5	22	3
26	2	43	7
27	8	41	7
27	3	25	5
27	6	45	8
27	7	35	8
28	5	24	5
29	5	53	9
30	7	43	7
30	7	44	6
31	6	23	4
31	5	41	5
32	4	34	7
32	6	37	6
33	7	40	7
33	6	39	3
33	4	22	3
33	6	25	2
33	5	34	6
34	7	32	7
34	5	31	6
34	6	27	3
35	3	37	8
38	6	35	9
38	5	31	5
39	4	29	4
39	5	30	5
40	4	41	9
40	9	47	8
40	6	42	10
40	4	20	4
41	6	33	9
41	4	27	7
43	7	27	6

(Continued)

SC		SC + CM	
Age	LDA	Age	LDA
43	4	45	7
44	6	42	9
45	3	50	9
49	6	59	11
53	4	27	6
57	6	43	7

SC	SC + CM	Total
$\sum(X_{\text{age}}Y_{\text{LDA}}) = 8{,}979$	$\sum(X_{\text{age}}Y_{\text{LDA}}) = 12{,}708$	$\sum(X_{age}Y_{\text{LDATot}}) = 21{,}687$
$\sum X_{\text{age}} = 1{,}814$	$\sum X_{\text{age}} = 1{,}981$	$\sum X_{\text{ageTot}} = 3{,}795$
$\sum Y_{\text{LDA}} = 273$	$\sum Y_{\text{LDA}} = 346$	$\sum Y_{\text{LDATot}} = 619$

$$\text{SSCOV}_{\text{Tot}} = \sum(X_{\text{age}}Y_{\text{LDATot}}) - \frac{(\sum X_{\text{ageTot}})(\sum Y_{\text{LDATot}})}{N_{\text{tot}}}$$

$$= 21{,}687 - \frac{(3{,}795)(619)}{114}$$

$$= 21{,}687 - 2{,}349{,}105/114$$

$$= 21{,}687 - 20{,}606$$

$$= 1{,}081$$

$$\text{SSCOV}_{\text{Within(group)}} = \sum(X_{\text{age}}Y_{\text{LDA}}) - \frac{(\sum X_{\text{age}})(\sum Y_{\text{LDA}})}{n}$$

$$\text{SC Group} = 8{,}979 - (1{,}814)(273)/57$$

$$= 8{,}979 - 495{,}222/57$$

$$= 8{,}979 - 8{,}688$$

$$= 291$$

$$SC + CM\,Group = 12{,}708 - (1{,}981)(346)/57$$
$$= 12{,}708 - 685{,}426/57$$
$$= 12{,}708 - 12{,}025$$
$$= 683$$
$$SSCOV_{Within} = SSCOV_{Within(SC)} + SSCOV_{Within(SC+CM)}$$
$$= 291 + 683$$
$$= 974$$

Step 4: Adjustment of LDA (DV, *Y*) Based on the Covariate of Age (*X*)

We are conducting calculations to remove (or adjust) the effects of the covariate (Age) on the dependent variable (LDA). We will use previous calculations to conduct the adjustments so they are summarized in Table 10.14 for easy access.

Adjustment of $SS_{Total(Y)}$

$$Adjusted\,SS_{Total(Y)} = SS_{Total(Y)} - (SSCOV_{Total})^2/SS_{Total(X)}$$
$$= 493.94 - (1{,}081)^2/9{,}145.45)$$
$$= 493.94 - 1{,}168{,}561/9{,}145.45$$
$$= 493.94 - 127.78$$
$$= 366.16$$
$$Adjusted\,SS_{Within(Y)} = SS_{Within(Y)} - (SSCOV_{Within})^2/SS_{Within(X)}$$
$$= 447.20 - (974)^2/8{,}900.98$$
$$= 447.20 - 948{,}676/8{,}900.98$$
$$= 447.20 - 106.58$$
$$= 340.62$$

TABLE 10.14 Summary of Previous Calculations

	Age (*X*)	LDA (*Y*)	Covariance
SS_{Total}	9,145.45	493.94	1,081
SS_{Within}	8,900.98	447.20	974
$SS_{Between}$	46.74		

$$\text{Adjustment of } SS_{\text{Between}(Y)} = \text{adj}\left(SS_{\text{Total}(Y)}\right) - \text{adj}\left(SS_{\text{Within}(g)(Y)}\right)$$
$$= 366.16 - 340.62$$
$$= 25.54$$

The summary table of the ANCOVA results is presented in Table 10.15. Figure 10.6 shows a visual representation of the findings. A critical value (CV) is obtained using an online calculator.

Go to www.danielsoper.com > select **Statistics Calculators** > select **F-Distribution** > select **Critical F-value Calculator** > type in 1 next to **Degrees of freedom 1:** > type 111 next to **Degrees of freedom 2:** > type 0.01 beside **Probability level:** > click on **Calculate!**

The F critical value is 6.86884699, rounded to 6.87. We place the F critical value on the abscissa (base of the curve) of the F-distribution curve. Then, we place the obtained omnibus ANOVA value of $F = 8.3$ on the curve. The area of rejection begins on the abscissa at the CV, and any obtained F to the right of the

TABLE 10.15 Summary of ANCOVA Results

Source	SS	df	MS	F	P
Adjusted means (Between)	25.54	1	25.54	8.3	P<.01
Adjusted error (Within)	340.62	111	3.07		
Adjusted total	366.16				

FIGURE 10.6 Hypothesis Testing Graph ANCOVA

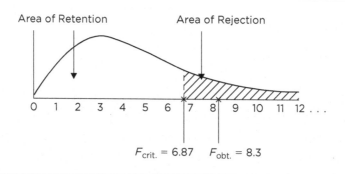

CV informs us to reject the null hypothesis. Our $F_{obtained} = 8.3$ falls in the area of rejection to the right of the $CV = 6.87$, so we reject the H_0, concluding that if the null hypothesis is true we would have obtained results like these less than 1 percent of the time.

Step 5: Calculation of Adjusted Means

$$B_{Within} = SSCOV_{Within}/SS_{Within(Age)}$$

$$= 974/8,900.98$$

$$= .11$$

$$M_{LDASC} \text{ Adjusted} = M_{LDASC} + (B_{Within})(M_{AgeSC} - M_{AgeTot})$$

$$= 4.79 + (.11)(31.82 - 33.29)$$

$$= 4.79 + (.11)(1.47 \text{ absolute value})$$

$$= 4.79 + (.16)$$

$$= 4.95$$

$$M_{LDASC+CM} \text{ Adjusted} = M_{LDASC+CM} - (B_{Within})(M_{AgeSC+CM} - M_{AgeTot})$$

$$= 6.07 - (.11)(34.75 - 33.29)$$

$$= 6.07 - (.11)(1.46)$$

$$= 6.07 - (.16)$$

$$= 5.91$$

	M_{Age}	M_{LDA}	M_{LDA} Adjusted
SC	31.82	4.79	4.95
SC + CM	34.75	6.07	5.91
Total	33.29	5.43	

Adjustment of $SS_{Total(Y)}$ Correlation r

$$r_{Tot.} = \frac{SSCOV_{Tot}}{sqrt([SS_{Tot(Age)}][SS_{Tot(LDA)}])}$$

$$= \frac{1,081}{sqrt([9,145][494])}$$

$$= 1,081/sqrt(4,517,630)$$

$$= 1,081/2,125$$

$$= .509$$

$$(r_{Tot})^2 = (.509)^2 = .259$$

Adjustment of $SS_{Within(Y)}$ Correlation (r)

$$r_{Within(LDA)} = \frac{SSCOV_{Within(LDA)}}{sqrt\left([SS_{Within(Age)}][SS_{Within(LDA)}]\right)}$$

$$= \frac{974}{sqrt([8,900.98][447.20])}$$

$$= 974/sqrt(3,980,518.26)$$

$$= 974/1,995.12$$

$$= .488$$

$$(r_{Within})^2 = (.488)^2 = .238$$

Post Hoc Effect Size

$$\eta_p^2 = \frac{\text{Treatment (Condition) sum of squares (SS)}}{\text{Treatment SS} + \text{Error SS}}$$

$$= \frac{25.570}{25.570 + 340.637}$$

$$= \frac{25.570}{366.207}$$

$$\eta_p^2 = .07$$

ANCOVA STUDY RESULTS

The purpose of this study was to determine if abstinence from using drugs is increased when a contingency management program is added to standard care with age as a covariate. The independent variable is a drug treatment program having two conditions: standard care, and standard care plus contingency management. The dependent variable is the longest duration of abstinence (LDA), operationally defined as the number of weeks of longest duration of objectively verified continuous abstinence. The legally documented age of the participants is used as the covariate in the study.

Data were collected from a sample of 114 substance abusers who were randomly assigned to receive the standard care condition ($n = 57$) or the standard condition plus contingency management condition ($n = 57$). The data were assessed for data accuracy and missing data. Also, the data were screened for underlying assumptions and were found to meet normality, homogeneity of variance, independence, and homogeneity of regression requirements.

The a priori power analysis was conducted using an average estimated effect size ($\eta^2 = .11$) from previous studies, $\alpha = .01$, $N = 114$, and a power criterion of .80. The analysis showed that we should be confident in correctly rejecting a false H_0 in favor of the alternative hypothesis in our study.

The omnibus null hypothesis was tested, and there was a significant difference in LDA among participants in the SC condition compared to those in the SC + CM condition with age used as a covariate, $F(1, 111) = 8.332$, $p < .01$. The participants in the SC + CM condition showed a higher number of days of abstinence ($M_{adj.} = 5.91$, SE $= .234$) than did participants in the standard condition ($M_{adj.} = 4.95$, SE $= .234$).

The post hoc effect size was $\eta^2 = .07$. The CI$_{.99}$ of the mean difference was $(.088) - (1.832)$, indicating that the probability is .99 that this interval will include the true mean difference between the population means of longest duration of abstinence between the standard care and standard care plus contingency management conditions adjusted for age.

In conclusion, a longer duration in abstinence from drugs was found when contingency management treatment was added to the standard care compared to the results of standard care only. Moreover, this finding is contingent on age being used as a covariate.

SUMMARY

An ANCOVA was conducted for this research problem. The independent variable (substance abuse treatment condition) included two levels: standard care and standard care plus contingency management. The dependent variable was the longest duration of abstinence and the covariate was the age of participants. Research questions and hypotheses were developed that incorporated independent, dependent, and covariate variables. We established a criterion alpha level considering Type I and Type II errors. An a priori power analysis was conducted to assess the dependability of the study.

Data were entered for computer analyses using the IBM SPSS statistical program (see Table 10.16). Data diagnostics were conducted to ensure we met univariate underlying assumptions of normality, homogeneity of variance, independence of scores, and homogeneity of regression (slope).

TABLE 10.16   Analysis of Covariance Data

ID#	IVTreatCond	COVAge	DVLDA
1	1	19	3
2	1	20	2
3	1	20	5
4	1	21	2
5	1	21	3
6	1	21	6
7	1	22	1
8	1	22	4
9	1	22	1
10	1	23	3
11	1	24	1
12	1	24	4
13	1	24	2
14	1	24	5
15	1	24	6
16	1	24	8
17	1	25	3
18	1	25	5
19	1	26	2
20	1	27	8
21	1	27	3
22	1	27	6

ID#	IVTreatCond	COVAge	DVLDA
23	1	27	7
24	1	28	5
25	1	29	5
26	1	30	7
27	1	30	7
28	1	31	6
29	1	31	5
30	1	32	4
31	1	32	6
32	1	33	7
33	1	33	6
34	1	33	4
35	1	33	6
36	1	33	5
37	1	34	7
38	1	34	5
39	1	34	6
40	1	35	3
41	1	38	6
42	1	38	5
43	1	39	4
44	1	39	5
45	1	40	4
46	1	40	9
47	1	40	6
48	1	40	4
49	1	41	6
50	1	41	4
51	1	43	7
52	1	43	4
53	1	44	6
54	1	45	3
55	1	49	6
56	1	53	4
57	1	57	6
58	2	36	7
59	2	33	2
60	2	23	4
61	2	53	6
62	2	41	6

(Continued)

TABLE 10.16 Analysis of Covariance Data (Continued)

ID#	IVTreatCond	COVAge	DVLDA
63	2	32	5
64	2	37	4
65	2	29	8
66	2	40	7
67	2	31	4
68	2	25	6
69	2	26	3
70	2	42	5
71	2	33	9
72	2	23	3
73	2	26	6
74	2	26	4
75	2	22	3
76	2	43	7
77	2	41	7
78	2	25	5
79	2	45	8
80	2	35	8
81	2	24	5
82	2	53	9
83	2	43	7
84	2	44	6
85	2	23	4
86	2	41	5
87	2	34	7
88	2	37	6
89	2	40	7
90	2	39	7
91	2	22	3
92	2	25	2
93	2	34	6
94	2	32	7
95	2	31	6
96	2	27	3
97	2	37	8
98	2	35	9
99	2	31	5
100	2	29	4
101	2	30	5
102	2	41	9
103	2	47	8

ID#	IVTreatCond	COVAge	DVLDA
104	2	42	10
105	2	20	4
106	2	33	9
107	2	27	7
108	2	27	6
109	2	45	7
110	2	42	9
111	2	50	9
112	2	59	11
113	2	27	6
114	2	43	7

Treatment conditions:
1 = Standard care
2 = Standard care plus contingency management

An ANCOVA analysis was conducted by hand and using IBM SPSS computer analysis. Post hoc effect size, power, and .99 confidence interval were calculated. Finally, a summary of the results was presented.

PROBLEM ASSIGNMENT

The steps involved in conducting an ANCOVA using IBM SPSS have been presented in this chapter. Now it is your turn to work independently through the steps of the hypothesis-testing process related to an ANCOVA using IBM SPSS. Go to the companion website and you will find a new ANCOVA research problem and data set along with a worksheet to complete. Use the problem presented in this chapter as a guide so you can complete the assignment. Your instructor will evaluate your completed worksheet when it is finished.

KEY TERMS

ANCOVA

continuous scale

covariates

discrete-nominal

error term

exploratory data analysis

extraneous variable

homogeneity of regression (slope)

G*Power 3.1

nominal-scaled

population mean

regression analysis

sample mean

two-group posttest-only randomized experimental design with covariate

variance

Chapter 11

RANDOMIZED CONTROL GROUP AND REPEATED-TREATMENT DESIGNS AND NONPARAMETICS

LEARNING OBJECTIVES

○ Demonstrate how to develop research questions and hypotheses as they relate to a research problem incorporating independent and dependent variables studies using nonparametric statistics.

○ Conduct data diagnostics to assess for parametric underlying assumptions and show how, when they are not met, nonparametric statistics provide alternatives.

○ Execute a Kruskal-Wallis test for independent samples, Mann-Whitney U test of two independent samples, Friedman's test for correlated samples, and Wilcoxon's test for two correlated samples.

○ Interpret post hoc analyses and understand the study findings combining the various analyses.

The use of four commonly used nonparametric statistics as alternatives to their parametric counterparts is covered in this chapter. Two research problem data sets are used to understand the application of nonparametric statistics. Kruskal-Wallis and Mann-Whitney *U* statistics will be used in the first data set and another data set will be used to illustrate the analyses of the Friedman and Wilcoxon tests.

RESEARCH PROBLEM

Multiple sclerosis (MS) is a central nervous system disease that affects the brain, spinal cord, and optic nerves (National Multiple Sclerosis Society, 2012). Chronic low back pain is one of the symptoms that individuals with MS can experience. In addition to medications to control pain, there are nonpharmacological methods used to manage pain. One method being tested by researchers is called transcutaneous electrical nerve stimulation (TENS) (Warke, Al-Smadi, Baxter, Walsh, & Lowe-Strong, 2006). TENS is administered as an electrical current applied to the participant's lumbar spine using a lumbar belt with self-adhering electrodes. Participants are trained on how and when to self-administer the TENS. This simulated study problem is designed to assess the effects of TENS on chronic low-back pain of persons with multiple sclerosis using the study by Warke et al. (2006) as a guide.

Persons with multiple sclerosis were recruited from an MS support group organization in a large city in the United States. Sixty persons who have multiple sclerosis comprise the sample. The average age of participants is 42.30 (SD = 4.20). There are 48 females (80 percent) and 12 males (20 percent). The participants have experienced low back pain over 11 years.

The 60 participants are randomly assigned to three condition groups. The participants in the first condition receive a low electric stimulation while the second group receives a placebo and the third group receives a high electric stimulation. The outcome variable is pain improvement as measured by the McGill Pain Questionnaire (MPQ).

STUDY VARIABLES

The independent variable is electric stimulation condition and has three conditions: (1) low electric stimulation, (2) placebo, and (3) high electric stimulation. The participants used a lumbar belt with neurostimulation electrodes positioned to emit a current to their lumbar spine region. The participants were trained in the use of the lumbar belt and how to self-administer their allotted electric stimulation level six days a week for 45 minutes at home over 24 weeks. The placebo condition participants received everything that the stimulation condition participants received except for the real electric stimulation.

The dependent variable is pain improvement, and it is operationally defined as scores on the McGill Pain Questionnaire (MPQ). An MPQ score is derived from patients rating their pain based on its location, what it feels like, pain change over time, and strength of pain from mild to excruciating. MPQ scores were obtained before treatment began. Improvement scores were recorded following treatment. In this study example, higher improvement scores translate to greater pain improvement.

RESEARCH DESIGN

The research design used for this research example is a *randomized pretest-posttest control group design* (Shadish, Cook, & Campbell, 2002) (see Figure 11.1). Each line in the diagram represents a group (three groups), and the R symbolizes random assignment to each group condition. The observations (O) before the treatment conditions represent a pretest on pain improvement using MPQ scores. The conditions by groups are represented by X_1 (low stimulation condition), C (placebo), and X_2 (high stimulation condition). The observations (O) following the treatment conditions represent the posttest pain level scores on the MPQ.

This design has utility for several statistical analyses. The pretest scores can be analyzed for differences (between-design) in pain improvement across the treatment conditions before the study is implemented. If there are differences in pain improvement across the groups, the pretest pain level scores can be used as a covariate to cancel out differences when comparing the posttest scores on pain improvement. Pretest and posttest scores can be analyzed for gains using a repeated-measures (within-design) statistic. Posttest scores can be analyzed for differences in pain improvement across the treatment conditions following treatment (between-design).

FIGURE 11.1 Randomized Pretest-
Posttest Control Group Design

R	*O*	X_1LowElectStim	*O*
R	*O*	C_2Placebo	*O*
R	*O*	X_2HighElecStim	*O*

Statistical Analyses

We begin with an analysis of the posttest pain improvement as measured by the MPQ scores to see if there were any differential treatment effects across the three conditions. The pain improvement scores were analyzed at the pretest and no significant differences were found. So the condition groups are starting out relatively equal on pain improvement before the treatment begins. We will find that the dependent variable does not meet the underlying assumptions of normality, so our choice will be to use a nonparametric *Kruskal-Wallis ANOVA* with a post hoc analysis using a *Mann-Whitney U (MWU) statistic.*

Parametric statistics use sample statistics to estimate population parameters requiring underlying assumptions that include normality and homogeneity of variance of the dependent variable from which the sample was drawn. *Nonparametric statistics* do not have the same stringent assumptions (Siegel, 1956). Salsburg (2001) says that a nonparametric statistic compares "the observed scatter of data with what might have been expected from purely random scatter" (p. 163).

Siegel (1956) identified several advantages of using nonparametric statistics. Nonparametrics use either exact probability or excellent approximations for large samples. Thus, the accuracy of probability statements does not rely on the shape of the population. When the sample size is quite small, say $N = 6$, nonparametrics are most effective. Nonparametric statistics can be used for dependent variable scores that are inherently in the form of ranks (ordinal) or categories (nominal).

PROGRESS REVIEW

1. The research problem that is focused on in this chapter relates to comparing the effects of electric stimulation (independent variable), operationally defined as a low electric stimulation condition, a placebo condition, and a high electric stimulation condition on pain improvement (dependent variable) among persons with multiple sclerosis who have chronic back pain.

---

2. Sixty participants were randomly assigned to the three treatment conditions using a randomized pretest-posttest control group design.

3. MPQ scores were obtained before treatment began. Improvement scores were recorded following treatment. Higher improvement scores indicate greater pain improvement.

4. A Kruskal-Wallis analysis of variance will be used to assess differences in the pain improvement scores across the three condition groups following treatment (posttest).

5. Next, the research question is stated and we begin completing the steps of the hypothesis-testing process.

STATING THE OMNIBUS (COMPREHENSIVE) RESEARCH QUESTION

The research question is stated first and then the steps of the hypothesis-testing process related to this research problem are presented.

Omnibus Research Question (RQ)

Will electric stimulation improve lower back pain when compared to a placebo condition among persons who have multiple sclerosis?

HYPOTHESIS TESTING STEP 1: ESTABLISH THE ALTERNATIVE (RESEARCH) HYPOTHESIS (H_a)

The omnibus (comprehensive) alternative hypothesis for the research problem is stated next in both narrative and symbolic formats.

Omnibus Narrative Alternative Hypothesis (H_a)

H_a: The low and high electric stimulation conditions will produce significantly more pain improvement when compared to the placebo condition among persons who have multiple sclerosis.

Symbolic H_a

$$H_a: \mu_{rankLowElectStim} > \mu_{rankPlacebo} < \mu_{rankHighElectStim}$$

This is a directional alternative hypothesis since it is expected that either low or high electric stimulation will improve low back pain when compare to the placebo condition.

Jones and Tukey Method of Possible Conclusions

Once the results are obtained, we will make one of the following decisions: (1) $(\mu_1 - \mu_2) > 0$, $(\mu_1 - \mu_3) > 0$, $(\mu_2 - \mu_3) > 0$; (2) $(\mu_1 - \mu_2) < 0$, $(\mu_1 - \mu_3) < 0$, $(\mu_2 - \mu_3) < 0$; or (3) the sign (< 0 or > 0) of $(\mu_1 - \mu_2)$, $(\mu_1 - \mu_3)$, $(\mu_2 - \mu_3)$ is indefinite. In this study, we are expecting that $(\mu_{rankLowElectStim} - \mu_{rankPlacebo}) > 0$ and that $(\mu_{rankHighElectStim} - \mu_{rankPlacebo}) > 0$, and that $(\mu_{rankLowElectStim} - \mu_{rankHighElectStim})$ is indefinite.

HYPOTHESIS TESTING STEP 2: ESTABLISH THE NULL HYPOTHESIS (H_0)

The omnibus null hypothesis is stated in narrative and symbolic formats in the second step of the hypothesis-testing process.

Omnibus Narrative Null Hypothesis (H_0)

H_0: There will be no significant mean rank differences in pain improvement (MPQ scores) across the electric stimulation conditions (low electric stimulation, placebo, high electric stimulation) following treatment implementation

Symbolic H_0

$$H_0: \mu_{rankLowElectStim} = \mu_{rankPlacebo} = \mu_{rankHighElectStim}$$

HYPOTHESIS TESTING STEP 3: DECIDE ON A RISK LEVEL (ALPHA) OF REJECTING THE TRUE H_0 CONSIDERING TYPE I AND II ERRORS AND POWER

We will use our chosen α level and combine it with anticipated sample size and an estimated (a priori) effect size, and determine if we have enough power (a priori) to conduct the study. Two power analyses for this problem will be conducted. The first will be for the comparison of the low electric stimulation condition to the placebo and the second will be comparing the high electric stimulation condition to the placebo.

Selecting Alpha (α) Considering Type I and Type II Errors

Since there have been previous studies and we are repeating their procedures, we will use a more strict alpha level of .01 to increase the probability of not making a Type I error, which is rejecting a true null. We will have more confidence that the low and high electric stimulation conditions are more effective in improving pain when compared to a placebo condition.

A Priori Power Analysis

We are going to conduct two a priori power analyses to make sure that our planned alpha, sample size, and estimated effect size will produce acceptable power probabilities necessary to find significant differences in pairs of mean ranks if they exist. The first power analysis will be conducted for the low electric stimulation compared to the placebo condition. A similar previous study resulted in a posteffect size of $d = .90$, where $.20 = $ small, $.50 = $ medium, and $.80 = $ large (Cohen, 1988). We are going to use G*Power 3.1 using our values of $N = 60$, $\alpha = .01$, and the estimated effect size of $d = 1.10$. We are assessing whether we meet or exceed our criterion of a power probability $= .80$ for the low electric stimulation versus placebo on pain improvement.

A Priori Power Analysis Using G*Power 3.1.2 for Low Electric Stimulation versus Placebo

1. Open up the G*Power 3.1.2 program.

2. Select **t tests** under **Test family** > under **Statistical test**, select **Means: Wilcoxon-Mann-Whitney test (two groups)** > under **Type of power analysis**, select **A priori: Compute required sample size - given α, power, and effect size**.

3. Select **One** beside **Tail(s)** > select **Normal** next to **Parent distribution** > type in 1.10 next to **Effect size d** > beside **α err prob**, type 0.01 > beside **Power (1-β err prob)**, type 0.80 > type 1 next to **Allocation ratio N2/N1** > click on **Calculate**. The results are in Figure 11.2.

FIGURE 11.2 A Priori Power Analysis Results for Low Electric Stimulation Versus Placebo

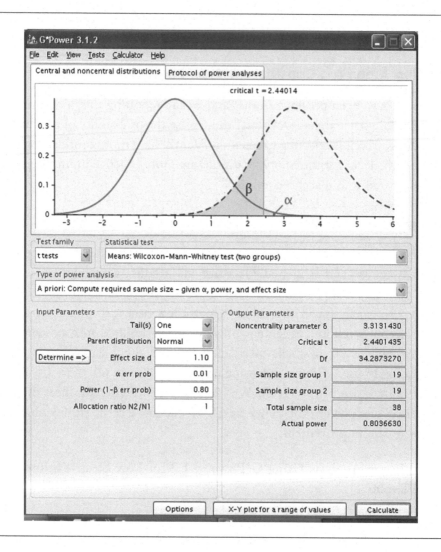

The power analysis results show that we would need a total sample size = 38 participants to reach a power ≥.80. Considering the combined elements in our study of total sample size of both groups, $n_1 + n_2 = 40, d = 1.10$, and $\alpha = .01$, a power of .80 should be achieved. We are therefore confident that we will correctly reject a false H_0 and avoid making a Type II error for the low electric stimulation condition compared to the placebo condition related to pain improvement. Next, we will do a similar power analysis for the high electric stimulation condition compared to the placebo condition. The only thing that will change will be the estimated effect size, which will be $d = 1.25$ from a previous study. We already know that the power value will be acceptable since we are increasing the estimated effect size, but let's run it anyway to see how sample size changes.

A Priori Power Analysis Using G*Power 3.1 for High Electric Stimulation versus Placebo

1. Open up the G*Power 3.1 program.

2. Select **t tests** under **Test family** > under **Statistical test**, select **Means: Wilcoxon-Mann-Whitney test (two groups)** > under **Type of power analysis**, select **A priori: Compute required sample size - given α, power, and effect size**.

3. Select **One** beside **Tail(s)** > select **Normal** next to **Parent distribution** > type in 1.25 next to **Effect size d** > beside **α err prob**, type 0.01 > beside **Power (1-β err prob)**, type 0.80 > type 1 next to **Allocation ratio N2/N1** > click on **Calculate**. The results are in Figure 11.3.

The results show that we would need a total sample size = 30 participants to reach a power = .801. The higher estimated effect size reduced the total participants needed by eight participants compared to the previous analysis.

PROGRESS REVIEW

1. The research question and hypotheses were identified for the study problem.

2. An $\alpha = .01$ was selected as the risk we are willing to take when rejecting a true null hypothesis. We believe this alpha to be a reasonable balancing point between the avoidance of making either a Type I or Type II error for the goal of this particular study.

3. We conducted two power analyses to assess the probability of correctly rejecting a false null hypothesis. Both power analyses, comparing the placebo condition to low electric stimulation condition and then to the high electric stimulation condition, resulted in power probabilities ≥.80.

FIGURE 11.3   A Priori Power Analysis Results for High Electric Stimulation Versus Placebo

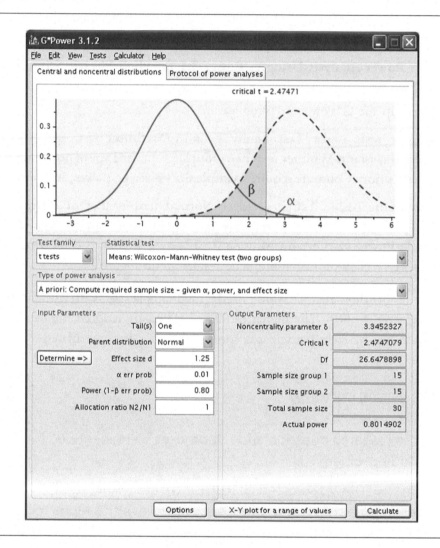

HYPOTHESIS TESTING STEP 4: CHOOSE APPROPRIATE STATISTIC AND ITS SAMPLING DISTRIBUTION TO TEST THE H_O ASSUMING H_O IS TRUE

We are using a Kruskal-Wallis (K-W) statistic to evaluate the omnibus null hypothesis and will follow up using the Mann-Whitney U statistics to compare paired-means rank differences.

We will discover during the data diagnostic process that the dependent variable does not meet the normality assumption across conditions. The nonparametric K-W one-way analysis of variance is appropriate to use as a good alternative to a parametric one-way ANOVA statistic when the assumption of normality is not met. Also, the K-W statistic is used when there are more than two groups being compared and the groups are independent from each other.

HYPOTHESIS TESTING STEP 5: SELECT SAMPLE, COLLECT DATA, SCREEN DATA, COMPUTE STATISTIC, AND DETERMINE PROBABILITY ESTIMATES

The sample consisted of 60 persons with multiple sclerosis who experienced chronic back pain. They were recruited from an MS support group organization in a large metropolitan area. The sample was selected using purposive sampling of typical instances (Shadish, Cook, & Campbell, 2002). The 60 participants were randomly assigned equally to the three conditions of the independent variable: (1) low electric stimulation, (2) placebo, and (3) high electric stimulation.

Study Data Diagnostics

Diagnostic assessments are conducted on the sample data after it has been collected but before the primary study hypothesis is tested to check for data accuracy, missing data, univariate outliers, and underlying assumptions.

Accuracy of Data Entry

The original data were compared to the entered data by two members of the research team. The accuracy of the data was corroborated by the two researchers. Moreover, the variable scores were in the expected range and the means and standard deviations appeared plausible.

Missing Data Analysis

There were no missing data in the original data set.

Means, Standard Deviations, Variances, and Assessing for Univariate Outliers IBM SPSS Commands

Enter the data from Table 11.1, K-W–MWU Data, into SPSS. Enter the data into three columns just as it appears in the table.

1. Click on **Data** > **Split File** > click on circle beside **Compare groups** > click on *ElectricStimulation* and click the arrow so that *Electric-Stimulation* is under **Groups Based on** > click on **OK** and don't save command output. You have told the program to provide output by the three groups (*ElectricStimulation*). You will need to change this command back later.

2. Click on **Analyze** > **Descriptive Statistics** > Descriptives > click over *PainImprovement* to **Variable(s)** > click on **Save standardized values as variables** > click on **Options** and check **Mean, Std. deviation**, and **Variance** > click on **OK** > save the output as *KW Descriptives*.

The descriptive statistics table (Table 11.2) lists the sample size of each group followed by the lowest (minimum) and highest (maximum) scores in each group. Valid N is the number of participant scores that do not having missing data. The average score (mean) of pain improvement for each group following electric stimulation condition is provided. Measures of variability (standard deviation and variance) designate how the scores in each condition distribution deviate from their group mean. Looking at the descriptive statistics, it is evident that high-frequency electric stimulation produced the most pain improvement ($M = 28.900$) followed by the low-frequency condition ($M = 28.700$) and then the placebo condition ($M = 26.750$).

The standard values (z-scores) requested for the analysis to assess for univariate outliers are produced in a new column on the **Data View** spreadsheet and named *ZPainImprovement*. These values represent the z-scores corresponding to the raw scores in each group. Since we used the "Split File" command, the z-scores are produced separately for each of the three electric stimulation conditions. The three highest positive and negative z-scores for each group are reported in Table 11.3.

TABLE 11.1 K-W-MWU Data

ID#	PainImprovement	ElectricStimulation*
1	28	1
2	38	1
3	26	1
4	29	1
5	26	1
6	27	1
7	29	1
8	29	1
9	28	1
10	27	1
11	30	1
12	31	1
13	27	1
14	28	1
15	32	1
16	26	1
17	25	1
18	29	1
19	30	1
20	29	1
21	26	2
22	19	2
23	30	2
24	25	2
25	27	2
26	26	2
27	29	2
28	28	2
29	26	2
30	27	2
31	28	2
32	27	2
33	27	2
34	28	2
35	26	2
36	29	2
37	26	2
38	25	2
39	29	2
40	27	2

(Continued)

TABLE 11.1 K-W-MWU Data (Continued)

ID#	PainImprovement	ElectricStimulation*
41	29	3
42	28	3
43	27	3
44	37	3
45	31	3
46	26	3
47	23	3
48	26	3
49	30	3
50	29	3
51	30	3
52	31	3
53	27	3
54	28	3
55	28	3
56	29	3
57	30	3
58	28	3
59	30	3
60	31	3

*1 = Low stimulation

 2 = Placebo

 3 = High stimulation

TABLE 11.2 Descriptive Statistics of Pain Improvement by Electric Simulation Condition

Descriptive Statistics						
ElectricStimulation		N	Minimum	Maximum	Mean	Std. Deviation	Variance
Low Elect Stim	PainImprovement	20	25.00	38.00	28.700	2.83029	8.011
	Valid N (listwise)	20					
Placebo	PainImprovement	20	19.00	30.00	26.750	2.29129	5.250
	Valid N (listwise)	20					
High Elect Stim	PainImprovement	20	23.00	37.00	28.900	2.77014	7.674
	Valid N (listwise)	20					

TABLE 11.3 Three Highest ±z-Scores of Pain Improvement by Electric Stimulation Condition

Condition	Highest +z	Outlier? > ±3.29	Highest −z	Outlier? > ± 3.29
Low Elect Stim	3.286*	Almost	−1.307	No
Placebo	1.418	No	−3.382	Yes
High Elect Stim	2.924	No	−2.130	No

*This number is rounded to three decimals.

One case (ID #22 = −3.382) has an outlying pain improvement score (19) that is significantly negatively skewed using the criterion of ±3.29 (< .001, two-tailed). Another case (ID #2) has a pain improvement score (38) as close as you can get to be significantly positively skewed, but if we rounded to two places, the $z = 3.286$ would be 3.29 and meet our criteria. We have to consider ID #2 a potential problem score, but we will look at additional information to help us assess normality.

Reset Split File Command

At this point, remove the **Split File** filter. **Data** > **Split File** > click on the **Reset** button and then click **OK** and click out of the output and don't save it.

Assessing for Underlying Assumptions

Next we will assess whether the dependent variable (pain improvement) distributes itself normally in each of the three electric stimulation conditions.

Normality SPSS Commands

1. **Analyze** > **Descriptive Statistics** > **Explore**.

2. Click over dependent variable *PainImprovement* to **Dependent List**.

3. Click over independent variable (*ElectricStimulation*) to **Factor List**. Factor is another term for independent variable.

4. Do not change **Display choices**—leave on **Both**.

5. To the upper right of Display are three buttons. Click on **Plots**. Then, select **Normality plots with tests**.

6. Under **Spread vs. Level with Levene Test** click on **Untransformed**.

7. Click on **Continue**.

8. Click on **OK**.

9. Save the output as *KW-assumptions-screen.*

Initially, we will obtain skewness and kurtosis information from the Descriptives table of the output, which is reproduced in Table 11.4.

Skewness Assessment

We proceed by dividing the skewness statistic value by its Std. Error value to obtain skewness z-scores. The skewness and standard error and their resulting skewness z-scores are presented in Table 11.5.

The dependent variable (pain improvement) in two of the condition distributions (low electrical stimulation and placebo) significantly ($p < .001$) depart from normality. The low electrical stimulation distribution is positively skewed with an extreme score to the right of the distribution as is evident in the histogram (see Figure 11.4). In the univariate outlier analysis, the outlying pain improvement score was 38, which was barely under the criterion of being a significant positively skewed outlier. However, the low electrical stimulation condition pain improvement clearly departs from normality when the skewness z-score is calculated.

The placebo condition also shows a significant departure on skewness ($z = -3.834$) from normality in the negative direction on pain improvement (see Figure 11.5). The extreme pain improvement score was 19, and it was found to be a significantly univariate outlier in our earlier analysis.

The distribution of pain improvement scores did not depart significantly from normality ($z_{\text{skew}} = 1.578 < \pm 3.29$, $p < .001$) based on the skewness of the distribution (see Figure 11.6).

TABLE 11.4 Skewness, Kurtosis, and Standard Error Values by Group

		Descriptives		Statistic	Std. Error
		ElectricStimulation		**Statistic**	**Std. Error**
PainImprovement	Low Elect Stim	Mean		28.7000	.63287
		95% Confidence Interval for Mean	Lower Bound	27.3754	
			Upper Bound	30.0246	
		5% Trimmed Mean		28.3889	
		Median		28.5000	
		Variance		8.011	
		Std. Deviation		2.83029	
		Minimum		25.00	
		Maximum		38.00	
		Range		13.00	
		Interquartile Range		2.75	
		Skewness		1.887	.512
		Kurtosis		5.473	.992
	Placebo	Mean		26.7500	.51235
		95% Confidence Interval for Mean	Lower Bound	25.6776	
			Upper Bound	27.8224	
		5% Trimmed Mean		27.0000	
		Median		27.0000	
		Variance		5.250	
		Std. Deviation		2.29129	
		Minimum		19.00	
		Maximum		30.00	
		Range		11.00	
		Interquartile Range		2.00	
		Skewness		−1.963	.512
		Kurtosis		6.482	.992
	High Elect Stim	Mean		28.9000	.61942
		95% Confidence Interval for Mean	Lower Bound	27.6035	
			Upper Bound	30.1965	

(Continued)

TABLE 11.4   Skewness, Kurtosis, and Standard Error Values by Group (Continued)

Descriptives		
ElectricStimulation	Statistic	Std. Error
5% Trimmed Mean	28.7778	
Median	29.0000	
Variance	7.674	
Std. Deviation	2.77014	
Minimum	23.00	
Maximum	37.00	
Range	14.00	
Interquartile Range	2.75	
Skewness	.808	.512
Kurtosis	3.516	.992

TABLE 11.5   Skewness z-Scores by Condition Group

Condition	Skewness z (Stat./Std. Error = Z)	Skewness Direction	Sig. Departure? (> ±3.29)
Low Elect Stim	1.887/.512 = 3.686	Positive	Yes
Placebo	−1.963/.512 = −3.834	Negative	Yes
High Elect Stim	.808/.512 = 1.578	Positive	No

Kurtosis Assessment

Below the skewness and standard error values in Table 11.4 are the kurtosis and standard error values. Next, we divide the kurtosis statistic by its standard error (values in Table 11.6) and compare the $z_{kurtosis}$ score resulting to ±3.29 to see if any condition distributions significantly depart from normality.

All three conditions produced significantly leptokurtic distributions that significantly departed from normality ($p < .001$). The three distributions are more narrow and peaked when compared to normally shaped distributions.

FIGURE 11.4   Histogram of the Low Electric Stimulation Condition on Pain Improvement

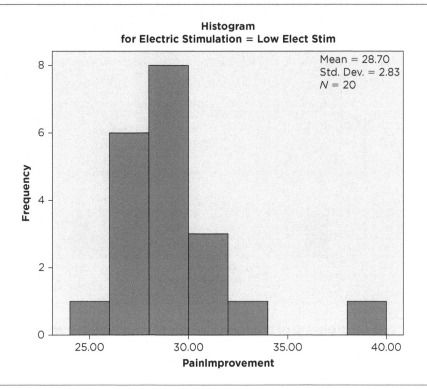

Histogram
for Electric Stimulation = Low Elect Stim

Mean = 28.70
Std. Dev. = 2.83
N = 20

Shapiro-Wilk Statistic Assessment

The S-W statistic information is found in the output under Tests of Normality (see Table 11.7). We will be comparing the significance values to our alpha of .01 to see if the distributions of pain improvement resulting from the conditions significantly depart from normality using the S-W statistics to corroborate previous evidence. We are testing H_0: The Sample Distribution = Normal.

The significance values of the low electric stimulation condition (p = .003) and the placebo condition (p = .001) are both less than α = .01, so we reject the null hypothesis for both conditions. Their distributions on pain improvement scores are significantly (p < .01) departing from normality. The distribution of pain improvement scores created by the high electric stimulation condition is not significant (p = .059 > α = .01). Thus, the distribution is considered normal enough using the S-W statistic.

FIGURE 11.5   Histogram of the Placebo Condition on Pain Improvement

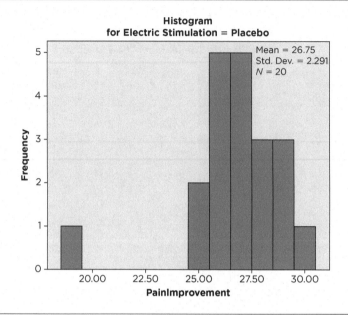

FIGURE 11.6   Histogram of the High Electric Stimulation Condition on Pain Improvement

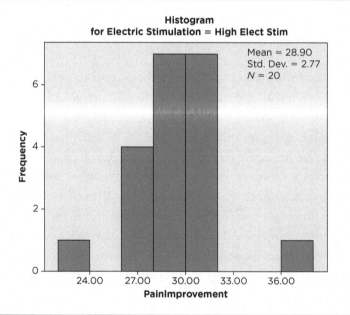

TABLE 11.6 Kurtosis z-Scores by Condition on Pain Improvement Scores

Condition	Kurtosis z (Stat./Std. Error = Z)	Kurtosis Direction	Sig. Departure? (> ±3.29)
Low Elect Stim	5.473/.992 = 5.517	Leptokurtic	Yes
Placebo	6.482/.992 = 6.534	Leptokurtic	Yes
High Elect Stim	3.516/.992 = 3.544	Leptokurtic	Yes

TABLE 11.7 Shapiro-Wilk Statistics by Conditions

		Kolmogorov-Smirnov[a]			Shapiro-Wilk		
	ElectricStimulation	Statistic	df	Sig.	Statistic	df	Sig.
PainImprovement	Low Elect Stim	.208	20	.024	.839	20	.003
	Placebo	.222	20	.011	.816	20	.001
	High Elect Stim	.174	20	.113	.908	20	.059

Tests of Normality

[a]Lilliefors significance correction.

Normal Q-Q Plots Analysis

The normal Q-Q plots in Figures 11.7, 11.8, and 11.9 provide another look at the three distributions. While the majority of the points are on or near the diagonal line, there is one point on the low electric stimulation condition and one point on the placebo condition that are a considerable distance from the line. These points represent the near outlier and the clear outlier that we discovered earlier. The evidence from the Q-Q plots supports the lack of normality of the two distributions.

Summary of the Normality Evidence

The evidence is consistent that two of the distributions of pain improvement scores do not meet the normality assumption. The low electric stimulation condition distribution of pain improvement scores had: (1) an observed score close to being an outlier, (2) a significant positive skew, (3) a significant leptokurtic kurtosis, (4) a significant S-W statistic, and (5) a problematic Q-Q plot.

All of the same indicators of normality for the placebo condition distribution of pain improvement scores were significant. Overall, the high electric condition produced pain improvement scores that were normal enough.

FIGURE 11.7 Normal Q-Q Plot of Pain Improvement Scores for the Low Electric Stimulation Condition

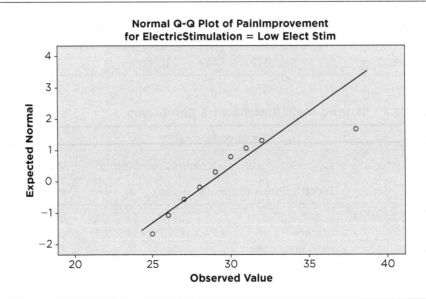

FIGURE 11.8 Normal Q-Q Plot of Pain Improvement Scores for the Placebo Condition

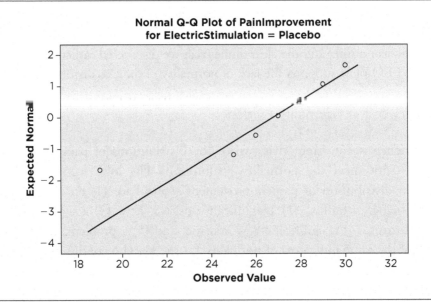

FIGURE 11.9 Normal Q-Q Plot of Pain Improvement Scores for the High Electric Stimulation Condition

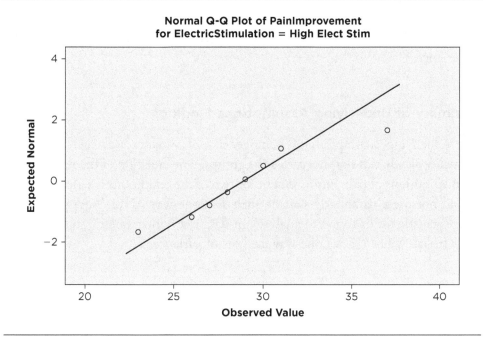

TABLE 11.8 Levene's Test of Homogeneity of Variance

Test of Homogeneity of Variance		Levene's Statistic	df1	df2	Sig.
PainImprovement	Based on mean	.300	2	57	.742
	Based on median	.360	2	57	.699
	Based on median and with adjusted df	.360	2	56.081	.699
	Based on trimmed mean	.380	2	57	.686

Homogeneity of Variance

The extent that the variances and error variances across the pain improvement scores by conditions are similar enough is assessed using Levene's test. The results are in the output results and reported in Table 11.8.

We are testing the null hypothesis that the variances and error variances are equal across the conditions with the Levene's test. The significance of .742 based on the mean is more than $\alpha = .01$, so we fail to reject the null hypothesis. We conclude that the variances and error variances are constant enough across conditions to meet the underlying assumption of homogeneity of variance.

Summary of Underlying Assumptions Findings

The underlying assumption of homogeneity of variance was met. However, normality clearly was not met across the groups. The violation of the normality of the distributions of pain improvement for two of the conditions is serious, and we should not use a parametric statistic such as a one-way ANOVA. A good alternative statistic for us to use to analyze our data is a nonparametric statistic called the Kruskal-Wallis (K-W) one-way analysis of variance.

PROGRESS REVIEW

1. Pain improvement data were collected on 60 persons with multiple sclerosis who experienced chronic low back pain. The sample members were randomly assigned to each of the three conditions.

2. Data diagnostics showed that the dependent variable of pain improvement as measured by the McGill Pain Questionnaire (MPQ) did not meet the underlying assumption of normality across the condition groups.

3. The decision was to use a nonparametric K-W analysis of variance to test the null rather than using a parametric one-way ANOVA since the data did not meet the underlying assumption of normality.

Kruskal-Wallis One-Way Analysis of Variance of the Omnibus H_0

Kruskal-Wallis One-Way ANOVA SPSS Commands

1. Click **Analyze** > click **Nonparametric Tests** > click **Legacy Dialogs** > click **K Independent Samples** > click over *PainImprovement* under **Test Variable List** and *ElectricStimulation* under **Grouping Variable** > click on **Define Range** > type a 1 beside **Minimum** and a 3 beside **Maximum** and click **Continue** > click on **Kruskal-Wallis H** under **Test Type**.

2. Click on the **Options** button > check the **Descriptive** box and then **Continue** and then **OK**.

3. Save generated output as *KW Results*.

The results of this analysis provide information to test the omnibus null hypothesis of the study:

H_0: There will be no significant mean rank differences in pain improvement (MPQ scores) across the electric stimulation conditions (low electric stimulation, placebo, high electric stimulation) following treatment implementation.

$$H_0: \mu_{rank1} = \mu_{rank2} = \mu_{rank3}$$

The results of the K-W one-way ANOVA are presented next. Additionally, interpretations are provided for the magnitude of treatment effects (effect sizes) and multiple comparisons of means. We are making an a priori decision to conduct two paired-means analyses comparing the low electric stimulation and the high electric stimulation conditions to the placebo condition regardless of whether the omnibus null hypothesis was significant.

K-W One-Way ANOVA Results

The table titled Ranks presents the mean ranks for each condition. The combined pain improvement scores in the three conditions are given a rank value representing their rank within all 60 scores. Lower scores receive lower ranks and higher scores receive higher ranks. Then the ranks of pain improvement scores are summed for each condition and divided by the group sample size $n = 20$; the results are the mean ranks for each condition group. The mean ranks for each group are presented in Table 11.9.

TABLE 11.9   Mean Ranks of Pain Improvement by Conditions

	Ranks		
	ElectricStimulation	*N*	Mean Rank
PainImprovement	Low Elect Stim	20	33.35
	Placebo	20	21.43
	High Elect Stim	20	36.73
	Total	60	

TABLE 11.10   K-W Results

Test Statistics[a,b]	
	PainImprovement
Chi-Square	8.663
df	2
Asymp. Sig.	.013

[a]Kruskal-Wallis Test.
[b]Grouping variable: ElectricStimulation.

The high electric stimulation has the highest mean rank ($M_{rank} = 36.73$), followed by the low electric stimulation ($M_{rank} = 33.35$) and placebo ($M_{rank} = 21.43$) conditions. In this study, a higher mean rank translates to greater pain improvement.

The K-W statistic tests for a significant difference among the mean ranks of pain improvement across the three conditions. Table 11.10 shows the results of the K-W statistic.

The difference among the mean ranks is not significant, $\chi^2(N = 60, df = 2) = 8.663$, $p > .01$. The asymptotic significance is $p = .013$, which is greater than $\alpha = .01$ so we fail to reject the null hypothesis. Asymptotic significance is a probability approximation of the parameters since it was not possible to obtain exact estimates (Norusis, 2004). Asymptotic approximation is based on large sample modeling.

HYPOTHESIS TESTING STEP 6: MAKE DECISION REGARDING THE H_0 AND INTERPRET POST HOC EFFECT SIZES

We were unable to reject the null hypothesis using the K-W statistic ($p > .01$). We made a decision prior to the K-W analysis that we would conduct two paired-means analyses comparing the low electric stimulation and the high electric stimulation conditions to the placebo condition regardless of whether the omnibus null hypothesis was significant.

Post Hoc Multiple Comparisons of Means

The K-W analysis did not result in a significant difference in the three means of the omnibus hypothesis using our criterion of $\alpha = .01$. The post hoc mean comparisons are: (1) H_0: $\mu_{rank1LowElectStim} = \mu_{rank2Placebo}$, and (2) H_0: $\mu_{rank2Placebo} = \mu_{rank3HighElectStim}$. We will be using the Mann-Whitney U (MWU) statistic, which is a nonparametric alternative to the independent t-test.

When we have conducted the K-W analysis, we assessed an overall set of mean ranks for differences. When we conduct a post hoc analysis of all paired means, there is a *family of conclusions* possible among the three pairs of means. We used an $\alpha = .01$ for the overall set of mean ranks for differences. When we conduct two more comparisons with the Mann-Whitney U statistic, the Type I errors for each of the three decisions combine to produce a higher level known as *inflated Type I error risk*. Making a Type I error is rejecting a null hypothesis when there is no difference. For example, we may reject H_0: $\mu_{rank1} = \mu_{rank2}$ at $\alpha = .01$ when alpha has been inflated to .02 (two comparisons times $\alpha = .01$).

To protect against making a Type I error decision on the three mean rank pairs being compared, we will use an *alpha correction* known as a *Bonferroni adjusted alpha* ($\alpha' = $ alpha prime). The Bonferroni adjustment is $\alpha' = \alpha/c$, where α is the alpha used for the overall set of mean ranks and c is the number of comparisons being made. Our overall alpha is .01 and there are two comparisons to be made, so $\alpha' = .01/2 = .005$. We will be using $\alpha' = .005$ as our criterion to determine if a pair of mean ranks is significantly different.

Mann-Whitney *U* Statistical Analysis

SPSS Commands for MWU

1. Select **Analyze** > **Nonparametric Tests** > click on **Legacy Dialogs** > **2 Independent Samples**.

2. Click over *PainImprovement* under **Test Variable List** and *ElectricStimulation* under **Grouping Variable** > click on **Options** > check **Descriptive** and click **Continue** > click on **Mann-Whitney U** under **Test Type**.

3. Click on **Define Groups** and type a 1 next to **Group 1** and a 2 next to **Group 2** > click continue > click **OK**. This will produce the output for the comparison of the first two groups. Next you need to conduct the other two group comparisons and add them to the output.

4. Go back to step 1 and select the same commands again but first change **Group 1 = 2, Group 2 = 3**. You will have the results of two pairs of groups (low stimulation vs. placebo and high stimulation vs. placebo) on the output.

The mean ranks of pain improvement produced by the low electric stimulation ($M_{rank} = 24.50$) and placebo ($M_{rank} = 16.50$) show more pain improvement descriptively in the low electric stimulation condition compared to the placebo condition (see Table 11.11). We will be using the exact significance ($p = .030$) value to compare to our $\alpha' = .005$. *Exact significance* is an observed significance used with small sample sizes. Exact probabilities are possible to obtain from various configurations of the data when the null hypothesis is true (Norusis, 2005a). The difference between the mean ranks is not significantly different, Z ($N = 40) = -2.195$, $p > .005$ (see Table 11.12).

We conclude that there is a significant difference between the mean ranks of pain improvement between the placebo condition ($M_{rank} = 15.43$) and the high electric stimulation condition ($M_{rank} = 25.58$), $Z(N = 40) = -2.775$, $p \leq .005$ (see Tables 11.13 and 11.14). Our decision is to reject if our calculated probability level is equal to or less than alpha. The exact significance is .005 and our $\alpha' = .005$, so we decide to reject the null hypothesis. There was significantly higher pain improvement among participants who received the high electric condition when compared to the placebo participants.

TABLE 11.11 Mean Ranks of the Low Electric Stimulation Condition Compared to the Placebo Condition

		Ranks		
	ElectricStimulation	*N*	Mean Rank	Sum of Ranks
PainImprovement	Low Elect Stim	20	24.50	490.00
	Placebo	20	16.50	330.00
	Total	40		

TABLE 11.12   MWU Results Comparing Low Electric Stimulation to Placebo

Test Statistics[a]

	PainImprovement
Mann-Whitney U	120.000
Wilcoxon W	330.000
Z	−2.195
Asymp. Sig. (2-tailed)	.028
Exact Sig. [2 × (1-tailed Sig.)]	.030[b]

[a]Grouping variable: ElectricStimulation.
[b]Not corrected for ties.

TABLE 11.13   Mean Ranks of the Placebo Condition Compared to the High Electric Stimulation Condition

Ranks

	ElectricStimulation	N	Mean Rank	Sum of Ranks
PainImprovement	Placebo	20	15.43	308.50
	High Elect Stim	20	25.58	511.50
	Total	40		

TABLE 11.14   MWU Results Comparing Placebo to High Electric Stimulation

Test Statistics[a]

	PainImprovement
Mann-Whitney U	98.500
Wilcoxon W	308.500
Z	−2.775
Asymp. Sig. (2-tailed)	.006
Exact Sig. [2 × (1-tailed Sig.)]	.005[b]

[a]Grouping variable: ElectricStimulation.
[b]Not corrected for ties.

Magnitude of Treatment Effect—Post Hoc Effect Size and Post Hoc Power

We are going to use G*Power again but this time to obtain post hoc effect sizes and power values.

Post Hoc Effect Size and Power Analyses Using G*Power 3.1.2 for Low Electric Stimulation versus Placebo

1. Open up the G*Power 3.1.2 program.

2. Select **t tests** under **Test family** > under **Statistical test**, select **Means: Wilcoxon-Mann-Whitney test (two groups)** > under **Type of power analysis**, select **Post hoc: Compute achieved power - given α, sample size, and effect size**.

3. Select **One** beside **Tail(s)** > select **Normal** next to **Parent distribution**.

4. Click on the **Determine** button and a new window is created > click on the button that says **n1 = n2** > Go to Table 11.2 in the text to obtain the means and standard deviations (SDs) of the condition groups that we will use in this new window.

5. From Table 11.2, type in 28.700 beside **Mean group 1** and 26.750 next to **Mean group 2** > type in 2.830 next to **SD σ group 1** and 2.291 next to **SD σ group 2** > **Calculate and transfer to main window** (this will produce a post hoc effect size for the comparison of low electric stimulation and the placebo).

6. Beside **α err prob**, type in 0.01 > next to **Sample size group 1** type in 20 > next to **Sample size group 2** type in 20 > click on **Calculate**.

The results in Figure 11.10 show a post hoc magnitude of treatment effect of $d = .7573863$, which is a high-medium effect size using Cohen's convention of small $= .20$, medium $= .50$, and large $= .80$. The post hoc power probability is .471, which means that we had only a 47.10 percent of correctly rejecting a false null hypothesis given our sample size of 40, $\alpha = .01$, and post hoc effect size of $d = .757$ (rounded to three places).

Earlier we conducted a post hoc comparison of the mean ranks of pain improvement between the low electrical stimulation condition and placebo condition using the Mann-Whitney U statistic. We did not find a significance difference using a corrected alpha level ($p = .030 > \alpha' = .005$), which is consistent with the low post hoc power. However, the post hoc effect size is meaningful at $d = .757$ (high-medium), so practical significance related to low electric stimulation producing pain reduction seems to exist even though the null was not found to be significant. It is possible that increasing the sample size or improving the treatment protocol to have more fidelity might result in a significant null in a future study.

FIGURE 11.10 Post Hoc Effect Size and Power Analysis for Low Electric Stimulation versus Placebo

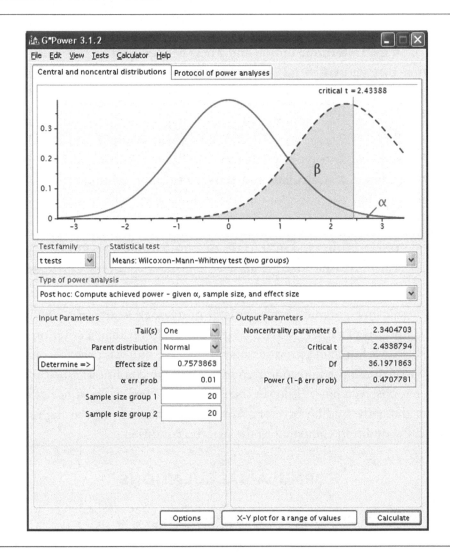

Post Hoc Effect Size and Power Analyses Using G*Power 3.1.2 for High Electric Stimulation versus Placebo

1. Open up the G*Power 3.1 program.

2. Select **t tests** under **Test family** > under **Statistical test**, select **Means: Wilcoxon-Mann-Whitney test (two groups)** > under **Type of power**

analysis, select **Post hoc: Compute achieved power - given α, sample size, and effect size**.

3. Select **One** beside **Tail(s)** > select **Normal** next to **Parent distribution**.

4. Click on the **Determine** button and a new window is created > click on the button that says **n1 = n2** > Go to Table 11.2 in the text to obtain the means and standard deviations (SDs) of the condition groups that we will use in this new window.

5. From Table 11.2, type in 26.750 beside **Mean group 1** and 28.900 next to **Mean group 2** > type in 2.291 next to **SD σ group 1** and 2.770 next to **SD σ group 2** > **Calculate and transfer to main window** (this will produce a post hoc effect size for the comparison of low electric stimulation and the placebo).

6. Beside **α err prob**, type in 0.01 > next to **Sample size group 1** type in 20 > next to **Sample size group 2** type in 20 > click on **Calculate**.

The results in Figure 11.11 reflect a large post hoc effect size ($d = .8458544$). The post hoc power value (.5751825), however, is lower than a criterion of .80. Nevertheless, we found in a previous analysis that the null was rejected comparing the high electric stimulation condition to the placebo condition ($p \leq .005$) even though our observed power is lower than expected. The large post hoc effect size supports the early finding of more pain improvement from the high electric stimulation condition compared to the placebo condition.

FORMULA CALCULATIONS

$$X^2_{KW} = 12/N(N + 1)\sum R^2_i - 3(N + 1)$$

where N = total sum of cases being analyzed

R_i = rank sum of each group

n_i = cases for each group

12 & 3 = constants that are always included in the formula

FIGURE 11.11 Post Hoc Effect Size and Power Analysis for High Electric Stimulation versus Placebo

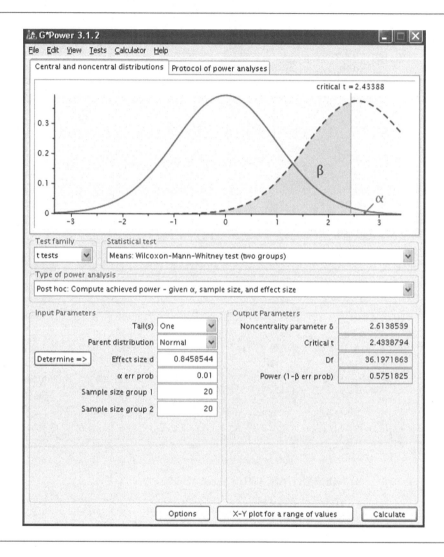

Mann-Whitney (MW) *U* Statistic

$$X^2_{KW} = 12/60(60 + 1)\sum[444,889/20 + 183,612.25/20$$
$$+ 539,490.25/20] - 3(60 + 1)$$
$$= 12/3,660\sum[22,244.45 + 9,180.61 + 26,974.51] - 183$$

TABLE 11.15 Formula Kruskal-Wallis and Mann-Whitney *U* Calculations of the Study Results

Kruskal-Wallis (K-W) One-Way Analysis of Variance					
Low Stimulation		Placebo		High Stimulation	
Score	Rank	Score	Rank	Score	Rank
28	30.50	26	10.50	29	41.00
38	60.00	19	1.00	28	30.50
26	10.50	30	50.00	27	20.50
29	41.00	25	4.00	37	59.00
26	10.50	27	20.50	31	55.50
27	20.50	26	10.50	26	10.50
29	41.00	29	41.00	23	2.00
29	41.00	28	30.50	26	10.50
28	30.50	26	10.50	30	50.00
27	20.50	27	20.50	29	41.00
30	50.00	28	30.50	30	50.00
31	55.50	27	20.50	31	55.50
27	20.50	27	20.50	27	20.50
28	30.50	28	30.50	28	30.50
32	58.00	26	10.50	28	30.50
26	10.50	29	41.00	29	41.00
25	4.00	26	10.50	30	50.00
29	41.00	25	4.00	28	30.50
30	50.00	29	41.00	30	50.00
29	41.00	27	20.50	31	55.50
	$R = 667.00$		$R = 428.50$		$R = 734.50$
	$R^2 = 444{,}889$		$R^2 = 183{,}612.25$		$R^2 = 539{,}490.25$

$$= (.00328)(58{,}399.57) - 183$$
$$= 191.55 - 183$$
$$X^2_{KW} = 8.6$$

Mann-Whitney *U* Test

$$U_{MW} = n_1 n_2 + [n_2(n_2 + 1)/2] - R_2$$
$$= (20)(20) + [20(20 + 1)/2] - 330$$
$$= 400 + [420/2] - 330$$

TABLE 11.16 Low Electric Stimulation Condition Compared to Placebo Condition on Pain Improvement

Low Stimulation		Placebo	
Score	Rank	Score	Rank
28	23.50	26	8.50
38	40.00	19	1.00
26	8.50	30	36.00
29	30.50	25	3.00
26	8.50	27	16.50
27	16.50	26	8.50
29	30.50	29	30.50
29	30.50	28	23.50
28	23.50	26	8.50
27	16.50	27	16.50
30	36.00	28	23.50
31	38.00	27	16.50
27	16.50	27	16.50
28	23.50	28	23.50
32	39.00	26	8.50
26	8.50	29	30.50
25	3.00	26	8.50
29	30.50	25	3.00
30	36.00	29	30.50
29	30.50	27	16.50
	$R = 490$		$R = 330$

$$= 400 + 210 - 330$$
$$= 610 - 330$$
$$U_{MW} = 280$$

$$Z_{MW} = \frac{(n_1 n_2/2) - U}{\sqrt{([(n_1)(n_2)(n_1 + n_2 + 1]/12)}}$$

$$= \frac{200 - 280}{\sqrt{([(20)(20)(20 + 20 + 1]/12)}}$$

$$= \frac{-80}{\sqrt{(16{,}400/12)}}$$

TABLE 11.17 High Stimulation Condition Compared to Placebo Condition on Pain Improvement

High Stimulation		Placebo	
Score	Rank	Score	Rank
29	28.500	26	8.000
28	22.000	19	1.000
27	15.000	30	34.000
37	40.000	25	3.500
31	38.000	27	15.000
26	8.000	26	8.000
23	2.000	29	28.500
26	8.000	28	22.000
30	34.000	26	8.000
29	28.500	27	15.000
30	34.000	28	22.000
31	38.000	27	15.000
27	15.000	27	15.000
28	22.000	28	22.000
28	22.000	26	8.000
29	28.500	29	28.500
30	34.000	26	8.000
28	22.000	25	3.500
30	34.000	29	28.500
31	38.000	27	15.000
	$R = 511.50$		$R = 308.50$

$$= \frac{-80}{36.969}$$

$$z_{MW} = 2.2$$

$$
\begin{aligned}
U_{MW} &= n_1 n_2 + [n_2(n_2 + 1)/2] - R_2 \\
&= (20)(20) + [20(20 + 1)/2] - 308.50 \\
&= 400 + [420/2] - 308.50 \\
&= 400 + 210 - 308.50 \\
&= 610 - 308.50 \\
U_{MW} &= 301.50
\end{aligned}
$$

$$Z_{MW} = \frac{(n_1 n_2 / 2) - U}{\sqrt{([(n_1)(n_2)(n_1 + n_2 + 1]/12)}}$$

$$= \frac{200 - 301.50}{\sqrt{([(20)(20)(20 + 20 + 1]/12)}}$$

$$= \frac{-101.50}{\sqrt{(16,400/12)}}$$

$$= \frac{-101.50}{36.969}$$

$$Z_{MW} = -2.7$$

Study Results

The purpose of this study was to determine if chronic low back pain experienced by persons who have multiple sclerosis can be improved by exposure to transcutaneous electrical nerve stimulation applied to the lumbar spine. A randomized control group design was used with low electric stimulation, placebo, and high electric stimulation conditions. The effects of treatment condition were assessed on pain improvement as measured by the MPQ. MPQ scores were obtained before treatment began. Improvement scores were recorded following treatment. Higher improvement scores represent greater pain improvement.

Sixty persons who have multiple sclerosis comprised the sample. The average age of participants was 42.30 ($SD = 4.20$). There were 48 females (80 percent) and 12 males (20 percent). The participants have experienced low back pain over 11 years.

Two a priori power analyses were conducted. A $\geq .80$ power was achieved for the low electric stimulation versus placebo and the high electric stimulation versus placebo conditions.

The data were screened as accurate with no missing data. The assessment of the underlying assumption of homogeneity of variance was met but normality was not met. There was a consistent pattern of the existence of outliers, significant skew, and significant kurtosis. Thus, the decision was made to use a nonparametric Kruskal-Wallis analysis of variance to test the omnibus null hypothesis.

The means, mean ranks, and standard deviations related to pain improvement across the conditions were: (1) low electric stimulation condition ($M = 28.700$, $M_{rank} = 33.35$, $SD = 2.830$); (2) placebo condition ($M = 26.750$, $M_{rank} = 21.43$,

$SD = 2.291$); and high electric stimulation condition ($M = 28.900$, $M_{rank} = 36.73$, $SD = 2.770$).

The participants with MS were tested for significant differences in pain improvement across the conditions (low electric stimulation, placebo, high electric stimulation) with a Kruskal-Wallis one-way analysis of variance using an alpha criterion of $\alpha = .01$. The omnibus K-W analysis was not significant, $\chi^2(N = 60, df = 2) = 8.663$, $p > .01$.

There was an a priori decision to conduct two paired-means analyses comparing the low electric stimulation and the high electric stimulation conditions to the placebo condition regardless of whether the omnibus null hypothesis was significant. The comparison between the low electric stimulation condition and the placebo did not generate a significant difference in pain improvement, $z(N = 40) = -2.195$, $p > .005$. Yet there was a high-medium post hoc effect size ($d = .757$), demonstrating practical significance related to the difference.

There was significant pain improvement resulting from the high electric stimulation condition compared to participants receiving the placebo, $z(N = 40) = -2.775$, $p \leq .005$, $d = .846$.

Overall, the results are mixed on the effectiveness of electrical stimulation on improving chronic low back pain of participants who have multiple sclerosis. The omnibus null hypothesis comparing the effects of all conditions together on pain improvement was not significant. The comparison of low electric stimulation on pain improvement compared to the placebo condition was not significantly different, although the practical significance of the difference was medium-high. The high electric stimulation condition did produce significantly higher pain improvement when compared to the participants in the placebo condition.

NONPARAMETRIC RESEARCH PROBLEM TWO: FRIEDMAN'S RANK TEST FOR CORRELATED SAMPLES AND WILCOXON'S MATCHED-PAIRS SIGNED-RANKS TEST

Two common nonparametric statistics used with correlated samples are *Friedman's rank test for correlated samples* and *Wilcoxon's matched-pairs signed-ranks test*. Friedman's test compares the mean ranks of two or more groups and is an analogue to the repeated measures analysis of variance. Wilcoxon's matched pairs test compares the mean ranks of two groups and parallels the parametric dependent *t*-test.

We are going to use the same research problem that we used for illustrating the K-W and MWU, but we are going to answer a different research question using new data. We want to know if pain improvement changes when high electric stimulation is added and removed with the same participants over time (24 weeks). The research design is a repeated-treatment design similar to the one used for the RM-ANOVA problem in Chapter 8 except that we have three repeated measures in this example compared to four repeated measures in the RM-ANOVA example.

The independent variable is high electric stimulation operationally defined with three conditions (first treatment, removed treatment, and restored treatment). Each treatment is provided over eight weeks. The dependent variable is pain improvement as measured by the McGill Pain Questionnaire (MPQ), which is the same DV used in the K-W analysis.

The study problem data set in Table 11.18, Friedman-Wilcoxon Data, does not meet the underlying assumption of normality. Thus, Friedman's statistic, the nonparametric analogue to the RM-ANOVA, would be more appropriate to use for

TABLE 11.18   Friedman-Wilcoxon Data

ID#	First Treatment	Removed Treatment	Restored Treatment
1	28	19	27
2	38	17	29
3	26	20	30
4	29	10	26
5	26	23	25
6	27	16	25
7	29	17	27
8	26	19	28
9	26	18	24
10	32	20	23
11	25	17	38
12	27	20	26
13	26	19	28
14	25	18	27
15	25	21	29
16	29	22	23
17	28	17	24
18	27	16	27
19	37	15	28
20	31	9	29

this problem. We will check a priori power before conducting the Friedman statistical analysis.

A Priori Power Analysis for Friedman and Wilcoxon Statistical Analyses

We will check the a priori power for the comparisons of the high electric stimulation first treatment and restored treatment conditions to the removed treatment condition using $N = 20$, $\alpha = .01$, and estimated effect size of $d = 1.0$. We will perform only one power analysis since we would use the same estimated effect size for both analyses and the answer would be the same.

A Priori Power Analysis Using G*Power 3.1.2 for High Electric Stimulation at First Treatment (or Restored Treatment) versus Removed Treatment

1. Open up the G*Power 3.1.2 program.

2. Select **t tests** under **Test family** > under **Statistical test**, select **Means: Wilcoxon signed-rank test (matched pairs)** > under **Type of power analysis**, select **A priori: Compute required sample size - given α, power, and effect size**.

3. Select **One** beside **Tail(s)** > select **Normal** next to **Parent distribution** > type in 1.0 next to **Effect size dz** > beside α **err prob**, type 0.01 > beside **Power (1-β err prob)**, type 0.80 > click on **Calculate**.

The results of the a priori power analysis show that to reach a power of .8211338 with an $\alpha = .01$, and estimated effect size of $d = 1.0$, we would need an $N = 14$ (see Figure 11.12). We are using an $N = 20$ in this study, so we met the criterion of desired power = $\geq.80$.

Friedman's Repeated Measures Analysis of Variance of the Omnibus H_0

Friedman's RM-ANOVA SPSS Commands

1. Click **Analyze** > click **Nonparametric Tests** > click on **Legacy Dialogs** > click **K Related Samples** > click over *First Treatment, Removed Treatment, Restored Treatment* under **Test Variable List** > click on **Friedman** under **Test Type**.

FIGURE 11.12 **A Priori Power Analysis Results for High Electric Stimulation at First Treatment (or Restored Treatment) versus Removed Treatment**

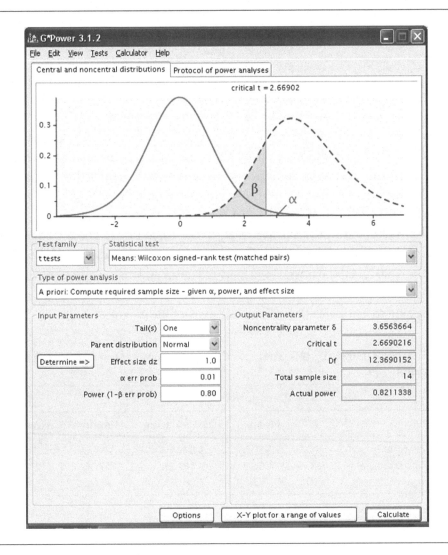

2. Click on the **Statistics** button > check the **Descriptive** box and then **Continue** and then **OK**.

3. Save generated output as *Friedman Results*.

The results of this analysis provide information to test the omnibus null hypothesis of the study:

H_0: There will be no significant mean rank differences in pain improvement (MPQ scores) across the high electric stimulation conditions (first treatment, removed treatment, restored treatment).

$$H_0: \mu_{rank1} = \mu_{rank2} = \mu_{rank3}$$

We are using an $\alpha = .01$ and plan to follow up Friedman's statistic analysis with a post hoc analysis using Wilcoxon's statistic.

The descriptive statistics in Table 11.19 show that the first treatment of high electric stimulation shows the highest pain improvement, closely followed by the restored treatment condition. Considerably less pain improvement was realized by the removed treatment condition. The mean ranks parallel these findings: (1) first treatment ($M_{rank} = 2.68$), (2) restored treatment ($M_{rank} = 2.33$), and (3) removed treatment ($M_{rank} = 1.00$) (see Table 11.20).

The results of testing the null hypothesis are in Table 11.21. There is a significant difference among the mean ranks of pain improvement, $\chi^2(N = 20, df = 2) = 31.620, p < .01$. Let's next assess which paired mean ranks are significantly different using Wilcoxon's statistic with a Bonferroni alpha correction of $.01/3 = \alpha' = .003$. We are going to compare all three possible pairs of mean ranks.

TABLE 11.19 Descriptive Statistics of Pain Improvement by High Electric Conditions

		Descriptive Statistics			
	N	Mean	Std. Deviation	Minimum	Maximum
FirstTreatment	20	28.3500	3.67459	25.00	38.00
RemovedTreatment	20	17.6500	3.46828	9.00	23.00
RestoredTreatment	20	27.1500	3.20113	23.00	38.00

TABLE 11.20 Mean Ranks of Pain Improvement by High Electric Conditions

Ranks	
	Mean Rank
FirstTreatment	2.68
RemovedTreatment	1.00
RestoredTreatment	2.33

TABLE 11.21 Friedman's Statistic of Pain Improvement by High Electric Conditions

Test Statistics[a]	
N	20
Chi-square	31.620
df	2
Asymp. sig.	.000

[a]Friedman test

Wilcoxon's Statistical Analysis

SPSS Commands for Wilcoxon's Statistic

1. Select **Analyze** > **Nonparametric Tests** > click on **Legacy Dialogs** > **2 Related Samples**.

2. Click over *FirstTreatment* next to Pair 1 under **Variable 1** and click over *RemovedTreatment* next to **Pair 1** under Variable 2.

3. Click over *FirstTreatment* next to Pair 2 under Variable 1 and click over *RestoredTreatment* next to **Pair 2** under **Variable 2**.

4. Click over *RemovedTreatment* next to **Pair 3** under **Variable 1** and click over *RestoredTreatment* next to **Pair 3** under **Variable 2**.

5. Click on **Options** > check **Descriptive** and click **Continue**.

6. Click on **Wilcoxon** under **Test Type** and click **OK**.

The Wilcoxon results in Table 11.22 show that two pairs of mean ranks of pain improvement are significant. The first treatment condition of high electric stimulation produced significantly higher pain improvement when compared to the removed treatment condition, $Z(N = 20) = -3.929$, $p < .003$. Additionally, the restored treatment condition was significantly higher in pain improvement compared to the removed treatment condition, $Z(N = 20) = -3.924$, $p < .003$. There was not a significant difference in pain improvement between the high electric stimulation conditions of first treatment and restored treatment $(p > .003)$.

TABLE 11.22 Wilcoxon Results

	Test Statistics[a]		
	RemovedTreatment – FirstTreatment	RestoredTreatment – FirstTreatment	RestoredTreatment – RemovedTreatment
Asymp. sig. (2-tailed)	–3.929[b] .000	–1.175[b] .240	–3.924[c] .000

[a]Wilcoxon Signed Ranks Test.
[b]Based on positive ranks.
[c]Based on negative ranks.

Magnitude of Treatment Effect—Post Hoc Effect Size and Post Hoc Power for Nonparametric Research Problem 2

We are using G*Power to obtain post hoc effect sizes and power values. However, before using G*Power we will need to obtain correlation coefficients on pain improvement between treatment conditions to use in the G*Power analyses.

Correlation Coefficients on Pain Improvement between Treatment Conditions

1. Open up the IBM SPSS data file called *Friedman-Wilcoxon-Data*.

2. **Analyze > Correlate > Bivariate**.

3. Click over **FirstTreatment** and **RemovedTreatment** under **Variables:** > click on the box beside **Spearman** only > click on **one-tailed** under **Test of Significance** > click **OK**. This will produce output and you will add the results of two additional analyses to it.

4. Keep output open and return to data set and click > **Analyze > Correlate > Bivariate**.

5. Click the **Reset** button > click over **FirstTreatment** and **RestoredTreatment** under **Variables:** > click on the box beside **Spearman** only > click on **one-tailed** under **Test of Significance** > click **OK**. This will produce output and you will add the results of one additional analysis to it.

6. Keep output open and return to data set and click > **Analyze > Correlate > Bivariate**.

7. Click the **Reset** button > click over **RemovedTreatment** and **RestoredTreatment** under **Variables:** > click on the box beside **Spearman** only > click on **one-tailed** under **Test of Significance** > click **OK**. You now have the Spearman correlation coefficients for all three pairs of conditions on pain improvement that will be used in the G*Power analyses.

Post Hoc Effect Size and Power Analyses Using G*Power 3.1 for High Electric Stimulation at First Treatment versus Removed Treatment

1. Open up the G*Power 3.1 program.

2. Select **t tests** under **Test family** > under **Statistical test**, select **Means: Wilcoxon signed-rank test (matched pairs)** > under **Type of power**

analysis, select **Post hoc: Compute achieved power - given α, sample size, and effect size**.

3. Select **One** beside **Tail(s)** > select **Normal** next to **Parent distribution**.

4. Click on the **Determine** button and a new window is created that we will be putting values in to arrive at our post hoc effect size > click on the button that says **From group parameters** > Go to Table 11.? in the text to obtain the means and standard deviations (SDs) of the condition groups that we will use in this new window.

5. From Table 11.19 type in 28.350 beside **Mean group 1** and 17.650 next to **Mean group 2** > type in 3.675 next to **SD σ group 1** and 3.468 next to **SD σ group 2** > type in −.387 next to **Correlation between groups** > **Calculate and transfer to main window** (this will produce a post hoc effect size for the comparison of high electric stimulation at first treatment versus removed).

6. Beside **α err prob**, type 0.01 > next to **Total sample size** type in 40 > click on **Calculate**.

The results in Figure 11.13 show a large post hoc magnitude of treatment effect ($d = 1.798$). The large effect size is consistent with our previous decision to reject the null hypothesis that pain improved significantly at the first high electric stimulation treatment compared to the removed treatment condition.

The post hoc power value of 1.0 shows that there was a 100 percent chance of correctly rejecting a false null hypothesis with a sample size of 40, $α = .01$, and post hoc effect size of $d = 1.798$.

Post Hoc Effect Size and Power Analyses Using G*Power 3.1.2 for High Electric Stimulation at First Treatment versus Restored Treatment

1. Open up the G*Power 3.1.2 program.

2. Select **t tests** under **Test family** > under **Statistical test**, select **Means: Wilcoxon signed-rank test (matched pairs)** > under **Type of power analysis**, select **Post hoc: Compute achieved power - given α, sample size, and effect size**.

3. Select **One** beside **Tail(s)** > select **Normal** next to **Parent distribution**.

FIGURE 11.13 Post Hoc Effect Size and Power Analysis for High Electric Stimulation at First Treatment versus Removed Treatment

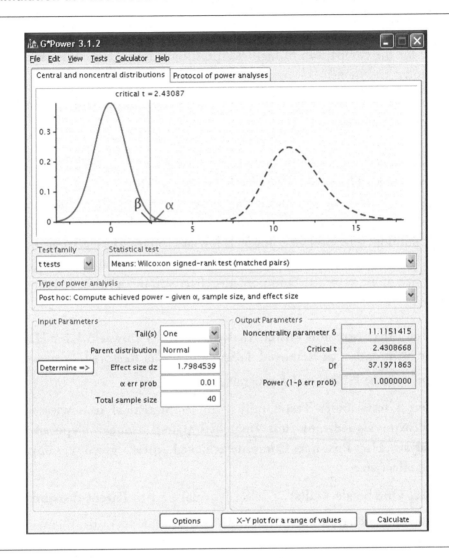

4. Click on the **Determine** button and a new window is created that we will be putting values in to arrive at our post hoc effect size > click on the button that says **From group parameters** > Go to Table 11.19 in the text to obtain the means and standard deviations (SDs) of the condition groups that we will use in this new window.

5. From Table 11.19, type in 28.350 beside **Mean group 1** and 27.150 next to **Mean group 2** > type in 3.675 next to **SD σ group 1** and 3.281 next to **SD σ group 2** > type in −.230 next to **Correlation between groups** > **Calculate and transfer to main window** (this will produce a post hoc effect size for the comparison of high electric stimulation at first treatment versus restored treatment).

6. Beside **α err prob**, type 0.01 > next to **Total sample size** type in 40 > click on **Calculate**.

The results in Figure 11.14 show an effect size of $dz = .2197599$, which is in the small range. The small effect size is consistent with the paired mean ranks analysis that showed no significant difference in pain improvement when comparing the high electric stimulation first treatment condition and restored treatment condition. The post hoc power is low at .1545664, suggesting there was only a 15.5 percent chance of correctly rejecting a false null hypothesis with a sample size of 40, $α = .01$, and post hoc effect size of $dz = .220$ (rounded).

Post Hoc Effect Size and Power Analyses Using G*Power 3.1 for High Electric Stimulation at Removed Treatment versus Restored Treatment

1. Open up the G*Power 3.1 program.

2. Select **t tests** under **Test family** > under **Statistical test**, select **Means: Wilcoxon signed-rank test (matched pairs)** > under **Type of power analysis**, select **Post hoc: Compute achieved power - given α, sample size, and effect size**.

3. Select **One** beside **Tail(s)** > select **Normal** next to **Parent distribution**.

4. Click on the **Determine** button and a new window is created that we will be putting values in to arrive at our post hoc effect size > click on the button that says **From group parameters** > Go to Table 11.19 in the text to obtain the means and standard deviations (SDs) of the condition groups that we will use in this new window.

5. From Table 11.19, type in 17.650 beside **Mean group 1** and 27.150 next to **Mean group 2** > type in 3.468 next to **SD σ group 1** and 3.281 next to **SD σ group 2** > type in −.209 next to **Correlation between groups** >

FIGURE 11.14   Post Hoc Effect Size and Power Analyses Using G*Power 3.1 for High Electric Stimulation at First Treatment versus Restored Treatment

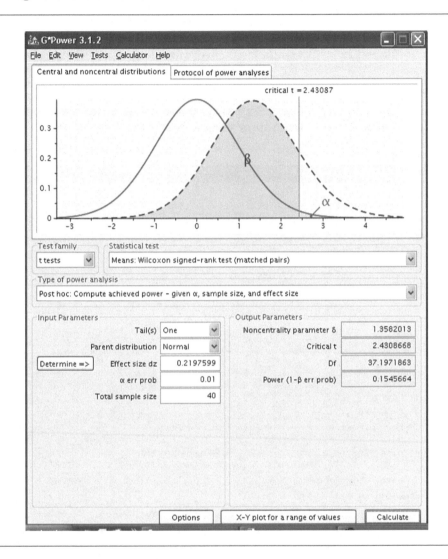

Calculate and transfer to main window (this will produce a post hoc effect size for the comparison of high electric stimulation at removed treatment versus restored treatment).

6. Beside **α err prob**, type 0.01 > next to **Total sample size** type in 40 > click on **Calculate**.

The results in Figure 11.15 show that the post hoc effect size was large ($dz = 1.8099934$) comparing the difference between the high electric stimulation removed treatment to the restored treatment. The post hoc power shows that we had a 100 percent chance of correctly rejecting a false null hypothesis with the same $N = 40$ and $\alpha = .01$ and a large effect size of $dz = 1.810$ (rounded).

FIGURE 11.15 Post Hoc Effect Size and Power Analysis for High Electric Stimulation at Removed Treatment versus Restored Treatment

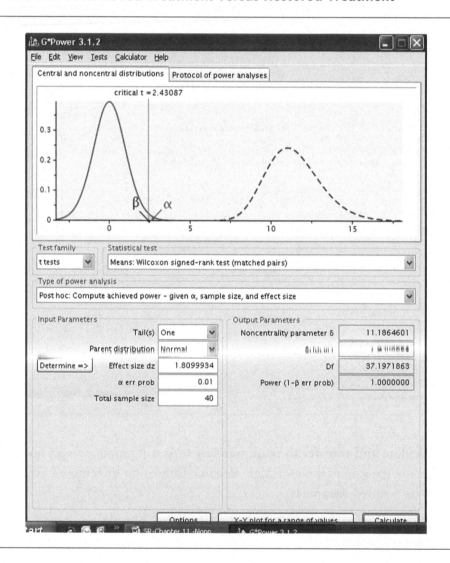

Formula Calculations for Friedman's Rank Test and Wilcoxon's Matched-Pairs Signed-Ranks Test

$$X_F^2 = 12/NK(K+1)\sum R_i^2 - 3N(K+1)$$

where
$N =$ total sum of cases being analyzed

$K =$ number of groups

$R_i =$ rank sum of each group

$n =$ sum of cases for each group

12 & 3 $=$ constants that are always part of the formula

TABLE 11.23 Friedman's Rank Test

First Treatment		Removed Treatment		Restored Treatment	
Score	Rank	Score	Rank	Score	Rank
28	3	19	1	27	2
38	3	17	1	29	2
26	2	20	1	30	3
29	3	10	1	26	2
26	3	23	1	25	2
27	3	16	1	25	2
29	3	17	1	27	2
26	2	19	1	28	3
26	3	18	1	24	2
32	3	20	1	23	2
25	2	17	1	38	3
27	3	20	1	26	2
26	2	19	1	28	3
25	2	18	1	27	3
25	2	21	1	29	3
29	3	22	1	23	2
28	3	17	1	24	2
27	2.5	16	1	27	2.5
37	3	15	1	28	2
31	3	9	1	29	2
	$R_i = 53.50$		$R_i = 20.00$		$R_i = 46.50$
	$R^2i = 2,862.25$		$R^2i = 400.00$		$R^2i = 2,162.25$

$$X_F^2 = 12/(20)(3)(4)\sum[(2{,}862.25 + 400 + 2{,}162.25)] - (3)(20)(4)$$

$$= 12/240[5{,}424.50] - 240$$

$$= .05[5{,}424.50] - 240$$

$$= 271.225 - 240$$

$$X_F^2 = 31.225$$

$$z = \frac{T - \dfrac{n(n+1)}{4}}{\sqrt{\dfrac{n(n+1)(2n+1)}{24}}}$$

TABLE 11.24 Wilcoxon's Matched-Pairs Signed-Ranks Test: First Treatment Scores Compared to Removed Treatment Scores

First Treatment Scores	Removed Treatment Scores	Difference Removed − First	Rank of Difference	Signed Rank
28	19	−9	11.00	−11.00
38	17	−21	18.00	−18.00
26	20	−6	3.00	−3.00
29	10	−19	17.00	−17.00
26	23	−3	1.00	−1.00
27	16	−11	13.00	−13.00
29	17	−12	15.50	−15.50
26	19	−7	6.00	−6.00
26	18	−8	9.00	−9.00
32	20	−12	15.50	−15.50
25	17	−8	9.50	−9.50
27	20	−7	6.00	−6.00
26	19	−7	6.00	−6.00
25	18	−7	6.00	−6.00
25	21	−4	2.00	−2.00
29	22	−7	6.00	−6.00
28	17	−11	13.00	−13.00
27	16	−11	13.00	−13.00
37	15	−22	19.50	−19.50
31	9	−22	19.50	−19.50
			$T = 210$	$T = -210$

TABLE 11.25 Wilcoxon's Matched-Pairs Signed-Ranks Test: Restored Treatment Scores Compared to Removed Treatment Scores

Restored Treatment Scores	Removed Treatment Scores	Difference Removed− Restored	Rank of Difference	Signed Rank
27	19	−8	13.50	−13.50
29	17	−12	5.00	−5.00
30	20	−10	7.50	−7.50
26	10	−16	3.00	−3.00
25	23	−2	19.00	−19.00
25	16	−9	10.50	−10.50
27	17	−10	7.50	−7.50
28	19	−9	10.50	−10.50
24	18	−6	16.50	−16.50
23	20	−3	18.00	−18.00
38	17	−21	1.00	−1.00
26	20	−6	16.50	−16.50
28	19	−9	10.50	−10.50
27	18	−9	10.50	−10.50
29	21	−8	13.50	−13.50
23	22	−1	20.00	−20.00
24	17	−7	15.00	−15.00
27	16	−11	6.00	−6.00
28	15	−13	4.00	−4.00
29	9	−20	2.00	−2.00
			$T = 210$	$T = -210$

$$= \frac{-210 - \dfrac{20(20 + 1)}{4}}{\sqrt{\dfrac{20(20 + 1)(2[20] + 1)}{24}}}$$

$$= \frac{-210 - 105}{\sqrt{717.50}}$$

$$= \frac{-105}{26.786}$$

$$z = -3.92$$

Nonparametric Research Problem Two Results

The aim of this study was to assess the effectiveness and stability of a high electric stimulation treatment on pain improvement of persons with MS. We evaluated whether pain improvement changes when high electric stimulation is added and removed with the same participants over time using a repeated-treatment design. The same 20 participants received three treatment conditions over 24 weeks. The participants first received a high electric stimulation (first treatment) for eight weeks, then the treatment was discontinued (removed treatment) for eight weeks, and finally the treatment was reinstated (restored treatment) for eight weeks. The participants' pain improvement from baseline was measured at the end of each treatment.

The a priori power analysis demonstrated that a desired power $\geq .80$ was achieved using $N = 20$, $\alpha = .01$, and estimated effect size of $d = 1.0$. The means, mean ranks, and standard deviations related to pain improvement across the high electric stimulation conditions were: (1) first treatment condition ($M = 28.350$, $M_{rank} = 2.68$, $SD = 3.675$), (2) removed condition ($M = 17.650$, $M_{rank} = 1.00$, $SD = 3.468$), and (3) restored condition ($M = 27.150$, $M_{rank} = 2.33$, $SD = 3.281$).

The Friedman statistic showed a significant difference among the mean ranks of pain improvement, $\chi^2(N = 20, df = 2) = 31.620$, $p < .01$. The post hoc comparisons of mean ranks using the Wilcoxon statistic showed that the high electric stimulation first treatment condition ($Z[N = 20] = -3.929$, $p < .003$, $d = 1.798$) and the restored treatment condition ($Z[N = 20] = -3.924$, $p < .003$, $d = 1.810$) resulted in significantly higher pain improvement than did the removed treatment condition.

In conclusion, a high electric stimulation to the lumbar region of the spine demonstrated effectiveness and stability in improving pain among persons with multiple sclerosis who are experiencing chronic low back pain.

SUMMARY

Two research problems were presented in this chapter demonstrating the use of nonparametric statistics. In the first study, a Kruskal-Wallis test for two or more independent samples and a Mann-Whitney U test of two independent samples were used. The variables and hypotheses were articulated within a randomized pretest-posttest control group design. A priori power and post hoc power were generated using G*Power. Data screenings were conducted. Interpretations were presented of the omnibus null hypothesis and the three mean rank pairs using a Bonferroni adjusted alpha to protect against making a Type I error decision. The results of the analyses were presented.

The Friedman's test for two or more correlated samples and the Wilcoxon's test for two correlated samples were illustrated in the second example. Again, a priori and post hoc power analyses were conducted. The omnibus null hypothesis was interpreted along with Bonferroni corrections to the paired mean ranks comparisons. The overall results of the second study were also presented.

PROBLEM ASSIGNMENT

The steps involved in conducting nonparametric statistics using IBM SPSS have been presented in this chapter. Now it is your turn to independently work through the steps of the hypothesis-testing process related to nonparametrics using IBM SPSS. Go to the companion website and you will find a new research problem and data set along with a worksheet to complete that relate to nonparametric statistics covered in this chapter. Use the problems presented in this chapter as guides so you can complete the assignment. Your instructor will evaluate your completed worksheet when it is finished.

KEY TERMS

alpha correction

asymptotic significance

Bonferroni adjusted alpha

exact significance

family of conclusions

Friedman's rank test for correlated samples

inflated Type I error risk

Kruskal-Wallis ANOVA

Mann-Whitney U (MWU) statistic

nonparametric statistics

randomized pretest-posttest control group design

Wilcoxon's matched-pairs signed-ranks test

Chapter 12

BIVARIATE AND MULTIVARIATE CORRELATION METHODS USING MULTIPLE REGRESSION ANALYSIS

LEARNING OBJECTIVES

- Identify the components and application of a bivariate correlation coefficient and multiple regression analysis.

- Conduct data diagnostics to assess for underlying assumptions.

- Execute a sequential multiple regression analysis using SPSS.

- Analyze the data and interpret the study findings combining the various analyses.

A study is presented that is suited for analyses using bivariate correlations and a sequential multiple regression analysis. The data are screened prior to analyses of the main study hypotheses. The null hypothesis is tested and interpreted. The written results are reported.

RESEARCH PROBLEM

In this study, a sample of 120 doctoral students in clinical psychology, counseling psychology, and counselor education program students completed the Scientist Practitioner Inventory (SPI) and the Dissertation Stress Inventory (DSI). High noncompletion rates of students in doctoral programs have been reported, including 50 percent (Kluever, 1997) and 43 percent (Denecke, 2006). Completing a dissertation is one of the most important milestones to reach in most doctoral programs. Dissertations tend to emphasize student skills of working productively with a dissertation chair and committee, persistence, organization, research, and analysis.

Doctoral students need to have interests and skills in both clinical and research areas to be successful in clinical and counseling psychology programs. However, doctoral students in clinically oriented programs often have more interests in clinical activities than in research activities. Completing a dissertation is a complex research process and, as Cone and Foster (2006) state, "your writing and methodological skills are the most important determinants of your success in the research process" (p. 21).

The researchers in this study want to assess whether doctoral students' lower interests in scientist activities more highly predict higher dissertation stress than do their interests in practitioner activities. The Scientist and Practitioner scales of the SPI are predictor variables, and higher scores reflect higher interests. The dependent variable in the study is the Dissertation Stress Inventory (DSI), and higher scores translate to higher dissertation stress perceived by the sample of doctoral students.

Bivariate correlation coefficient, multiple correlation coefficient, and sequential multiple regression analyses will be conducted. An $\alpha = .05$ is used for all analyses.

STUDY VARIABLES

The predictor variables (independent variables) and dependent variable (criterion variable) are identified in this section. Additionally, the operational definitions of the variables are described.

The two *predictor variables (PVs)* are measured by the Scientist and Practitioner scales of the Scientist Practitioner Inventory (SPI) (Leong & Zachar, 1991). The SPI consists of 21 items that measure interests in scientist activities and 21 items assessing interests in practitioner activities. A five-point (1 = very low interest to 5 = very high interest) Likert-type scale is used for each item. The Scientist scale measures student interests in activities related to research, statistics and design, teaching/guiding/editing, and academic ideas. The Practitioner scale assesses interests in activities involving therapy, clinical expertise and consultation, and testing and interpretation. Higher scores on the SPI reflect higher interests.

The DSI is comprised of 53 items using a seven-point Likert-type scale ranging from 1 (strongly disagree) to 7 (strongly agree). The DSI measures dissertation stress reported by doctoral students in counseling and clinical psychology programs. The specific areas assessed are chair and committee functioning, student organization and task commitment, statistics and research methodology competence, and relationship and financial functioning. High scores on all of the DSI scales represent more perceived dissertation-related stress.

RESEARCH METHOD

The purpose of this correlation research is to explore *bivariate relationships* and *multiple relationships* and predictions among variables. We will use bivariate correlations (r) to assess the relationships between all pairs of variables in the study. A multiple correlation (R) will be used to assess the relationship of the two predictor variables to the dependent variable. We will use a *sequential multiple linear regression* to predict the criterion variable (dissertation stress) (Y) from the two predictor variables (Xs).

In this study we will assess the extent that two predictor variables individually and collectively predict a criterion variable. Each individual PV will be assessed for its significant prediction to the DV, and the combination of the PVs will be evaluated as to how they predict the CV. The research model to be used can be written symbolically as dissertation stress is a function of interests in scientific activities and practitioner activities.

$$Y_{\text{DissStress}} f\left(X_{1\text{SPIScientInterests}}, X_{2\text{SPIPractInterests}}\right)$$

The statistical prediction model can be written:

$$Y' = A + B_1X_1, B_2X_2$$

where $Y' =$ predicted value on the dependent variable (dissertation stress)

           $A =$ intercept, the value of Y when all the X values are zero

           $B =$ unstandardized regression coefficient assigned to each X value

           $X =$ measured value of the independent variables.

Statistical Analysis: Bivariate Correlation and Multiple Regression

The Pearson product-moment correlation coefficient is the most commonly used correlation coefficient, and it is used to generate bivariate correlations and is the basic statistic in the multiple regression analyses (MRAs) in this study. There are three types of linear multiple regression analysis.

One MRA type is called *standard MRA (simultaneous MRA)*. All predictor variables (PVs) are entered into the regression equation at once. Each PV is evaluated in terms of what it adds uniquely to the prediction of the criterion variable (CV). Standard MRA is best used in exploratory and hypothesis-building regression models. Standard MRA can explain the basic multiple correlation, but its use may be less theoretically based and may be criticized for being a shotgun approach.

Another approach is called *sequential MRA (hierarchical MRA)*. The PVs enter the equation in an order specified by the researcher. Each is assessed in terms of what it adds to the equation when it is added to the model. This is the favored MRA by many researchers because it requires linking the analysis to previous research, theory, and logic rather than just throwing variables into a model. Sequential MRA is useful to designate the portion of variance associated with some variables while holding others constant.

Finally, *statistical MRA (stepwise MRA)* uses a procedure in which the entry of variables is based on statistical criteria in the statistical software program. In this procedure, a PV is selected and removed as a model predictor based on its statistical and probability values in relation to other PVs. This approach has been criticized if researchers do not use theory to guide the statistical MRA process.

STATING THE OMNIBUS (COMPREHENSIVE) RESEARCH QUESTION

Initially the ominibus research question is stated. Then the research and null hypotheses are developed as logical extensions of the research question.

Omnibus Research Question (RQ)

The omnibus research question is: To what extent will lower interests in scientific activities be a better predictor of higher dissertation stress reported by counseling and clinical psychology doctoral students when compared to their interests in practitioner activities?

HYPOTHESIS TESTING STEP 1: ESTABLISH THE ALTERNATIVE (RESEARCH) HYPOTHESIS (H_a)

The omnibus (comprehensive) alternative hypothesis for our research problem is stated next in both narrative and symbolic formats. We also will be addressing subquestions and subhypotheses following the overall analysis.

Omnibus Narrative Alternative Hypothesis (H_a)

H_a: Lower interests in scientific activities will be a better predictor of higher dissertation stress reported by counseling and clinical psychology doctoral students when compared to their interests in practitioner activities.

Symbolic H_a

$$Yf(X_1, X_2) \neq 0$$

where $Y =$ dissertation stress

$f =$ function of

$X_1 =$ interests in scientific activities

$X_2 =$ interests in practitioner activities

HYPOTHESIS TESTING STEP 2: ESTABLISH THE NULL HYPOTHESIS (H_0)

The omnibus null hypothesis is stated in narrative and symbolic formats in the second step of the hypothesis-testing process.

Omnibus Narrative Null Hypothesis (H_0)

H_0: Neither interests in scientific activities nor interests in practitioner activities will significantly predict dissertation stress reported by counseling and clinical psychology doctoral students.

Symbolic H_0

$$Yf(X_1, X_2) = 0$$

HYPOTHESIS TESTING STEP 3: DECIDE ON A RISK LEVEL (ALPHA) OF REJECTING THE TRUE H_0 CONSIDERING TYPE I AND II ERRORS AND POWER

There has been little data-based research in the area of identifying significant predictors of dissertation stress, so this is an exploratory study. As such, an alpha of .05 provides a reasonable balance between avoiding rejecting the H_0 when there really are no significant relationships (Type I [alpha] error) and not rejecting the H_0 when there really are significant relationships (Type II [beta] error).

A Priori Power Analysis

We are planning to use $N = 120$, two predictor variables, and $\alpha = .05$. A previous similar study resulted in a squared multiple correlation of $R^2 = .09$, which we will use to determine an estimated effect size for the a priori power analysis. We will conduct the a priori power analysis using G*Power 3.1.2.

A Priori Power Analysis Using G*Power 3.1 for the Multiple Regression Analysis

1. Open up the G*Power 3.1.2 program.

2. Select **F tests** under **Test family** > under **Statistical test**, select **Linear multiple regression: Fixed model, R^2 increase** > under **Type of power**

analysis, select **A priori: Compute required sample size - given α, power, and effect size**.

3. Click on the **Determine** box > in the newly created window click on **Direct** circle > type in 0.09 next to **Partial R^2** > click on the button **Calculate and transfer to main window** > click on **Close** button.

4. Type in 0.05 next to **α err prob** > type in 0.80 next to **Power (1-β err prob)** > type in 2 next to **Number of predictors** > type in 2 next to **Total number of predictors** > click **Calculate**.

The estimated effect size ($f^2 = .0989011$) to use in the power analysis was calculated from the R^2 ($\rho^2) = .09$. The estimated effect size is transferred to the full a priori power analysis. The planned $\alpha = .05$, two predictors, desired power $= .80$ are added to the analysis and the results show that a total sample size of 101 is needed to reach a .8022579 power (see Figure 12.1). We meet the power criteria with the planned sample size of 120 participants.

HYPOTHESIS TESTING STEP 4: CHOOSE APPROPRIATE STATISTIC AND ITS SAMPLING DISTRIBUTION TO TEST THE H_0 ASSUMING H_0 IS TRUE

We will be using bivariate correlations calculated using the Pearson product-moment correlation coefficient and a sequential multiple regression analysis to test the null hypothesis: $Yf(X_1, X_2) = 0$. We are going to assess the individual and combined relationships of interests in scientist and practitioner activities in predicting dissertation arrons among doctoral students in counseling and clinical psychology programs. Sequential multiple regression analysis is appropriate to use because: (1) there is one continuously scaled dependent variable, and (2) there are two or more predictor variables.

HYPOTHESIS TESTING STEP 5: SELECT SAMPLE, COLLECT DATA, SCREEN DATA, COMPUTE STATISTIC, AND DETERMINE PROBABILITY ESTIMATES

Data are collected from a sample of participants during Step 5 of the hypothesis-testing process. The data are assessed for data accuracy, missing values, and univariate

FIGURE 12.1 A Priori Power Analysis of MRA Problem

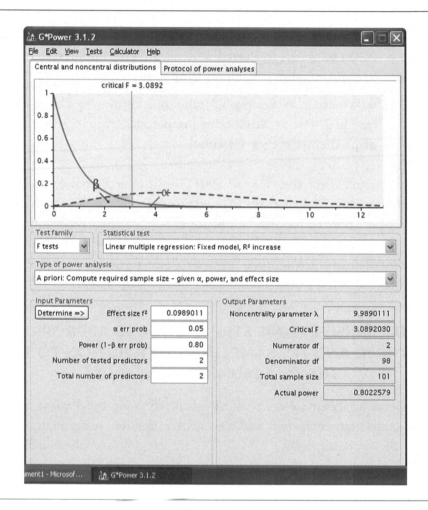

and multivariate outliers, and to determine whether the underlying assumptions of the statistic are met. If needed, data modifications are made. Then, the null hypothesis is testing using statistical analyses.

Sample Selection and Assignment

The sample in this study is selected using purposive sampling of typical instances (Shadish, Cook, & Campbell, 2002), also called homogeneous sampling. In purposive sampling of typical instances, we define the characteristics that reflect the persons, settings, times, independent variables, and dependent variables we intend to use to generalize our findings. We then select participants who match the targeted characteristics.

The persons being studied in this sample are doctoral students in counseling psychology, clinical psychology, and counselor education programs throughout the United States.

Study Data Diagnostics

There are new screening procedures that we will use for the sequential MRA analysis. Descriptions of these procedures will be discussed as we are using them. Many of these procedures are selected when we run the sequential MRA main analyses.

Univariate Outlier Analysis

There are two predictor variables and one dependent variable that will be used in this analysis. It is important to assess each variable for participant scores that may represent significantly extreme high or low scores, so we will conduct an analysis for univariate outliers. We will start with a familiar procedure, checking for univariate outliers.

SPSS Commands for Identifying Univariate Outlier

1. **Analyze > Descriptive Statistics > Descriptives**.

2. Click over *DSI*, *SPIPract*, and *SPIScient* under **Variable(s):** > click on the box called **Save standardized values as variables** > click **OK**.

3. You can click out of the output produced and go to **Data View**, where new variables have been created that represent the *z*-scores for the participants' observed scores for all variables.

The highest $\pm z$-score for each variable taken from the Data View is presented in Table 12.1. None of the *z*-scores reach the criterion of ± 3.29 ($<.001$, two-tailed), so we conclude that there are no univariate outliers.

Next, we determine if there are any multivariate outliers in which one or more cases have an "unusual combination of scores on two or more variables" (Tabachnick & Fidell, 2007). Mahalanobis distance values are used to assess for multivariate outliers, and they are produced as values in a new column on the IBM SPSS Data View spreadsheet. Also, output is produced from the following commands that will be used for all other screening and sequential MRA analyses.

TABLE 12.1 Highest ±z-Scores for DSI, SPIPract, and SPIScient

Variable	Highest +z	Outlier? >±3.29	Highest −z	Outlier? >±3.29
DSI	2.50291*	No	−2.01254	No
SPIPract	1.73182	No	−2.74452	No
SPIScient	2.55536	No	−1.86080	No

*This number is rounded to three decimals.

Sequential (Hierarchical) MRA Example SPSS Commands

1. Open up SPSS Data File called *MRA-Data* and click on **Analyze** > **Regression** > **Linear**.

2. Click over *DSI* under **Dependent:**.

3. Under **Independent(s):** > click over *SPIScient* then click on the **Next** button to the upper right. The *SPIScient* disappears and the program stores the variable as the first predictor variable in the model you are developing. Then, click over *SPIPract* and click on the **Next** button and it too disappears. You now have set up the model we want to test.

4. Click on the **Statistics** button > check on **Estimates, Confidence intervals**, and type in 95 beside **Level(%):** > check on **Model fit, R squared change, Descriptives, Part and partial correlations**, and **Collinearity diagnostics** and click on **Continue**.

5. Click on the **Plots** button and click over ***ZRESID** to the **Y:** box and ***ZPRED** to the **X:** > under **Standardized Residual Plots** click on **Histogram** and **Normality probability plot** and click **Continue**.

6. Click on the **Save** button > under **Distances** click **Mahalanobis** and click **Continue** and click **OK**.

7. Save the results as *Sequential-MRA-Results*.

Multivariate Outlier Analysis

We are assessing the impact of two predictor variables on a dependent variable in this study. We are concerned that participants may have combinations of extreme scores on two or more variables that represent *multivariate outliers*. We use the

Mahalanobis distance values that were produced from our MRA commands to determine if we have multivariate outliers. A new column in the Data View called **MAH_1** is comprised of Mahalanobis values. Also, the output has a table called Residuals Statistics in which the largest Mahalanobis distance (maximum) is presented as 9.034 (see Table 12.2). We are going to compare the Mahalanobis distance values (beginning with the largest) to a chi squared (χ^2) critical value to determine if any of the values are significant. To find the χ^2 critical value to compare to the Mahalanobis values we will need degrees of freedom (*df*) and alpha level. The *df* for this analysis is the number of predictor variables, which is two, and the alpha we use is .001 (Tabachnick & Fidell, 2007).

Go to www.danielsoper.com > select **Statistics Calculator** > select **Chi Square Distribution** > select **Critical Chi Square Value Calculator** > type in 2 next to **Degrees of freedom** > type .001 next to **Probability level:** > click on **Calculate!**

You see that $\chi^2_{.999}$ (2 *df*) = 13.81551056, rounded to 13.816. Any participant who has a Mahalanobis value that is equal to or greater than 13.816 is considered to be a multivariate outlier. The largest Mahalanobis value is 9.03410,

TABLE 12.2   Largest (Maximum) Mahalanobis Distance Value

Residuals Statistics[a]					
	Minimum	Maximum	Mean	Std. Deviation	N
Predicted value	146.66	194.07	174.98	10.630	120
Std. predicted value	−2.664	1.797	.000	1.000	120
Std. error of predicted value	3.245	9.691	5.075	1.458	120
Adjusted predicted value	149.29	195.03	175.07	10.533	120
Residual	−73.149	72.419	.000	33.105	120
Std. residual	−2.191	2.169	.000	.992	120
Stud. residual	−2.215	2.181	−.001	1.003	120
Deleted residual	−74.740	73.325	−.097	33.900	120
Stud. deleted residual	−2.253	2.217	−.002	1.010	120
Mahal. distance	.132	9.034	1.983	1.851	120
Cook's distance	.000	.060	.008	.012	120
Centered leverage value	.001	.076	.017	.016	120

[a]Dependent variable: DSI.

which is fairly close to but less than our criterion of 13.816, so we conclude that there are no participants who have scores that reflect being a multivariate outlier.

General Screening of Correlation Coefficients

A look at the bivariate Pearson product-moment correlation coefficients between the predictor variables and the dependent variable and just between the predictor variables provides information on whether the multiple regression analysis is suggesting the existence of a viable solution.

A correlation coefficient is an index of the relationship between and among variables. A correlation coefficient between two variables is a *bivariate correlation (r)*, and it is designated with the symbol (*r*). A correlation coefficient representing a relationship among more than two variables is called a *multiple correlation (R)*. Values for correlation coefficients (*r*) like the Pearson product-moment correlation range from -1.0 to $+1.0$; however, multiple correlations (*R*) are only positive values.

A -1.0 reflects a perfect negative relationship. As the scores of one variable increase, the other variable scores decrease at the same rate. A 0 reflects no correlation; there is no consistent increase or decrease in scores between two or more variables. A $+1.0$ reflects a perfect positive relationship. As the scores of variables increase or decrease, the scores of other variables do the same at the same rate.

There are several useful ways to descriptively interpret correlation coefficients. The *strength of the correlation* coefficient can be interpreted as *low* ($\leq\pm.39$), *moderate* (between $\pm.40$ and $\pm.69$), and *large* ($\geq\pm.70$) (Grimm, 1993).

The *coefficient of determination* is obtained by squaring the bivariate correlation (r^2) or multiple correlation (R^2), which is an index of the strength of the relationship. The *percentage of shared variance* between two or more variables can be obtained by calculating $r^2 \times 100$ or $R^2 \times 100$.

The *coefficient of alienation* is obtained by subtracting the coefficient of determination from $1.0(1.0 - r^2$ or $1.0 - R^2)$, which is an index of unexplained variance in the relationship. The *percentage of unexplained variance* is obtained by $1.0 - (r^2 \times 100)$ or $1.0 - (R^2 \times 100)$.

An illustration of these interpretation is: (1) $r = .40$ is a moderate correlation, (2) the coefficient of determination is $r^2 = (.40)^2 = .16$, (3) there is 16 percent shared variance between the variables, (4) the coefficient of alienation is $(1.0 - .16) = .84$, and (5) the percentage of unexplained variance between the variables is 84 percent.

The row for Pearson Correlation—DSI in Table 12.3 shows the bivariate correlations of the predictor variables to the dependent variable. We want these correlations to show some degree of strength, which suggests that there may be a meaningful solution when all the variables are combined in the MRA. The correlations of the predictor variables to the dependent variable are below moderate SPIScient and DSI ($r = -.302$) and SPIPract and DSI ($r = .104$). However, looking at the Sig. (1-tailed) DSI row, one of the predictors (SPIScient) reflects a significant relationship ($p = .000$ or $p < .05$) with DSI. So, the MRA may reflect a meaningful model that predicts dissertation stress. If all of the predictors were very low and not significant, it is likely there would not be meaningful results from the MRA.

It also is important to review the correlation coefficient between the predictor variables. If any correlation between two predictor variables is around .70 (high), that means that there is *redundancy of information* between the variables. The two variables would appear to be measuring the same thing, and one of the variables may not need to be in the combined variable solution. This is called *multi-collinearity* when several redundant pairs of variables overly explain ($r = .90$) each other and complicate meaningful interpretation of the actual relationships among variables.

The bivariate correlation between the two predictor variables in Table 12.3 is low ($r = -.199$). The $r^2 = .040$, so there is less than 4 percent shared variance between the two variables. There is no indication of redundancy between the two predictor variables.

TABLE 12.3 Bivariate Correlation Coefficients between the Study Variables

Correlations

		DSI	SPIScient	SPIPract
Pearson Correlation	DSI	1.000	−.302	.104
	SPIScient	−.302	1.000	−.199
	SPIPract	.104	−.199	1.000
Sig. (1-tailed)	DSI	.	.000	.129
	SPIScient	.000	.	.015
	SPIPract	.129	.015	.
N	DSI	120	120	120
	SPIScient	120	120	120
	SPIPract	120	120	120

Assessment of Multicollinearity and Singularity

The bivariate correlations do not seem to suggest the presence of redundancy among the predictor variables. There are other measures used to directly assess whether multicollinearity or singularity exist. Singularity is an extreme case of multicollinearity when a predictor variable is perfectly predicted (± 1.0). The presence of singularity is rare and usually a result of mistakes in data entry or analysis such as using the same variable twice.

Tolerance is defined as $(1 - SMC)$ where SMC is a squared multiple correlation (R^2) and ranges from 0 to 1.0. The higher the SMC, the more redundancy there is between variables and the lower the tolerance value will be. A lower SMC reflects less redundancy and the tolerance will be higher. So, we want high tolerance values; multicollinearity is more of a concern if tolerance values are below .20 and are more acceptable when they are above .50.

The reciprocal (opposite) of tolerance is the variance inflation factor (VIF). The VIF is obtained by dividing 1 by tolerance, so we want VIF values to be low, which is opposite of tolerance values that we want high. Variance inflation factors are of more concern when they are greater than 10 and most acceptable when they are less than 5.

Looking at the collinearity results in Table 12.4, the tolerance values are high, 1.00 in Model 1 (SPIScient only) and .960 in Model 2 (SPIScient and SPIPract). These tolerance values are much higher than criteria of $>.20$ or $>.50$, so the evidence does not support the presence of multicollinearity. This finding is supported by the low VIF values of 1.00 in Model 1 (SPIScient only) and 1.041 in Model 2 (SPIScient and SPIPract), which are considerably lower than

TABLE 12.4 Multicollinearity Measures of Tolerance and Variance Inflation Factor (VIF)

	Coefficients[a]		
		Collinearity Statistics	
Model		Tolerance	VIF
1	SPIScient	1.000	1.000
2	SPIScient	.960	1.041
	SPIPract	.960	1.041

[a]Dependent variable: DSI.

<5 or <10. We conclude that there is no presence of severe redundancy among the predictor variables. Parenthetically, the two tolerance values in Model 2 and the VIF values are the same. This is true because there are only two predictor variables in the model that are being analyzed with each other twice. There would be different tolerance and VIF values if there were more than two predictor variables in the model. One predictor variable would be compared to all other predictor variables in the model.

Assessment of Normality, Linearity, and Homoscedasticity of Residuals

We are going to analyze residuals to assess normality, linearity, and homoscedasticity. *Residuals* represent error variances of prediction, which are differences between obtained and predicted dependent variable scores. Residuals are the portion of the score on the dependent variable that is not explained by the predictor variable. In order to use MRA, it is assumed that the residuals have normal distributions (normality), and a straight-line relationship (*linearity*) with predicted dependent variable scores. Also, the variance of the residuals related to the dependent variable scores is consistent for all the predicted scores (*homoscedasticity*).

The *normal distribution of residuals* can be assessed from the histogram in Figure 12.2. The residuals appear reasonably symmetrical and within the superimposed normal distribution outline. Also, the P-P (probability-probability) plot in Figure 12.3 is interpreted similarly to Q-Q plots where we want the points on or close to the graph line. This shows that the observed *cumulative probability of the residuals* is congruent with the expected cumulative probability of the residuals.

The residual scatter plot in Figure 12.4 provides information about normality, linearity, and homoscedasticity. Normality is indicated when there is an accumulation of residuals in the center of the plot in relation to each value of the predicted score, with residuals trailing off symmetrically from the center (Tabachnick & Fidell, 2007). There is more of a concentration of residuals in the middle of the plot, and they disperse from the center somewhat evenly in smaller numbers.

The variance of residuals about the predicted dependent variable scores is the same for all predicted scores when homoscedasticity exists. Visualize a band around the residuals, and the residuals should be approximately equal in width at all values of the predicted dependent variable. The residuals do appear to be

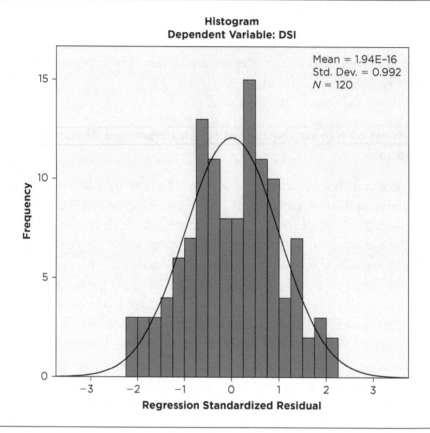

approximately equal in width at the values of the regression standardized pre-dicted values on the abscissa.

When residuals have a straight-line relationship with predicted DV scores, then the linearity exists, which is desired. The band surrounding the residual scatter plot will approximate the form of a rectangle. If the band around the residuals is a shape other than a straight line, such as a U shape, then variables or combinations of variables may have curvilinear relationships with the dependent variable, and then linear MRA may not be the best choice for analysis. No curvilinear relationship of residuals is evident in the scatter plot, and a rectangular shape surrounding the residuals can be visualized. Evidence suggests that the assumptions of normality, homoscedasticity, and linearity have been met.

FIGURE 12.3 Normal P-P Plot of Residuals of DSI Predicted by SPIScient and SPIPract

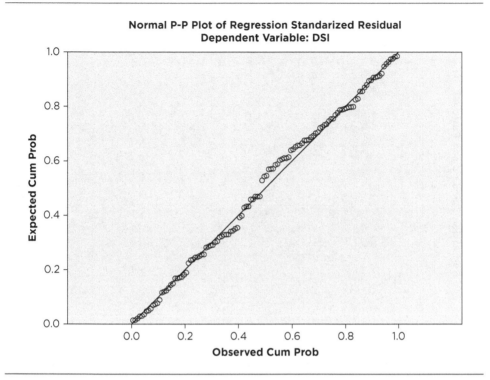

Sequential Multiple Regression Analysis

The results of the sequential MRA are in the *Sequential-MRA-Results* output. Initially, we interpret the Model Summary table (see Table 12.5) The first row is Model 1 and has one predictor variable (SPIScient) predicting DSI. The multiple correlation is $R = .302$, showing that the model with SPIScient has a moderate correlation to DSI. Model 1 has only two variables (SPIScient and DSI) that should produce a similar correlation coefficent to the bivariate correlation in Table 12.3, with one important difference: a minus value reflecting an inverse relationship between the two variables; the bivariate correlation is $r = -.302$. A multiple correlation coefficient (R) is always a positive value, so it is essential to refer to the bivariate correlation coefficients table to see what direction (positive or negative) the relationship is between pairs of variables.

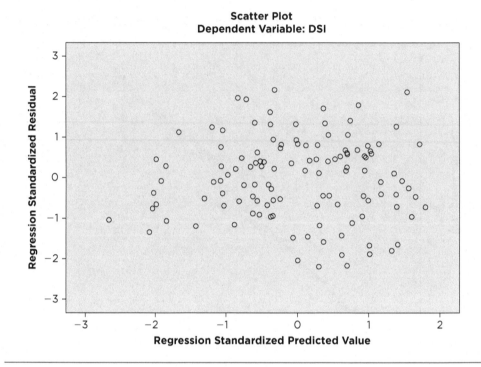

The *R-squared* (R^2) value = .091 [(SS$_{regression}$/SS$_{total}$) or (.302)^2], showing that 9.10 percent of the variability in higher dissertation stress can be explained by lower interest in scientific activities. We know that SPIScient and DSI have an inverse relationship, because the bivariate correlation between SPIScient and DSI is −.302. We also know that high scores on DSI translate to higher dissertation stress and low scores on SPIScient mean lower interest in scientific activities.

The *adjusted* R^2 = .084 [1 − (SS$_{Resid.}$/SS$_{Tot.}$)(df$_{Tot.}$/df$_{Resid.}$)] corrects the R^2 to be a better estimate of how well the model fits the population parameters. The adjusted R^2 is more conservative and is lower than the R^2.

The *standard error of the estimate (SEE)* (Sqrt of SS$_{residual}$/N − # of predictor variables − 1) is the standard deviation of the residuals (prediction errors). The moderate correlation of the predictor variable to the dependent variable is not perfect (±1.0). The standard error of estimate (SEE) is an index of how far off our prediction is. The larger the SEE value, the less confident we are in prediction.

TABLE 12.5 Model Summary of Sequential MRA

Model Summary[a]

Model	R	R-Squared	Adjusted R-Squared	Std. Error of Estimate	Change Statistics				
					R-Squared Change	F Change	df1	df2	Sig. F Change
1	.302[b]	.091	.084	33.281	.091	11.880	1	118	.001
2	.306[c]	.093	.078	33.386	.002	.258	1	117	.612

[a]Dependent variable: DSI.
[b]Predictors: (Constant), SPIScient.
[c]Predictors: (Constant), SPIScient, SFIPract.

According to Norusis (2005), the SEE should be considerably lower than the standard deviation of the dependent variable for a successful regression model.

The *R-squared change* value ($R^2_{change} = .091$) represents the amount of change to the model's R^2 when a variable is added to the previous model. In this situation, this is Model 1 and there was no previous model, so the $R^2_{change} = .091$ is the same as $R^2 = .091$. The *F change* value $= 11.880$ is a statistical *F*-test assessing whether the R^2_{change} in the model is a significant addition to the model. The assessment of the *F* change results in a *Sig. F change* $= .001$, which is significant, $p < .05$.

Model 2 combines both SPIScient and SPIPract as a multiple correlation to DSI. The multiple correlation is $R = .306$, reflecting moderate relationships among the two predictor variables (or independent variables) and one criterion variable (or dependent variable). The $R^2 = .093$ and the $R^2_{change} = .002$ by adding the new variable, SPIPract, in Model 2. This small amount of R^2_{change} was not significant *F* change $= .258$, with a Sig. *F* change $= .612$, $p > .05$.

In the ANOVA table (see Table 12.6), the information relates to testing the null hypotheses that the population value for the multiple *R* is 0 in each model using the *F* test of the model. The *regression sum of squares* is variability explained by the regression, and the *residual sum of squares* is variability not explained by the regression. The *total sum of squares* is the total of the two. We want to compare the Sig. value of the *F* ratio ($MS_{Regres.}/MS_{Resid.}$) to our $\alpha = .05$ to determine if we reject the null hypothesis. In Model 1, the significance (Sig.) value of .001 is less than the $\alpha = .05$, so we reject the null that the population value for multiple

TABLE 12.6 Analysis of Variance of the Two Sequential MRA Models

ANOVA[a]						
Model		Sum of Squares	df	Mean Square	F	Sig.
1	Regression	13,158.483	1	13,158.483	11.880	.001[b]
	Residual	130,702.442	118	1,107.648		
	Total	143,860.925	119			
2	Regression	13,446.116	2	6,723.058	6.032	.003[c]
	Residual	130,414.809	117	1,114.656		
	Total	143,860.925	119			

[a]Dependent variable: DSI.
[b]Predictors: (Constant), SPIScient.
[c]Predictors: (Constant), SPIScient, SPIPract.

R is 0. There $R = .302$ represents a significant correlation, $F(1, 118) = 11.880$, $p < .05$. Model 2 has both predictor variables (SPIScient and SPIPract) predicting DSI, and it also reflects a significant model, $F(2, 117) = 6.032$, $p < .05$.

The significance of individual predictors on dissertation stress is assessed next (see Table 12.7). The *constant* is the intercept, which is the expected value of the dependent variable when all the independent variables are zero. The *unstandardized beta coefficient (B)* is an estimate of the likely change in the dependent variable for each one-unit change in the predictor variable. The unstandardized beta coefficient values are scaled in the original metric of the variables used. The unstandardized beta coefficient is also referred to as the regression coefficient. The Std. Error (standard error of the estimate) is a value that estimates the standard deviation of the dependent variable for any value of the predictor variable. It is a standard deviation of residuals (Norusis, 1999).

The *standardized beta coefficient (beta weight) (β)* is a regression coefficient for a sample expressed in standard deviation units (i.e., z-scores). The mean is 0 and the standard deviation is 1. The standardized beta coefficient indicates the change in the dependent variable for each one standard deviation change in the predictor variable. So scores are reported as standard scores on IVs rather than using the original metric. These beta weights allow for easier comparisons of the relative influence of other PVs used in the regression. Standardized beta coefficients provide guidance as to the relative importance of predictor variables in the model—however, not in an absolute sense because they are contingent on the other PVs in the model.

The *t-statistic* is a test of significance to determine if the coefficients for individual variables are different from 0. Each variable is tested for significant contribution in the model.

An examination of the significance of the standardized beta coefficient SPIScient to DSI in Model 1 shows that it is significant, $\beta = -.302$, $t(118) = -3.447$, $p = .001$ ($p < .05$). You notice that the $\beta = -.302$ is equal to $r = -.302$. Standardized regression coefficients and correlation coefficients are the same when one predictor variable is used with the dependent variable. When we have more than one predictor variable used with a dependent variable, the regression and correlation coefficients are no longer equal.

Model 2 has SPIPract added to SPIScient to predict DSI. Again, SPIScient is significant, $\beta = -.293$, $t(117) = -3.266$, $p = .001$ ($p < .05$). However, SPIPract is not a significant predictor variable with SPIScient of DSI, $\beta = .046$, $t(117) = .508$, $p = .612$ ($p > .05$).

TABLE 12.7 Significance Values of Each Predictor Variable

Coefficients[a]

Model		Unstandardized Coefficients		Standardized Coefficients			95% Confidence Interval for B	
		B	Std. Error	Beta	t	Sig.	Lower Bound	Upper Bound
1	(Constant)	213.510	11.586		18.429	.000	190.567	236.453
	SPIScient	−.654	.190	−.302	−3.447	.001	−1.030	−.278
2	(Constant)	202.345	24.862		8.139	.000	153.107	251.584
	SPIScient	−.634	.194	−.293	−3.266	.001	−1.019	−.250
	SPIPract	.132	.259	.046	.508	.612	−.381	.644

[a]Dependent variable: DSI.

The 95 percent confidence interval for B (unstandardized coefficients) tells us that the probability is .95 that the intervals obtained in this way encompass the true value of B.

It is evident that Model 1 is the best model. It contains the interests in science variable (SPIScient), which is the only predictor that is significantly predicting dissertation stress (DSI) and in an inverse relationship. Practitioner interests do not significantly predict dissertation stress.

HAND CALCULATIONS OF STATISTICS

Several analyses are calculated next to show the equations used in obtaining results in the multiple regression example. The first analysis is to calculate the Pearson product-moment correlation coefficient.

Pearson Product-Moment Correlation Coefficient

The formula of the Pearson product-moment correlation coefficient that we will be using follows.

$$r_{XY} = \frac{\Sigma XY - (\Sigma X)(\Sigma Y)/N}{\text{Sqrt}[\Sigma X^2 - (\Sigma X)^2/N][\Sigma Y^2 - (\Sigma Y)^2/N]}$$

SPIScient and DSI Pearson Product-Moment Correlation

The data used to calculate the Pearson product-moment correlation for SPIScient and DSI are presented next. The data are followed by the correlation calculations.

ID#	YDSI	XSc	XY	X^2	Y^2
1	107	58	6,206	3,364	11,449
2	183	35	6,405	1,225	33,489
3	125	62	7,750	3,844	15,625

(Continued)

ID#	YDSI	XSc	XY	X^2	Y^2
4	130	43	5,590	1,849	16,900
5	170	29	4,930	841	28,900
6	203	51	10,353	2,601	41,209
7	212	44	9,328	1,936	44,944
8	177	34	6,018	1,156	31,329
9	174	38	6,612	1,444	30,276
10	105	57	5,985	3,249	11,025
11	110	46	5,060	2,116	12,100
12	162	69	11,178	4,761	26,244
13	150	70	10,500	4,900	22,500
14	161	70	11,270	4,900	25,921
15	155	64	9,920	4,096	24,025
16	205	55	11,275	3,025	42,025
17	221	32	7,072	1,024	48,841
18	139	66	9,174	4,356	19,321
19	132	92	12,144	8,464	17,424
20	204	80	16,320	6,400	41,616
21	188	32	6,016	1,024	35,344
22	232	69	16,008	4,761	53,824
23	203	76	15,428	5,776	41,209
24	191	60	11,460	3,600	36,481
25	230	50	11,500	2,500	52,900
26	244	63	15,372	3,969	59,536
27	167	74	12,358	5,476	27,889
28	203	58	11,774	3,364	41,209
29	155	57	8,835	3,249	24,025
30	244	47	11,468	2,209	59,536
31	205	52	10,660	2,704	42,025
32	193	53	10,229	2,809	37,249
33	262	32	8,384	1,024	68,644
34	166	38	6,308	1,444	27,556
35	139	70	9,730	4,900	19,321
36	215	65	13,975	4,225	46,225
37	188	49	9,212	2,401	35,344
38	167	41	6,847	1,681	27,889
39	120	84	10,080	7,056	14,400
40	224	52	11,648	2,704	50,176
41	141	72	10,152	5,184	19,881
42	141	86	12,126	7,396	19,881
43	186	63	11,718	3,969	34,596
44	135	39	5,265	1,521	18,225

ID#	YDSI	XSc	XY	X^2	Y^2
45	203	45	9,135	2,025	41,209
46	219	58	12,702	3,364	47,961
47	232	72	16,704	5,184	53,824
48	181	72	13,032	5,184	32,761
49	153	65	9,945	4,225	23,409
50	148	66	9,768	4,356	21,904
51	195	89	17,355	7,921	38,025
52	199	47	9,353	2,209	39,601
53	189	76	14,364	5,776	35,721
54	161	72	11,592	5,184	25,921
55	159	78	12,402	6,084	25,281
56	190	71	13,490	5,041	36,100
57	183	67	12,261	4,489	33,489
58	112	100	11,200	10,000	12,544
59	200	61	12,200	3,721	40,000
60	170	44	7,480	1,936	28,900
61	140	63	8,820	3,969	19,600
62	139	50	6,950	2,500	19,321
63	203	60	12,180	3,600	41,209
64	191	50	9,550	2,500	36,481
65	165	55	9,075	3,025	27,225
66	129	34	4,386	1,156	16,641
67	232	36	8,352	1,296	53,824
68	173	68	11,764	4,624	29,929
69	206	61	12,566	3,721	42,436
70	225	63	14,175	3,969	50,625
71	183	73	13,359	5,329	33,489
72	218	46	10,028	2,116	47,524
73	184	42	7,728	1,764	33,856
74	126	53	6,678	2,809	15,876
75	152	90	13,680	8,100	23,104
76	153	42	6,426	1,764	23,409
77	118	46	5,428	2,116	13,924
78	176	39	6,864	1,521	30,976
79	197	61	12,017	3,721	38,809
80	179	69	12,351	4,761	32,041
81	151	74	11,174	5,476	22,801
82	144	81	11,664	6,561	20,736
83	147	73	10,731	5,329	21,609

(Continued)

ID#	YDSI	XSc	XY	X^2	Y^2
84	215	36	7,740	1,296	46,225
85	146	45	6,570	2,025	21,316
86	193	37	7,141	1,369	37,249
87	215	51	10,965	2,601	46,225
88	179	65	11,635	4,225	32,041
89	165	68	11,220	4,624	27,225
90	173	77	13,321	5,929	29,929
91	207	45	9,315	2,025	42,849
92	134	50	6,700	2,500	17,956
93	206	39	8,034	1,521	42,436
94	191	46	8,786	2,116	36,481
95	214	66	14,124	4,356	45,796
96	139	67	9,313	4,489	19,321
97	120	86	10,320	7,396	14,400
98	196	53	10,388	2,809	38,416
99	128	54	6,912	2,916	16,384
100	169	86	14,534	7,396	28,561
101	182	51	9,282	2,601	33,124
102	203	66	13,398	4,356	41,209
103	159	52	8,268	2,704	25,281
104	128	96	12,288	9,216	16,384
105	183	68	12,444	4,624	33,489
106	182	59	10,738	3,481	33,124
107	127	78	9,906	6,084	16,129
108	177	66	11,682	4,356	31,329
109	163	65	10,595	4,225	26,569
110	164	55	9,020	3,025	26,896
111	123	45	5,535	2,025	15,129
112	165	87	14,355	7,569	27,225
113	208	38	7,904	1,444	43,264
114	236	53	12,508	2,809	55,696
115	160	32	5,120	1,024	25,600
116	202	48	9,696	2,304	40,804
117	153	70	10,710	4,900	23,409
118	202	42	8,484	1,764	40,804
119	193	52	10,036	2,704	37,249
120	108	87	9,396	7,569	11,664

$\Sigma Y = 20,997 \quad \Sigma X = 7,070 \quad \Sigma XY = 1,216,955 \quad \Sigma X^2 = 447,300 \quad \Sigma Y^2 = 3,817,811$

$$r_{XY} = \frac{\Sigma XY - (\Sigma X)(\Sigma Y)/N}{\text{Sqrt}[\Sigma X^2 - (\Sigma X)^2/N][\Sigma Y^2 - (\Sigma Y)^2/N]}$$

$$= \frac{1,216,955 - (7,070)(20,997)/120}{\text{Sqrt}[447,300 - (7,070)^2/120][3,817,811 - (20,997)^2/120]}$$

$$= \frac{1,216,955 - 1,237,073}{\text{Sqrt}[447,300 - 416,541][3,817,811 - 3,673,950]}$$

$$= \frac{-20,118}{\text{Sqrt}(30,759)(143,861)}$$

$$= \frac{-20,118}{\text{Sqrt}\,4,425,020,499}$$

$$= -20,118/66,521$$

$$r_{XY} = -.302$$

SPIPract and DSI Pearson Product-Moment Correlation

ID#	YDSI	XSc	XY	X^2	Y^2
1	107	72	7,704	5,184	11,449
2	183	87	15,921	7,569	33,489
3	125	86	10,750	7,396	15,625
4	130	81	10,530	6,561	16,900
5	170	77	13,090	5,929	28,900
6	203	94	19,082	8,836	41,209
7	212	84	17,808	7,056	44,944
8	177	90	15,930	8,100	31,329
9	174	70	12,180	4,900	30,276
10	105	91	9,555	8,281	11,025
11	110	70	7,700	4,900	12,100
12	162	95	15,390	9,025	26,244
13	150	84	12,600	7,056	22,500
14	161	69	11,109	4,761	25,921
15	155	81	12,555	6,561	24,025
16	205	80	16,400	6,400	42,025
17	221	85	18,785	7,225	48,841

(Continued)

ID#	YDSI	XSc	XY	X^2	Y^2
18	139	80	11,120	6,400	19,321
19	132	75	9,900	5,625	17,424
20	204	81	16,524	6,561	41,616
21	188	65	12,220	4,225	35,344
22	232	67	15,544	4,489	53,824
23	203	74	15,022	5,476	41,209
24	191	95	18,145	9,025	36,481
25	230	93	21,390	8,649	52,900
26	244	70	17,080	4,900	59,536
27	167	70	11,690	4,900	27,889
28	203	72	14,616	5,184	41,209
29	155	89	13,795	7,921	24,025
30	244	88	21,472	7,744	59,536
31	205	97	19,885	9,409	42,025
32	193	82	15,826	6,724	37,249
33	262	71	18,602	5,041	68,644
34	166	88	14,608	7,744	27,556
35	139	79	10,981	6,241	19,321
36	215	75	16,125	5,625	46,225
37	188	83	15,604	6,889	35,344
38	167	70	11,690	4,900	27,889
39	120	82	9,840	6,724	14,400
40	224	74	16,576	5,476	50,176
41	141	56	7,896	3,136	19,881
42	141	43	6,063	1,849	19,881
43	186	89	16,554	7,921	34,596
44	135	94	12,690	8,836	18,225
45	203	85	17,255	7,225	41,209
46	219	70	15,330	4,900	47,961
47	232	72	16,704	5,184	53,824
48	181	92	16,652	8,464	32,761
49	153	78	11,934	6,084	23,409
50	148	76	11,248	5,776	21,904
51	195	87	16,965	7569	38,025
52	199	67	13,333	4,489	39,601
53	189	72	13,608	5,184	35,721
54	161	52	8,372	2,704	25,921
55	159	73	11,607	5,329	25,281
56	190	89	16,910	7,921	36,100
57	183	73	13,359	5,329	33,489
58	112	59	6,608	3,481	12,544
59	200	68	13,600	4,624	40,000

ID#	YDSI	XSc	XY	X^2	Y^2
60	170	79	13,430	6,241	28,900
61	140	68	9,520	4,624	19,600
62	139	58	8,062	3,364	19,321
63	203	91	18,473	8,281	41,209
64	191	89	16,999	7,921	36,481
65	165	93	15,345	8,649	27,225
66	129	63	8,127	3,969	16,641
67	232	78	18,096	6,084	53,824
68	173	50	8,650	2,500	29,929
69	206	85	17,510	7,225	42,436
70	225	65	14,625	4,225	50,625
71	183	81	14,823	6,561	33,489
72	218	71	15,478	5,041	47,524
73	184	89	16,376	7,921	33,856
74	126	77	9,702	5,929	15,876
75	152	71	10,792	5,041	23,104
76	153	68	10,404	4,624	23,409
77	118	64	7,552	4,096	13,924
78	176	92	16,192	8,464	30,976
79	197	67	13,199	4,489	38,809
80	179	84	15,036	7,056	32,041
81	151	64	9,664	4,096	22,801
82	144	77	11,088	5,929	20,736
83	147	78	11,466	6,084	21,609
84	215	58	12,470	3,364	46,225
85	146	71	10,366	5,041	21,316
86	193	80	15,440	6,400	37,249
87	215	73	15,695	5,329	46,225
88	179	79	14,141	6,241	32,041
89	165	87	14,355	7,569	27,225
90	173	77	13,321	5,929	29,929
91	207	77	15,939	5,929	42,849
92	134	83	11,122	6,889	17,956
93	206	64	13,184	4,096	42,436
94	191	90	17,190	8,100	36,481
95	214	62	13,268	3,844	45,796
96	139	72	10,008	5,184	19,321
97	120	58	6,960	3,364	14,400
98	196	90	17,640	8,100	38,416
99	128	64	8,192	4,096	16,384
100	169	46	7,774	2,116	28,561

(Continued)

ID#	YDSI	XSc	XY	X^2	Y^2
101	182	62	11,284	3,844	33,124
102	203	83	16,849	6,889	41,209
103	159	88	13,992	7,744	25,281
104	128	90	11,520	8,100	16,384
105	183	82	15,006	6,724	33,489
106	182	85	15,470	7,225	33,124
107	127	97	12,319	9,409	16,129
108	177	57	10,089	3,249	31,329
109	163	57	9,291	3,249	26,569
110	164	86	14,104	7,396	26,896
111	123	91	11,193	8,281	15,129
112	165	62	10,230	3,844	27,225
113	208	58	12,064	3,364	43,264
114	236	77	18,172	5,929	55,696
115	160	76	12,160	5,776	25,600
116	202	80	16,160	6,400	40,804
117	153	79	12,087	6,241	23,409
118	202	72	14,544	5,184	40,804
119	193	64	12,352	4,096	37,249
120	108	43	4,644	1,849	11,664

$\Sigma Y = 20,997 \quad \Sigma X = 9,133 \quad \Sigma XY = 1,603,236 \quad \Sigma X^2 = 712,415 \quad \Sigma Y^2 = 3,817,811$

$$r_{XY} = \frac{\Sigma XY - (\Sigma X)(\Sigma Y)/N}{\text{Sqrt}[\Sigma X^2 - (\Sigma X)^2/N][\Sigma Y^2 - (\Sigma Y)^2/N]}$$

$$= \frac{1,603,236 - (9,133)(20,997)/120}{\text{Sqrt}[712,415 - (9,133)^2/120][3,817,811 - (20,997)^2/120]}$$

$$= \frac{1,603,236 - 1,598,047}{\text{Sqrt}[712,415 - 695,097][3,817,811 - 3,673,950]}$$

$$= \frac{5,189}{\text{Sqrt}[17,318][143,861]}$$

$$= \frac{5,189}{\text{Sqrt}\ 2,491,384,798}$$

$$= 5,189/49,914$$

$$r_{XY} = .104$$

TABLE 12.8   Matrix of Correlation Coefficients, Means, and Standard Deviations

	SPIScient	SPIPract	DSI
SPIScient	1		
SPIPract	−.199	1	
DSI	−.302	.104	1
Mean	58.92	76.11	174.98
SD	16.077	12.063	34.769

Next, a summary table of data is presented that is used for hand calculations of other formulas for the sequential MRA (see Table 12.8).

Partial Regression Coefficients

$$b_1 = \frac{r_{y1} - r_{y2}r_{12}(s_y/s_1)}{1 - r_{12}^2}$$

SPIScient and DSI

$$b_1 = \frac{-.302 - (.104)(-.199)}{1 - (-.199)^2} \frac{(34.769)}{(16.077)}$$

$$= \frac{-.302 - (-.021)}{1 - .040}(2.163)$$

$$= (-.281/.96)(2.163)$$

$$= -.293(2.163)$$

$$b_1 = -.634$$

SPIPract and DSI

$$b_2 = \frac{.104 - (-.302)(-.199)}{1 - (-.199)^2} \frac{(34.769)}{(12.063)}$$

$$= \frac{.104 - (.060)}{1 - .040}(2.882)$$

$$= (.044/.96)(2.882)$$

$$= .046(2.882)$$

$$b_2 = .1326$$

Squared Multiple Correlation for Model 2

$$R^2 = \frac{r_{y1}^2 + r_{y2}^2 - 2r_{y1}r_{y2}r_{12}}{1 - r_{12}^2}$$

$$= \frac{.091 + .011 - 2(-.302)(.104)(-.199)}{1 - (-.199)^2}$$

$$= \frac{.102 - .013}{1 - .040}$$

$$= .089/.96$$

$$R^2 = .093$$

Significance of R^2 Using Analysis of Variance for Model 2

$$F = \frac{(N - p - 1)R^2}{p(1 - R^2)}$$

where N = number of score

   p = number of predictor variables

$$F = \frac{(120 - 2 - 1).093}{2(1 - .093)}$$

$$= \frac{(117).093}{2(.907)}$$

$$= 10.88/1.81$$

$$F = 6.0$$

F-Test of Change in R^2

$$F_{change} = \frac{sr_i^2}{(1 - R^2)/df_{res}}$$

where sr^2 = squared semiparital correlation of the added variable in Model 2 to the variable in Model 1. The sr^2 is obtained by $(R^2_{\text{Model 1}} - R^2_{\text{Model 2}})$.

R^2 = squared multiple correlation of Model 2

df_{res} = residual degrees of freedom for Model 2

$$F_{\text{change}} = \frac{.002}{1 - .093/117}$$

$$= \frac{.002}{.907/117}$$

$$= .002/.00775$$

$$F_{\text{change}} = .258$$

Study Results

The purpose of this study was to assess whether doctoral students' lower interests in scientist activities more highly predict greater dissertation stress when compared to their interests in practitioner activities. A national sample of 120 doctoral students in counselor education, counseling psychology, and clinical psychology programs was studied.

The two predictor variables used in the study were identified from anecdotal experiences of faculty and a limited number of studies. Both interests in scientist and practitioner activities were measured using the Scientist Practitioner Inventory. The Dissertation Stress Inventory was used to measure the dependent variable and assesses perceived stress related to completing the doctoral dissertation

An a priori power analysis was conducted that showed that a total sample size of 101 was needed to reach a .80 power. The a priori power criterion was met using an $\alpha = .05$, a priori effect size of $R^2(\rho^2) = .09$, and a planned sample size of 120 participants.

No missing values and univariate or multivariate outliers were found in the data set. Moreover, multicollinearity was not present, and normality, linearity, and homoscedasticity of residuals were all within acceptable ranges.

A sequential multiple regression analysis was conducted. The bivariate correlations of the predictor variables to the dependable variable of dissertation stress were: (1) SPIScient and DSI ($r = -.302$, $p < .05$) and (2) SPIPract and DSI ($r = .104$, $p > .05$).

Model 1 of the sequential MRA included the SPI Scientist scale only, and it was a significant predictor variable of DSI, $R = .302$, $F(1, 118) = 11.880$, $p < .05$. Then, the SPI Practitioner variable was added to the SPI Scientist variable, resulting in a significant Model 2. However, the SPI Practitioner variable added little to the model and was not significantly contributing to the model, $\Delta R^2 = .002$, $F(1, 117) = .258$, $p > .05$.

The findings indicate that lower interests in scientist activities of doctoral students in counseling and clinical psychology programs significantly predicted higher perceived dissertation stress, $\beta = -.293$, $t(118) = -3.266$, $p < .05$. Moreover, the relationship of interests in practitioner activities did not significantly predict dissertation stress, $\beta = .046$, $t(118) = .508$, $p > .05$. The alternative hypothesis was supported; lower interest in scientific activities was a better predictor of higher dissertation stress reported by counseling and clinical psychology doctoral students when compared to their interests in practitioner activities.

SUMMARY

Correlation research methods were covered in this chapter to assess relationships and predictions among variables. The steps of the hypothesis-testing process were applied to a research problem using bivariate correlations and sequential multiple regression analysis. Data are provided in Table 12.9 to conduct the several analyses related to this bivariate and multivariate correlation research problem.

PROBLEM ASSIGNMENT

The steps involved in conducting a sequential MRA using IBM SPSS have been presented in this chapter. Now it is your turn to independently work through the steps of the hypothesis-testing process related to a sequential MRA using IBM SPSS. Go to the companion website and you will find a new sequential MRA research problem and data set along with a worksheet to complete. Use the problem presented in this chapter as a guide so you can complete the assignment. Your instructor will evaluate your completed worksheet when it is finished.

TABLE 12.9 Sequential MRA Data

ID#	DSI	SPIScient	SPIPract
1	107	58	72
2	183	35	87
3	125	62	86
4	130	43	81
5	170	29	77
6	203	51	94
7	212	44	84
8	177	34	90
9	174	38	70
10	105	57	91
11	110	46	70
12	162	69	95
13	150	70	84
14	161	70	69
15	155	64	81
16	205	55	80
17	221	32	85
18	139	66	80
19	132	92	75
20	204	80	81
21	188	32	65
22	232	69	67
23	203	76	74
24	191	60	95
25	230	50	93
26	244	63	70
27	167	74	70
28	203	58	72
29	155	57	89
30	244	47	80
31	205	52	97
32	193	53	82
33	262	32	71
34	166	38	88
35	139	70	79
36	215	65	75
37	188	49	83
38	167	41	70
39	120	84	82

(*Continued*)

TABLE 12.9   Sequential MRA Data (Continued)

ID#	DSI	SPIScient	SPIPract
40	224	52	74
41	141	72	56
42	141	86	43
43	186	63	89
44	135	39	94
45	203	45	85
46	219	58	70
47	232	72	72
48	181	72	92
49	153	65	78
50	148	66	76
51	195	89	87
52	199	47	67
53	189	76	72
54	161	72	52
55	159	78	73
56	190	71	89
57	183	67	73
58	112	100	59
59	200	61	68
60	170	44	79
61	140	63	68
62	139	50	58
63	203	60	91
64	191	50	89
65	165	55	93
66	129	34	63
67	232	36	78
68	173	68	50
69	206	61	85
70	225	63	65
71	183	73	81
72	218	46	71
73	184	42	89
74	126	53	77
75	152	90	71
76	153	42	68
77	118	46	64
78	176	39	92
79	197	61	67
80	179	69	84

ID#	DSI	SPIScient	SPIPract
81	151	74	64
82	144	81	77
83	147	73	78
84	215	36	58
85	146	45	71
86	193	37	80
87	215	51	73
88	179	65	79
89	165	68	87
90	173	77	77
91	207	45	77
92	134	50	83
93	206	39	64
94	191	46	90
95	214	66	62
96	139	67	72
97	120	86	58
98	196	53	90
99	128	54	64
100	169	86	46
101	182	51	62
102	203	66	83
103	159	52	88
104	128	96	90
105	183	68	82
106	182	59	85
107	127	78	97
108	177	66	57
109	163	65	57
110	164	55	86
111	123	45	91
112	165	87	62
113	208	38	58
114	236	53	77
115	160	32	76
116	202	48	80
117	153	70	79
118	202	42	72
119	193	52	64
120	108	87	43

KEY TERMS

adjusted R^2

bivariate correlation (r)

bivariate relationships

coefficient of alienation

coefficient of determination

constant

cumulative probability of the residuals

F change

homoscedasticity

linearity

Mahalanobis distance values

multicollinearity

multiple correlation (R)

multiple relationships

multivariate outliers

normal distribution of residuals

percentage of shared variance

percentage of unexplained variance

predictor variables (PVs)

redundancy of information

regression sum of squares

residuals

residual sum of squares

R-squared (R^2)

R-squared change

sequential MRA (hierarchical MRA)

sequential multiple linear regression

Sig. F change

singularity

standard error of the estimate (SEE)

standardized beta coefficient
(beta weight) (β)

standard MRA (simultaneous MRA)

statistical MRA (stepwise MRA)

strength of the correlation

tolerance

total sum of squares

t-statistic

unstandardized beta coefficient (B)

variance inflation factor (VIF)

Chapter 13

UNDERSTANDING

QUANTITATIVE LITERATURE

AND RESEARCH

LEARNING OBJECTIVES

○ Learn guidelines to interpret quantitative research articles in the professional literature.

○ Apply the interpretation guidelines to a quantitative research article.

t **is** essential for members of a professional discipline to understand the purpose of methods and the meaning of results from quantitative research. Learning and applying guidelines for interpreting quantitative research is the focus of this chapter. We will use the information learned in the previous chapters to analyze a published research article. We will be interpreting the methods and findings of the research article but not evaluating the research as to weaknesses and strengths of the study. Research consumers need first to understand fully what happened in a study before they are in a position to coherently evaluate a study. Initially, you are asked to read a guide to interpret research developed by Gay (1976). Then you will retrieve and read a specified article. Finally, you will apply knowledge that you have learned from previous chapters and the consumer guide.

INTERPRETATION OF A QUANTITATIVE RESEARCH ARTICLE

Retrieve and read the article that will be used for interpretation: Steele, K. M., Bass, K. E., & Crook, M. D. (1999). The mystery of the Mozart effect: Failure to replicate. Psychological Science, 10, 366–369.

Then, read through the following interpretation of the article. The discussion items used to organize the interpretation of the article were drawn for the most part from the *Research Interpretation for Consumers Guide* of Professor Dennis Gay.

1. Identify the **theme** of the study. What is the basic idea, subject, topic, or argument of the study? The theme usually can be identified from the title, abstract, and purpose statement of an article.

The title provides clear thematic information with the words "the mystery of the Mozart effect" and "failure to replicate." The abstract indicates that several laboratories have been unable to replicate the existence of a Mozart effect. The purpose statement says, "to confirm the existence of the Mozart effect" by following the recommendations of the initial researchers. The theme of the research article is to determine whether the Mozart effect has a real effect on spatial reasoning, and if it does not, whether there is another explanation for the Mozart effect.

2. What is the **significance** of this study? Why is the study important? Has previous research on this topic been done? If so, what more is being contributed by this study? Will the findings of this study impact theory, knowledge, or practice? This information is usually found in the introduction and discussion sections of an article.

The original researcher of the Mozart effect reported that the hypothesis that musical experience of short duration can have a direct causal influence on spatial reasoning on both a short-term and a long-term basis is important for both practical and theoretical reasons. The expansion of teaching interventions to improve cognitive development would be astounding if an aspect of measured intelligence can be increased by listening to Mozart's music. In fact, an industry associated with the Mozart effect has been developed and can be found readily on the web.

3. How does this study relate to **previous research**? How does this research emanate from and add to key conceptual and methodological issues in the field related to the topic? This information is found in the introduction and discussion sections. A brief summary of the previous research is presented next using information from the article.

- Rauscher, Shaw, and Ky (1993) found Mozart increased spatial reasoning by eight or nine IQ points as measured by portions of the Stanford-Binet Intelligence Scale, Fourth Edition, after listening to 10 minutes of a Mozart sonata. The effect was temporary and disappeared in 10 to 15 minutes.

- Rauscher, Shaw, and Ky (1995) reported findings related to replicating the effect.

- Fifteen other research laboratories could not confirm the findings of Rauscher et al.

- Rauscher et al. reviewed some of the negative results of the researchers from other laboratories and recommended key components necessary to produce a Mozart effect.
  - Use an appropriate DV (paper folding and cutting items [PF&C]).
  - Tend to the order of presentation of the listening and task conditions.
  - Increase the time between pretest and treatment so there are no carry-over effects.

RESEARCH INTERPRETATION FOR CONSUMERS

The following guide is intended as a practice device for the interpretation of published research in education and the behavioral sciences.

I. The Initial Exposure

The initial exposure to a research study should begin by reading the entire study with a rather casual, relaxed approach with little attention to given details. The objective at this point is to gain a general overview. As one progresses through the five guidelines that follow, more and more attention to detail will become necessary; however, one should not stop and spin wheels at any point where a particularly difficult problem presents itself. Instead, continue on through until more clarification is gained and then return to the difficult problem when a more comfortable solution is available.

1. Read the entire study through rather casually to gain a general overview.

2. Ascertain the central theme of the study, the basic rationale for the research, and the relationship of the study to other research.

3. Determine the existing theory, if any, to which the research is addressed, or speculate as to the basic theoretical framework.

4. Identify the subject(s) of the study and the research setting or environment if it is localized.

5. Determine the basic nature of the research (e.g., historical, descriptive, or experimental). Studies of an inferential nature can usually be detected at this point.

II. The Research Question(s)

Every research study should have a question or questions formulated prior to its initiation. It is the nature of the question or questions and the approach toward resolution that distinguish one form of research from another. Quite often a primary question will be subdivided into subquestions. This is a matter of style and can be helpful for both the researcher and the consumer. All too often, however, the research questions (RQs) either are not stated or are stated poorly. In the event that the research questions are not stated, it is necessary for the consumer to speculate by formulating a tentative guess. One may then return later and revise the question as more information is gained.

- Ascertain the question(s) asked.

- Determine whether the criteria for good research questions are met, and if not, restate the RQs as you believe the researcher intended them to be stated, applying the criteria. This is an important step toward a clearer interpretation of the remainder of the study. A good research question must be clear, unambiguous, and in question form. It must ask about the relationship between two or more variables and must imply the possibility of empirical testing.

III. Follow a Single Question All the Way Through

The research question is the primary reference point for interpretation and evaluation of any research study. It is for this reason that all of the guidelines that are presented here should be applied to each research question individually and completely, one RQ at a time. It is quite easy for the consumer of research to become lost in the middle of the study among all the jargon, charts, and statistics. When this happens, simply return to the specific research question and start over.

IV. The Hypotheses

Just as every research study should have at least one question, it should also have some systematic means of answering the question. This is usually, though not always, accomplished through the use of hypotheses. In that it is conceivable that more than one hypothesis is required to help answer a single research question, depending on the style of the author and how broadly the question is formulated, each hypothesis should be followed through individually and completely. All four of these guidelines should be followed by the consumer before starting on a second hypothesis.

1. For each research question identified in the study, ascertain the hypothesis (or hypotheses) intended by the researcher to help answer that research question. Formal hypotheses should be stated in two forms: the research or alternative hypothesis (H_a), which is what the researcher is actually guessing the true situation to be, and the null hypothesis (H_0), which provides a mathematical zero reference point for a formal statistical test.

2. For each research hypothesis (H_a), determine the corresponding null hypothesis (H_0) that is actually tested.

3. Determine whether the stated alternative and null hypotheses meet the criteria for good hypotheses, and if not, state or restate them applying the criteria. They should be stated as you feel the researcher meant to state them.

4. If only the null hypothesis is stated, which is unfortunately too often the case, speculate and state the research

hypothesis (H_a) in an acceptable manner. Usually when only the null hypothesis (H_O) is presented it is safe to assume that the alternative hypothesis (H_a) is a nondirectional hypothesis. This means that the researcher is not predicting a greater-than or less-than relationship, but instead is simply waiting to see what will happen. In this case a two-tailed test of statistical significance will be used in hypothesis testing.

V. The Variables

Because the very essence of research is centered on the relations between and among variables, a thorough knowledge of variables and their classifications is imperative for research interpretation. Very generally, variables are classified into three categories according to their relative purpose or existence in a study: independent variable (IV), dependent variable (DV), and extraneous variable (EV). Extraneous variables are contaminating, are unwanted, and need to be controlled in some way.

- Identify each variable important to the hypothesis and research question, and classify it as independent or dependent if appropriate within the context of the study. Some studies are more concerned with simply the association of a large number of variables, in which case this may not be appropriate. If independent, classify as either *active* or *attribute*.

- Identify all extraneous variables mentioned by the researcher for each hypothesis. These are variables that behave like independent variables and confound or contaminate the study. Determine any steps taken by the researcher to control for those extraneous variables mentioned.

VI. The Operational Definition (OD)

Every variable in a study must have an operational definition (OD). The OD is specific (though not necessarily unique) to the study. It is the precise way the variable is measured in the study, and its nature is the prerogative of the researcher.

- Identify the operational definition of each variable.

- The consumer should take time to learn about any operational definitions with which he or she is unfamiliar at this point (e.g., Q-sort technique, semantic differential, various published psychological instruments, etc.).

- Keep notes for later use.

- Determine the level of measurement (scaling) of each variable's operational definition, and distinguish between those considered continuous and those considered discrete.

VII. The Population under Study

At this point the consumer should take a closer look at exactly whom the study is concerned with.

- Determine the precise population under study. Quite often the researcher does not define the population clearly. If this is the case, one must speculate the best one can.

- Determine the actual subjects comprising the sample in the study, the number acquired, and the method of acquiring the subjects (sampling).

VIII. The Basic Research Design

The nature of the design of the research is dependent upon the research questions asked and the researcher's approach toward answering those questions. Because of the large number of possible designs, the consumer should have some background knowledge of general research designs to assist him or her in identification. The simpler experimental or quasi-experimental attempts are usually the easiest to detect because of their emphasis on matched or random assignment and control or comparison groups. Other designs may be more difficult for the consumer to discern. At any rate, the consumer should glean what information is possible regarding the basic design from the context of the study. It may also prove helpful to diagram the design if possible.

IX. The Collection of the Data

- Determine precisely how the data were collected for each variable.

- Familiarize yourself with any procedures mentioned that are unknown to you at this point (e.g., survey techniques, mechanical devices, psychometric instruments, etc.). This is obviously related to operational definitions in many instances.

- Keep notes on new information for later use.

X. The Analysis of the Data

Most research studies are fairly clear as to how the data were analyzed. However, adequate interpretation requires some knowledge of basic statistics and the common symbols encountered. In addition, one should be familiar with the basic hypothesis-testing process. The serious consumer of published research will keep a notebook handy with acquired information that can be added to and drawn from continuously. The consumer must eventually acquire an interpretive knowledge of the most commonly seen statistics (e.g., Z, t, F (the simpler models), chi-square, and r). These statistics, along with their use and the information they yield, may be found in any elementary statistics text. When more sophisticated techniques are encountered (e.g., multiple regression, factor analysis, discriminate analysis, or canonical correlation), use information resources related to multivariate statistics.

- Identify and define each statistical procedure employed and note the specific variables involved.

- Identify and define each symbolic expression encountered and determine the precise meaning with respect to the analysis presented.

- Take notes on information gained for future use.

XI. The Presentation of the Results

The presentation of the results is necessarily related to the analysis of the data and will usually be a combination of narrative and tables or graphs. It is important for the consumer to pay careful attention to exactly what the researcher has presented.

- Identify and define all terms and symbols presented in the results.

- Determine which null hypotheses, if any, were rejected and the level of significance for rejection.

- Stay with a table or graph until you know you understand what is presented.

XII. The Conclusions and Interpretations

The conclusions of the study should be based on the analysis of the hypotheses, if hypotheses were tested, and should be clearly related to the original research question(s). The consumer's focus of attention should be on whether the research questions were answered, and on the final conclusions of the study regarding the questions.

- Ascertain the specific conclusion for each finding presented.

- Determine the researcher's interpretation with respect to each conclusion individually and in concert with respect to the research question(s).

Source: From Dennis A. Gay, PhD, University of Northern Colorado. By permission of Professor Gay.

The researchers of this study used the Rauscher et al. recommendations to plan a replication study to "be a faithful replication of the central conditions of the Rauscher et al. experiment." However, there were differences in this replication study that included: (1) only one posttreatment assessment was used, (2) random assignment to condition group was used to create equivalent groups, (3) the time interval was lengthened by 24 hours to 48 hours between pretest and treatment condition.

4. What conceptual, methodological, and measurement **theories** undergird this study? This information can be found in the introduction but also throughout the article.

- The overarching theory relates to cognitive learning theory.

- The more immediate theories are:
  - Musical (complexly structured) experience of short duration (long duration) improves spatial abilities.

  - Music as a mood-induction technique affects performance on cognitive tasks.

5. Who are the **participants** and what is the **research setting**? Describe the characteristics of the sample participants.

- There were 125 introductory psychology students who comprised the study sample. There were 42 males and 83 females. The students received credit for participation.

Describe the research setting.

- The students participated in the study in a university psychology building in the early evening when the building was quiet. There were 15 persons in each session with a projector in the room.

6. What **research method(s)** are used in this study? Different general categories of research methods include survey, descriptive, causal-comparative, correlation, multivariate correlation, experimental, quasi-experimental, case study, single-case designs, qualitative, historical, evaluation, and action research.

The general method of research used in the study was experimental. The experimental design used a manipulated independent variable, random assignment to condition, and a control group.

7. Diagram the overall **research design** used in the study. There is an overall experimental design used in the study. However, it is modified for different questions. For example, there is no pretest on Profile of Mood States (POMS) scores.

The design is a randomized pretest-posttest multiple treatments control group design.

$$
\begin{array}{cccc}
R & O & X_{Mozart} & O \\
R & O & C_{silence} & O \\
R & O & X_{Glass} & O
\end{array}
$$

8. Identify the steps used to **collect data** for this study. Brief summaries of the 14 steps are presented next.

1. The researchers in this study used one posttest assessment, unlike the Rauscher study.

2. They used random assignment, not assignment by PF&C scores, to improve the design and to create equivalent groups.

3. They allowed 48 hours to elapse between sessions.

4. The study was conducted in the early evenings in a university psychology building where it was quiet.

5. The researchers used 15 students per group session to assure visibility of the projected PF&C items.

6. Acceptable deceit was used by telling participants during the first session that they were participating in a puzzle experiment.

7. The researchers used sample PF&C items to explain the task.

8. They answered student questions.

9. The 16 PF&C items were projected for 1 minute each.

10. The second session was 48 hours later, and the students were reminded of the task.

11. The participants were exposed to the stimulus condition and immediately tested on a new set of 16 PF&C items.

12. The PF&C items were counterbalanced to avoid an order effect or difficulty issues (systematic bias).

13. Exposure to music is an established mood-induction technique, so it was incorporated into the study. After the PF&C task, the participants were given a mood assessment instrument and were asked to identify their mood when the PF&C task began.

14. Performance on the PF&C task and mood were analyzed at a later time.

Identify the Research Questions in the Study

The research questions stated next were not stated in the article. They were created by reviewing the analyses and results reported. Two research questions were written to reflect the analyses and results of the study. The first research question has subquestions A, B, and C and focuses on several analyses that relate to spatial reasoning. The second question is stated with one subquestion (A).

Research Question for RQ1

RQ1: Will participants who receive the Mozart listening condition produce greater spatial reasoning performance (mean number of paper folding and cutting items answered correctly) when compared to participants who receive the listening conditions of silence or Glass?

Research Question for RQ1 Subquestion A

RQ1 subquestion A: Will there be differences in pretest spatial reasoning performance (mean number of paper folding and cutting items answered correctly) across the three listening conditions (Mozart, silence, and Glass)?

What Are the Hypotheses for RQ1 Subquestion A?

H_{aS-QA}: There will there be differences in pretest spatial reasoning performance (mean number of paper folding and cutting items answered correctly) across the three listening conditions (Mozart, silence, and Glass).

$$\text{Symbolic } H_{aS-QA}: \mu_{Mozart} \neq \mu_{silence} \neq \mu_{Glass}$$

H_{0S-QA}: There will there be no differences in pretest spatial reasoning performance (mean number of paper folding and cutting items answered correctly) across the three listening conditions (Mozart, silence, and Glass).

$$\text{Symbolic } H_0: \mu_{Mozart} = \mu_{silence} = \mu_{Glass}$$

Variables and Operational Definitions for RQ1 Subquestion A
Independent variable (IV): Listening condition.

Condition 1 (or OD_1): Mozart

Condition 2 (or OD_2): silence

Condition 3 (or OD_3): Glass

Active IV? Yes. Attribute IV? No. Fixed IV? Yes. Random IV? No.
Scale of measurement? Discrete-nominal.
Dependent variable (DV): Pretest spatial reasoning performance.
Operational definition (OD): Mean number of paper folding and cutting items answered correctly.
Scale of measurement? Continuous-ratio.

What Was the Analysis of the Data and Presentation of the Results for RQ1 Subquestion A?

1. Identify statistical procedure employed: One-way analysis of variance.

2. Findings and values for testing the $H_0(s)$: The following finding is reported in the left column at the top of page 368 of the article, $F(2, 122) = .05, p = .95$. This finding assesses the pretest means for significant differences. The pretest means are listed in Table 1 of the article.

Conclusion and the Interpretation for RQ1 Subquestion A   There are no significant differences in pretest spatial reasoning across the listening condition groups of participants. The groups were equivalent at the beginning of the study on spatial reasoning, confirming that the random assignment to condition worked.

What Is the Research Question for RQ1 Subquestion B?   This question reflects a factorial ANOVA statistical design, more specifically a 2×3 ANOVA. There are three analyses embedded within it. First, the differences between all groups' scores from pretest to posttest are assessed, which is also referred to as the main effect of session (pretest-posttest). Second, the differences on spatial reasoning among the three conditions groups at the posttest on spatial reasoning are assessed, called the main effect of listening condition. Third, the interaction effect between session (pretest-posttest) and listening condition (Mozart, silence, Glass) on spatial reasoning is assessed.

RQ1 subquestion B(1): Will there be session (pretest-posttest) main effect differences, treatment (listening condition) main effect differences, and an interaction effect difference (session × treatment) on the spatial reasoning performance of participants?

What are the hypotheses for RQ1 subquestion B(1)?

$H_{aB(1)}$: There will be main effect differences on the spatial reasoning performance of participants across the sessions (pretest-posttest).

$$\text{Symbolic } H_{aB(1)}: \mu_{\text{pretest}} \neq \mu_{\text{posttest}}$$

$H_{0B(1)}$: There will be no main effect differences on the spatial reasoning performance of participants across the sessions (pretest-posttest).

$$\text{Symbolic } H_{0B(1)}: \mu_{\text{pretest}} = \mu_{\text{posttest}}$$

$IV_{B(1)}$: Session.

Condition 1 (or OD_1): Pretest

Condition 2 (or OD_2): Posttest

$DV_{B(1)}$: Pretest spatial reasoning performance.
OD: Mean number of paper folding and cutting items answered correctly.

$H_{aB(2)}$: There will be main effect differences on post spatial reasoning performance of participants across the treatment listening conditions (Mozart, silence, Glass).

$$\text{Symbolic } H_{aB(2)}: \mu_{Mozart} \neq \mu_{silence} \neq \mu_{Glass}$$

$H_{0B(2)}$: There will be no main effect differences on the post spatial reasoning performance of participants across the treatment (listening conditions).

$$\text{Symbolic } H_{0B(2)}: \mu_{Mozart} = \mu_{silence} = \mu_{Glass}$$

$IV_{B(2)}$: Listening condition.

Condition 1 (or OD_1): Mozart

Condition 2 (or OD_2): silence

Condition 3 (or OD_3): Glass

$DV_{B(2)}$: Posttest spatial reasoning performance.
OD: Mean number of paper folding and cutting items answered correctly.

$H_{aB(3)}$: There will be an interaction effect (session × treatment) difference on the post spatial reasoning performance of participants.

$$\text{Symbolic } H_{aB(3)}: \mu_{session} \times \mu_{ListeningCondition} \neq 0$$

$H_{0B(3)}$: There will be no interaction effect (session × treatment) difference on the spatial reasoning performance of participants.

$$\text{Symbolic } H_{0B(3)}: \mu_{session} \times \mu_{ListeningCondition} = 0$$

$IV_{1B(3)}$: Session.

Condition 1 (or OD_1): Pretest

Condition 2 (or OD_2): Posttest

$IV_{2B(3)}$: Listening condition.

Condition 1 (or OD_1): Mozart

Condition 2 (or OD_2): silence

Condition 3 (or OD_3): Glass

$DV_{B(3)}$: Posttest spatial reasoning performance.
OD: Mean number of paper folding and cutting items answered correctly.

Analysis of the Data and Presentation of the Results for RQ1 Subquestion B   Identify statistical procedure employed: 2×3 ANOVA.
Identify the findings and values for testing the $H_0(s)$:

Main effect of session: $F(1, 122) = 76.1$, $p < .001$.

Main effect of listening condition: $F(2, 122) = 0.11$, $p = .89$.

Interaction effects of session and listening conditions: $F(2, 122) = 0.48, p = .62$

Conclusions and Interpretations for RQ1 Subquestion B   The main effect of the session (pretest-posttest) was a significant indication that overall the participants in the three groups showed a gain in spatial reasoning from the pretest to the posttest. The main effect of the listening condition was not significant, reflecting that the spatial reasoning means were not significantly different across the three listening condition groups at the end of the study. This is the finding that is the most important as to whether there was a Mozart effect in this study, and there was not. The interaction effect of the session and listening condition was not significant, indicating that there was no differential effect at different levels of the independent variables.

What Is the Research Question for RQ1 Subquestion C?   RQ1 subquestion C: Will participants who receive the Mozart listening condition produce greater spatial reasoning performance (mean number of paper folding and cutting items answered correctly) when compared to participants who receive the listening conditions of silence or Glass when adjusted for an individual's initial performance on the PF&C task (pretest)?

What Are the Hypotheses for RQ1 Subquestion C?

$H_{aSQ\text{-}C}$: Participants who receive the Mozart listening condition will produce greater spatial reasoning performance (mean number of paper folding and cutting items answered correctly) when compared to participants who receive the listening conditions of silence or Glass when adjusted for an individual's initial performance on the PF&C task (pretest).

$$\text{Symbolic } H_{aSQ-C}: \mu_{adj.Mozart} > \mu_{adj.silence} > \mu_{adj.Glass}$$

$H_{0SQ\text{-}C}$: There will there be no differences in spatial reasoning performance (mean number of paper folding and cutting items answered correctly) across the three listening conditions (Mozart, silence, and Glass) when adjusted for an individual's initial performance on the PF&C task (pretest).

$$\text{Symbolic } H_{0SQ-C}: \mu_{adj.Mozart} = \mu_{adj.silence} = \mu_{adj.Glass}$$

Variables and Operational Definitions for RQ1 Subquestion C

$IV_{SQ\text{-}C}$: Listening condition.

Condition 1 (or OD_1): Mozart

Condition 2 (or OD_2): silence

Condition 3 (or OD_3): Glass

$DV_{SQ\text{-}C}$: Posttest spatial reasoning performance when adjusted for an individual's initial performance on the PF&C task (pretest).

OD: Mean number of paper folding and cutting items answered correctly.

Identify the analysis of the data and presentation of the results for RQ1 subquestion C.

Identify statistical procedure employed: One-way analysis of covariance where the pretest scores on spatial reasoning were used as the covariate.

What are the findings and values for testing the H_0(s)? $F(2, 121) = 0.61, p = .55$.

Conclusion and Interpretation for RQ1 Subquestion C   Again, there was no significant difference in spatial reasoning ability across the three listening conditions (Mozart, silence, Glass) when the pretest scores on spatial reasoning were used as the covariate. This outcome is another confirmation that there was no Mozart effect in this study.

Research Question for RQ2

RQ2: Will participants who receive the Mozart listening condition produce different mood factor scores (depression, tension, anger, vigor, fatigue, and confusion) when compared to participants who receive the listening conditions of silence or Glass?

Hypotheses for RQ2

H_{a1-6}: There will there be differences in mood factor scores (depression, tension, anger, vigor, fatigue, and confusion) across the three listening conditions (Mozart, silence, and Glass).

(There were actually six hypotheses analyzed reflecting the comparisons for differences across the listening conditions on each of the six mood factor scores. For the sake of brevity, we will write only one hypothesis, knowing, though, that six were tested.)

Symbolic H_{a1-6}: $\mu_{1(Moz)} \neq \mu_{2(silence)} \neq \mu_{3(Glass)}$

(This alternative hypothesis is used for each of the six mood factor scores that are each a different dependent variable.)

H_{01-6}: There will be no differences in mood factor scores (depression, tension, anger, vigor, fatigue, and confusion) across the three listening conditions (Mozart, silence, and Glass).

Symbolic H_{01-6}: $\mu_{1(Moz)} = \mu_{2(silence)} = \mu_{3(Glass)}$

(This null is used for each of the six mood factors.)

Variables and Operational Definitions for RQ2
IV: Listening condition.

Condition 1 (or OD_1): Mozart

Condition 2 (or OD_2): silence

Condition 3 (or OD_3): Glass

Active IV? Yes. Attribute IV? No. Fixed IV? Yes. Random IV? No.
Scale of measurement: Discrete-nominal.

DVs: The six mood factors (depression, tension, anger, vigor, fatigue, and confusion). Each mood factor is analyzed as a separate dependent variable.

OD: There were three questions drawn from each of the six mood factors of the 65 questions of the Profile of Mood States (POMS), which is a psychometric test.

Scale of measurement of the DV: Continuous-interval.

Analysis of Data and Presentation of the Results for RQ2   Identify statistical procedure employed: The researchers most likely used a series of six one-way ANOVAs.

Findings and values for testing the H_0(s): Only two of the six mood factors were significantly different across the three conditions; they were:

1. Tension $F(2, 122) = 6.32$, $p = .002$

2. Anger $F(2, 122) = 7.21$, $p = .001$

Conclusions and Interpretations for RQ2   There were significant differences in the mood factors of tension and anger across the listening conditions. A post hoc Tukey HSD was conducted to determine which paired means were different from each other. The researchers found that the Mozart condition produced the lowest tension and anger scores compared to the silence and Glass conditions. The Mozart condition produced significantly lower tension ($p = .001$) and lower anger ($p = .001$) when compared to the Glass condition.

Conclusions and Interpretations for RQ 2 Subquestion A   Unlike the spatial reason findings, there was a Mozart effect on the moods of tension and anger. Mozart produced significantly lower tension and anger mood scores when compared to music by Glass.

TABLE 13.1 Comparisons of Effect Sizes of the Mozart Effect

Study	Effect Size d	Size of Effect
Rauscher et al. (1995)	$d = .72$	High medium
This study	$d = .06$	Very small
Average of 15 other studies	$\overline{d} = .16$	Small

Discuss the comparisons of effect sizes of previous studies and this study relative to the Mozart effect. In the discussion section of the article, the authors present and discuss the effect sizes from the original study by Rauscher et al. (1995), this study, and 15 other Mozart-versus-silence studies (see Table 13.1). Cohen's effect size convention for d is small (.20), medium (.50), and large (.80).

Identify the major conclusions from the study.

- No significant Mozart effect on spatial reasoning ability was found using replication procedures recommended by Rauscher. The procedures were not exactly like the ones that Rauscher et al. (1995) used. Essential experimental procedures were added by the researchers, including random assignment of participants to condition, and the PF&C items were used in a counter-balanced order across sessions and groups.

  Steele, Bass, and Crook (1999) stated, "We conclude that there is little evidence to support basing intellectual enhancement programs on the existence of the causal relationship termed the Mozart effect" (p. 368).

- There was an effect on mood (tension and anger). Tension and anger scores were significantly lower for the participants receiving the Mozart condition compared to the Glass condition. The participants were less happy listening to the Glass selection reflecting amelodic and repetitive music compared to the Mozart selection. Other studies have found that mood can affect performance in other cognitive tasks indirectly through differences in mood.

Identify recommendations for future studies.

- There need to be improved specifications of the class of music selections that are likely to produce effects. Rauscher et al. used the term "complexly structured music" to depict Mozart music. It would be valuable to conduct additional studies focusing on other stimulus variables to see if they have an effect on spatial reasoning.

- Another issue relates to the dependent variable of spatial reasoning as measured by the PF&C items. The early research by Rauscher reported that some studies did not find a Mozart effect because they used spatial pattern-recognition tasks (Raven Progressive Matrices) rather than spatial-temporal tasks (PF&C). However, two studies used both types of tasks and found no difference. So, more research is needed using and comparing different cognitive ability tasks.

SUMMARY

The information learned in previous chapters has been applied to the analysis of a published quantitative research article. A structured format using the *Research Interpretation for Consumers* (Gay, 1976) was used to interpret the article.

PROBLEM ASSIGNMENT

The process of analyzing a quantitative research article was presented in this chapter. Now it is your turn to independently analyze a quantitative article. Retrieve the following article for review, study, and analysis.

Pace, T. M., & Dixon, D. N. (1993). Changes in depressive self-schemata and depressive symptoms following cognitive therapy. *Journal of Counseling Psychology, 40, 288–294.*

Go to the companion website and you will find an Article Analysis Worksheet to use for analyzing this new article. Use the information in this chapter to guide you as you complete the assignment. Your instructor will evaluate your completed worksheet when it is finished.

REFERENCES

American Psychological Association. (2006). Evidence-based practice in psychology: APA task force on evidence-based practice. *American Psychologist, 61*, 271–285.

Brown, K. W., & Ryan, R. M. (2003). The benefits of being present: Mindfulness and its role in psychological well-being. *Journal of Personality and Social Psychology, 84*, 822–848.

Campbell, D. T. (1957). Factors relevant to the validity of experiments in social settings. *Psychological Bulletin, 54*, 297–312.

Campbell, D. T., & Stanley, J. C. (1963). *Experimental and quasi-experimental designs for research*. Chicago, IL: Rand McNally.

Cohen, J. (1988). *Statistical power analysis for the behavioral sciences* (2nd ed.). Hillsdale, NJ: Erlbaum.

Cohen, J. (1994). The earth is round ($p < .05$). *American Psychologist, 49*, 997–1003.

Cone, J. D., & Foster, S. L. (2006). *Dissertations and theses from start to finish* (2nd ed.). Washington, DC: American Psychological Association.

Cook, T. D., & Campbell, D. T. (1979). *Quasi-experimentation: Design and analysis issues for field settings*. Chicago, IL: Rand McNally.

Cook, T. D., & Steiner, P. M. (2010). Case matching and the reduction of selection bias in quasi-experiments: The relative importance of pretest measures of outcome, of unreliable measurement, and of mode of data analysis. *Psychological Methods, 15*, 56–68.

Denecke, D. (2006). *The Ph.D. completion project*. Washington, DC: Council of Graduate Schools.

Dennis, M. L., Scott, C. K., Funk, R., & Foss, M. A. (2005). The duration and correlates of addiction and treatment careers. *Journal of Substance Abuse Treatment, 28*, S51–S62.

Erdfelder, E., Faul, F., & Buchner, A. (2010, January 2). GPOWER. Retrieved from www .psycho.uni-duesseldorph.de/aap/projects/gpower/.

Faul, F., Erdfelder, E., Lang, A. G., & Buchner, A. (2007). A flexible power analysis program for the social, behavioral, and biomedical sciences. *Behavior Research Methods, 39*, 175–191.

Fisher, R. A. (1925). *Statistical methods for research workers*. Edinburgh, Scotland: Oliver & Boyd Publishers.

Fisher, R. A. (1973). *Statistical methods for research workers* (14th ed.). New York, NY: Hafner Publishing Company.

Gay, D. (1976). *Research interpretation for consumers.* Greeley, CO: Department of Human Rehabilitation, University of Northern Colorado.

Gorin, A., Phelan, S., Tate, D., Sherwood, N., Jeffery, R., & Wing, R. (2005). Involving support partners in obesity treatment. *Journal of Consulting and Clinical Psychology, 73,* 341–343.

Grimm, L. G. (1993). *Statistical applications for the behavioral sciences.* New York, NY: John Wiley & Sons.

Hair, J. F., Jr., Black, W. C., Babin, B. J., Anderson, R. E., & Tatham, R. L. (2006). *Multivariate data analysis* (6th ed.). Upper Saddle River, NJ: Pearson Prentice Hall.

Hays, W. L. (1963). *Statistics.* New York, NY: Holt, Rinehart, & Winston.

Horowitz, J. L., & Garber, J. (2006). The prevention of depressive symptoms in children and adolescents: A meta-analytic review. *Journal of Consulting and Clinical Psychology, 74,* 401–415.

Horowitz, J. L., Garber, J., Ciesla, J. A., Young, J. F., & Mufson, L. (2007). Prevention of depressive symptoms in adolescents: A randomized trial of cognitive-behavioral and interpersonal prevention programs. *Journal of Consulting and Clinical Psychology, 75,* 693–706.

Howell, D. C. (2007). *Statistical methods for psychology* (6th ed.). Belmont, CA: Thomson Wadsworth.

Howell, D. C. (2010). *Statistical methods for psychology* (7th ed.). Belmont, CA: Wadsworth, Cengage Learning.

Jones, L. V., & Tukey, J. W. (2000). A sensible formulation of the significance test. *Psychological Methods, 5*(4), 411–414.

Kerlinger, F. N., & Lee, H. B. (2000). *Foundations of behavioral research* (4th ed.). Ft. Worth, TX/Orlando, FL: Harcourt.

Kerlinger, F. N., & Pedhazur, E. J. (1973). Multiple regression in behavioral research. New York, NY: Holt, Rinehart & Winston.

Kirk, R. E. (1995). *Experimental design: Procedures for the behavioral sciences* (3rd ed.). Pacific Grove, CA: Brooks/Cole Publishing Company.

Kluever, R. C. (1997). Students' attitudes toward the responsibilities and barriers in doctoral study. *New Directions for Higher Education, 99,* 5–16.

Leong, F. T. L. (1991). Development and validation of the Scientist-Practitioner Inventory for psychology. *Journal of Counseling Psychology, 38,* 331–341.

Little, R. J. A., & Rubin, D. B. (2002). *Statistical analysis with missing data* (2nd ed.). Hoboken, NJ: John Wiley & Sons.

Lowry, R. (2011). Concepts and applications of inferential statistics. Retrieved from http://faculty.vassar.edu/lowry/webtext.html.

Martin, W. E., Jr., & Bridgmon, K. D. (2009). Essential elements of experimental and quasi-experimental research. In S. D. Lapan & M. T. Quartaroli (Eds.), *Research essentials: An introduction to designs and practices* (pp. 35–58). San Francisco, CA: Jossey-Bass.

National Multiple Sclerosis Society. (2012). *What is multiple sclerosis?* Retrieved from www.nationalmssociety.org/about-multiple-sclerosis/what-we-know-about-ms/what-is-ms/index.aspx.

Neff, K. D. (2003). The development and validation of a scale to measure self-compassion. *Self and Identity, 2,* 223–250.

Nickerson, R. S. (2000). Null hypothesis significance testing: A review of an old and continuing controversy. *Psychological Methods, 5,* 241–301.

Norusis, M. J. (1994). *SPSS 6.1 base system user's guide, part 2.* Chicago, IL: SPSS.

Norusis, M. J. (1999). *SPSS 9.0: Guide to data analysis.* Upper Saddle River, NJ: Prentice Hall.

Norusis, M. J. (2003). *SPSS 12.0: Statistical procedures companion.* Upper Saddle River, NJ: Prentice Hall.

Norusis, M. J. (2004). *SPSS 13.0 advanced statistical procedures companion.* Upper Saddle River, NJ: Prentice Hall.

Pace, T. M., & Dixon, D. N. (1993). Changes in depressive self-schemata and depressive symptoms following cognitive therapy. *Journal of Counseling Psychology, 40,* 288–294.

Pagano, R. R. (1998). *Understanding statistics in the behavioral sciences* (5th ed.). Pacific Grove, CA: Brooks/Cole Publishing Company.

Rash, C. J., Alessi, S. M., & Petry, N. M. (2008). Contingency management is efficacious for cocaine abusers with prior treatment attempts. *Experimental and Clinical Psychopharmacology, 16*(6), 547–554.

Rauscher, F. H., Shaw, D. I., & Ky, K. N. (1993). Music and spatial task performance. *Nature, 365,* 611.

Rauscher, F. H., Shaw, D. I., & Ky, K. N. (1995). Listening to Mozart enhances spatial-temporal reasoning: Towards a neurophysiological basis. *Neuroscience Letters, 185,* 44–47.

Rosenbaum, P. R., & Rubin, D. B. (1983). The central role of the propensity score in observational studies for causal effects. *Biometrika, 70,* 41–55.

Rossello, J., Bernal, G., & Rivera-Medina, C. (2008). Individual and group CBT and IPT for Puerto Rican adolescents with depressive symptoms. *Cultural Diversity and Ethnic Minority Psychology, 14,* 234–245.

Salsburg, D. (2001). *The lady tasting tea: How statistics revolutionized science in the twentieth century.* New York, NY: W. H. Freeman & Company/Henry Holt & Company.

Seashore, H. D. (1955). Methods of expressing test scores. *Test Service Notebook,* 148. San Antonio, TX: The Psychological Corporation, NCS Pearson.

Shadish, W. R., & Cook, T. D. (2009). The renaissance of field experimentation in evaluating interventions. *Annual Review of Psychology, 60,* 607–629.

Shadish, W. R., Cook, T. D., & Campbell, D. T. (2002). *Experimental and quasi-experimental designs for generalized causal inference*. Boston, MA: Houghton Mifflin Company.

Siegel, S. (1956). *Nonparametric statistics for the behavioral sciences*. New York, NY: McGraw-Hill Book Company.

Snedecor, G. W. (1934). *Analysis of variance and covariance*. Ames, IA: Collegiate Press.

Snedecor, G. W., & Cochran, W. G. (1967). *Statistical methods* (6th ed.). Ames: Iowa State University Press.

Steele, K. M., Bass, K. E., & Crook, M. D. (1999). The mystery of the Mozart effect: Failure to replicate. *Psychological Science, 10*, 366–369.

Stevens, J. (1996). *Applied multivariate statistics for the social sciences*. Mahwah, NJ: Erlbaum.

Student [William Gossett]. (1908). The probable error of the mean. *Biometrika, VI*(1), 1–25.

Tabachnick, B. G., & Fidell, L. S. (2007). *Using multivariate statistics* (5th ed.). Boston, MA: Pearson Allyn & Bacon.

Tabak, J. (2005). *Probability and statistics: The science of uncertainty*. New York, NY: Checkmark Books.

Vacha-Haase, T., & Thompson, B. (2004). How to estimate and interpret various effect sizes. *Journal of Counseling Psychology, 4*, 473–481.

Warke, K., Al-Smadi, J., Baxter, D., Walsh, D. M., & Lowe-Strong, A. A. (2006). Efficacy of transcutaneous electric nerve stimulation (TENS) for chronic low-back pain in a multiple sclerosis population. *Clinical Journal of Pain, 22*, 812–819.

Wegner, D. M., & Zanakos, S. (1994). Chronic thought suppression. *Journal of Personality, 62*, 615–640.

Weisz, J. R., Southam-Gerow, M. A., Gordis, E. B., Connor-Smith, J. K., Chu, B. C., Langer, D. A., . . . Weiss, B. (2009). Cognitive-behavioral therapy versus usual clinical care for youth depression: An initial test of transportability to community clinics and clinicians. *Journal of Consulting and Clinical Psychology, 77*, 383–396.

INDEX

233; treatment status, 233; 2 × 2 factorial design, 234, 237; two-way analysis of variance data, 291–294; two-way ANOVA computer analysis results, 265–271; two-way ANOVA formula calculations, 278–284; two-way ANOVA SPSS commands, 264–265; underlying assumptions, assessing for, 250–255; underlying assumptions findings, summary of, 263–264; univariate outliers IBM SPSS commands, assessing for, 249–250; variances, 249–250; within-subjects ANOVA design, 235

Coefficient of determination, 412

Coefficient of variation (C), 10

Cognitive-behavioral therapy (CBT), 131–132

Cohen's d statistic, 45

Cohen's strength: of η^2 effect sizes, 46; of r effect sizes, 47

Composite mean variable of two variables, creating, 95–96

Composite summed variable of two variables, creating, 93–94

Compound symmetry, 196

Confidence intervals, 37

Confidence intervals of mean differences, 160, 165–166; cocaine abusers in treatment study, 273–278

Constant, 421

Continuous-interval scale, 5

Continuous-ratio scale, 5

Continuous scale, 299

Controlling extraneous variance (MaxMinCon), 54

Corrected effect sizes, 45, 47

Correction: alpha, 371; Bonferroni alpha, 386; Lilliefors, Kolmogorov-Smirnov test with, 114–115

Correlation coefficient, defined, 412

Correlation designs, 61

Correlational research methods, 66

Correlational research models, 54

counconfid variable, 85, 97

Covariances, 196, 208–209

Covariates, 298, 299, 343

Criterion variable (CV), 5, 31, 66

Critical value, 20

Cubic trend, 214

Cumulative probability of residuals, 415

D

Data analysis commands, 78

Data diagnostics, 100, 177; adolescent depression treatment program study, 145–148; doctoral student dissertation study, 409; erroneous data entries, detecting, 100–103; histograms, 110; kurtosis, 109–110; missing data, identifying/dealing with, 103–106; multiple sclerosis (MS) study, 355–368; multivariate outliers, 107–108; procedures, 35; purposes of, 145; research example, 100–127; skewness, 109–110; univariate assumptions, screening and making decisions about, 108–109; univariate outliers, 106; weight gain among women with bulimia study, 35; weight loss treatment with support partners study, 196–205

Data preparation, 100, *See* Data diagnostics

Data screening, 34–35, 37, 100, *See* Data diagnostics

Data transformation, 108, 120, 122, 125

Data View screen, IBM SPSS 20 program, 79–80, 86–87

Data View tab, IBM SPSS 20 program, 86

dealdiff variable, 85, 89

Deception, 59

Degrees of freedom (df), 9, 162, 169

Dependent (outcome) variables, 54

Dependent *t*-test, 23

Dependent variables (DVs), 4, 30–31, 445; adolescent depression treatment program study, 131; cocaine abusers in treatment study, 233; drug treatment program study, 299; weight loss treatment with support partners study, 186

Depression treatment program study, *See* Adolescent depression treatment program study

Descending, 97

Descriptive statistical applications of normal distribution, 17–18

Descriptive statistics, 89–90

Directional alternative hypothesis, 31–32

Evidence-based practice in psychology (EBPP), 3
Exact significance, 372
Exclusion criteria, 17–18, 144
Expectation maximization (EM), 105
Experimental conditions, formulating, 54–55
Experimental designs, 56; experimental research procedures, 64; internal validity, 59–61; randomized multiple treatments and control with posttest-only design, 62; randomized multiple treatments and control with pretest and posttest design, 63; rules/symbols used to describe, 61
Experimental research: procedures, 64; purpose of, 54
Exploratory data analysis (EDA), 37, 100, 306, 307–327, *See also* Data diagnostics; drug treatment program study, 306, 307–327
Explore Analysis, 88
Extraneous experimental influences, controlling, 57–59
Extraneous variables (EVs), 4, 298, 445; blinded procedures, 58–59; building into the design, 58–59; matching participants, 58
Extraneous variance, controlling, 54

F

F change value, 420
Factor: defined, 69; use of term, 235
Factorial ANOVA, 231–295
Factorial design, 233
Factors, *See* Independent variable (IV)
Family of conclusions, 371
Fisher, R., 134
Fisher's protected least significant differences (PLSD), 222–226
Foundational research concepts: active independent variable, 4; attribute independent variable, 4; categorical variable, 5; classification variable, 5; dependent variable (DV), 4; extraneous variable (EV), 4; independent variable (IV), 4
Foundational statistical information, 6–14; coefficient of variation (C), 10; measures of central tendency, 6–8; measures of variability (dispersion) of scores, 8; standard deviation of the sample (s), 9; variance of the sample (s^2),

8–9; visual representations of a dataset, 10–14
Free statistics calculators, 18
Frequency analysis, 87–88
Frequency distribution, 10
Frequency table, 88
Friedman repeated measures analysis of variance, 71
Friedman RM-ANOVA, 72
Friedman's rank test, 382–387; formula calculations, 395–396

G

gender variable, 84
Glass's Δ (delta) statistic, 46
G*Power, 47–48, 50
G*Power 3.1, 48, 303
Grand mean (M_{TOT}), 167–168
Greenhouse-Geisser, 209, 211

H

Histograms, 12–13, 110–112, 121
Homogeneity of regression (slope) assumption, 317–318
Homogeneity of variance, 134, 154–156; adolescent depression treatment program study, 154–156; cocaine abusers in treatment study, 260; drug treatment program study, 312–316; evidence, 156; multiple sclerosis (MS) study, 367–368; screening for, 115–116
Homogeneous sampling, 408
Homoscedasticity, of residuals, 415
Honestly significant difference (HSD) statistic, 130, 163; post hoc analysis, 164
Huynh-Feldt, 209, 211
Hypothesis significance testing (NHST), 36–37
Hypothesis-testing process, 29–38; defined, 29; steps in, 28–37

I

IBM SPSS 20 program, 3, 77–98; *age* variable, 84; Align column, 82; AMOS (Analysis of Moment Structures), 104; basic analyses, examples of, 87–96; Columns column, 82; *counconfid* variable, 85, 97; data, entering, 86–87; Data View screen, 79–80, 80,

variances, 356; Wilcoxon's matched-pairs signed-ranks test, 382–389, 396–397
Multivariate ANOVA, 134
Multivariate correlation methods, using multiple regression analysis, 401–438
Multivariate outliers, 107–108, 410–412

N

National Multiple Sclerosis Society, 346
Negative side, 17
Negatively skewed, 110
Nil null hypothesis, 32
No-treatment control condition, 133
No-treatment waiting-list control, 132
Nominal scale, 82
Nominal-scaled variables, 83
Nondirectional, 19; alternative hypothesis as, 22
Nonequivalent no-treatment control group time-series design, 66
Nonparametric statistics, 348; as alternatives to parametric counterparts, 346
Normal distribution, 14–26, 15–17; abscissa, 17; characteristics of, 15–17; defined, 14–15; descriptive statistical application so, 17–18; inferential statistical application so, 18–26; negative side, 17; peak, 15; positive side, 17; of residuals, 415; shoulders, 15; in standardized scores, 16; tails, 15
Normal probability plot (Q-Q plot), 114–115, 117; after log10 transformation, 125; assessing normality of control condition scores, 117; assessing normality of treatment condition scores, 116; cocaine abusers in treatment study, 256, 258–259
Normality, 108–109, 114, 134, 151–154, 176–177; assessing normal Q-Q plots for, 114–115
Normality IBM SPSS commands, 148–149
Null hypothesis (H_0), 19, 32; cocaine abusers in treatment study, 240–241; doctoral student dissertation study, 406; drug treatment program study, 302; establishing (H0), 137; inferential statistical application so, 19; multiple sclerosis (MS) study, 350; statistical testing process, 40; weight loss treatment with support partners, 191

Null hypothesis significance testing (NHST) process, 36–37
Nullification, 32

O

Observed score, 56
Omega-squared (ω^2), 47, 173–174; cocaine abusers in treatment study, 285–287
Omnibus research question (RQ): cocaine abusers in treatment study, 237–238; doctoral student dissertation study, 405; drug treatment program study, 301; multiple sclerosis (MS) study, 349; stating, 135–136; weight loss treatment with support partners study, 186–189
One-sample t-test (student's t-test), 21–23
One-way, defined, 69
One-way analysis of variance (ANOVA), 67–69, 130, 133–135; IBM SPSS commands, 159–160; Kruskal-Wallis, 70–71; results, 160–162
One-way analysis of variance (ANOVA) results: for log10 transformed data, 126; nontransformed, 119; and transformed screening, 119–128
Operational definition (OD), 5, 54, 131–132
Ordinal scale, 82
Ordinate, 10, 17
Orthogonal cells, 234
Outliers, 145, 153, 176

P

Paired-sample t-test, 23
Parameters, 19; parameter statistics, 35
Partial-blind procedure, 59
Partial eta-squared ($\eta2$): cocaine abusers in treatment study, 284–285; use of term, 162
Peak, 15
Pearson's product-moment bivariate correlation coefficient, 46
Pearson's product-moment correlation coefficient, 73, 423
Percentage of shared variance, 412
Percentage of unexplained variance, 412
Percentile rank, 17
Platykurtic, 110, 151

402; drug treatment program study, 298–299; multiple sclerosis (MS) study, 382–398; weight loss treatment with support partners study, 184–185

Residual sum of squares, 420

Residuals, 13–14; assessment of normality, linearity, and homoscedasticity of, 415–417; defined, 415

returndate variable, 83

Rival hypotheses, 64

S

Sample mean, 302

Sample variances to be approximately equal, 108

Sampling distribution, 34; of mean, 19

Sampling error, 19, 55–56; random sampling, 56; standard error of the mean, 55

Scale, 82

Scatter plot, 93–94

Scientist Practitioner Inventory (SPI), 402–403

Scientist Scale of the Scientist Practitioner Inventory (SPI), 67

Self-Compassion Scale (SCS), 23

Sequential MRA (hierarchical MRA), 404, 417–423

Shapiro-Wilk (S-W) statistics, 151–152; after log10 transformation, 124; cocaine abusers in treatment study, 255, 257; by condition group, 152

Shapiro-Wilk (S-W) test, 114

Shoulders, 15

Sig. F change, 420

Simple effects analysis, 235; cocaine abusers in treatment study, 268–271

Simple linear regression, 66

Single-blind procedure, 58

Singularity: assessment of, 414–415; defined, 413

Skewness, 109–110, 113; cocaine abusers in treatment study, 255; screening, 110–111; values, 111–112

Slope, 317–318

spconfidence variable, 97

Sphericity, 196, 208–209; Mauchly's test of, 209

Sphericity assumed, 216

Spreadsheet, 78

SPSS Data View spreadsheet, 157

sqcounconfid variable, 97

Standard care plus contingency management condition, 302

Standard deviation: cocaine abusers in treatment study, 249–250, of the sample, 9

Standard error: of the estimate (SEE), 418; of the mean, 20, 55

Standard MRA (simultaneous MRA), 404

Standardized beta coefficient (beta weight) (β), 421

Standardized differences effect sizes, 45, 47

Statistical designs, 54, 61

Statistical nullification, 33

Statistical software, 2–3

Statistical techniques, learned within the context of research, 4

Statistics calculators, 18

Strength of correlation coefficient, 412

Study data: diagnosing for inaccuracies/assumptions, 99–128; erroneous data entries, detecting, 100–103; histograms, 110; kurtosis, 109–110; missing data, identifying/dealing with, 103–106; multivariate outliers, 107–108; purposes of, 145; research example, 100–127, 100–128; skewness, 109–110; univariate assumptions, screening and making decisions about, 108–109; univariate outliers, 106

Study sample, cocaine abusers in treatment study, 289

Study variables. cocaine abusers in treatment study, 231–232

Substance abuse treatment program study, *See* Drug treatment program study

Sum of squares, 8; error, 46

Suspending judgment, 32

Symmetry, 12; compound, 196

Systematic error, 56–57

T

t critical value, 22–23

t-distribution, 21–22

T-scores, 17

t-statistic, 421

222–226; formula calculations of study results, 218–228; histograms of weight loss by weight loss intervention, 200–201; independent variable (weight loss intervention), 185–186; kurtosis z-scores by condition group, 204; magnitude of treatment effect—post hoc effect size, 197, 216; missing data analysis, 197; normal evidence, summary of, 205; normal Q-Q plots of weight loss by weight loss intervention conditions, 205–207; null hypothesis (H_0), establishing, 191; omnibus narrative, null hypothesis (H_0), 191; omnibus research question (RQ), 186–189; post hoc effect size—partial eta-squared, 221–222; post hoc multiple comparisons of means, 212–213; post hoc paired-means comparisons, 222–227; post hoc power, 216; power analysis using G*Power, 193; a priori power analysis, 192–193; *Removesupport* condition, 199; repeated-measures analysis of variance, 205; research design, 186–189; research problem, 184–185; risk level of rejecting the true (H_0), 192; RM-ANOVA results, 210–212; RM-ANOVA summary table specifications, 218, 221; sample selection/assignment, 196; selecting alpha (α) considering type I and Type II errors, 192; Shapiro-Wilk (S-W) statistics by condition group, 204; skewness/kurtosis/standard error values by condition group, 202–203;

skewness z-scores by condition group, 203; sphericity, 208–209; standard deviations, 197; study results, 227–228; study variables, 185–186; sum of squares calculation, 220; trend analysis, 213–215; trends of weight loss means across the condition groups, 215; using RM-ANOVA to test the null hypothesis, 195; variances, 197; *Withsupport* condition, 198, 199, 216; *ZAddsupport* condition, 198; *ZContinuesupport* condition, 198; *ZRemovesupport* condition, 198; *ZWithsupport* condition, 198

Weighted by sample size, 140
Weschler Adult Intelligence Scale—IV, 19–20
White Bear Suppression Inventory (WBSI), 25
Width column, IBM SPSS 20 program, 81
Wilcoxon's matched-pairs signed-ranks test, 72–73, 382–389, 396–397
Within-group design, 69
Within-subjects ANOVA design, 186–187; cocaine abusers in treatment study, 235

X
x-axis, 10, 17

Y
y-axis, 10, 17

Z
z-scores, 17–18